RICHARD SAKWA is Professor of Russian and European Politics, and Head of the School of Politics and International Relations at the University of Kent. He is also an associate fellow of the Russia and Eurasia Programme at Chatham House and the author of *Putin* Redux: *Power and Contradiction in Contemporary Russia*; *The Crisis of Russian Democracy*; *Putin: Russia's Choice*; *Communism in Russia*; *Russian Politics and Society*; *The Rise and Fall of the Soviet Union* and *Gorbachev and his Reforms*.

PUTIN AND THE OLIGARCH

OLIGARCH

The Khodorkovsky–Yukos Affair

RICHARD SAKWA

I.B. TAURIS

LONDON · NEW YORK

Published in 2014 by I.B.Tauris & Co. Ltd

6 Salem Road, London W2 4BU
175 Fifth Avenue, New York NY 10010
www.ibtauris.com

Distributed in the United States and Canada
Exclusively by Palgrave Macmillan
175 Fifth Avenue, New York NY 10010

ISBN: 978 1 78076 459 7

A full CIP record for this book is available from the British Library
A full CIP record is available from the Library of Congress

Library of Congress Catalog Card Number: available

Typeset by Tetragon, London

Printed and bound in Sweden by ScandBook AB

To the victims of the Yukos affair

CONTENTS

LIST OF ILLUSTRATIONS

ACKNOWLEDGEMENTS

This book builds on the work published as *The Quality of Freedom: Khodorkovsky, Putin and the Yukos Affair* (Oxford: Oxford University Press, 2009). I am grateful to OUP, and in particular Dominic Byatt, for transferring full copyright privileges. This book, though, is not simply a second edition but a thoroughly reworked and updated study. Since the first book was delivered to the publishers in July 2008 much has occurred, notably Mikhail Khodorkovsky's second trial between March 2009 and December 2010 and a 'castling' of president and prime minister in 2012, whereby Vladimir Putin returned to the presidency, while Dmitry Medvedev, the president since 2008, became prime minister. There has also been a financial and economic crisis, the consolidation of authoritarian features in Russian politics and the deterioration of relations with the West. The emphasis of this book has also changed: it focuses more narrowly on Khodorkovsky the man and much less on the rise and fall of the Yukos oil company (which is the subject of a forthcoming companion volume). The book still covers some of the big issues in Russian politics, notably the struggle between the defenders of the rule of law and those claiming prerogative rights for the state. It is in this sense that the struggle for Russia continues. The Khodorkovsky case puts the country on trial, and not only in the court of world opinion; above all it is a trial of strength between defenders of the constitutional state and those ready to use the law for instrumental purposes.

I am most grateful to Joanna Godfrey, the commissioning editor for History and Politics, and her team at I.B. Tauris for their readiness to take on this project. It is my pleasure to acknowledge the support of the British Academy for two Small Research Grants: 'The Yukos affair and the development of Russian energy policy' and 'Business raiding in contemporary Russia'. I am also happy to thank the Norwegian Institute of

International Affairs (NUPI) and the Norwegian Research Council (project number 209365/H30) for their support within the framework of the project 'Modernizing the Russian north: politics and practice'. I am pleased to acknowledge the support of the Kennan Institute of the Woodrow Wilson International Center for Scholars, Washington, DC, which provided a stimulating environment in which to work on this project while undertaking a short-term fellowship there. The award of an Honorary Senior Research Fellowship at the Centre for Russian and East European Studies (CREES) at the University of Birmingham allowed me access to electronic materials. I am particularly grateful to Pavel Ivlev, who offered many useful suggestions to improve the text. My thanks for secretarial and other assistance go to Gemma Chapman, Rob Chapman, Nicola Cooper, Suzanne Westhead and Jessica Shepheard, and also to Frances Pritchard, the school administrative manager in the School of Politics and International Relations at the University of Kent. It has been a privilege, although not always a pleasure, to work on this book, and it is dedicated to all those who have suffered as a result of the Yukos affair.

NOTE ON TRANSLITERATION AND TRANSLATION

The transliteration system employed throughout this book is a modified version of British Standard, and is used in all cases except those where convention decrees otherwise. Thus the Russian letter 'ю' becomes 'yu', 'я' becomes 'ya', and at the beginning of names 'e' becomes 'ye' (i.e. Yevgeny rather than Evgeny). For the sake of reader-friendliness the '-ий' or '-ый' at the end of words is rendered simply as '-y' (i.e. Dmitry rather than Dmitrii); similarly, in forenames 'кс' has been rendered 'x' (i.e. Alexei rather than Aleksei). Diacritics representing the Russian hard and soft signs have been omitted in proper nouns.

Transliteration in bibliographical references will largely follow the more precise Library of Congress system (albeit with 'ya' for 'я' and 'yu' for 'ю'), and so the reader may at times notice variances between the spelling in the text and that found in the references.

All translations, unless otherwise indicated, are by the author.

INTRODUCTION

In a dawn raid on his plane in Novosibirsk on 25 October 2003, Mikhail Khodorkovsky, the CEO of the Yukos oil company, was arrested. This event provoked a controversy that continues to this day. By then Khodorkovsky had become one of the world's richest and most powerful business leaders, while Yukos had been transformed from a ramshackle conglomeration of Soviet production, refining and distribution units into a vertically integrated oil company that was set to go global. It was Russia's second-largest producer and, if the plans to merge with Sibneft had been completed, it would have become the biggest, with up to 40% of its stock to be sold to an American company. On all counts, this looked like a success story, but it was precisely at this moment that the authorities struck. Arrested in October 2003, Khodorkovsky was sentenced in May 2005 to nine years in jail (reduced to eight on appeal); the Yukos oil company was broken up, its name removed from share registers, and its cheery yellow-and-green strip, once so common in petrol stations across Russia, disappeared. In March 2009 a second trial began, and in December 2010 Khodorkovsky and his close business associate Platon Lebedev were given another long sentence, to be served concurrently with the first, that would have seen them in jail until 2016. In December 2012 the Moscow City Court reduced their sentences by two years, and on 6 August 2013 the Supreme Court cut a further two months from their sentences, bringing forward their anticipated release to 23 August and 2 May 2014, respectively. However, on 19 December 2013 President Vladimir Putin pardoned Khodorkovsky, and early the next morning he was released and flew to Berlin.

The purpose of this book is to explain why all this occurred. It will provide some theoretical discussion as well as analysis of the rise and fall of Yukos, and will examine the relationship between the state and big business during Russia's traumatic shift from the Soviet planned economy to a free-market system. Since 1985 Russia has been engaged in one of the most ambitious acts of political and economic reconstitution undertaken by any nation in history. Mikhail Gorbachev's perestroika tried to remake the Union of Soviet Socialist Republics (USSR) into a democratic socialist state, but the more successful his reforms, the less was left of the system that he was trying to save. In the end, by December 1991, the country disintegrated into 15 separate republics, of which Russia was by far the largest. This was then followed by the accelerated disbursement of state property, a process that has remained controversial to this day. The collapse of the USSR and the shift to national capitalism represented yet another revolution for Russia and its people.

This work will trace the story of Khodorkovsky's emergence during perestroika in the late 1980s as one of the country's leading entrepreneurs, the development of Yukos under Boris Yeltsin in the 1990s into one of the country's most dynamic oil majors, the transformation of the company into a modern corporation in the early Putin period, and then the epochal confrontation between business and state that culminated in Khodorkovsky's arrest and imprisonment and the destruction of the Yukos company. Like Henry II, Putin turned on 'this turbulent priest', and the confrontation between the state and temporal power that led to the murder of Thomas Becket on 29 December 1170 reappeared in a new guise as a struggle between political and economic power. Equally, as John Harvey's study of the Plantagenets demonstrates, in Becket's behaviour as Archbishop of Canterbury 'there is a sad atmosphere of cant'.[1] This did not prevent Becket becoming a saint, and while a strain of cant can be found in some of Khodorkovsky's utterances, his status as a political victim of the Russian regime is no less evident. This extraordinary confrontation between the two great forces of modernity, the state and the market, with their associated conceptions of freedom, was at the same time a struggle for Russia.

A revolution has its own laws and dynamics, its victims and its idealism, its heroes and villains, and these were vividly in evidence in Russia's era of transformation. With Yeltsin as president between 1991 and 1999, Russia became a capitalist democracy, but it did so in a revolutionary way – that is, law, constitutionality and the regular operation of institutions were subordinated to the imperative of change. This was a hybrid revolution, since part of the transformation was designed precisely to create the conditions where extraordinary politics no longer applied and where the law and institutions would be able to operate autonomously. The Yukos affair demonstrated just how entrenched the subversion of law and constitutionalism had become. This gave rise to a distinctive type of dual state. Freedom would be granted to the nation, but this freedom could be exercised only within the constraints of the logic of the transformative process itself. In other words, while the typical panoply of democratic institutions was created within the framework of a constitutional order, a parallel system emerged at the same time, claiming certain prerogatives that transcended the rules and constraints of the constitutional state.[2] This 'prerogative state', or, as it will be called in this work, the 'administrative regime', represented a classic case of a system where the rules that applied to the rest of society did not apply to itself.[3] These administrative powers were unleashed against Khodorkovsky and his associates.

Vladimir Putin's assumption of the presidency in 2000 represented a new stage in Russia's hybrid revolution, when contradiction itself became a mode of governance. Putin launched his presidency proclaiming the 'dictatorship of law', by which he meant that all special interests – above all, oligarchs and regional governors – would have to obey the law, but the regime itself ended up subverting the constitutionalism that it proclaimed. Even worse from the point of view of normative development, the administrative regime proved adept at using the instruments of the constitutional state – principally the courts – to achieve its goals. Putin's first two-term presidency (2000–8) was committed to restoring the prerogatives of the state against the declared wilfulness of 'oligarchs', the conventional name for the small group of super-rich individuals who profited from the revolutionary change in property ownership in the 1990s and who sought to dictate their will to ministers and presidents (we shall use the term in this conventional sense), as well as against regional leaders and other political and social actors. Putin's regime, however, was unwilling to subordinate itself to the constraints of the constitutional state or the supervision of popular representative institutions, notably parties and parliament, and thus it stood outside the process that it declared as its goal. Revolutionary expediency once again came into contradiction with the regime's declared ambition to transform Russia into a law-based, democratic capitalist state.

Khodorkovsky himself was no stranger to the contradictory essence of Russia's democratic revolution, and thus he was not only Putin's antagonist, but also, at the same time, he was a protagonist of the contradictions that Putin's regime reflected. In the 1990s he had not hesitated to use the courts and political leverage, and to abuse the rights of minority shareholders in order to consolidate his business empire. We should be wary, therefore, of unduly romanticising Khodorkovsky's resistance to the consolidation of Putin's statism and model of political economy, while giving due weight to his dignity and courage in adversity. To make this point does not mean aligning with the Putinite view that this 'over-mighty subject' embodied a threat to the government's ability to forge policies and strategies that represented the interests of the many and not the few. By the 2000s Khodorkovsky was advancing an alternative vision of a pluralist democracy with an active civil society within the framework of national liberalism, thus challenging the administrative regime's basis of power. The response of the statists and *siloviki* – those with a security-service background or orientation, who made up an important constituency in Putin's power base – was not long in coming.

The personal attack on Khodorkovsky and the assault against the Yukos oil company are two separate processes, although at the beginning they were entwined. The logic of the two campaigns had a common source: to remove a challenge to the regime's claimed prerogatives in the political sphere and to assert those same prerogatives in economic life, above all through the sponsorship of 'national champions' in the energy sector and elsewhere. The destruction of Yukos was a consequence of the personal attack on Khodorkovsky, but Khodorkovsky's persecution was prompted by concerns about the direction that Yukos was taking in a number of policy areas. The *silovik* faction reasserted the claimed prerogatives of the state over economic policy and political economy as a whole. The result was a partial revision of the property settlement of the 1990s, allowing the state-sponsored national champions Rosneft and Gazprom to flourish at the expense of the dismembered Yukos company. This did not signal wholesale nationalisation or a review of the capitalist system as it had developed in Russia; it did, however, enhance the powers of the state bureaucracy in economic matters and merged political power and economic wealth, increasing the opportunities for the ruling elite to enrich itself. The other oligarchs were cowed and as a class subordinated to the administrative regime. Although full-scale state capitalism was not established, this was *statist* capitalism reminiscent of the *dirigisme* practised in the 1960s by Charles de Gaulle in France and the developmental statism deployed by Park Chung-hee in South Korea at the same time.

The Yukos affair had systemic consequences: the other oligarchs were tamed and the regime emerged with no serious competitors. The autonomous power of the select few (*hoi oligoi*) gave way to the rule of a camarilla of officials centred on the power system. The attack took place under the slogan of strengthening the state, but instead the regime eliminated one of the last major sources of independent power. The state's role in the economy was reinforced, but fell short of state capitalism. Putin's industrial policy focused on creating a number of 'national champions' and state corporations in what were considered strategic sectors of the economy, but these did not become the motors of a consistent developmental strategy. In keeping with the 'regime' character of the attack on Yukos, the strategy allowed a number of 'beneficiaries' to prosper, while the national economy suffered from the deterioration in the business climate. The short-term consequences included a dip in inward investment, a rise in capital flight and some disruption in oil output, but these soon recovered. The most important long-term outcome was the consolidation of a *dirigiste*, or 'directive', political economy – bolted on to the neo-liberalism of the 1990s – in which a more interventionist state asserted its presumed right to oversee the national economy, a type of neo-patrimonialism that is characteristic of developing economies. *Dirigisme* in the economy was accompanied by regime consolidation at the political level, although this was not full-blown authoritarianism but heavy-handed political management accompanied by the creation of greedy distributional coalitions. A dual economy emerged to accompany the dual state: a private sector operating according to the logic of the market, and a state-sponsored sector acting as 'national champions'.

The focus of this book is Khodorkovsky's personal and intellectual journey, covering his early years as an entrepreneur, his acquisition and development of the Yukos oil company, and his fall and arrest in October 2003. Much of the book is devoted to what happened after that, as Khodorkovsky became one of the world's most renowned political prisoners. From jail he issued a stream of commentary and publications, examining developments in Russia and the world. Indeed, from various places of incarceration he became one of the most acute observers of contemporary Russia. He remained as much if not a greater threat to the regime than at liberty. Even though Khodorkovsky repeatedly stated that he would not seek revenge, a second trial was staged from March 2009, in which he was accused of stealing the oil on which he allegedly had not paid the appropriate taxes, the subject of the first trial.

The regime ensured that Khodorkovsky was not at liberty during the crucial succession operation in 2011–12. In May 2008, at the end of his constitutionally allowed two terms, Putin transferred the presidency to his protégé Dmitry Medvedev. Putin took up the post of prime minister, although he continued to act as 'national leader'. The 'tandem' was created, with Medvedev espousing a gradualist reform agenda while Putin guaranteed the power and privileges of the elites who had benefited from his earlier period of rule. As the election approached, it became clear that Medvedev wished to run for a second presidential term (now extended to six years). Instead, in September 2011, at the congress of the ruling party United Russia, a 'castling' move was announced: Putin would run for the presidency while Medvedev would be designated prime minister. The move provoked disappointment and anger in equal measure, since the prospect of six years more of 'Putinism' filled even many of his supporters with misgivings. The flawed parliamentary election of 4 December 2011 brought thousands to the streets in protest, gathering on Bolotnaya Ploshchad and Prospekt Akademika Sakharova in Moscow. However, the protestors lacked a single charismatic leader or a coherent programme. One can only imagine what would have happened if Khodorkovsky had been able to address the crowds, as a unifying point of opposition to the stifling Putinite system of rule. Having regained his freedom in December 2013, Khodorkovsky rejoined his family and friends in Berlin, and began to rebuild his life after ten years in jail.

The story of Khodorkovsky is one of competing narratives: Khodorkovsky as the hero who built up one of Russia's most successful companies, who was brought down in his prime since his success threatened the prerogatives of a narrow political elite and the bureaucracy; Khodorkovsky as a speculator, who levered his Communist Youth League (Komsomol) and political connections to become one of Russia's powerful oligarchs, who treated politicians and the state as just another commodity and who made every effort to avoid paying taxes, while the mass of the people sank into poverty; Khodorkovsky as a Soviet individual, who, through luck and skill, built up a successful company no different from a dozen others, was brought low by political enemies, and in jail found himself and became the conscience of the nation. In his study of Khodorkovsky's time in prison, Panyushkin writes: 'Khodorkovsky is like a forum in which we, people living in Russia, argue about what we are. Half assert that we are a great nation. The other half affirm that we are slaves without rights. The choice is yours.'[4] He goes on to say that 'the Khodorkovsky affair is not about how they jailed an oligarch, or about how unfair are the Russian courts. It is about how someone in Russia can become free, and what happens to them when they do.'[5] It is also, we may add, about recognising the responsibilities that freedom brings.

CANTERBURY, DECEMBER 2013

CHAPTER 1

RISE OF THE CITIZEN OLIGARCH

By the time of his arrest in 2003 Mikhail Khodorkovsky was Russia's richest man. Publication of details of the ownership structure of Yukos in June 2002 revealed that Khodorkovsky's share in the company amounted to $7.7 billion,[1] and in the following year he topped the *Forbes* Russia list.[2] For many he represented the exemplary 'oligarch', the colloquial term for the economic magnates who made their fortunes during the period of anarchic privatisation (known in Russian as *prikhvatizatsiya*, 'piratisation') in the 1990s.[3] In contrast to the 'grey privatisation' typical in central Europe, where relatively few insiders managed to leverage political influence for property, the 'black privatisation' in Russia was far more blatantly slanted to benefit a handful of insiders. This was to cast a long shadow over the succeeding decade, and capitalist democracy in the country is tainted even to this day by the excesses of this period.

ORIGINS

Khodorkovsky was born in Moscow to a Jewish–Russian family of modest means on 26 June 1963. Like Putin, he spent his first years in a cramped communal apartment, in this case two rooms off Prospekt Mira in northern Moscow (on Ulitsa Kosmonavtov), and his family only moved into a separate flat in 1971 (it would be another six years before Putin's family received a flat of their own). This was a tough area of the city and, like Putin in Leningrad a decade earlier, Khodorkovsky spent his childhood in various gangs, with street ranged against street. His parents were typical of the Moscow technical intelligentsia. His father, Boris Moiseevich, and his mother, Marina Filippovna, were both chemical engineers and spent their working lives at the Kalibr factory, turning out precision measuring equipment. Neither joined the Communist Party, and both endured Soviet power without enthusiasm. In year seven (aged 13) the young Mikhail took extra lessons in maths in the evenings, and for two summers, from the age of 15, he refused to go to Pioneer camp, 'saying he was tired of the childish games there', working instead in a local bread factory.[4] Like another of the leading oligarchs, Roman Abramovich, he started earning extra income from an early age. After the bakers he worked as a carpenter in his local housing cooperative, then for four years headed a building brigade (a group of *shabashniki*), which involved work in Moldova and on the Baikal–Amur Mainline (BAM) railway to the north of the Trans-Siberian line. He engaged in a number of sports – including boxing, karate and sambo, a mix of judo and wrestling – until the age of 18, but, unlike Putin, he dropped them when he went to college, and thereafter his only sporting activity was jogging.[5]

Khodorkovsky's favourite subject was chemistry, and he changed specialist schools three times until he found one with what he considered the appropriate level of expertise.[6] In 1980 he entered the renowned Mendeleev Moscow Institute of Chemical Engineering (now the D. Mendeleev University of Chemical Technology of Russia), graduating in 1986 with top marks. He joined the defence faculty in an early manifestation of his patriotic and idealistic instincts,[7] specialising as a technical engineer rather than in chemistry as such, and thus he was trained to become a factory manager. He would undoubtedly have had a successful career in the Soviet system. He was a model citizen and rose to become deputy head of the Komsomol (Communist Youth League) organisation in his institute; in 1986 he was elected a member of the Sverdlovsk Komsomol District Committee. He was a typical 'Soviet man', not too bothered by ideology, but he nevertheless stated: 'I believed in the Party. […] If one objectively observes the majority of the "then" dissidents and even human rights defenders, they did not look convincing.'[8] His college career inculcated a deep patriotism that would never leave him.[9]

In the Sverdlovsk district he got to know Boris Yeltsin, the first secretary of the Moscow Communist Party and later, following his fall from grace in Autumn 1987, head of the committee for state construction, until he began his spectacular march to power that took him to the Kremlin at the head of an independent Russia in December 1991. As a result Khodorkovsky always considered himself a Yeltsinite, defending the White House (the seat of Russian government) in August 1991 and October

1993, and was part of the presidential re-election team in 1996.[10] Khodorkovsky went on to become deputy head of the Frunze Komsomol District Committee, at which time he joined the Communist Party of the Soviet Union (KPSS). It was in this district that all the top members of the Komsomol Central Committee were registered, providing many contacts who later came in useful. He was responsible for expelling the then wife of Gleb Pavlovsky – who later headed the pro-Kremlin Effective Politics Foundation – from the Komsomol when her husband was arrested for 'dissident' activities in the early 1980s.[11] Pavlovsky did not bear a grudge and later opposed Khodorkovsky's arrest.

Party membership did not help Khodorkovsky when it came to postgraduate studies or job allocation (*raspredelenie*) after graduating. He was considered too much of a risk-taker to be allowed into graduate school, with a reputed penchant for explosives. He wrote his final-year dissertation under the supervision of Alexander Fogelzang, who considered Khodorkovsky unsuited for research work in experimental chemistry. The rector Gennady Yagodin is alleged to have stated: 'If the Jew Fogelzang won't take on the Jew Khodorkovsky, then so be it.'[12] Khodorkovsky to this day speaks warmly of Yagodin and insists: 'I never had any problems on nationality grounds,' although he admits that 'in systemic terms there were conflicts.'[13]

Khodorkovsky stressed, 'I feel Russian'; although he did recognise that his refusal to consider himself Jewish could be taken as a betrayal: 'I never thought of myself as a Jew.' He notes that if he had any national self-identification (apart from Soviet), it was as a Russian. He goes on: 'I never thought of my father as being from any other nation than that around us. [...] He was a postwar Moscow homeless child [*besprizornik*]. What has "Jewishness" got to do with that?'[14] Receiving his first passport at the age of 16, he was faced with the choice of how to fill in the notorious 'point 5', the section pertaining to nationality. Stating that 'I did not consider myself a Jew', he put down Russian. Summing up, he insisted: 'I devoted my strength and talent in Russia and for Russia', counting himself both part of the intelligentsia and a capitalist, in the sense of a manager and entrepreneur.[15] The roots of his 'national liberalism' thus came from early convictions, combining first Soviet, then Russian patriotism, accompanied by a strong belief in individual autonomy that was inculcated, paradoxically, by the formally collectivist Soviet Union.

The Jewish factor may have played a part in Khodorkovsky's choice of career, since in the late Soviet years an unofficial *numerus clausus* operated on the basis of nationality. The system applied a perverse type of 'affirmative action' to reduce the assumed disproportionate number of Jews in leading professions. As one of the best students in his class, Khodorkovsky had first choice of jobs on offer, and he choose to go to a 'P.O. Box', a closed defence-related region, but because of 'point 5' he was advised to enter an open establishment.[16] Failing to enter graduate school or to be appointed to his chosen post, Khodorkovsky instead turned his energies to business.

THE BIRTH OF RUSSIAN CAPITALISM

Khodorkovsky graduated at a time when opportunities were dramatically expanding as a result of Gorbachev's perestroika. In December 1986 Gorbachev allowed Andrei Sakharov to return from exile in Gorky (now once again Nizhny Novgorod), and thereafter glasnost and democratising reforms advanced at a dizzying, and increasingly uncontrollable, pace. On 25 July 1986 the Central Committee of the KPSS adopted rules to establish centres for the scientific and technical creativity of youth (NTTMs), an idea proposed by the Central Committee of the Komsomol, with further regulations adopted on 28 January 1987, and again on 11 and 13 March of the same year.[17] The green light was given for the massive development of a 'Komsomol economy' to act as the seedbed for the post-Communist entrepreneurial class, functioning as a privileged auxiliary to the formal economy. The sponsor of this Chinese-style Party capitalism was the moderate reformer Yegor Ligachev, but the initiative turned out very differently to what he had anticipated. Youth entrepreneurship quickly turned into a massive money-making exercise.

With a dozen partners from the Mendeleev Institute, by December 1986 Khodorkovsky had opened a private café, was trading new technologies to Soviet enterprises and importing computers; he was also selling Polish, Armenian and French cognac. This was the 'primary accumulation of capital' phase of Russian capitalism. In 1987 legislation was adopted allowing the creation of private commercial banks. In that year he created an NTTM, formally headed by Sergei Monakhov, the head of the Frunze District Komsomol.[18] It was registered with the Moscow Soviet by Yelena Baturina, the wife of Yury Luzhkov, the future mayor of Moscow, and a formidable entrepreneur in her own right.[19] Although intended to introduce scientific innovation into production, the cooperative instead bought and sold computers and made a lot of money. As Khodorkovsky wryly notes, none of the progenitors of perestroika 'could imagine the effect these decisions would have on social and economic life'.[20]

A lucrative contract with the High Temperatures Institute of the Academy of Sciences (IVTAN) provided an early boost to fuel further development.[21] With a delay of 60 years they took up Nikolai Bukharin's slogan of the New Economic Policy

(NEP) in the 1920s: '*Enrichissez-vous.*' By December 1987 over 60 city and district NTTMs had been established, and their rights were extended soon after. By spring 1990 there were about 600 NTTMs and over 17,000 youth, student and academic cooperatives sponsored by the Komsomol, employing about a million people.[22] Attempts to rein in the Komsomol economy by that time were futile. Nevertheless, up to the August 1991 coup Khodorkovsky considered himself 'a loyal Communist Party member'.[23] If the Soviet order had not dissolved he would no doubt have been at the head of Chinese-style capitalism within a socialist framework.

Soon after entering business, Khodorkovsky was joined in 1987 by Leonid Nevzlin, who answered an advertisement for young entrepreneurial staff. Born on 21 September 1959, Nevzlin graduated from the Gubkin Moscow Institute of the Petrochemical and Gas Industries in 1981, and later from the Plekhanov Moscow Institute of Economics with a higher degree in management and marketing. At that time he was working as a programmer in Zarubezhgeologiya. Nevzlin ably fulfilled all of Khodorkovsky's tasks and quickly rose to become his deputy. The team was joined by Vladimir Dubov, the son of a baking magnate Matvei Dubov. Another of Khodorkovsky's associates in this early period was Vladislav Surkov, who, under Putin and Medvedev, worked as deputy head of the presidential administration.[24] By the end of 1987 Khodorkovsky was working full-time as director of a network of NTTMs, employing 5,000 people on various research contracts. By the end of 1988 he had created the country's biggest NTTM with a turnover of 80 million roubles (over $100 million at the official exchange rate), a colossal sum for the time, when a car cost 10,000–20,000 roubles and a computer 40,000 roubles.[25]

The Law on Cooperatives was adopted in May 1988, and Nevzlin and Mikhail Brudno registered one under the name Nigma, trading in computers and software. Like Roman Abramovich, Mikhail Prokhorov, Vladimir Gusinsky and many others, cooperatives were one of the major routes to wealth for Russia's budding entrepreneurs. The Moscow commission for cooperatives and individual labour was headed by Yury Luzhkov, who would go on to become the city's mayor from 1992 to 2010. In August 1988 the Commercial Innovation Bank for Scientific and Technical Progress – chaired by Khodorkovsky until 1990 – was co-founded by Zhilsotsbank and the State Committee for Science and Technology, operating in partnership with the Moscow Soviet as a cooperative based on NTTM principles. Khodorkovsky used his leadership of the Scientific and Youth Union to merge various organisations into the trading company, which on 29 December 1988 was launched as a bank (Interbank Association for Scientific and Technological Development, Menatep). This was arguably Russia's first private commercial bank since the October revolution.

The bank formally adopted the name Menatep on 14 May 1990 when it was registered with the Moscow Soviet, and in December of that year it was one of the first
companies in Russia to issue what at the time passed for shares. By then Menatep
encompassed some 40 commercial structures, including 18 banks, investment and
trading companies, with over 200 million roubles in capital.[26]

Persistent rumours suggest that some of Menatep's early funds were provided by
the Komsomol Central Committee, and even by the KPSS.[27] Khodorkovsky brushes
off this accusation by arguing that Menatep was ready to take money from any client
without checking their passport.[28] He later admitted that he relied on protection
from the State Committee on Science and Technology to ward off challenges from
the police and security services. The company was greatly helped by Khodorkovsky's
Komsomol colleague Alexei Golubovich, whose parents held top positions in the
Soviet State Bank and thus allowed one of its subsidiaries, the Frunze district branch
of Zhilsotsbank, to help Menatep; it was also aided by the elite connections of the
parents of his associate Vladimir Dubov, who gave Khodorkovsky access to political
figures all the way up to Gorbachev.[29] These political links allowed Menatep to handle
the accounts of the Chernobyl disaster committee. At the same time Khodorkovsky
continued his studies, and in 1988 he graduated as a specialist in finances from the
Plekhanov Moscow Institute of Economics. Only later, in January 1990, was the bank
joined by Platon Lebedev, who would go on to become its chairman. Lebedev was also
a graduate of the Plekhanov Institute and worked as a planner in Zarubezhgeologiya
before demonstrating that he was a financier of genius.[30]

Menatep soon overtook most of its competitors. By mid-1991 Menatep encompassed 18 independent commercial banks, two insurance companies, a trading
company and some 30 industrial and other enterprises.[31] There were a number of
reasons for this rapid growth. First, the bank's area of specialisation (foreign trade)
was one where capital accumulation grew fastest. Second, Menatep was one of the
first private banks to receive a licence to deal in the foreign currency market, handled
by Menatep SA, established in late 1989 for this purpose, which had subsidiaries
in Gibraltar (which from 1997 became the financial holding Group Menatep Ltd,
later GML) and Budapest. Third, and most importantly, if state enterprises diverted
virtual rouble resources through the accounts of NTTMs they could receive in
exchange hard cash. In effect, this was a licence to print money, as state companies
used the bank to convert nominal rouble accounts into currency. Khodorkovsky
dismisses as 'myth' the influence of this on Russian economic development.[32] The
golden days of this particular scheme did not last long once everyone jumped on the
bandwagon, but Khodorkovsky had plenty of other ideas to keep him busy. Fourth,

the company was also active in domestic trade, including the import of computers and cognac from France. Fifth, from 1990 the bank took in money from the public (some 2.5 million roubles), who heeded the warnings broadcast in Menatep advertising campaigns that inflation would eat away their life savings. Very few ever saw returns from the allegedly high-dividend earning vouchers (*veksely*) that they bought, and most lost the capital they invested. Menatep now became a household name, with a reputation not much better than Sergei Mavrodi's MMM pyramid scheme.[33] Finally, and perhaps most crucially, the company enjoyed strong links with the government. On one occasion in its early days Menatep took a $1 million state loan, sold it at commercial rates and returned the loan in roubles, making a handsome profit of 9 million roubles on the deal.[34] Menatep acted on behalf of the state to conduct transactions, serving as a delegated authority. By 1991 Menatep was one of the first banks licensed to service trade with Ukraine and Belarus.[35] There are also rumours that the bank played a part in handling the mythical Communist 'Party gold' transactions in the final period of Soviet power.[36] As noted, there were persistent rumours that Menatep had been founded on 'Party money', and by the time of the August 1991 coup the Central Committee of the KPSS had created over 100 banks and commercial structures, many of them headed by active or reserve KGB officers.[37]

The August 1991 coup placed Khodorkovsky in a quandary. By inclination he was a statist and he was also a Party member, and like his colleagues he feared the disintegration of the Soviet Union; however, like the rest of the country, they were unclear about the aims of the putschists. As Khodorkovsky later put it, 'I was unequivocally in favour of preserving the USSR, but the question at the time was: for reforms or against.'[38] Khodorkovsky and Nevzlin finally chose to defend Yeltsin and the White House, although they retained close links with those 'on the other side of the barricades'.[39] On 21 August, once it was clear that the coup had failed, Khodorkovsky returned his Party card. The subsequent shift of power from the Soviet Union to the Russian Federation, accompanied by the dissolution of state power in its entirety, horrified him. He notes that the 'market is a fine mechanism, but in certain circumstances it can cost the lives of millions […] hence the need for the state. But the state must be professional […] and outside ideology […] and personal interests.'[40] These beliefs lay at the core of what he described as his 'liberal statism', which in an earlier era was called national liberalism. It was for this reason that when the raid started in late 2003 Khodorkovsky did not stop the work of Yukos, on which the country, and certain regions specifically, depended. He describes himself as an 'ideological person': in other words, someone who is governed by strong beliefs.[41]

His liberal statist convictions led him to criticise the headlong rush to the market launched by Yegor Gaidar, deputy prime minister between November 1991 and May 1992, and then acting prime minister until December of that year. Khodorkovsky's belief in a strong state-managed industrial policy later inclined him to support Viktor Chernomyrdin, prime minister between December 1992 and March 1998, and then Yevgeny Primakov, premier from September 1998 to May 1999, and Yury Maslyukov, the only Communist minister during Yeltsin's presidency, serving as a deputy prime minister in Primakov's cabinet.[42]

With the fall of Communism and Yeltsin's coming to power, Menatep's fortunes soared.[43] Khodorkovsky's links served the company well; like many banks of the time, Menatep was sponsored by a business group, and they in turn provided the flexibility and resources for the group to expand. Khodorkovsky's trading operations included international commodity shipments – notably a major oil-for-sugar deal with Cuba – and he also dealt with the commodity trader Marc Rich, head of global commodities trading company Glencore International. His offshore operations pre-dated the fall of Communism by a year. Above all, Menatep was authorised to handle the funds of the finance ministry, the state taxation service and – with Most Bank, headed by Vladimir Gusinsky, who was also head of the banking consortium handling Moscow's budget – the city of Moscow. Menatep also handled the funding of a number of federal programmes; as well as managing the cash for the Chernobyl clean-up, it was involved in the reconstruction of Chechnya, which was accompanied by the usual allegations of embezzlement.[44]

This was the golden age of bank capital in Russia, with the number of private banks rising from five in 1989 to 2,500 in 1994. Khodorkovsky remained chair of Menatep's board of directors until April 1996, but from 1991 Lebedev had operational control as the bank's president. In 1990–1 Khodorkovsky acted as an adviser to the Russian prime minister Ivan Silaev, giving him access to privileged information, and this was one factor prompting him to defend the White House in August 1991.[45] In 1992 Khodorkovsky became head of the fuel and energy industry's investment fund, with the status of deputy minister of fuel and energy of the Russian Federation and responsibility for private investment. Surkov, head of advertising for Menatep, was also an adviser on public relations to the Russian government;[46] he devised Menatep's first campaigns and made Khodorkovsky famous.[47] In their 1992 book *Man with a Rouble*, Khodorkovsky and Nevzlin are lavish in their praise of Surkov's abilities and 'non-standard mindset', and quote a press report stating: 'Every new step taken by this man is a sensation!'[48] Little did they know quite how sensational Surkov would be when he entered presidential service and perfected the art of 'managed democracy'. In late 1999 Surkov himself noted: 'Sooner or later I always come into conflict with the system in which I find myself, even if I have been part of its creation.'[49] He would leave Menatep in 1997 under strained circumstances, not having been offered a partnership; in 2011 he even fell out with the Putin team and joined Medvedev's 'modernisers'.

Menatep won the lucrative contract to handle the foreign-currency accounts of Rosvooruzhenie, the arms-export monopoly created by presidential decree on 18 November 1993. In March 1993 Khodorkovsky was appointed deputy to the fuel and energy minister, Yury Shafranik, as well as acting as an adviser on finances to Chernomyrdin. In a meeting in the Kremlin at that time Khodorkovsky called on entrepreneurs to go into industry, since it was shameful, he claimed, to make money out of trade.[50] In 1994 Khodorkovsky joined the council of authorised banks under the Moscow mayor's office; at the same time he was working as the deputy head of the Russian government's Council for Industrial Policy and Entrepreneurship and until 1996 was part of a government group set up to improve wage payments.

In 1992 Menatep shifted its focus from financial activities and established Rosprom, a holding company to manage its industrial interests. Khodorkovsky became chair of the board of directors, which was registered as a stock company on 1 September 1995. In the early 1990s Menatep was flooded with more money than it knew how to handle, and thus Menatep was an active player in investment auctions, winning controlling shares in a number of companies. Khodorkovsky characteristically thought in grandiose terms and, following his own advice, used the new wealth to create a major industrial empire. He bought up any available company, including the Apatit mineral-fertiliser company in Murmansk oblast that was later to play such a fateful role in the Yukos affair, as well as the Uralelektromed, the Sredneuralsky and Kirovogradsky copper-works, the Volga pipe plant, Russia's largest producer of titanium AO Avisma, in addition to various textile, wood and food plants, including the Ust-Ilimsky wood-processing concern. By March 1996, through Rosprom, Menatep had controlling shares in 29 industrial enterprises and major holdings in another 50.[51] Nevzlin insists that most purchases were consensual, and there was no question of Rosprom engaging in 'raiding' attacks.[52] Nevertheless, Menatep was the only bank mentioned by name in a 1994 CIA report warning that 'the majority of Russian banks are controlled by the dreaded Mafia'.[53]

Menatep devoted considerable efforts to public relations (PR) and to what Russians delicately call 'government relations' (GR). As Surkov put it at the time, the company sought to forge a 'clan' with its major clients, including regular contacts and the creation of a special department in Menatep to lobby the interests of its clients in state structures.[54] It was in this context that Lebedev first used the term 'oligarch' to describe the new elite when on 11 November 1992 Menatep announced the creation of a special department 'to provide banking services for the financial–industrial oligarchy'.[55] In other words, Menatep created one of the most powerful lobbying structures in post-Communist Russia and offered to leverage its unique links with the state on behalf of its clients. The relationship was largely one-way, with Menatep shaping government policy, while the nascent state had few levers with which to exert influence in the other direction. The lobbying power of the company was its pride in the early days, but it also later proved its Achilles heel when the regime changed.

This activity was overseen by Nevzlin and Dubov, who enjoyed particularly close relations with Boris Fedorov, finance minister until January 1994. The 'merger' of state and business was evident when in October 1994 Konstantin Kagalovsky was appointed deputy head of Menatep's board of directors. From November 1991 Kagalovsky negotiated on behalf of the Russian government with international financial institutions, and he was, from October 1992 until he joined Menatep, Russia's nominated IMF director. Khodorkovsky enjoyed good relations with Gaidar despite differences on policy, and he was one of the main financial sponsors of his party – Russia's Choice – in the December 1993 elections.[56] There was already evidence of tension between Nevzlin's more neo-liberal views and Khodorkovsky's statist liberalism. According to John Lloyd, Khodorkovsky 'was a supporter of a strong, centrist government and a powerful state in partnership with the financial sector'.[57] The election, taking place in the shadow of the bloodshed of October 1993 (when Khodorkovsky unequivocally supported Yeltsin in his confrontation with parliament), proved a disappointment for organised liberalism, and thereafter all parties declined as instruments of political intermediation as the regime relied increasingly directly on the support of big business and the security apparatus.

Thane Gustafson is sceptical about the 'myth of the all-powerful Russian banks', but concedes that banking power was strongly in evidence in the case of Yukos and Sidanco.[58] Professional oilmen in these companies were subordinated to the rule of financiers with no experience in the industry. With the abolition of state financing for capital investment in the oil industry in 1993–4, accompanied by the conversion of state oil enterprises into joint-stock companies and their subsequent privatisation, the opportunities for Moscow banks expanded. The initial partner for Yukos was Promradtekhbank, which managed the company from its inception in 1993. However, as the drive to convert ramshackle holding companies into vertically integrated operations began, Promradtekhbank lacked the size and skills and was marginalised, in the end becoming the depositary for Yukos shares.

Although Yukos would later fall victim to the *siloviki*, the company was no stranger to the security establishment, having become one of the largest employers of ex-KGB officials.[59] In the 1990s most companies employed former security officials, usually organised as an 'analytical department'.[60] Menatep proved an attractive soft landing for displaced KGB officers, employing some 230 people in its security service in the early 1990s. One of these was Victor Ivanenko, who was for a brief period the head of the KGB's successor agency, the Federal Security Service (FSB). Another was former KGB general Alexei Kondaurov, who joined Menatep in 1994 as deputy head of security and then director of Rosprom's analytical office before in 1997 moving over full-time to lead the analytical office in Yukos and becoming an adviser to Khodorkovsky.[61] He balloted as a Communist Party deputy in 1999 but only entered parliament in 2003. Both Ivanenko and Kondaurov, subordinates to Khodorkovsky, outranked Putin, who had risen no higher than lieutenant-colonel in the service.

Menatep's grandiose neo-Gothic headquarters in Kolpachny Pereulok had formerly hosted the city and regional Komsomol committees, and its transfer to private entrepreneurs symbolised this new era. The huge cars of Menatep officials blocked the pavements, forcing pedestrians (the 'little people' who have to pay taxes, in Leona Helmsley's vivid phrase) to navigate between moving traffic. There was a new power in the land, and it was not bashful in announcing its presence.

FROM BANKS TO OIL

Khodorkovsky was ideally placed to take advantage of the break-up of the integrated Soviet oil industry. The Ministry of Fuel and Energy in September 1991 became the joint stock company Rosneftegaz, which in November 1992 simply became Rosneft, and the same decree opened the way for the privatisation of the industry, effectively hiving off companies from Rosneft.[62] The oil industry was broken up into 32 production associations and 29 refineries.[63] The plan was for them to be consolidated into regionally concentrated, vertically integrated companies on the Western model.[64] The ministry itself was no longer allowed to manage companies, and instead Rosneft was intended to become one of the vertically integrated companies. In the event, it lost most of its assets in the privatisation frenzy, something that its leadership never forgave and for which it later took revenge.[65]

Yukos was created in April 1993 out of the merger of two state-owned companies, the West Siberian oil producer Yuganskneftegaz (henceforth YNG) based in the

Khanty-Mansi autonomous *okrug* (district) of Tyumen oblast, and the Volga-based refining company Kuibyshevnefteorgsintez. The former contributed the 'Yu' and the latter the 'kos' (KuibyshevnefteOrgSintez) to Yukos. The production company Samaraneftegaz, three refineries in Samara oblast, eight oil-distribution networks and various geological and technical service agencies also joined the conglomerate.[66] The company was registered on 12 May 1993 and was formally known as OAO Yukos Oil Company. The company had the largest oil reserves in Russia and was the second-largest producer. Sergei Muravlenko, the company's general director, was a professional *neftyanik* ('oilnik') who had earlier headed YNG.

YNG provided 62% of Yukos's oil output and held around 70% of its reserves. Although Muravlenko had come from YNG, this did not prevent tension between the two organisations as YNG resisted attempts to merge it into the Yukos structure. Government contacts were deployed to resolve the problem, in this case through Vladimir Lopukhin, who had been minister of fuel and energy in Gaidar's government in 1991–2. Khodorkovsky also enjoyed good relations with Chernomyrdin, the founder of Gazprom, who was appointed deputy prime minister responsible for the fuel and energy complex on 30 May 1992, and in December of that year he became prime minister. The 1992 privatisation programme for the oil industry stipulated that the state would initially retain a controlling interest, a period that came to an end in early 1996. The pressing financial needs of the state, with the budget deficit reaching 10% of GDP by 1995, led to the disbursement of the state's share.

Taking advantage of the administration's financial woes, a number of leading banks offered credit to the government on security of government shares in privatised enterprises. At a cabinet meeting on 30 March 1995 some leading oligarchs, including Khodorkovsky and Vladimir Potanin, head of Onexim Bank, outlined a plan to allow investors to take over a share of trust stakes for a set period in exchange for extending credit to the government, the notorious 'loans for shares' scheme.[67] A presidential decree of 31 August 1995 formalised the plan, with shares to be allocated through auctions from which foreigners were excluded. Investment tender competitions in state-owned oil companies would also take place, so the winner would pay for shares and also commit to investment in the relevant company.[68] Khodorkovsky recalls the relatively random way in which he became an oil magnate, even though he had worked with the energy ministry at the beginning of the transition and had an academic background in chemistry, while his colleagues Brudno and Nevzlin were oil-industry computer specialists, and Lebedev was a geologist.[69] Nevertheless, none could claim to be a professional oilman. Khodorkovsky argues that he never set himself the task of becoming a *neftyanik*; his job as an 'engineer–technologist' was to organise the business.[70]

The first loans-for-shares and investment auctions were held in late 1995, accompanied by accusations that the auctions had been rigged. This transfer of public assets into the hands of a small group of oligarchs remains one of the most contested issues in Russian politics, and was the focus of many of Khodorkovsky's later writings. With oil prices at the time ranging between $16 and $25 a barrel, it was unclear how much a company like Yukos was actually worth. Khodorkovsky argues that 'the situation was very simple: pay as much as you can, and take as much as you can deal with'. He dismisses the view that foreigners would have paid more, noting that he had conducted interminable negotiations with various potential partners to share the risk, but none was 'mad enough' to enter the Russian market.[71] In absolute terms the programme involved a relatively small proportion of the Russian economy, and Treisman correctly points out that the beneficiaries were not just a group of brash oligarchs but also a number of 'red directors'. In the circumstances the prices were not too wildly out of kilter with relevant comparators, yet the whole incident was more than a 'public relations disaster' and came to symbolise the flawed transition as a whole.[72] As late as 2012, in his 'state of the nation' speech on 12 December, Putin warned that the new round of privatisations planned by the government 'must be nothing like those of the 1990s, with the notorious loans-for-shares auctions'.[73] Anatoly Chubais, the master strategist behind rapid privatisation, stresses the political aspect, with the auctions allowing the 'conclusive destruction of the Communists in the 1996 elections'.[74] Yeltsin was returned to the presidency for a second term despite clear indications of physical and political degeneration.

Menatep was put in charge of processing bids for the Yukos auction. It was represented in the auction on 8 December 1995 by the two permitted bids (primarily the Laguna company, created especially for the purpose since Yukos could not represent itself);[75] while a third, which offered more money than Khodorkovsky's team, was disqualified on technical grounds.[76] Menatep thus won 45% of Yukos stock for $159 million, $9 million above the starting price. The associated investment tender in December 1995 saw a further 33% of Yukos shares going to Menatep for $150 million, with the bank pledged to invest a further $300 million over the next three years. In sum, Khodorkovsky and his partners paid a total of $350 million up front for control of 78% of Yukos stock, suggesting that the total value of the company was $450 million. At the same time they were taking on some $3 billion of debt, including some $2 billion in tax arrears, and employees had not been paid for six months. Later share emissions further diluted the state's holding, so by autumn 1996 Menatep owned 90% of Yukos stock. When the shares began trading in 1997, Yukos's market capitalisation was $9 billion, and reached some $15 billion by early 2002. In 1996, however, Khodorkovsky was still joking that the winners of the loans-for-shares auction were 'a collection of bankrupts'.[77]

Menatep already had close relations with Yukos, so it was an insider at the time of the auctions. Menatep then played a major part in the further development of the company.[78] For this it used Rosprom, effectively a financial–industrial group (FIG), but one created from below, which already by late 1994 controlled about 60 companies.[79] FIGs were formally established by the law of 27 October 1995 as a way of bringing together financial and industrial organisations and were to be officially registered as a specific form of organisation, although there were many unregistered ones.[80] Yukos in 1996 owned only some 38–40% of the shares in its subsidiaries, with many of the other owners resistant to being bought out. The struggle to achieve vertical integration was accompanied by the scandals that made Yukos notorious but was basically achieved by 1999.

Yukos was Russia's largest oil company in terms of total recoverable reserves, but its financial performance was disastrous. YNG in particular was deeply indebted to the government and owed substantial wage arrears to its workers, caused largely by consumer payment arrears. Just weeks before the August 1998 default, the first deputy prime minister, Boris Nemtsov, with the government desperate for funds, set a two-week deadline for the oil companies to clear their debts. Even with low oil prices, energy export duties made up a very large proportion of government revenue. In the first quarter of 1998 these fell by 25% as world oil prices plummeted to $10 per barrel. The government's drive to collect back taxes in 1998 forced Yukos and other companies to impose major job cuts. Yukos targeted administrative posts and cut social spending on housing, hospitals and welfare programmes.[81] Given that many fields were in effect 'company towns', the result was devastating and, as we shall see, provoked considerable tensions, leading even to accusations of the murder of Vladimir Petukhov, the mayor of Nefteyugansk, the hometown of YNG. From 1999 oil prices began an upward trajectory, with various short-term dips, peaking at $147 a barrel in May 2008. These boom years allowed Yukos to thrive and Khodorkovsky's vision to expand, but also provoked the envy of state officials.

THE OLIGARCHS ARE BORN

At the World Economic Forum in Davos, on 2–5 February 1996, Khodorkovsky overheard the conversation in which international financier George Soros warned Boris Berezovsky that if the Communists returned to power the liberal economy and democracy would be destroyed. He advised the oligarchs to emigrate.[82] Berezovsky instead joined with his arch-enemy, Gusinsky, to save Yeltsin.[83] Presidential elections were due in June, and it was clear that Yeltsin's re-election campaign was floundering. Yeltsin enjoyed no more than 4% of support, while Gennady Zyuganov, at the head of the Communist Party of the Russian Federation (KPRF) held 35%. Alexander Korzhakov, Yeltsin's confidant and powerful bodyguard, and the *siloviki* called for the Communist Party to be banned and the elections to be cancelled.[84] A fortnight after the Davos meeting Khodorkovsky was one of the group of business and media leaders who went to see Yeltsin and offered not only money but also experienced political strategists.[85] Yeltsin gave one of his famous long pauses, prompting Khodorkovsky to wonder whether 'the tsar was thinking about whether to send us all to the execution block'.[86] In the event, an 'analytical group' was created and Chubais was brought in to mastermind Yeltsin's re-election.[87]

Uncertain of the outcome, a group of top oligarchs on 27 April 1996 issued the notorious 'Appeal of the Thirteen', urging Yeltsin to come to terms with Zyuganov.[88] 'Society is divided,' they argued.

> The rift that divides us into reds and whites, ours and theirs, runs through Russia's heart. [...] We entrepreneurs of Russia, propose to [...] all those in whose hands real power is concentrated that they pool their efforts in searching for a political compromise that can prevent acute conflicts that threaten Russia's basic interests and its very existence as a state.[89]

Whoever won the election would have to implement policies 'categorically rejected by a large part of society', and the 'mutual repulsion of political forces was so great' that it could lead to 'civil war and the break-up of Russia'. The letter warned that for many 'the word "democracy" has become all but synonymous with an anti-state attitude', but 'we cannot allow the great ideas of freedom, civic spirit, justice, law and truth – the main elements of true people's rule – to be discredited.'[90] The plan was for Zyuganov to become prime minister with extended powers, while Yeltsin would remain as president as a 'guarantee of democratic freedoms and human rights'.[91] That was rejected, but the oligarchs made unquantified sums available to Yeltsin's campaign and were not too concerned about democratic niceties.

The oligarchs thus announced their presence as a political force. *Semibankirshchina*, or the 'group of seven bankers', came to the fore, and by the end of the decade a 'family' group around Yeltsin had emerged. While the 'bureaucratic' component of Yeltsin's power system favoured a postponement of the election and the 'security' bloc sought outright repression, the 'oligarchic' leg in alliance with reformists such as Chubais resolved on a frontal attack on the Communist opposition, in which perhaps a billion dollars were spent. The consequences were not long in coming. As Paul Klebnikov notes, 'Entering into politics, he [Berezovsky] outdid everyone even here. Having privatised a vast swathe of Russian industry, Berezovsky now privatised the state.'[92] In a notorious interview Berezovsky claimed that the seven had been responsible for Yeltsin's re-election and controlled 50% of the Russian economy: 'We hired Chubais and invested huge sums of money to ensure Yeltsin's election. Now we have the right to occupy government posts and enjoy the fruits of our victory.'[93] Their grip on the media was no less tight, controlling 70% of the Moscow press and radio and 80% of national television. Berezovsky put it starkly: 'If the media had not been free or private, we would not win elections.' The group saw themselves as 'an embattled elite pooling their efforts to steer Russia through a difficult transition'.[94]

No less humiliating for the authorities was an interview with *Nezavisimaya gazeta* in which Khodorkovsky made no bones about the relationship between politics and business: 'Politics is the most lucrative field of business in Russia. And it will be that way forever. We draw lots in order to pick out a person from our milieu for work in power.'[95] Potanin, head of Onexim Bank, was indeed delegated by the oligarchs to work as first deputy prime minister in charge of the economy from August 1996 until March 1997, and Berezovsky was deputy head of the Security Council from October 1996 until sacked on 4 November 1997. Oligarchs now firmly entered the ranks of the most influential politicians in the country, with Berezovsky between 1997 and 2000 consistently ranking as the top oligarch and in 1998 and 2000 listed as the fourth most influential person in the country. Of all the major oligarchs Khodorkovsky was ranked lowest, in those years placed only 25th and 60th respectively.[96] According to Satter, 'By 1997 a ruling criminal business oligarchy was in place.' They included Berezovsky, the head of the LogoVaz car dealership; Potanin; Gusinsky, the head of Most Bank; and 'Mikhail Khodorkovsky, the head of the Menatep Bank'.[97] The investment auctions and loans-for-shares scheme endowed a small group with an enormous concentration of economic power. They soon flexed their political muscles, provoking critics to suggest that only authoritarian methods could stop them.[98]

'THE EXPERIMENT IS OVER'

By late 1997 Russia's foreign debt reached $123.5 billion, and its domestic debt, mainly in treasury bills, reached $95 billion. Debt servicing alone swallowed 5% of GDP, with over a quarter of budget spending not backed by revenues. Most of the oligarchs were tax delinquents, and although the government had established a short-lived Emergency Tax Collection Commission (the 'Cheka'), it lacked the will and power to bring the new entrepreneurs to heel.[99] Faced with mounting budget shortfalls exacerbated by falling energy prices, the government tried to cover its debts by issuing bonds at ever higher interest rates. The whole system collapsed on 17 August 1998, when the government declared a moratorium on debt repayments and companies were forced to default on foreign loans. The financial crisis dealt a severe blow to Russian investors and signalled the end of the golden age of oligarchic capitalism. Companies dependent on the financial sector suffered most, including Gusinsky's Most Group and Potanin's Onexim Bank, while Smolensky's SBS-Agro and Vladimir Vinogradov's Inkombank were ruined. The Moscow branch of Bank Menatep, with 70% of its assets in state securities on the eve of the default, lost its banking licence. It transferred what was left to its sister bank, the St Petersburg branch of Bank Menatep, in a 'bridge' operation that hindered depositors' ability to gain redress.

The bank still faced a $250 million claim from its creditors, including some foreign banks, which had lent Menatep $266 million, secured by a 32% stake in Yukos. Lebedev, the director of Group Menatep, and Khodorkovsky tried to convince them to accept a three-year repayment plan secured against oil exports rather than Yukos shares. The largest creditors – Daiwa Bank, West Merchant Bank (a subsidiary of Westdeutsche Landesbank) and Standard Bank of South Africa – refused, and took over the collateral, representing 29% of Yukos shares. Their main concern was to cover their losses, but in mid-1999 the two companies precipitously sold their stake, reputedly receiving only half the amount of their loan, scared into dumping their shares by Khodorkovsky's threat of a share offering in Yukos that would have diluted their holdings to insignificance. At the same time Yukos was selling some of its prime assets to offshore companies, and it appeared to be in danger of becoming little more than a shell company.

The aim according to Yukos's defenders was to fight off the maverick American investor Kenneth Dart, heir to the Styrofoam fortune and leading private investor in Yukos, with some $2 billion committed by 1998 in various affiliated oil-producing companies including YNG, Samaraneftegaz and Tomskneft.[100] Dart reputedly practised what is called 'greenmail', the purchase of relatively small stakes in companies, typically 10–15%, which allowed him to block management proposals at shareholders' meetings until he was bought out, usually at 2–3 times the real value of his stock.[101] Dart was thus able to thwart Khodorkovsky's plans to streamline the management of the company, resulting in one of the major battles of the era, fought in innumerable court cases and media wars, but which irrevocably tarnished Khodorkovsky's reputation. One tactic employed by Khodorkovsky to win undivided control over Yukos assets was to issue millions of shares and move the real assets abroad, leaving minority shareholders with little more than empty shells.[102] Once the foreign companies were off the scene, Khodorkovsky and his associates repurchased most of the stock, the share offering was cancelled, and the assets that had been moved offshore were returned to Russia.[103] These methods were employed against Dart, whose stock in late 1998 was diluted using rising oil revenues, leading to Dart's losing of up to half of his investment, although in 1999 a settlement was reached. These machinations, and there were many more, gave the company a particularly unsavoury reputation, and it was only in 2003 that Yukos dared to go back to Western capital markets.[104]

Yukos ended the 1990s with arguably the worst reputation of all. The liberal paper *Novaya gazeta* in 1999 ran a story called 'Chronicle of an ideal crime', arguing that the privatisation of the oil industry had turned into the 'theft of the century', and noted that if most of the newborn oil magnates at least tried to keep up the appearance of honesty, there were some who did not even do this.

> The list of open cynics in the domestic oil market is led by Mikhail Khodorkovsky, a chemical engineer by training and a financial alchemist by nature. It was he who achieved in the oil sector what criminals throughout the ages have called an 'ideal crime'.

The report noted that what he had done with Yukos and VNK (Eastern Oil Company, acquired by Yukos for $850 million in 1997) in just 2–3 years 'is unprecedented in the history of oil piracy'. The report stressed: 'The main thing is that he is now closer than any other oil oligarch to achieving his cherished and genius plan to deprive the country of an enormous part of its oil resources.'[105] Coming from a paper that would later be Khodorkovsky's staunchest defender, this was strong stuff. Equally ironic, when Khodorkovsky took the paper to court, it was none other than the Basmanny District Court, whose name would later become synonymous with the subordination of law to power, that on 3 October 2000 found in his favour, declaring that the article had 'defamed his honour, dignity and business reputation'.[106]

On the morrow of the 1998 partial default, Luzhkov announced the end of an era: 'Ladies and gentlemen,' he declared, 'the experiment is over.'[107] Luzhkov's announcement was premature, but he was right in so far as the nature of Russian capitalism had changed, as had the economic conditions. The crisis marked the shift from financial to industrial capitalism, from speculation to production. Khodorkovsky underwent some sort of an 'internal reorientation of values',[108] reflected in the various missives from prison (see Chapters 9 and 10). He later wrote that from the default he learnt that 'not only laws but also ethics are important': 'I decided that I must not only repay all debts, but also do something so people live better'. Production stopped being his main aim and he stated: 'I understood that I would have to leave business, and that I would have to spend more time on public affairs.'[109] Like all other export-oriented Russian companies, Yukos benefited from the fivefold devaluation of the rouble following the default since oil was priced in dollars. The company sharply increased production and export volumes, drawing on Western expertise to exploit so-called 'easy oil' – output from wells that had been poorly tapped during the Soviet period.[110] Yukos took advantage of the rise in energy prices, tripling in just two years to reach $33 per barrel in 2000. Its stock value rose sharply and the sector's disposable revenues began an upward trajectory that was to fund Putin's state-building projects, although Yukos in the end became a victim of that process.

CORPORATE TRANSFORMATIONS

Big business began to transform itself from morally dubious 'oligarch capitalism' into respectable national capital. As world oil prices and exports rose, Khodorkovsky in October 1999 announced an ambitious investment programme.[111] Most major Russian oil companies launched a transparency drive, with the notable exception of Surgutneftegaz.[112] Khodorkovsky was in the vanguard of this transformation, changing Yukos from one of the most ruthless and predatory companies to a symbol of a more open and transparently managed enterprise. It adopted Western accounting standards and issued clear financial accounts every three months, and in 2002 Menatep published a list of its main shareholders. Pumping 1.1 million barrels of oil per day, the company was one of the world's leading producers, with 2% of global oil output. As one of Russia's best-performing companies, Yukos gained significant sympathy in the West in its later struggle with the Kremlin. In an interview in the late 1990s Khodorkovsky announced that if the prime minister were to ask him to resign as head of his bank, he would do so without hesitation: 'That's how Russia is organized. The state is always the dominant force in the economy.'[113] Khodorkovsky later forgot his own insight.

Khodorkovsky survived the shipwreck of the default and Putin's early attack on the most egregiously political of the oligarchs (see Chapter 2). Of the seven 'boyars' originally listed by Berezovsky in 1996, only three were still active in Russia in 2001: Mikhail Fridman, Vladimir Potanin and Khodorkovsky. In 2000 Yukos returned to the Moscow stock market, from which it had been delisted a year earlier for regulatory offences. At a Russian investment conference in London in June 2000, Khodorkovsky insisted that Yukos had outgrown its poor corporate governance record and sought to issue internationally traded shares. He dismissed Berezovsky's claims that Russian oligarchs exercised significant political influence: 'If we had just 10 per cent of the political influence that Berezovsky claims, we would never have allowed the government to impose the unbearable tax burden on business that it has.' He was open about his lobbying activities in parliament and the press, which would later provoke his downfall: 'I don't really see the difference, politically, between Yukos and General Motors. Both have about 2 per cent of [their country's] GDP. Both lobby in parliament for their interests. Both propagandise in the press.' Khodorkovsky stressed the need to reduce the tax burden on business, arguing that 'As long as the tax regime is unjust, I will try to find a way round it', and he agreed with Putin's moves to reduce the powers of Russia's regional leaders.[114]

PERSONAL LIFE

Khodorkovsky was just 19 when he married his first wife, Yelena Dobrovolskaya. She was also a member of the Mendeleev Institute's Komsomol committee. They had a son, Pavel, in June 1985, who later studied at a Swiss boarding school and then went to university in the United States, where he remains to this day at the head of the Institute of Modern Russia. After they divorced, Khodorkovsky supported his former wife to set up her own travel business. His second wife, Inna Valentinovna, was only 17 when she joined the night-school department of the Mendeleev Institute in 1986, and she later worked as a laboratory assistant before joining the Institute's

Komsomol organisation on 22 October of that year to handle the accounts. There she met Khodorkovsky, and a few months afterwards they became partners. Later she worked in the currency operations department of Menatep. Their daughter Anastasia was born on 26 April 1991, and they were married soon after. In 1999 they had twin sons, Ilya and Gleb. Inna did not complete her studies and gave up paid work to devote herself to the children. In June 1991 they moved out of the city to share a country house with Nevzlin's family on the Uspensky highway, and soon after rented a number of cottages on the campus of the International University at Skolkovo.

By 2002, aged only 38, Khodorkovsky was ranked number 101 (the highest of Russia's seven billionaires) of the world's rich with a net worth of $3.7 billion.[115] By 2003 *Forbes* estimated that his personal wealth had risen to nearly $8 billion, consolidating his top-ranking position in Russia and seeing him 26th in the global rankings, while the 2004 rankings saw him climb to 16th place with a purported net worth of $15.2 billion.[116] Khodorkovsky 'used to personify the predatory Russian oligarch', but his own image had been burnished along with that of his company.[117] Khodorkovsky liked to describe himself as three generations of Rockefellers rolled into one: robber baron, respected business leader and philanthropist (see Chapter 9). In 1999 Khodorkovsky and his team set up home in the elite exurb of Zhukovka, about an hour's drive west from Moscow city centre and once the home of Soviet generals and top Party officials. A number of his associates and Yukos executives also built houses in a closely guarded gated community called 'Yablonevy sad' ('Apple Orchard'), set among pine trees and gently rolling hills. According to Klebnikov, 'the compound itself bears a resemblance to a prison camp. It is surrounded by high walls, with powerful lights every 30 paces. Guards with machine guns patrol the perimeter.'[118]

The transformation of Yukos in the new millennium was accompanied by a physical transformation in Khodorkovsky. Up to the end of the 1990s he had a pallid Soviet look about him, with heavy-rimmed glasses, a rather thickset body, a moustache and persistently ill-kempt hair, but in the 2000s he had a makeover – with shorter hair, the moustache gone, his glasses changed to a rather Lennon-like rimless style – and he looked fitter.[119] He also joined the international jet-set lifestyle, with Savile Row suits but no fancy yachts. Addressing a meeting of the American Chamber of Commerce in Moscow in May 2001, Khodorkovsky didactically explained to his American guests why Russian business leaders dealt so brutally with shareholder rights: 'It's the mentality. Twenty years ago, under Soviet power, to be honest meant to die of hunger, and in some regions this mentality continues.'[120] This was probably not the message that the Americans wanted to hear.

Khodorkovsky had long been a member of the Rand US–Russia Business Leader Forum, an invitation-only organisation with which the veteran Sovietologist Jeremy Azrael was closely involved. The body met twice a year, alternately between Russia and America, and sought to acquaint Russian CEOs with the ways of Western business, including acclimatising them to the notion of corporate social responsibility while improving their image and influence in America and over civil society. Khodorkovsky was one of the original members from the early 1990s, along with Gusinsky, while on the American side members included Donald Rumsfeld (from 2001 to 2006 secretary of defence under President George W. Bush) and Kenneth Lay, who was later to achieve notoriety at the head of Enron Corporation. It was in this forum that Khodorkovsky got to know Bruce Jackson, formerly of Lockheed Martin, who became head of the Project on Transitional Democracies in 2002 and was an influential figure in Washington, lobbying for NATO enlargement. Jackson was married to a Belarusian and had close ties to the Democrats as well as the Republicans. Following Khodorkovsky's arrest, the Yukos affair became a battle of the lobbies, notably in trying to influence the US administration. Khodorkovsky was also a member of the US–Russia Business Council headed by Gene Lawson, with whom Khodorkovsky maintained strong personal relations.

Khodorkovsky also joined the Carlyle Group, the world's largest private-equity firm specialising in military–industrial investments, enjoying close ties with the Pentagon and, it almost goes without saying, the Bush (father and son) White House. Other members included the former secretary of state James Baker, the former defence secretaries William Perry and Frank Carlucci, the former British prime minister John Major, as well as a number of other prominent figures. In the 'war on terror' following the 11 September 2001 (9/11) attack on America the group used its contacts to shape the security agenda of the new era. Menatep was also able to lever these contacts into support for Yukos once the assault on the company began in 2003. Earlier that year Menatep had set up an international advisory board to create a global lobbying network on behalf of Yukos. One of the advisory-board members was Stuart Eizenstat, who had worked in the US treasury under President Bill Clinton, who himself was also an adviser to the lobbying company APCO and whose law company in October 2003 agreed to work with Kissinger McLarty Associates; Mack McLarty had been chief of staff under Clinton and was a member of the Carlyle Group. In spring 2002 Menatep announced that it would invest $50 million in the Carlyle Group. Following Khodorkovsky's arrest, Eizenstat, who had also served as US ambassador to the European Union, sprang to his defence.[121]

Khodorkovsky had risen from a poor boy growing up in the rough streets of Moscow to international financier and global capitalist. His rise coincided with the fall of Communism and the disintegration of the Soviet state. Khodorkovsky was an exemplary Soviet citizen, active in its Komsomol youth organisation, and imbued with a certain idealism that persisted into the new era; however, he also reflected the other side of Soviet citizenship, the ability to dissimulate and to break rules to survive. Opportunities could not have been grander from the late 1980s as the Soviet economic order was destroyed and whole industries came to the market. The state retreated into an enclave based on the Kremlin, while the country fell prey to criminal–economic entrepreneurs. With the rule of law in abeyance, the distinction between criminal and legitimate business activity was blurred. A powerful new force emerged, the super-wealthy oligarchs, who were prepared to dictate to the state. Conflict with a resurgent Russian state was inevitable.

CHAPTER 2

THE STATE AND THE OLIGARCHS

In his address to the Federal Assembly on 8 July 2000 Putin argued that 'an era is beginning in Russia where the authorities are gaining the moral right to demand that established state norms should be observed' and that 'strict observance of laws must become a necessity for all people in Russia by their own choice'.[1] He argued that the close relationship between big business and government should be broken. In an interview soon after, he insisted that he sought to put an end to the situation in which Russians appeared to have become subjects of different regions rather than citizens of a single country.[2] Oligarchs and regional barons were the two categories that he primarily had in his sights. The Russian state had suffered from the very reforms that it had sponsored, and now the state fought back. The oligarchs spent the latter part of the 1990s fighting among themselves; their class power had not been consolidated, and so they now proved defenceless when the government turned to the attack.

EQUIDISTANCE AND UNIFORMITY

The problem was recognised generally. As the lawyer and US government adviser Lee Wolosky put it at the time, before Putin could do anything else 'he must first rein in a dangerous posse of plutocrats riding roughshod over the country [...] these oligarchs – Boris Berezovsky, Mikhail Khodorkovsky, Roman Abramovich, Mikhail Fridman and others – largely co-opted Yeltsin's governments, silencing most opposition to their conduct'.[3] Wolosky in particular targeted Khodorkovsky, accusing him of numerous crimes including stripping value from the production companies and their stakeholders, stealing assets from Amoco and paying off law-enforcement officials; he even intimated complicity in murder. He called on the Russian government to renationalise the company and for the West to launch a transnational law-enforcement campaign against Khodorkovsky and his associates. The case was a powerful one but in numerous aspects overdrawn (certainly when it came to murder). In the end his appeal had greater resonance in Moscow than in Washington.

Putin repeatedly returned to the question. As the presidential election on 26 March 2000 approached, Putin asked: 'What then should be the relationship with the so-called oligarchs? The same as with anyone else. The same as with the owner of a small bakery or a shoe-repair shop.'[4] In a later interview, asked what would be the future for the oligarchs, Putin answered that if one meant 'those people who fuse, or help the fusion of, power and capital, there will be no oligarchs of this kind as a class'.[5] This was a clear allusion to Stalin's threat in 1929 to 'liquidate the kulaks as a class'. In an interview later that year Putin noted: 'In our country representatives of big business who try to influence political decision-making while remaining in the shadows have been regarded as oligarchs. There must be no such group of people.' He defended the need for big business, but absolutely refused to allow them a privileged political role: 'I cannot imagine people anywhere near me who try to exert influence from the shadows.'[6] Coming from someone surrounded by a camarilla of informal associates, this was rather rich.

In a crucial meeting with business representatives on 28 July 2000 he formalised the principle of 'equidistance' in relations between the state and the oligarchs: 'We will prevent anyone attaching themselves to political authority and using it for their own goals. No clan, no oligarch should come close to regional or federal authorities – they should be kept equally distanced from politics.' At that meeting he noted the 'highly politicised' actions of law-enforcement agencies against certain oligarchs, but stated: 'you yourselves to a significant degree formed this state through the politi-cal and quasi-political structures that you control.'[7] The basic deal was a 'pragmatic exchange of political restraint for secure property rights', and, as Tompson notes, the meeting assumed the character of a 'foundational political myth', even though the basic framework had been shaped by a whole series of actions since Putin's assumption of power.[8]

The consolidation of oligarch power would have rendered Russia a 'domain democracy', where certain groups (such as the military or entrepreneurs) could exercise veto powers by taking 'certain political domains out of the hands of demo-cratically elected representatives'.[9] The plutocratic social order of the 1990s was repudiated, although the scope for enrichment by individual oligarchs remained. Putin imposed an informal 'social contract' on big business: as long as the oligarchs paid their taxes and stayed out of politics, they would be left to get on with their affairs. The state would deal with oligarchs on the basis of equidistance, ending the phenomenon of court oligarchs stalking the corridors of power and using the state to advance their business interests. The new policy of equidistance was imposed by making an example of two of the most egregiously political of the oligarchs. Berezovsky, at the head of a major media and energy holding company, was forced into exile, together with Gusinsky, the founder of the NTV television channel, part of the Media-Most banking and media conglomerate that owned a string of newspapers. By the same token, the Putin administration imposed uniformity on the main electronic mass media.

MUDDY WATERS

Even before assuming the presidency Putin sought to reassert the state's authority in the energy sector. In late October 1999, as prime minister, he signed a decree accord-ing to which energy magnates could no longer be voting participants in the Ministry of Fuel and Energy. The likes of Rem Vyakhirev (Gazprom), Chubais (RAO UES, the electricity monopoly) and Vagit Alekperov (Lukoil) were thus excluded from direct participation in formulating policies of the ministry that provided Russia's single largest source of revenue. The debate in 1999 over the budget demonstrated the power of the oil lobby and just how entwined politics and oil had become in the country. The struggle to oust Vyakhirev from Gazprom had begun, so as to ensure that the Kremlin could control the revenues from the energy giant directly as well as to isolate Gusinsky, with whom Vyakhirev had forged a close relationship.[10] Gazprom funded Gusinsky's heavily indebted NTV to the tune of some half a billion dollars. Chubais's attempts to oust Sergei Bogdanchikov and place someone more amena-ble at the head of Rosneft were blocked. Khodorkovsky met Putin twice before the latter's formal election in March 2000 to discuss energy issues; although forming a favourable impression, Khodorkovsky rather condescendingly noted that Putin was 'more of a politician than an economist'. He called on the new administration to end talk of a group of well-connected oligarchs running the Kremlin: 'I hope the legends about the oligarchs will die along with the changing of presidents'; he also warned that 'Anyone who calls him [Berezovsky] an entrepreneur is mistaken'. He declared that the influence of American companies lobbying in Washington was much greater than anything seen in Moscow: 'We are like children in comparison.'[11] This was an imbalance that he ill-advisedly sought to rectify.

The first to feel the cold wind was Gusinsky, and the attack on him prefigured that on Khodorkovsky later. The Media-Most offices were raided on 11 May 2000, just four days after Putin's inauguration, and on 13 June Gusinsky was arrested and held in solitary confinement for four days. Gusinsky effectively bought his freedom, transferring ownership of NTV and other media outlets to a Gazprom subsidiary in return for permission to leave the country. Putin was in Spain at this time and gave the appearance, not for the last time, of being puzzled by what was happening at home. For Khodorkovsky, the attack on NTV's independence and thus media diversity represented the crossing of the Rubicon, hence he granted the company a loan that would later figure in his first trial.[12] He was one of 17 leading Russian entrepreneurs who actively spoke in defence of Gusinsky.[13] Few of them would return the compliment when he was arrested three years later. Putin did not forget this act of resistance to his authority; while for Khodorkovsky the attack on media diversity forever tainted the Putin regime in his eyes.

The tax affairs of a number of other companies, including Gazprom, Norilsk Nickel, Lukoil, and the biggest car manufacturer, AvtoVAZ, became objects of scrutiny in late 2000. Norilsk Nickel had fallen into Potanin's possession (through his holding company Interros) as a result of his loans-for-shares plan of 1995–6. Now the authorities called for repayment of $140 million in compensation for alleged underpayment when the plant was privatised in the auction that he had organised. The inclusion of AvtoVAZ in the list indicated the renewal of investigations into the affairs of Berezovsky, who had made his first millions by association with the hugely loss-making car company through his car-dealership business, LogoVaz. Berezovsky's interests had by now diversified to include Aeroflot, Sibneft and the media (including a controlling stake in ORT, Russia's main television station).[14] As Berezovsky put it in June 2000, the way that business had been conducted in the last decade meant that no one 'could survive a serious government effort to find something to charge them with'.[15]

In July 2000 Putin criticised 'people who feel comfortable in conditions of disorder, catching fish in muddy waters and wanting to keep things as they are'. Yeltsin had also occasionally talked in these terms, and, as prime minister, Primakov had launched an investigation against some business leaders, notably Berezovsky and Smolensky. In April 1999 Berezovsky had been charged with 'illegal business activity', but these charges were dropped in November (when Putin was already prime minister). The investigation into Berezovsky's activities – at the time of the takeover, Aeroflot's cash flow was diverted through a Swiss intermediary – had been conducted by Yury Skuratov when he was prosecutor general; however, Skuratov was dismissed from his post in Yeltsin's last year, with Putin's help.[16] Berezovsky was notorious for allegedly using his businesses as cash cows, running down their capitalisation for immediate benefit. Berezovsky (with his business partner Roman Abramovich) had acquired Sibneft in 1995 at a significant discount, and although it produced 40% as much oil as Surgutneftegaz, the market capitalisation of the latter (one of the best-managed oil majors in Russia) was 11 times higher. Berezovsky, as Khodorkovsky well understood, was always more interested in politics than business. Primakov's efforts to investigate Berezovsky and others in fact prompted the oligarchs to close ranks, and Primakov was dismissed as premier on 12 May 1999. A few days later Berezovsky's nominees were settling into ministerial posts, notably Nikolai Aksenenko, encouraging the notion of 'family' power, a union of oligarchs and Yeltsin's entourage.

Even at the time Putin's attack against leading businesses was condemned as 'absolutely illiterate'. The letter of 7 July 2000 by Deputy Prosecutor Yury Biryukov (who gained further notoriety in the Yukos case) calling for Potanin to reimburse what the state had lost through his 'criminal actions' and accusing him of acting 'in conspiracy' with Alfred Kokh (the former head of the State Property Committee) lacked evidence and rather pre-empted a judicial process that could have proved the charges.[17] This behaviour characterised the Yukos affair. Even by 2000 the attacks on such a range of disparate figures (Smolensky took the opportunity to flee abroad shortly after Gusinsky) and conducted in such an unprofessional manner aroused considerable speculation about the motivation: 'What is the driving force of this openly aggressive behaviour by the executive authorities against big Russian business?'[18] A number of options were suggested, ranging from the attempt to impose the 'dictatorship of law', a campaign that would affect other businesses (Sibneft and Yukos were named), to the simple attempt by the regime to gain financial resources for its political line. But why open up a second front at a time when Putin was locked in struggle with governors to change the federal system?

According to Olga Kryshtanovskaya, the leading Russian expert in elite studies:

> The destruction of the media empires of Berezovsky and Gusinsky led to the under-
> standing that the present regime would not allow itself to be blackmailed. Only
> those working with the authorities would be able to influence the media. Loyalty
> had become the new slogan of the oligarchs.[19]

A further explanation was that despite Putin's promise during the presidential campaign that 'We will not allow the results of privatisation to be reviewed', his hand was forced by factional struggles within the Kremlin. The demonstration effect of the use of selective justice was clearly a factor, which took on much more clearly delineated forms in the later attack on Khodorkovsky. As Voltaire put it in *Candide*, referring to the court martial and execution of Admiral John Byng following the Battle of Minorca in 1756, 'It is wise to kill an admiral from time to time to encourage the others.' Times had changed, and it was now the turn of oligarchs to be 'encouraged'. Putin defended actions by the tax police and the Prosecutor General's Office (PGO) against companies like Media-Most, AvtoVAZ, Lukoil and Interros. He insisted that 'the state has the right to expect entrepreneurs to observe the rules of the game', and argued that the state 'would act more vigorously to change the environment in which business operates. I am referring first and foremost to the tax sphere and the restoration of order in the economy.'[20] Putin stated that all the oligarchs would be kept equally at arm's length from the government.

Berezovsky's rather inglorious political career in Russia was now fast coming to an end. In the December 1999 parliamentary elections he won a seat from the single-member constituency in the North Caucasian republic of Karachai-Cherkessia, and thus gained immunity from prosecution. On 17 July 2000 he announced that he planned to resign his Duma seat in protest against 'the establishment of the authoritarian regime in Russia'. He argued that the campaign against the oligarchs was not selective, since none could consider themselves immune. 'Whether you are the first or last to be hanged is a dubious honour', he noted. 'I intend to play on equal terms with other oligarchs in this campaign launched by the state against Russian business.'[21] He described the guarantee of immunity as 'worthless', which in his case it probably was since most deputies would have been only too glad to strip him of his immunity and see him in court. He noted, 'Only those people who have been asleep for the past 10 years have avoided willingly or unwillingly breaking the law.'[22] His official letter of resignation of 19 July condemned both the attempt to rein in regional leaders and the criminal cases opened against businessmen. He called for an amnesty for all past economic crimes and denounced the anti-corruption drive as 'an orchestrated campaign, directed at destroying major independent businesses'.[23] In November 2000 he went into exile in London from where he plotted Putin's overthrow. He was granted political asylum in September 2003 and committed suicide on 23 March 2013.

Gusinsky joined Berezovsky in his condemnation of Putin's government. He asserted that the anti-oligarch campaign signalled the end of the democratic freedoms that Russia had enjoyed in the 1990s. As he put it, 'In Russia there used to be a police regime. It disappeared temporarily and now it is being rebuilt.'[24] Gazprom had provided considerable financial backing for NTV, and many considered that this was the real reason for the firm coming under investigation.[25] It was documentation dealing with the company's links with Media-Most that were seized when Gazprom's headquarters were raided on 11 May 2000. Similarly, Alekperov, the head of Lukoil, was associated with a number of television stations and held a joint stake with Potanin in the liberal daily *Izvestiya*. Some of the other oligarchs, notably Abramovich, not only avoided scrutiny but, with his associate Oleg Deripaska, was able during Putin's rise to amass an empire that brought 70% of Russia's aluminium industry under their control. In 2000 Abramovich levered out the arch-manipulator Berezovsky from his share of Sibneft, with the latter allegedly selling out at a discount. The matter became the subject of a $5.1 billion lawsuit in London in 2011–12, which Berezovsky spectacularly lost.

The methods used against Gusinsky and Berezovsky were similar to those applied at first against Yukos in 2003, including various public signals, heavy-handed searches and attempts at resolving issues through informal mechanisms. After having agreed in July 2000 to transfer his property to the state in exchange for an end to the case, Gusinsky later claimed that he had been blackmailed into signing by the press minister Mikhail Lesin and other officials. The mix of political motives and straightforward commercial greed was also to be repeated later. In the end Gusinsky lost his economic assets but kept his freedom, albeit in exile; while Berezovsky fled once it became clear that Putin would continue Primakov's struggle against him. The close involvement of the regime in all the attacks is another common feature, although sometimes disguised by tax, criminal or debt charges accompanied by the use of crude coercion. The differences between the cases are also significant: NTV faced major solvency questions, whereas Yukos in 2003 was enjoying a period of unprecedented growth.

BUSINESS AND THE STATE

Not since the Bolshevik revolution of 1917 had Russia seen an autonomous bourgeoisie, and Soviet prejudices against their independence as a class persisted. Twenty-one top figures of Russia's business elite met with the president on 28 July 2000 to lay down the ground rules of relations between government and business. This was not the first meeting between the business elite and the Kremlin, and under Yeltsin four had been held. In the wake of the Svyazinvest privatisation scandal, on 15 September 1997 top oligarchs had been invited to meet Yeltsin to lay down the rules of engagement.[26] Not much had come of the initiative, and the Kremlin now sought to ensure that the business leaders were disabused of the notion that they were equal political interlocutors with the elected presidency. The bureaucratic consolidation of the state was accompanied by the destruction of alternative centres of power.[27]

The aim of the July 2000 meeting was to establish a level economic playing field in which the role of the state as referee would be enhanced and respected. The agenda was set by Nemtsov, the leader of the liberal Union of Right Forces (SPS) Duma faction. He insisted: 'Business and power should not attack or blackmail each other, they should be partners working towards the economic recovery of Russia.' The business leaders presented a three-point declaration to the government: first, for the Kremlin to declare a moratorium on any investigations into the legitimacy of privatisation over the past decade and not to initiate any redistribution of former state property; second, the business community must undertake to play by the rules, pay taxes and scrupulously obey the law; and third, the government must rid itself of corrupt bureaucrats, while business tycoons for their part must undertake not to use government institutions or bribe state officials to fight their competitors.[28] The link between power and property was hardly challenged by such an extra-constitutional 'pact', which in any case left out some of the key players.

The 'new deal' did not contract big business to keep out of politics, but warned them not to use political instruments in their struggles or against the state. Many went on to pursue quasi-political careers, notably Abramovich as governor of Chukotka. In addition, Putin made clear that he would prefer a more institutionalised framework for relations with business, signalling a reversion to neo-corporatist forms of interest representation. After the meeting most leading oligarchs joined the Russian Union of Industrialists and Entrepreneurs (RSPP), which had hitherto been not much more than a club of 'red directors' and middle-ranking industrial managers. It was led by the veteran survivor of Soviet and Russian politics Arkady Volsky, who had served as an aide to both Yury Andropov and Gorbachev in the 1980s. The 'new RSPP' now acted as the collective voice of big business, lobbying its interests while at the same time constraining its membership. Putin addressed the group on an annual basis, and it was at one of these meetings, on 19 February 2003, that the fateful encounter between Khodorkovsky and Putin took place. The Delovaya Rossiya ('Business Russia') organisation represented medium and large 'neo-oligarchic' capital, while OPORA Rossii spoke for small and medium businesses. A 'consultative regime', to use Alexei Zudin's term, was created on the basis of a system of collective representation.[29] The 'silent acquiescence' of the business community reflected the new balance of power between the oligarchs and the state.[30]

An essential aspect of the new social contract was the emphasis on the 'social responsibility' of big business. While Putin persecuted some oligarchs on a selective and partial basis, with others he struck a bargain: invest your ill-gotten gains in the manufacturing ('real') part of the Russian economy or else face the consequences. A notable example of this business–state alliance was the involvement of Deripaska's Rusal company in the purchase and subsequent restructuring of the Gorky Automotive Works in Nizhny Novgorod. Putin thereby hoped to see filched assets return from offshore haunts and invested to revive the economy. Companies forged in the corrupt era of 'piratisation' were encouraged to become good capitalists based on transparent accounting standards and responsibility to shareholders (including minority ones) and legally accountable directors. These legitimate goals were soon subverted as the state turned towards a more *dirigiste* model and the regime's officials entered into business. The regime sponsored 'national champions' and intervened actively in the management of economic life. While Putin's policy was logical from a short-term perspective, this model of economic development effectively represented what I call 'meta-corruption', the state-sanctioned distortion of the economic sphere, often to the personal benefit of regime acolytes.

The shift to statism was accompanied by the proliferation of venal corruption. From early on in Putin's presidency there were endless stories of business owners being visited by senior officials in uniform (described by Boris Gryzlov as 'werewolves in epaulettes') who demanded money for Putin's re-election campaign or other purposes. They were invited to pay up in exchange for not having criminal cases opened concerning ancient business dealings.[31] Following the Yukos affair this type of raiding (*reiderstvo*) became a mass phenomenon, although no longer intended to fulfil political purposes but merely the personal enrichment of officials.[32] One of the most spectacular cases was the raid against the investment company Hermitage Capital, which ended in the violent death, after nearly a year in jail, of Sergei Magnitsky in November 2009. This was a natural continuation of the 'violent entrepreneurship' of the 1990s.[33]

The reaction of big business to the new dispensation was not always complaisant. As Konończuk notes, 'the oligarchs' political activity in 2000–3 did not so much decrease as transform in nature.'[34] Big business shifted the focus of its lobbying activity from the presidential administration to parliament and regional governments. In the State Duma the 'Russian Energy' cross-party bloc, with several dozen deputies, represented the interests of the energy lobby. A group sponsored by Yukos, but also including Lukoil, TNK and Surgutneftegaz, was coordinated by Vladimir Dubov, a Menatep shareholder who had been elected on what became the United Russia ticket. Dubov took over as head of the Duma's tax committee in December 1999 and actively worked to shape a fiscal regime favourable to the big oil companies (see Chapter 3).[35] In the regions the oil companies backed their candidates in gubernatorial elections and sought to shape elections to regional legislatures. Some companies were more circumspect. Abramovich's Sibneft, for example, simply closed down its political department.

BETWEEN ASSAULTS

With the most offensively political of the oligarchs out of the way, a period of quiet ensued in relations between the state and big business. The regime focused on other matters, notably reforming the party system. It also enjoyed the dramatic rise in oil income, growing from $14 billion in 1999 to $140 billion in 2005–6, allowing it to pay back the bulk of its debts to the London and Paris Clubs and, later, to squirrel revenue away into a Stabilisation Fund created on 1 January 2004. However, habits of the 1990s had certainly not disappeared. The sale of Slavneft in late 2002 was accompanied by traditional claims of insider dealing and favouritism. The director, Mikhail Gutseriev, was ousted in May 2002 in a boardroom coup instigated by the prime minister, Mikhail Kasyanov, and replaced by former Sibneft official Yury Sukhanov. Sibneft then proceeded to buy up shares in alliance with TNK. The ugly scenes in May 2002, when the Slavneft offices in the centre of Moscow were seized by private security guards in an attempt to restore Gutseriev, were reminiscent of the 'wild East' days of the 1990s, especially when Kasyanov sent in the police to evict the intruders. In October Kasyanov hastily pushed through the privatisation of Slavneft, with all 75% of the state's stake sold as a single block with a reserve price of $1.3 billion (later raised to $1.7 billion). In the days preceding the auction (set for 19 December) the competitors – Lukoil and Surgutneftegaz – were encouraged to withdraw their bids, while the China National Petroleum Corporation (CNPC) was barred on a technicality. Sibneft and TNK went on to win the auction as the sole joint bidders for $1.86 billion. The case recalled the insider dealings of the Yeltsin years, above all the loans-for-shares scandal.

As Barnes notes, 'leading economic actors […] are still engaged in a complex struggle for property that transcends simple processes of privatization or consolidation and shows no sign of abating.'[36] Although investment rose after 2000, it remained very low, and the remodelled RSPP was certainly far from an independent collective voice able to ensure the impartial exercise of the rule of law. Business magnates entered the RSPP en masse in autumn 2000 and eclipsed the old guard of Soviet industrial directors, much to Volsky's displeasure.[37] The RSPP now became known as 'the oligarchs' trade union'.[38] Writing on the eve of the Yukos affair, Barnes notes that 'economic groups in Russia are still strong enough to manipulate governmental decisions to their advantage, use selective legal enforcement in pursuit of assets, or simply ignore laws when it suits them'.[39] Big business had modified its behaviour, but the bounds of the new 'equidistance' deal were far from clear. The Yukos affair would provide the answer.

The 1998 crash reduced the role of banking conglomerates, and instead companies sought to take over assets, using a range of dubious methods including forced bankruptcies. Yukos pursued an aggressive acquisition strategy in the early 2000s, which confirms Barnes's argument that although these companies were no longer tied to banks they still sought to grow both deeper and wider. The struggle for property continued, and no post-transition period of consolidation had yet arrived. Tensions between statist and market-driven energy policy came to a head in 2003, as did the contradiction between companies becoming international or transnational. The prime example of the latter was the $6.7 billion deal completed in August 2003, whereby BP joined forces with Alfa Group, Access Industries and Renova Group (collectively known as AAR) to create TNK–BP, with shares split equally between the British company and its Russian partners. When in the same year Khodorkovsky sought to protect his assets by transnationalising the company through the sale of a large stake in Yukos to a foreign company, the government stepped in.

In his annual address to the nation on 16 May 2003 Putin advanced the ambitious plan to double Russian GDP in the space of a decade.[40] This would require annual growth in excess of 7%; although widely ridiculed at the time as a throwback to the exhortatory style of Soviet central planning, the target was basically met by the end of the decade. This was achieved primarily on the back of high natural-resource prices, and less by the state corporations established in Putin's second presidency to provide a developmental impetus. More immediately, the speech warned that 'monopolists are suffocating the competitive part of our economy'. It signalled a new activism by the state in economic life, to which Yukos fell victim.

FROM EQUIDISTANCE TO SUBORDINATION

The Yukos affair was not a Stalinist-type operation planned in advance and implemented methodically; it was provoked by a set of actions and reactions without a single common cause. The July 2000 'concordat' between business and the state, as well as the defeat of Berezovsky and Gusinsky, gave the regime the whip hand. From the summer of 2003, however, a new force emerged from within the system, intending to modify the administration's policies. The intra-systemic radicals, combining *siloviki* and statist bureaucrats, sought to achieve a redistribution of property, a change of elites at the national and regional levels, and the development of an activist ideology that would allow a 'state oligarchy' to consolidate power. Pavlovsky stressed that if these 'new oligarchs' won, then Putin's position would be immeasurably weakened and he would become their hostage.[41] Although the group that I shall call the 'politburo' (see below), had no independent legitimacy and relied on Putin, it was able to push through its agenda. In part this was possible because of the weakening of the outer bulwarks of the new property order, 'the liberal parties, the liberal press and the liberal bureaucracy'.[42] Ultimately, the case depended on Putin's decision to endorse the radicals, who sought to destroy independent business leaders through an anti-oligarch campaign, while fostering a new statist oligarchy of which they were part.

The radicalisation of policy came not from the right (the liberals) but from the securitised left. The 'left revanche' against the privatisation of the 1990s was sustained by the incomplete revolution in Russia's transition from the Soviet system to the new order. The semi-Soviet Russian ruling elite had developed considerably since 1991, and, while cognisant of the global context, when faced by perceived threats they reverted to stock neo-Soviet securo-bureaucratic responses. The Russian system had developed as a peculiar amalgam of a modern constitutional state (the 'stationary bandit' described by Mancur Olson) and a semi-autonomous administrative regime (the 'roving bandits').[43] The Yukos case exposed the fault lines in this construction as well as the split identity of the regime itself. Factions within the regime had different agendas, but gradually an 'affair' took shape embedded within a narrative that evolved as the case advanced.

One of the key bodies shaping this evolving narrative was the Council for National Strategy (SNS), founded in 2002 by Stanislav Belkovsky and Iosif Diskin.[44] In May 2003 the SNS issued a notorious report called 'The state and the oligarchs', which signalled the beginning of the assault on Yukos.[45] The SNS had already issued two reports raising similar concerns. The first in October 2002 was called 'The great game in Russia' and examined the key groups in Russian politics and how they affected the decision-making process. It argued that since 1995 Russia had been pursuing the path of 'oligarchic modernisation', and as the economic power of the oligarchs increased, so too did their political influence:

> As a result the 'oligarchs' are turning into a 'super-elite', concentrating political and economic influence, limited today by only one barrier – the prohibition on direct conflict with the president as a person. In this sense the federal government is not an independent subject. It de facto fulfils the function of executive committee for oligarch affairs (an instrument to balance oligarchic interests).[46]

A further report issued on 1 January 2003, 'Risks and threats facing Russia in 2003', developed the theme, warning that Russia was losing influence in the world and that business groups were eclipsing the autonomy of political actors.[47] The ruling layer, consisting in the report's view of 'oligarchs' and their political structures, was willing to trade Russia's influence as a regional power and as a partial continuer of Soviet global status in return for the legitimation of the capital seized in the 1990s. Only the United States, as the world's remaining superpower, could provide this external legitimation, while at home Putin's 'stable and popular regime', as the report put it, guaranteed the existing economic order.

By the time 'The state and the oligarchs' came out, the Council was even more alarmist, warning that the oligarchs had moved on to the offensive, looking to usurp the domestic regime while consolidating their external legitimacy. The importance of this report for the later development of the case can hardly be overstated. Reputedly sponsored by the *silovik* faction in the Kremlin, it signalled that the Yukos affair was framed as a way of resisting the encroachments of big business on the prerogatives of the state. Having completed the privatisation of the economy, the document argued, the oligarchs were now privatising politics. The authors warned of 'a creeping oligarchic coup' to change the country's system of governance to ensure 'the union of super-big business and executive power'. Khodorkovsky was named ten times in the report and Yukos 25 times, with Abramovich coming in second with nine and 22 mentions for Sibneft. In the end, though, only Khodorkovsky was singled out for attack.

The oligarch system had been created outside market mechanisms, where wealth had effectively been handed over by the government. Yukos was a prime example. Bought in the loans-for-shares auction in 1995 for $350 million, the report noted that after shares became publicly traded in 1997 'the corporation's market capitalisation reached $9 billion', accentuating that the rise occurred before the new Yukos management had done much in the way of adding value to the company, and on the eve of the planned merger with Sibneft in early 2003 Yukos's capitalisation approached $15 billion. The presidency was the major obstacle to their plans, hence the oligarchs favoured a shift to a more parliamentary system, with Khodorkovsky named as the main proponent of rebalancing the constitution, and probably the main beneficiary: 'The front-runner to be prime minister of such a government, formed under a new constitution, is considered to be Mikhail Khodorkovsky.'

The report stressed the 'anti-national' character of the oligarch system. Its property tended to be registered abroad, often in offshore companies. This was not just for tax minimisation and cash-flow purposes, but because 'in the collective understanding of the oligarchs foreign property in Russia is defended substantially more than domestic'. Thus the oligarchs were 'drawing on the resources of foreign states to guarantee their interests in Russia's political–economic space'. They also noted that most oligarchs kept their families abroad (although this did not apply to Khodorkovsky). The document identified what it called 'oligarchic autism', the inability to recognise that the interests of the mass of the people should be taken into account in governmental policy, or indeed that anything that took place outside the oligarch's narrow world had any strategic or even tactical significance. In sum, in the report's view the 'capitulationist state, wreathed in liberal rhetoric, today does not even fulfil the role of "nightwatchman", but opens the path for strengthening the power and influence of the oligarchs'. The idea of 'equidistance', the report insisted, acted as little more than a cover for the consolidation of oligarch power.

Although Putin had begun to reverse state capture, the report warned that oligarchs were now attempting to subvert the state by stealthier means – an 'oligarch's coup'. Economic magnates had privatised the economy, and they now sought to privatise the political system by winning a Duma majority sympathetic to their interests. If they pushed through constitutional changes rendering the government responsible to the parliamentary majority, then, in the authors' view, the presidency would be diminished and the seizure of power would be complete. To this end, parties had to be brought under oligarch control, and hence Yukos ramped up its political contributions. The report identified Khodorkovsky as the chief ideologue of the strategy, supported by some other oligarchs including Abramovich, Deripaska (head of the Base Element holding group) and Mikhail Fridman (chair of Alfa Group and TNK–BP). A new government under the control of parliament would be created, with Khodorkovsky the leading contender for the post of premier.

The report was presented to Putin by Igor Sechin, deputy head of the presidential administration and a leading *silovik*, and Viktor Ivanov, the administration official responsible for personnel appointments. The report was the political manifesto of the *siloviki*, a group of whom came together to create the 'politburo', since in their behaviour and views they hark back to the Soviet era. The 'politburo' faction was the driving force behind the Yukos affair, pushing Putin further than his own initial inclinations may have taken him.[48] Andrew Wilson speaks of the Yukos affair as an act of grand dramaturgy designed to reshape the orientations of the political system and for Putin to stamp his authority on the elite.[49] In practice, Putin's administration did not enter into this unholy struggle with clear intentions, let alone a grand design, but stumbled from event to event, torn by the factional fights that were characteristic of his presidency. This gave rise to the version that the whole Yukos affair was a giant provocation by the *siloviki* against both Khodorkovsky and Putin, a 'conspiracy' that succeeded far beyond any possible original intention.

OPENING RUSSIA

Khodorkovsky began as an ardent exponent of the view that the economy should be freed from social and state control; as Karl Polanyi noted, however, there is a natural cycle, and when pushed too far towards the market there is a 'counter-movement' towards some form of embedded economy constrained by social limits.[50] Khodorkovsky pushed the Polanyian elastic band far to the side of the view that economic life should enjoy an autonomous existence and, indeed, should shape the socio-political sphere. Kimmage puts this well: 'Once upon a time, a Russian oil company called Yukos and a man named Mikhail Khodorkovsky embodied a dream – that the free market, perhaps more than any other force, could and would complete Russia's transformation from a struggling post-Communist question mark into an economically prosperous democracy ruled by reasonable laws and anchored in the institution of private property.'[51] The partisans of this view, Kimmage notes, were always more numerous in the West than in Russia. The transformation of Yukos appeared to demonstrate the redemptive power of transparent corporate governance, international accountants and investment in social projects. Khodorkovsky himself had also undergone a transformation: 'With an almost messianic fervor, he had adopted his new cause to the point where he seemed to be waging a quest for martyrdom. No longer the young man who would give up his bank if the government asked', Putin's sanctions against the oligarchs 'had turned Khodorkovsky into a quixotic crusader almost eager for prison'.[52]

Even while leading the crusade for business, Khodorkovsky's horizon broadened beyond issues of day-to-day management, and he turned his talents to other spheres.

Khodorkovsky's concern for Russia's long-term future led to major investments in Russian education, culture and research, combined with attempts to improve the governance of his own corporation. In April 2003 Putin sent greetings to celebrate the tenth anniversary of Yukos: 'The effective organisation of labour and the high professionalism and responsibility of staff allow the company not only to maintain but to strengthen its position in domestic and foreign markets.'[53] All of this was cut short by the assault against his company and his person.

From the early 2000s Yukos developed a broad range of activities in society, and it took the path trodden by major oligarchs earlier by entering the media market. In 2003 Yukos bought *Moscow News* for $2 million and hung on to the paper until 2005. The veteran reporter and latterly editor, Viktor Loshak, was fired in September 2003 and in his place Khodorkovsky appointed Yevgeny Kiselev, a harsh critic of the regime and a refugee from the state's assault against NTV and TVS, where many of the independent journalists from NTV had sought shelter. Nevzlin took over current management, and the paper became Yukos's cheerleader. Kiselev proved a poor editor, provoking conflicts with most of his staff and sacking a number of its longest-serving journalists, leading to the mass resignation of its oversight board.[54]

In 2001 Yukos provided nearly one third of the $150 million donated for charitable purposes by Russian businesses, including funds for 1,000 scholarships and $743,000 to repair flood damage in Lensk.[55] In January 2002 the government removed tax breaks for donations, which stalled the shift towards corporate philanthropy. This did not stop Khodorkovsky. In December 2001 he established the Open Russia Foundation as an independent international charitable foundation, operating as a private endowment. It was modelled on George Soros's Open Society Institute (OSI) and shared the goal of developing civil society in Russia. Open Russia addressed social welfare, public health, cultural and civic education, as well as other issues, including working with partner bodies, community development and support for small businesses. Like OSI, it funded programmes in education and internet development. The goal, as Khodorkovsky put it, was to help create a 'normal country',[56] but it also transformed his image from robber baron to international philanthropist. Khodorkovsky later called this 'political philanthropy';[57] while Nevzlin observes that this was the moment when 'we moved beyond business'.[58]

Within months Open Russia had opened branches in 50 Russian regions, and was beginning to fill the ideological vacuum that Putin's technocratic style of governance encouraged. Open Russia was the first public association to sign an agreement with the Ministry of Culture, and in May 2002 a memorandum of understanding was approved for joint work on modernising village libraries.[59] In 2003 the budget for Yukos's philanthropic work reached $45 million.[60] The management board on 14 March 2002 noted that 'The target audience are youths between 12 and 18, whose world views are just forming. The aim is to create a positive informational field around Open Russia and its leadership.'[61] In effect, the philanthropic organisation became a new type of 'party surrogate', while Open Russia never made a secret of its support for 'democratic parties'. From the outset, Open Russia was managed by Irina Yasina, and the former American secretary of state Henry Kissinger was appointed to its management board, along with Senator Bill Bradley and the director of the Hermitage, Mikhail Piotrovsky. Its mission statement declared: 'The founders of the Open Russia Foundation believe that openness is the first principle of substantial and mutually enriching communication between the peoples of Russia and the West.'[62] Its fundamental aim was to cultivate a new generation that could participate in business and politics with the confidence to act as equals. For this purpose Khodorkovsky sponsored 'schools for public policy', which developed into a network of over 50 organisations. It also sponsored a 'club of regional journalists', which among other things met annually as a group. Addressing the second such convocation in April 2003, attended by 120 journalists from 53 regions, Khodorkovsky argued that the KPRF was the only party worthy of the name and noted that the Iraq War would have negative consequences for Russia, but he stressed that oil comprised only 15% of the country's GDP.[63] The club continued to work even after the demise of Yukos, now sponsored by Soros and USAID.[64]

The UK-based Khodorkovsky Foundation supported a range of philanthropic activities in Russia, including the Koralovo orphanage and lycée in Odintsovo district, located 60 kilometres from Moscow in an old country estate. Established by Khodorkovsky in 1994 and run by his parents, at any one time it shelters some 150 children aged 11–16. They come from some of Russia's worst tragedies, including the Chechen wars and the Dubrovka *Nord-Ost* theatre and the Beslan school sieges.[65] In a particularly vindictive twist, some of the school's graduates after the demise of Yukos were charged by the authorities for alleged tax irregularities. The foundation also supported Yelena Nemirovskaya's Moscow School of Political Studies, providing summer schools for young officials and politicians. Speaking in a seminar at the school on 26 July 2003 Khodorkovsky noted that the developing conflict was 'between business and authoritarianism'; he insisted, 'I will never surrender. If I do, they will go for others,' and in discussing the media he extolled the 'civic courage' of journalists, a term that he used frequently at this time.[66] The foundation sponsored the Russian Booker literary prize until 2006.

Critics suggested that Open Russia usurped state functions and opposed, as Valery Fadeev, the editor of the *Ekspert* weekly, put it, 'the main trend in the country's development – gaining autonomy, sovereignty and a new identity'. In Fadeev's view, Russia could not become just another Poland or Czech Republic: that would be to misunderstand 'the mission and meaning of Russia's existence'.[67] Like Soros's OSI, Open Russia came to be seen as a type of opposition party.[68] As a network structure, the regime feared that it could mobilise an anti-Putin movement, and thus even before the Orange revolution of late 2004 in Ukraine the authorities became alarmed. Both organisations came under pressure. Soros himself insisted that Khodorkovsky 'acted within the constraints of the law in supporting political parties. I am doing the same in the United States'.[69] Khodorkovsky portrayed his philanthropic and educational activities as representing an epochal transformation of Russia and trumpeted his achievements.[70]

Khodorkovsky was particularly assiduous in cultivating his image in America. He made a number of donations in the United States to burnish his image as an enlightened capitalist. In November 2001 he donated $1 million to the Library of Congress and forged close links with influential policy institutions in Washington by giving generous grants to the Carnegie Endowment for International Peace, the American Enterprise Institute and other non-profit institutions, although the Brookings Institution refused his offer of support.[71] His $500,000 grant to the Carnegie Moscow Center was openly declared, but some of the other recipients were less forthcoming. In 2002 Khodorkovsky contributed $100,000 for First Lady Laura Bush's favoured venture, the National Book Festival. Khodorkovsky's largesse was not confined to foreign beneficiaries, and he contributed to a number of civic projects for the development of Khanty-Mansiisk, the capital of the Khanty-Mansi oil-producing region, including an impressive art gallery stocked with nineteenth- and twentieth-century masters as well as some remarkable modernist European art. Khodorkovsky helped fund Alexander Yakovlev's book on the Gulag.[72]

One of the more audacious projects was the election of Nevzlin as rector of the Russian State Humanities University (RGGU) on 17 June 2003. Long led by Yury Afanasev, one of the radical democrats who helped Yeltsin to power, the university took over the premises of the former Higher Party School. In April 2003 the Yukos team offered the university $100 million over ten years. For Afanasev, the funds would allow the university 'to dramatically improve the level of scholarship and methodology in the humanities'. Staff resistance at a meeting on 24 April quickly gave way to support for the project, and the initiative was welcomed by Minister for Education Vladimir Filippov.[73] In the event, even though an office was prepared to his specifications, Nevzlin barely entered the building and left for Israel in late July. On 14 November 2003 Filippov personally tried to convince RGGU's Educational Council (*Uchenyi sovet*) to dismiss Nevzlin, but the professors, in a rare act of courage, refused. Although the academics had not been keen to see Nevzlin, a man with no scholarly reputation, take up the post, once installed it became a matter of principle to defend him. Nevzlin himself resigned as rector on 17 November 2003 to avoid damaging the university. The university had by then received $5 million, which was used for some infrastructural developments but above all to enhance staff salaries, which as a result became among the highest in Russia. The leadership of RGGU would have given Nevzlin and his associates an enhanced role in public and political life. The Yukos leadership had a 'business plan for Russia':

> They attacked corruption, they were removing one of the biggest oil companies from state control, they funded the opposition, they were educating a new genera-tion of free citizens, and they were developing humanities education. Just a little bit more and Russia would move out of President Putin's personal control and become a Western country.[74]

Their ambitions can be seen in the relations with Tomsk oblast. The company's head-quarters were directly opposite the regional administration's office, symbolising the contrasting realities of economic and political power. There are persistent allegations that Yukos failed to invest in the oilfields in the region, and instead extracted in a manner that did not secure the long-term viability of the field. Attempts by local scholars to write a history of the oil industry in the region were not supported.[75] However, the regional branch of Open Russia was extremely active and funded a number of projects. The company also invested heavily in the Tomsk Polytechnic Institute, training specialists in the petroleum industry. The company also sponsored the local television company, ensuring favourable coverage when Khodorkovsky visited the region about once every two months. Relations with the Khanty-Mansi oblast were more ambivalent. Vladimir Karasev, the deputy head of the regional government, noted:

> There was no such thing as the Khodorkovsky era here. Yukos was simply one of the vertically integrated companies – not the best, in some respects the worst. These people [the Yukos management] did not understand that one cannot endlessly extract profits. They understood too late that one should also invest in people. They had more accidents than anyone else. Other companies built social infrastructure

here from the very beginning. Yukos did finally understand all this and changed its mentality, but it was too late.[76]

Given more time it is possible that Yukos would have rehabilitated its reputation and gone on to become one of Russia's great companies and a continuing sponsor of philanthropy, but for this less haste and more modesty would have been required. Instead Khodorkovsky conducted his good works in a classically Soviet campaigning spirit, and the respect that he won with the one hand was lost with the other.

Although the policy of equidistance remained in operation, a number of Russian oligarchs appeared to have forgotten the other part of the new social contract – investment in the domestic economy and society, on the Kremlin's terms. The purchase of Chelsea Football Club by Abramovich attracted much negative comment and was contrasted with the purchase for the nation of Fabergé eggs by Viktor Vekselberg. Capital flight remained high, suggesting that the new business elite had little confidence in the country, while the purchase of extravagant properties abroad reinforced this impression. The support given to Western educational and cultural institutions aroused particular ire. Potanin provided generous funds to the Guggenheim Museum in New York, while Fridman gave a large donation to the Jewish Museum there. In 2003, moreover, Yukos planned to distribute some $3 billion in dividends, more than four times as much as in the previous year, and this meant fewer resources to invest in the business. With Western support for oligarchic capitalism in Russia increasingly perceived to be the final stage of the Cold War, Khodorkovsky was fast running out of friends in the country.

THE REVENGE OF THE STATE

The 1998 financial crisis signalled the end of a distinctive period. Rutland argues that 'the demise of oligarchic capitalism was due to deep contradictions in the model, and not merely to contingent factors such as Yeltsin's incompetence or the August 1998 crash'. He singles out two main contradictions: 'First, the oligarchs were parasitic on the Russian state.' They not only drained the exchequer of financial resources, but also undermined the working of state institutions. Second, 'the oligarchs were deeply divided among themselves.'[77] There had been suicidal conflict over the Svyazinvest privatisation in 1997, and no sense of self-preservation prevented the feuding, in spite of Yeltsin's attempts to arbitrate some sort of truce. The competitive nature of oligarch power almost by definition precluded collective action, even in self-defence.

By the early 2000s a third contradiction was becoming evident: the challenge to the autonomy of state power itself. The Putinite 'social contract' of 2000–3 was inherently unstable, if only because none of the fundamental issues had been resolved. The balance of power between the oligarchs and the bureaucracy as well as the moral high ground remained in contention. Khodorkovsky won plaudits by adopting Western accounting standards and social activism, but the accompanying self-promotion antagonised the authorities as well as other oligarchs.

At the heart of Putin's thinking was a reactionary–remedial narrative about the 1990s. While the 1990s in Russia was accompanied by massive inequality and the rise of the magnates, it was also the decade when capitalism in the main was built. Nevertheless, Putin returned frequently to the idea that in the 1990s business had accrued powers that were not legitimate and had thus encroached on the prerogatives of the state. Although Berezovsky's influence on the Kremlin leadership was not as great as he boasted, the ability of big business, and Yukos in particular, to shape and block legislation is a classic case of overweening business power.[78] This is certainly part of the picture, but does not by any means cover the complexity of the relationship. A survey conducted by Timothy Frye of 500 company managers in late 2000 identified a system of mutual 'exchange' between businesses and the state.[79] The 'state capture' model is at best a simplification, a view confirmed by various cases launched against companies by state agencies in arbitration courts.

Hence Putin at first devised his policies in reaction to the alleged excesses of the 1990s, but from 2003 a more remedial element came to the fore. The 'social contract' between business and the Kremlin was being rethought. It was no longer enough for big business to stay out of politics: the economic sphere was to be reshaped by the authorities, and the oligarchs were to understand that their historic role as independent creators of capitalism was over. A new model of political economy was to emerge in which the notion of an 'oligarch' as a politically independent entrepreneur was to become anachronistic. Putin's attempts to restructure Russian political economy signalled a sea change in the legal environment. Oligarchs like Berezovsky had long warned of the danger from the traditional left, epitomised above all by the return to power of the Communists, but the oligarchs were now outflanked by a new type of securo-leftism in alliance with the presidency.

The anti-oligarch campaign was accompanied by suspicions that one set of tycoons was using the law and the presidency against another set. In particular Abramovich, who in early 2000 had participated in the creation of a holding that controlled most of Russia's aluminium production, was known to covet Norilsk Nickel. Abramovich had made his fortune when he teamed up with Berezovsky in 1995 to acquire Sibneft in one of the most notorious loans-for-shares deals, and later Berezovsky sold his stake to Abramovich as he fled to London. Other oligarchs, notably Fridman at the head of TNK, and Deripaska at the head of the rambling metals conglomerate Basic Element, turned over a new leaf and gradually brought their companies up to international levels of corporate governance. They accepted the new rules of the game and thus prospered in the new era of Kremlin-sponsored oligarchy.

Khodorkovsky came to be seen as an obstacle to the creation of the new system. One of the companies bought in an investment auction in the early 1990s now came back to haunt the Yukos team. The giant Apatit plant, established in 1929, was the country's largest phosphate company. It was bought in a tender by Menatep's AOZT Volna subsidiary in 1994 for $280 million, accompanied by strict investment conditions, which in technical terms were not fulfilled. Yukos argues that they feared that the old Apatit management would simply steal and squander the money, so Menatep took over the management of the company, paid the wages, optimised taxes and invested in infrastructure. These indirect investments were the basis for the amicable settlement of the dispute on 19 November 2002 with the state privatisation authority, with the Moscow Arbitrazh court soon after endorsing the view that Menatep had made the requisite investment in Apatit. However, in response to a letter from the governor of Pskov oblast to Putin, condemning the allegedly unfavourable terms of the settlement, the case was reopened. Putin requested that the prosecutor general examine whether any criminal offence had been committed in the acquisition of Apatit and the subsequent trading practices.[80] On 28 April 2003 the prosecutor general reported that he found no grounds to take action.[81] The investigation had included Kasyanov and took evidence from numerous governmental bodies including the Federal Anti-Monopoly Agency, the Ministry of Internal Affairs (MVD), the FSB, the taxation ministry, the Federal Tax Police, the Ministry of Finance, the Federal Agency for State Property Management and the Moscow branch of the MVD's Economic Crimes Department. One would have thought that this would have satisfied Putin's concerns, yet on 20 June 2003 a full criminal investigation was launched that eventually led to Khodorkovsky, Lebedev and some of their past subordinates, including Natalya Chernysheva, who by 2003 was an official of Putin's own administration, being charged of conspiring with others to defraud the Property Fund of Murmansk.

The attack signalled the Kremlin's determination to impose its authority in the country, but it was part of a broader political change. The December 2003 parliamentary-election campaign was characterised by an anti-business animus, with almost all political parties engaged in populist oligarch-bashing. Sergei Glazev, one of the leaders of the Kremlin-sponsored Rodina party, a left-populist project party designed to draw votes away from the Communists, called for the introduction of a 'resource tax', a punitive and retrospective levy on big business intended to recuperate some of the losses endured by the state in the loans-for-shares auctions and other privatisations. Already from March 2003 the mass electronic media was dominated by the question of how to make the oligarchs pay for the sins of the 1990s.[82] The remedial agenda was also a feature of the March 2004 presidential campaign.

On 19 June 2003 the head of one of the units of Yukos's economic-security department, Alexei Pichugin, was arrested and later charged with organising up to five contract killings.[83] On 26 June the PGO conducted a search of Yukos's Moscow headquarters. Finally, signalling the beginning of the 'Yukos affair' proper, on 2 July the head of Group Menatep (Yukos's main shareholder), Platon Lebedev, was arrested in connection with Apatit and tax evasion by Menatep subsidiaries.[84] Nevzlin and Khodorkovsky were questioned as witnesses in the Lebedev case. Months of pressure culminated in Khodorkovsky's arrest on 25 October. We shall return to these events later. At the same time various threats were made against other oligarchs. A long-running case against Deripaska at the head of Russian Aluminium was resurrected, while the Kremlin made clear to Abramovich that his extravagant purchase in 2003 of the Chelsea Football Club in London was frowned upon. Even the Kremlin ultra-loyalist Potanin was not immune when it became known that he was looking for ways to transfer some of his assets abroad. Thus, in the early stages of the Yukos affair it was unclear whether the aim was to remove a single troublesome oligarch or to resume the struggle against the oligarchs as a class. In September 2003 Putin insisted that there would be no review of the results of privatisation and that the attack on Yukos was an exceptional case, yet forces had been unleashed that even he could not control.

CHAPTER 3

WHY KHODORKOVSKY?

The arrest of Mikhail Khodorkovsky on 25 October 2003, following months of pressure against Yukos, on charges of tax evasion and irregularities during privatisation, demonstrated that a new model of state–economy relations was emerging. The arrest signalled the breakdown of Putin's policy of 'equidistance', in which the oligarchs would no longer have privileged access to political power. It also signalled an attempt by the so-called *siloviki* to break the hold on government still exercised by Yeltsinite 'old Muscovite' ideas and elites. Kononchuk fairly notes that analysis of the Yukos affair is complicated by 'the overlap of its numerous plots and aspects', and that its 'multidimensionality and ambiguity makes it difficult to restrict oneself to one particular interpretation or one decisive cause'.[1] A mix of objective issues, notably the prospective sale of a large part of the company to a foreign corporation; subjective factors, above all Yukos's involvement in politics and civic affairs; and personal issues, with Khodorkovsky emerging as an independent politician, combined to provoke the attack. With the eclipse of Berezovsky and Gusinsky and the political self-restraint exercised by the other magnates, Khodorkovsky emerged as the leader not only of the nascent bourgeoisie but also of a quasi-political movement.

A STATE WITHIN THE STATE

As the state strengthened in the early 2000s, so too did the counter-state in the form of Yukos and its multifarious endeavours. State consolidation took the form of bureaucratic aggregation on the basis of a technocratic policy agenda accompanied by factional conflict. Andrei Piontovsky asks why Khodorkovsky was singled out, and not Deripaska or Chubais. He, like them, was a child of the original sin of the merger of power and money, and, like the others, he was appointed as one of the super-rich. However:

> Unlike the others, he has recently tried to draw a line under his past and to play the game according to different rules. [...] That is, he has let it be understood that he no longer wanted to be dependent on the authorities. This could not please either the bureaucracy or the *siloviki*, who are the armed wing of the bureaucracy.

Echoing Khodorkovsky's own sentiments, Piontovsky argued that in ten years he had travelled the path that took American businesspeople three generations. He notes the paradox that 'The former oligarch Khodorkovsky is fighting today against oligarchical capitalism'.[2]

The transformation was indeed radical, advancing a remedial programme of its own. Khodorkovsky's activities assumed the expansive characteristics of an 'empire', generating its own rules and purposes, constantly expanding into new spheres of social, political and economic life. Menatep became a microcosm of Russia's transition as a whole, with enormous achievements inadequately inscribed into the constitutional state. The polymorphic Menatep empire came into conflict with the administrative regime because of their functional similarities, however contrasting their dynamics and purposes. In their study of the 'shadow' economy in Russia, Klyamkin and Timofeev argue: '[T]he Russian system of shadow relations is nothing other than a privatised state, developing as an all-encompassing *para-state*, which at the same time falls well within the conceptual framework of the "shadow economy".'[3] In other words, the widespread development of informal relations and survival strategies bypassing formal social and constitutional institutional structures generated a type of alternative state, with codes of meaning and political practices of its own. Since the official state was incapable of doing its job properly, Yukos executives claimed the moral right to create their own.

The complex of social relations that we call Yukos generated an extraordinarily concentrated form of para-state. Just like the state itself, the company maintained a distinctive 'administrative resource' of its own, developing its policies on a number of important issues and pursuing them with a single-minded determination that was characteristic of all Khodorkovsky's endeavours. Indeed, on a number of occasions 'Khodorkovsky ignored budgetary and regional politics, and subordinated the state to himself on the grounds that the state was corrupted and he,

Khodorkovsky, was more effective than the state.'[4] Khodorkovsky did not hesitate to defend his views on the Russian tax system.[5] Like Putin, but from the opposite end of the state–society spectrum, Khodorkovsky found existing institutions constraining and sought para-constitutional solutions to practical problems. The company became a type of 'corporate state', acting as a miniature entity pursuing its own interests in a hierarchical state-like manner while mobilising horizontal networks (including the media, civil-society organisations and representative bodies) implicitly against Putin's regime. The regime, in turn, feared that the merger of vertical and horizontal axes of power would in due course threaten the autonomy of the state itself.

A distinctive Yukos spirit was generated within the company, and this shaped its external relations and its employees. Even after Alexei Golubovich – the head of Menatep's investment operations in the mid-1990s and later the director of Yukos's strategic planning and corporate finances – left the company in 2001, he continued to attend Menatep's investor meetings 'so that I was not suspected of disloyalty'.[6] Yuliya Latynina notes this characteristic of the 'Khodorkovsky clan': 'In the team no one ever betrayed another,' but outsiders were considered expendable.[7] Unlike the Yeltsin 'clan', where family relations became important, Khodorkovsky's group was based on an abstract loyalty to 'the firm', although paying deeply personalised forms of obeisance to the company's executives and in particular to the charismatic figurehead. Access to the body of the leader became increasingly limited to a small band of loyalists.[8] A cult of personality in one company developed.

Yukos ran an extensive security service overseen by Nevzlin, which engaged in analysis as well as protection activities. As Olga Kostina, who worked with Nevzlin, recalls, when a Yukos employee bought an apartment, it was not unusual for a security operative to check its dimensions and to ask about the source of funding, concerned whether any Yukos secrets had been sold. Nevzlin in her view had great faith in the special services, and she argued that he believed in the power of fear to manage people. She left the company to work in the Moscow mayor's office, but even there Nevzlin called frequently to find out what she was doing, and when she answered that she no longer worked for him, he responded: 'No, you are mistaken. You will always work for me.'[9] In November 1998 a bomb exploded outside her door, for which Pichugin (see Chapter 6) was charged in his first trial.

Unlike many businesses in the 1990s, which acted as predators focused on certain limited ends (usually the capture of cash flows), Khodorkovsky's empire took on increasingly stable forms.[10] Its vaulting ambition in the early 2000s and the proliferation of social and political initiatives meant that the company began to traverse the path taken by the modern state itself, from roaming to stationary bandit; in other words, to take on state-like characteristics. The company in the early 2000s negotiated with China as if it was a sovereign state, and in his various dealings with foreign powers 'Khodorkovsky was acting like a king, not a subject'.[11] Another account puts it as follows: 'He even started appearing in foreign capitals – often acting more like a head of state than like an oil magnate.'[12] State-like formations substituted for under-developed political parties and operated according to a zero-sum exclusive logic. Khodorkovsky's expanding empire began to claim a society-forming capacity and at that point became a direct threat to Putin's regime.[13]

Yelena Tokareva, the head of the *Stringer* journal and website established in 2000 specialising in political information, argues: 'From 2002 the Yukos corporation entered the political phase of its development and its main efforts were no longer directed even to producing oil but focused on buying power in the country as a whole, and whole regions.' Yukos launched a whole range of political projects that, in Tokareva's view, provoked the state to respond, and the tax question was no more than a tactic to avoid talking about political issues.[14] From this perspective, consumed by hubris, the Menatep–Yukos leaders ignored the warning signs.

Thane Gustafson adduces elements of this argument in his magisterial study of the Russian oil industry. He argues that Yukos's drive to increase short-term production exploited oilfields in a Soviet manner, taking the easy oil and moving on, thus alienating the oil professionals. The aggressive use of transfer pricing, the high-handed pipeline negotiations with China, the attempts to shape the oil tax regime in parliament and above all Khodorkovsky's arrogant personal manner and his increasingly accentuated interest in political and social affairs broke with the imposed conventions of the Putin system and provoked the attack. Thus Gustafson eschews systemic explanations, such as the consolidation of a predatory state or fears associated with the sale of Yukos–Sibneft shares to an American company, and instead focuses on the personal factor:

> Without the factor of personality, in short, the contest and the privatized oil industry would arguably not have descended into such a bitter confrontation among a small group of powerful men, which in turn served as the convenient instrument for one leadership faction to gain the edge in the making of policy.[15]

Khodorkovsky thought he was leading a crusade for the soul of Russia; instead, as so often in Russian history, he came to be seen as alien and threatening: 'Khodorkovsky and Yukos were attacked because they were seen by a wide range of Russian elite opinion as a foreign body and a threat.'[16]

In his characteristically ironic manner, Khodorkovsky is alleged to have commented more than once that he could not respect a state that had not yet put him in jail.[17] If this is true, then Putin in the end decided to teach Khodorkovsky to respect the state. However, the constitutional state was weakened as a result of the attack, with the judicial system manifestly engaged in a political trial. In other words, the Yukos affair not only damaged state development but also strengthened the arbitrariness of the administrative regime. Equally, the destruction of Yukos damaged society-forming processes, undermining the investment and business climate and the consolidation of civil society and a ramified business class. Khodorkovsky and Yukos, as we have seen, sponsored the development of civil society and public politics, but it did so in a state-like manner, a contradiction that lies at the heart of the whole Yukos affair. On the other side, the state in the Yukos affair acted as business corporations had done earlier in their struggle for property, including the instrumental use of law and the application of coercive power. In mimicking the para-state behaviour of the shadow economy, the regime itself, permeated by the venal concerns that are the essence of business, began to take on para-societal characteristics, another contradiction that inhibited the development of a classic rule-of-law state. As for the economy, the anarcho-oligarchy of the 1990s had given way by the late Putin presidency to a bureaucratic oligarch system characterised by the creation of state corporations and an internally differentiated oligarchy. Conflict between business and the state was replaced by a dangerous merger of the state and business.

The Yukos affair exposed two types of corruption in Russia. The commercialisation of services intended to operate for the public good manifested itself in what can be called 'venal' corruption. However, when the logic of one sphere (the market) invades another sphere (the state), we are dealing with something far more profound, and I call this 'meta-corruption'. The flow of meta-corruption in the Putin years was reversed: the logic of the state (in the degenerated form of the regime) invaded the market, a process which in broad terms can be described as the change from state capture to business capture.[18] The systemic breakdown of the boundary between the state and the market in the Yeltsin era continued in an inverted form into the Putin period. The Yukos affair represented an attempt to put an end to one type of meta-corruption, and to that extent it gained a degree of elite and popular support, but it gave rise to another type.

KHODORKOVSKY'S DEFECTION

The case against Yukos has a grimly personal element, directed against Khodorkovsky as a business leader and as an individual. In the 1990s Khodorkovsky amassed a vast fortune and paid little tax, but as a *Financial Times* leader puts it, 'so did other oligarchs'; however, 'Mr Khodorkovsky was chosen because he was the richest and politically the most outspoken. That decision was arbitrary and immoral.'[19] Andrew Jack describes in detail the strained relations between Yukos and the government and in particular Khodorkovsky's refusal to subordinate himself to Putin.[20] A tendentious study argues that Khodorkovsky was always motivated by envy and considered it unfair that Putin, who had never risen higher than a lieutenant colonel in the KGB, 'was occupying a post higher than that of a marshal'.[21]

Khodorkovsky recounts how in December 2000, at the request of the RSPP, in whose bureau he had been since October, he prepared a report for the president on the bureaucratic burden on business, 'imposed above all by the law and order agencies'. Khodorkovsky warned that a major company could become the object of attention and thereby 'lose millions of dollars of potential investment for the country'.[22] Yukos was delegated by an informal business trade union (above all representing a cartel of oil companies) to advance their interests in parliament, a mission that Khodorkovsky rather ill-advisedly took on.[23]

Lord Browne, the head of BP, describes meeting Khodorkovsky at his house in Cambridge on 17 February 2002:

> Bespectacled, soft-spoken Khodorkovsky could at first glance be mistaken as unassuming. But as the conversation progressed, I became increasingly nervous. He began to talk about getting people elected to the Duma, about how he could make sure oil companies did not pay much tax, and about how he had many influential people under his control. For me, he seemed too powerful. It is easy to say this with hindsight, but there was something untoward about his approach.[24]

Khodorkovsky offered BP a 25% stake in Yukos, motivated in part by the need for international expertise, but also to act as an insurance policy against state attack. Browne recalls that shortly before Khodorkovsky's arrest Putin remarked to him: 'I have eaten more dirt than I need to from that man.' Browne comments that

> Khodorkovsky did what Putin regarded as unforgiveable. He started meddling in the political arena when he was only a businessman. Putin's rule was 'stay out of

politics, just do business and you will be all right'. Khodorkovsky crossed that line. When you do that in Russia there is no coming back.[25]

Browne then goes on to describe the tribulations attending the creation and management of TNK–BP, including the sudden imposition of back taxes. He noted that 'it is easy to think there are no rules in Russia. [...] The problem is not the lack of laws but their selective application. And this is what creates this sense of lawlessness'.[26]

Khodorkovsky reveals that some time before 2003 the Sochi-coast sanatorium Rus, which Yukos inherited from the purchase of Tomskneft and which was used for their workers and managers, was expropriated by Putin's presidential administration. For him this was a 'breaking point': not so much over the facility itself, but the way in which the administrative system simply decided to take it over. There was no recourse to law or due process.[27] Equally, Khodorkovsky at first did not believe that Putin had been personally responsible for Gusinsky's and NTV's travails, until insiders convinced him otherwise. At that point 'I lost my internal loyalty to the authorities, which I had retained from Yeltsin's time [...] [they] stopped being mine, dividing people into allies and enemies'.[28] Even so, Khodorkovsky stresses that up to August 2003 'I did not fight against Putin, but for the choice between Putin and society. And only in August I understood: Putin has made his choice'. He describes how a deal could probably have been made, and authoritative people did offer them, but the price, both financial and moral, would have been intolerable.[29] 'I could never agree to [the return of] an Asiatic police state, a "sovok", at whatever price'.[30] Khodorkovsky stressed that his fundamental disagreement with Putin lay in their differing views of 'managing state affairs and visions of the future', with Putin favouring 'the vertical of power', which Khodorkovsky considered 'archaic'.[31]

Personal relations between Putin and Khodorkovsky were for the most part proper, but as 2003 advanced they became increasingly strained. A trivial but perhaps psychologically important point is that Khodorkovsky attended various meetings with the president in his trademark rollneck sweater, whereas Putin is a stickler for formality on these occasions.[32] Khodorkovsky's informality was seen by the presidential administration as a sign of his arrogance and contempt not only for the president but also for the dignity of the office and the state that he represented. The political was becoming personal. As a later commentary put it, Khodorkovsky addressed Putin 'in the manner he would with owners of the businesses that caught his fancy. Putin took offence, and as far as Putin is concerned, offending the president is no better than offending the state itself'. Khodorkovsky not only posed a threat to the Russian state but 'had the capacity to turn this threat into reality'.[33] Khodorkovsky certainly maintained an *hauteur* in his relations with Putin and underestimated the latter's determination and qualities as a statesman, let alone his touchiness and sensitivity to slights. Among his friends he allegedly referred to Putin dismissively as 'lieutenant Vova' (in this context, a derogatory diminutive of Vladimir, the mid-ranking secret policeman). Khodorkovsky had hired former security officials like Putin by the dozen and he was used to dealing with them as subordinates; this attitude spilt over into his relations with the president.[34]

These accumulating tensions boiled over into open confrontation at a fateful meeting of business leaders with Putin in St Catherine's Hall in the Kremlin on 19 February 2003. Khodorkovsky's reckless streak was on full display. He was the second of the main speakers, after Alexei Mordashov of Severstal reported on administrative pressure on small and medium businesses. This was the fifth such meeting since Putin had come to power. The first, on 28 July 2000, as we have seen, set the rules of the game, and the next three – on 31 May 2001, focusing on legal, pension, administrative and tax reforms and Russia's entry into the WTO; on 6 June 2001, on the motor industry; and on 23 May 2002, on accelerating economic growth – were all low key. If not for later events, the fifth meeting, whose theme was administrative reform, would also have been unremarkable.[35] In his opening remarks Putin noted that the struggle against corruption was essential, not through coercive means but by ensuring that rules were easier to obey than to avoid.[36] Khodorkovsky's speech on behalf of the RSPP was titled 'Corruption in Russia: a brake on economic growth', and was sanctioned by Alexander Voloshin, the head of the presidential administration, and his deputy, Medvedev, who was responsible for organising the meeting.[37] It should have been delivered by the head of Alfa Bank, Fridman, but two days before the meeting he had refused to take on the role. When asked later by Kondaurov why he had done so, Khodorkovsky replied: '*Buinykh malo* [There are not enough rebellious spirits].'[38]

It is clear from the video of the meeting that Khodorkovsky was extremely nervous, pale, his voice breaking. He provided some opinion-polling data and other statistics, including the assertion that corruption had reached $30 billion per year, a quarter of the state budget and some 10% of GDP, and that according to the Indem Foundation 72% of Russians feared going to court since the bribes were too high. He noted that even children had been corrupted, detailing the stiff competition for places in institutes training low-paid tax inspectors and other civil servants, and suggested that some arithmetic other than wages entered their calculations – obviously the bribes that they would be able to receive on graduating.[39] As Khodorkovsky went on Putin's expression hardened, and at this comment he exclaimed that it was wrong to presume guilt like this.

Khodorkovsky continued, criticising the unequal rules of the game between state and private corporations. He cited the example of Rosneft's takeover of Severnaya Neft, headed by the insider Andrei Vavilov (a former deputy finance minister and a senator in the Federation Council), an asset that both Yukos and Sibneft had tried to win. The price paid by Rosneft looked excessive, $600 million instead of its estimated top value of around $300 million, with the surplus then allegedly spread between Vavilov, Bogdanchikov and government officials, and possibly designated to fund Putin's re-election campaign.[40] Khodorkovsky demanded that German Gref (who at the time was chair of Rosneft's board) explain how Rosneft had won control of the firm. If in the 1990s the state had sold its companies too cheaply, in the 2000s it was paying too much to buy them back. Khodorkovsky admitted that business had in part been responsible for corruption in the 1990s, but it was now time to stamp it out from whatever source. In effect Khodorkovsky was saying that those around the table, including the president, were guilty of corruption.[41] Putin noted in a steely voice that Rosneft 'is a state company and needs to increase its inadequate reserves', whereas companies like Yukos had 'super-reserves' anyway.[42] The question was: how did it get them? Putin paused, allowing the threat to sink in, and then added that Yukos had some tax problems 'which it had to sort out, and think why they arose in the first place'.[43]

According to Viktor Gerashchenko, the former chair of the Central Bank of Russia, who would go on to head the Yukos board, Khodorkovsky spoke again and appealed to Putin for his approval for an oil pipeline to China. Putin unequivocally said 'no'; there was a project to build a line to Nakhodka on the Pacific coast, 'and that was the plan that would be implemented'. Khodorkovsky continued to object, insisting that his pipeline would use private capital and not state funds, but Putin was adamant. Still Khodorkovsky refused to remain silent, and to the astonishment of those present he declared: 'Vladimir Vladimirovich, you do not understand the importance of establishing relations with China,' and sat down. 'After this meeting,' according to Gerashchenko, 'Khodorkovsky was told unequivocally to leave Russia. He would not budge an inch. "What did I say that was wrong?" he demanded.'[44] Pipeline politics are a matter of the highest state interest, and the regime resented Yukos's attempts to shape policy. Conflict in particular focused on Yukos's plans to build a privately owned pipeline to China, challenging the prerogatives of Transneft, the state-owned pipeline monopoly.

Bystanders reported that the exchange had been marked by a high degree of personal animosity. Nevzlin alleges that as a result Sechin and Ivanov were instructed by Putin to gather evidence against Yukos, and Biryukov was the chief investigator of the Yukos case, with Yury Zaostrovtsev, head of the economic-security department at the FSB, given an equivalent job in the security service. They began investigating various murder and assault cases and tried to link them to Yukos managers.[45] In an attempt to pre-empt reprisals, Khodorkovsky suggested that the oligarchs who had benefited from gaining assets on the cheap in the 1990s should pay a one-off windfall tax amounting to some $20 billion. Kasyanov was attracted by the idea, but the Kremlin already had other plans and the idea was dropped.[46] Khodorkovsky himself realised that Yukos faced difficult times, and soon after warned a meeting of Yukos managers that the company would be attacked and that those who were not ready should leave.

As for Putin's motivations, as he himself noted, he had been trained to keep his feelings under control. Although he condemned the excesses of the 1990s, he made no attempt to challenge the property settlement of that era. In his book of interviews published in 2000 he categorically rejected the idea of a new redistribution of property, although he accepted a role for 'state property on a limited scale'.[47] As Belkovsky notes, the roots of the contemporary Russian political system lie in the attack on the White House in October 1993 and then the presidential election of 1996: 'Oligarchs like Berezovsky, Gusinsky, Abramovich and Khodorkovsky came to power, and then divided Soviet property among themselves.' Belkovsky argues that Putin

> was placed in his present position by precisely these people. Berezovsky, Abramovich and others made him president to fulfil one task – to guarantee the inviolability of the results of privatisation, to permit the conversion of the privatised enterprises into 'cash flow', as well as to legalise its capital in Russia and abroad.[48]

These comments were made in 2007, when Belkovsky had been disappointed that Putin did not press the attack against the 1990s property settlement further. The Yukos affair remained by and large an isolated event and did not signal a new property revolution. Putin's first public comment on the Yukos arrests came in his 20 September 2003 meeting with American journalists, when he portrayed the affair as a purely legal matter with criminal overtones, the latter no doubt a reference to the Pichugin case. The *New York Times* quoted him as saying, 'Nobody can be free from complying with the laws,' and he noted that the investigation was examining 'assassinations or murders in the merger of companies'.[49] This was typical of the pseudo-legalism with which the case against Yukos was pursued.

THE MERGER OF YUKOS AND SIBNEFT

In early 2003 there were fears that oil prices would collapse once the full potential of Iraqi reserves were released following the anticipated overthrow of Saddam Hussein, pushing some of Russia's indebted oil companies, together with the Russian banking system, into insolvency. This is one reason why Putin gave the go-ahead for the sale on 2 February 2003 by Vekselberg (Access/Renova), Fridman (Alfa Group) and Len Blavatnik on behalf of TNK to BP to create Russia's third-largest oil company, TNK–BP, and one in which a foreign company was a major strategic investor.[50] The deal was formally signed on 26 June in London in the presence of Tony Blair and Putin, and finalised on 29 August 2003.[51] By then it was clear that post-Saddam Iraq would remain in chaos, ensuring high oil prices.

It was against this background that the merger of Yukos and Sibneft was announced on 22 April and signed on 14 May 2003. The deal created Russia's biggest and the world's fourth-largest oil company in terms of production, pumping 2.3 million barrels of crude a day, and it was the world's second in terms of reserves at 19.5 billion barrels. In an interview on 16 June Khodorkovsky explained the various advantages of the merger.[52] The new company would control 35% of oil refining and 39% of petrol production through its six major refineries in Russia (Omsk, Achinsk, Angarsk, and the three in Samara oblast, in addition to Mazeikiu Nafta in Lithuania) as well as Russia's largest distribution network with 2,500 petrol stations.[53] Yukos–Sibneft would dominate 'big oil' in East Siberia and the Russian Far East. Starting with a relatively low capitalisation of $35 billion, the stock of the joint company could only go up. Yukos received a 92% stake in Sibneft in exchange for 26% of Yukos shares and $3 billion in cash, effectively representing a friendly Yukos takeover of Sibneft, with 55% of the new company controlled by Menatep. The merger was completed on paper by 3 October 2003, and the physical merger was due to be completed by 1 January 2004. The creation of the new super-company was, among other things, a way of insuring against the arbitrariness of the state.[54]

Abramovich at this time was disbursing his assets, selling his stake in Sibneft to Khodorkovsky for $3 billion, and soon after announced his intention to sell his share of Basic Element (Russian Aluminium) for much the same amount. The apparent sell-out by oligarchs influenced the Kremlin's view of the merger. Abramovich's motive in suggesting the merger also remains unclear. When in 1997–8 there had been discussions to create Yuksi (Yukos–Sibneft), the deal was opposed by Abramovich, and he did not enjoy warm relations with Khodorkovsky. Nevzlin suspected that

Abramovich had set a trap, allegedly planning to use a shareholders' meeting to take over the merged company and present it to the Kremlin.[55] Following Khodorkovsky's arrest Abramovich did try to take over the conglomerate, but when rebuffed by the new team he called off the merger, leaving Khodorkovsky and the demerged Yukos to their fate. In September 2005 he sold Sibneft to Gazprom. Managing his companies was left to others: 'It is the task of squaring the authorities that requires Abramovich's particular form of genius,' whereas Berezovsky, Gusinsky and Khodorkovsky 'allowed their egos to cloud their judgement'.[56] Khodorkovsky refused to be a divisional manager of Russia Inc., and he paid the price.

At first the merger was condoned by the Kremlin. Khodorkovsky met Putin on 26 April 2003 and explained the terms, and Putin gave the go-ahead.[57] The merger was approved by the Federal Anti-Monopoly Agency on 14 August, and on 28 August a consortium of Western banks led by Société Générale agreed a $1 billion loan to Yukos at the best rates ever offered to a Russian company. It looked as if the arrests of Pichugin and Lebedev were no more than a passing storm. However, powerful wheels had already been set in motion. Fears that the Yukos–Sibneft company would create a giant beyond the Kremlin's influence tilted the balance. The new company would have challenged the state's claimed prerogatives over energy and broader security questions, and the attack on Yukos was the outcome. Above all, the merger sought to repeat the TNK–BP transnationalisation strategy, but on a far larger scale. As early as July 2002 discussions began with ChevronTexaco;[58] by the autumn parallel talks were being pursued with ExxonMobil.[59] Khodorkovsky's plan to sell a 25% stake – possibly even up to a 40% one – of the new super-company to an American company deeply alarmed the Kremlin. Even the most liberal of Russian commentators noted that 'Obviously, this sale is not in Russia's interests'.[60]

As was seen later with the attempt by Sinopec to buy America's Unocal in June 2005 or the sale of American ports to Dubai, such large deals in what are considered strategic sectors are blocked by national governments. As Ajay Goyal puts it:

By July [2003], even Putin comprehended that Russia's place in the world would become threatened by a sale of Yukos to an American company. Worse, Kremlin officials warned the boss, if Yukos were allowed to proceed, the sell-out would become a stampede, an even greater flight of capital than Russia's vulnerable economy had suffered to date, as every one of the oligarchs offloaded the country's largest, most important natural assets to foreign buyers.[61]

Khodorkovsky at some point met with American vice president Dick Cheney and discussed the sale. It would have made him independent from the Kremlin, backed not only by foreign oil but also by a foreign power. At a meeting with Lee Raymond, the head of ExxonMobil, at the World Economic Forum in Moscow on 1 October 2003, the American company offered $25 billion for 25% of Yukos–Sibneft. Khodorkovsky planned to retain 30% of the capital of the merged company, which according to Western practice represents a blocking minority. By 3 October Khodorkovsky could announce that the Yukos–Sibneft merger was substantially complete, but he dismissed rumours of plans to sell a 25% stake to ExxonMobil.[62]

In an interview in early October, Putin seemed to take a relaxed approach to the sale of a quarter and even 40% of the new company, since 'we favour foreign capital investment', and indicated that the Yukos sale could go ahead 'if preliminary discussions take place with the Russian government'.[63] Appropriate consultation did not take place, and it appears that Putin twice privately told Khodorkovsky that he disapproved of the planned sale.[64] Later, during his 2012 presidential campaign, Putin returned to the issue and made the following fundamental argument:

> The struggle then [early 2000s] was between those who had captured the main financial flows in the 1990s (which were based on the sale of raw materials and energy sources) and those who wanted to return them to the state and use them for the good of all society. I believe that we acted correctly then, increasing the state's influence in the raw materials sector. And not only because some oligarchs tried to continue buying politics directly. At the very start of my first presidential term we faced persistent attempts to sell key assets abroad. The retention of the country's key strategic resources in the private hands of a few people for 5–10 years meant that control of our economy would be exercised from outside.[65]

This was an extraordinary admission. It discounted the 'political' motivation for the assault on Yukos – that Khodorkovsky and his associates were funding a suspiciously eclectic range of political parties to ensure a strong 'Yukos' lobby in parliament – although of course a company with Western shareholders controlling a bloc of votes in the Duma would be even worse from the regime's point of view. Crucially, it admitted that the charges of tax evasion, fraud and embezzlement were applied instrumentally against Yukos managers. Putin conceded that the privatisations of the 1990s could not be reversed, since they did not violate the laws of the time, and many of the new owners turned into effective managers. Khodorkovsky may well have been one of these, but the attempt to sell a large stake of his company abroad alarmed the Kremlin.

This may have been Putin's conviction at the time, but he kept his views to himself. On 7 October the Russian press reported that the government saw 'no legal objections to the deal'. Temporising by the Russian leadership over the issue may well have been provoked by anticipation of President Bush's visit to Putin's dacha in Sochi on 14 October. Bush, with his close links to the Texas oil industry, was lobbying hard for the sale to go ahead. His mother and former first lady, Barbara Bush, had close links with Texaco and the company had been one of the main sponsors of Bush's election campaign in 2000, and until early 2001 Condoleezza Rice had sat on the board of ChevronTexaco. As far as the American leadership was concerned this was the favoured company, whereas ExxonMobil was considered more sympathetic to the Democrats. It appears that Khodorkovsky demanded the release of Lebedev (arrested on 2 July) as the price for selling to ChevronTexaco, but Putin declared that if he conceded this he would stop being president; it was at this point that Khodorkovsky activated negotiations with ExxonMobil.[66] Such a sale would have set Putin against Bush, and this was something that Putin sought to avoid at all costs. It was then that Putin took the 'politburo' off the leash.[67]

Having given its public blessing for the sale to go ahead, yet considering the sale against the national interest and in danger of souring relations with the Americans, the Russian leadership appeared to have boxed itself in. The attack on Yukos and its leadership was one way of breaking out of the impasse. In due course, and after considerable delay and controversy, a law regulating foreign investment in 'strategic companies', requiring all large deals between Russian and foreign companies to be formally approved by the Russian government, was drafted.[68] A law on investment in strategic sectors was adopted in the last days of Putin's first presidency in 2008. In 2003, however, there was a danger that the sale could be achieved by Menatep, located offshore, hence possibly the firmness with which the attack was launched.[69] Fear that the oligarch was undermining Russia's national interests and subordinating Russian budget revenues to the whims of Texan boardrooms alarmed a broad swathe of elite opinion. Khodorkovsky did not listen, and paid the penalty.

The Russian government ultimately came to the view that while it favoured the globalisation of the Russian economy, with Russian companies entering world capital markets and buying up foreign companies, and certainly encouraged foreign direct investment in Russia itself, it was wary of allowing foreign companies leverage in Russia. The tie-in of BP and TNK was a classic case of transnationalism, with TNK firmly locked into the strategic thinking of the British company. The creation of

TNK–BP, according to one expert, 'gave Britain a powerful instrument for lobbying its interests in Russia'.[70] However, the model did not catch on, and the attempt by Yukos to transnationalise itself by bringing in a large-scale American partner was stopped. Gazprom too was encouraged to go global, but its shares could only be traded freely on the international market after the state had gained a majority interest (51%), securing Gazprom's core interests in Russia. Very few companies, even Gazprom, met the criteria of transnationalism.[71] Talks on the sale of Yukos to a foreign company were suspended in the wake of Khodorkovsky's arrest and never restarted.[72]

PARLIAMENT AND LOBBYING

In the 1990s it was impossible for big business not to be involved in politics, and this gave rise to what Hale calls 'politicized financial–industrial groups' (PFIGs) at both the national and regional levels.[73] This was Khodorkovsky's forte, with close links between Menatep–Yukos managers and government officials. The Menatep–Yukos PFIG made a notable intervention during Yeltsin's re-election campaign in 1996, and Yukos supported Primakov when he became prime minister in September 1998. Later, despite Khodorkovsky's doubts, others in Yukos forged close ties with the challengers in the 1999–2000 succession struggle. Khodorkovsky was ambivalent about the creation of Luzhkov's Fatherland (Otechestvo) party in January 1999, a core element of what became Fatherland–All Russia (OVR), which combined Moscow capitalism with regional leaders and aspired to seize power as part of a coalition headed by Primakov. In the event, they were outwitted by the Kremlin. Berezovsky and Putin allied to ensure a smooth succession and the creation of a pro-presidential bloc of deputies in the form of Unity (later United Russia) in the Duma. Khodorkovsky kept his options open in this campaign and did not align himself with either contending faction.

Khodorkovsky provided personal funds to support the social-liberal party Yabloko, headed by Grigory Yavlinsky, in the December 1999 parliamentary election.[74] He also made funds available for the SPS – headed collectively by Nemtsov, Irina Khakamada and Chubais – the movement Golos Rossii, and apparently Unity as well as the KPRF.[75] Financial support was accompanied by the election of business executives to legislatures and governorships. The billionaire Vladimir Dubov, a Yukos manager with a 4.2% stake in the company, was elected to parliament in December 1999 on the OVR list, which was later subsumed into United Russia, and he became head of the tax committee; in April 2001 Yukos deputy managing director Boris Zolotarev was elected governor of the Evenk autonomous *okrug.*

By 2003 it was clear that Khodorkovsky was no longer willing to abide by the 'social contract' established earlier. Putin was informed that 226 deputies in the Third Duma (1999–2003) owed allegiance to Yukos: a majority of the total of 450.[76] This figure is exaggerated and the real figure was closer to a hundred, encompassing not just Yukos but all the energy companies.[77] 'Lobbying' barely describes what was going on, with activists running about with packets of money on the eve of important votes. The budget committee chaired by Alexander Zhukov had 'practically turned into a structural sub-unit of Yukos', although, as is always stressed, this did not come about because of him.[78] A particularly sharp bone of contention was the government's attempts to modify the December 1995 production-sharing agreements (PSA) law. Khodorkovsky was deeply opposed to the whole principle of PSAs, since he considered them a form of unfair competition by giving advantages to foreign investors, a view to which Putin's government came round once Khodorkovsky was safely in jail.[79] Of the 21 PSA projects originally mooted in 1994–5, only three were signed: Sakhalin-1 led by what became ExxonMobil in 1999, Sakhalin-2 headed by Shell, and Total's project in the Kharyaga field in Timan-Pechora before the scheme was abolished in late 2003.

Various pieces of legislation were shaped according to Yukos's preferences, including revisions to the PSA law, the indexation of the natural-resource tax, access to pipelines, export taxes on crude and oil products, and petrol distribution.[80] In the debate on amendments to the PSA law on 14 May 2003 Khodorkovsky spoke via mobile phone to his partisans with points to be made.[81] The Kremlin was clearly angered in June 2003 by its inability to introduce a new unified petroleum tax as a result of vigorous lobbying by energy companies. Two attempts to raise excise taxes were blocked, and it is estimated that the government may have lost up to $2 billion in revenue from Yukos alone because of the favourable tax regime. Khodorkovsky is alleged to have warned Gref: 'If you push through these oil taxes, I'll have you fired.'[82] Gref recalls that on the eve of the vote he was visited by Vasily Shakhnovsky, the president of Yukos-Moscow, who warned him that the law would not be adopted and that 'if you insist on it, we will write a collective letter from all oil producers asking for the resignation of you and Mr Kudrin [minister of finance] for lack of professionalism'.[83]

The passage of the law was indeed blocked in the Duma the next day by an unholy alliance of liberals and Communists, and thus at a time of budget deficits the government was unable to take advantage of the rising price of oil. It took another year and Yukos's downfall for the oil-taxation law to be passed. Yukos supported other legislation in its favour, notably modifications to the tax code that left in a 'grandfather' clause allowing exemptions on profit tax in agreements between regional governments and businesses. Mordovia and Evenkia signed such agreements with Yukos, while other companies had agreements with Chukotka and Kalmykia, saving them over $1.5 billion a year.[84] Andrew Jack reports that a senior Yukos executive warned that if the company did not get its way with a new law 'we will start a war against the government'; Khodorkovsky himself is alleged to have boasted, 'With money, you can ultimately buy anything.'[85] Following Khodorkovsky's arrest the government wasted no time in abolishing 'onshore offshore' tax havens on 18 November 2003, and closed other tax loopholes at this time.

The Kremlin feared that Khodorkovsky would give no quarter in ensuring a bloc of loyal parliamentary deputies. Other companies also engaged in lobbying, but Yukos's activity was more than just about blocking individual laws but represented a broader attempt to shape the legislative agenda. Ivan Grachev, a Duma deputy and the leader of the Party for the Development of Entrepreneurship, was unequivocal that 'Yukos was chosen [for attack] out of political considerations. Its level of activity in the present [Third] Duma, above all in the budget committee, is incomparable with the activity of all other companies.' He noted that Yukos effectively enjoyed a majority in the finance committee, and 'one cannot deny that they abused the position', with their behaviour raising questions not only among committee members but also in the business community. This explains why, in his view, the attack on Yukos aroused such a weak reaction among both businesspeople and politicians. The attack was provoked, in his view, because 'Khodorkovsky openly declared his intention of continuing the practice and even to develop it by winning a blocking vote, no longer in a single committee but in the whole Duma'. Grachev stressed that Yukos deputies, including Dubov (the chair of the tax committee), worked within the law, 'but extremely aggressively'. In his view the company sought to create a system that would uniquely serve its interests, often against the interests of the business community as a whole, as with the planned profit tax.[86]

FINANCING PARTIES

2003 was the year of Yukos, with the company seldom out of the news on a whole range of issues. Particularly controversial was business support for parties, which, although nothing new, became politicised as the 7 December 2003 parliamentary election approached. Dominance over the Duma was crucial for Putin as he consolidated his hold on power, and Yukos was particularly exposed since it funded a range of parties and activities. The pluralism sponsored by Khodorkovsky was countered by the practices of 'managed democracy'. The Yukos candidate list, according to Mikhail Grishankov (the head of the Duma's anti-corruption committee), ran to over 200 names.[87] As far as the exponents of managed democracy were concerned, 'Khodorkovsky has failed to pay tribute and to separate the things that belong to God from the things that belong to Caesar.' Khodorkovsky was adamant that there was no deal concerning the funding of political parties, and thus that he could not have broken the alleged truce: 'What was discussed was that large companies should not become involved in political life. I support this'; but he ignored the issue of 'men with large wallets'.[88]

Khodorkovsky made no secret of his 'investment' in various parties.[89] On 7 April 2003 Khodorkovsky declared: 'My political sympathies lie with SPS and Yabloko and I am willing to provide personal funds to finance them'; he noted also that a minority shareholder and former manager of Yukos (he did not give the name but Veretennikova suggests that it was Muravlenko, chair of the Yukos board of directors) would provide personal support for the KPRF.[90] Yavlinsky admitted that Yukos contributed 'several million dollars' for the campaign in 2003.[91] Khodorkovsky repeatedly stressed that the money did not come directly from Yukos but from personal funds.[92] The party lists showed that Yukos hoped to enter about 30–40 deputies 'to form their own faction by the name of Yabloko'.[93] As Yabloko's main sponsor, Yukos nominees occupied prominent positions on its party list.[94] Alexander Osovtsov, director of the Open Russia Foundation, Yukos executive Kagalovsky and Galina Antonova, head of strategic planning in Yukos, ran on the Yabloko list.[95] Yukos was also active in funding a corps of Yabloko single-mandate deputies. Already in January Khodorkovsky exerted considerable effort to unite the two main liberal parties, Yabloko and SPS, but to no avail.[96] Khodorkovsky understood that unless they campaigned together they would hang separately.[97] Nevertheless, he denies that he attempted to 'buy' parliament and insists that he engaged in normal lobbying behaviour and not politics.[98]

Yukos was not the only oil company fighting for a presence in parliament, but it was unusual for the balance of its nominees to be in oppositional groupings. There is much speculation that Khodorkovsky resisted 'invitations' to provide support for Kremlin-backed United Russia. This was levied as a type of 'loyalty tax', and Khodorkovsky's repeated refusal singled him out from other oligarchs. State-friendly Lukoil, for example, had five people on the United Russia list, and TNK also had five with United Russia and two running with the KPRF; whereas with Yukos the proportion was reversed, with five on the KPRF list and only two with United Russia. At least five Yukos associates were on the KPRF party list, notably the Yukos shareholder and chair of the Yukos supervisory board, Muravlenko, and Kondaurov.[99] Kondaurov had run in 1999 but had been too far down the list (No. 4 in the Far East) to make it into the Duma, but in 2003 he was placed 13th and remained in parliament until December 2007. He was one of the key figures running the KPRF's Duma campaign in 2003 and acted as the link with Yukos. He also tried to close down a special issue of *Stringer*, the investigative journal edited by Tokareva, which was critical of Yukos.[100] According to Boris Kagarlitsky, Yukos 'bought 13 places on the KPRF's list of candidates for its own people, at a cost of $12 million'.[101] Viktor Kazakov, a former director of Yukos EP, was one of the few Yukos people to run on the United Russia list. As one study puts it, 'Yukos's enormous wealth could be converted into real power by recruiting parliamentarians and creating its own caucus in the Duma.' The aim, the authorities alleged, was 'to privatise parliament and the government'.[102] Khodorkovsky suggests that Putin had been deliberately misinformed about the scale of the 'Yukos lobby' in parliament, making one group where in fact there were many.[103] This helps explain why Putin was so angry: like Gorbachev in the final phase of perestroika, he was being misinformed by his security officials.

The entry of Yukos as a major political player was perceived by the Kremlin as a threat to its political prerogatives. Following the meeting in Novo-Ogarevo on 26 April 2003, when the merger of Yukos and Sibneft was approved, Khodorkovsky was left on his own with Putin. The latter suddenly asked Yukos to stay out of politics and not to finance the opposition. Khodorkovsky answered that it was not Yukos that was providing finance but executives were doing so out of their own pockets, something that any citizen had the right to do. Putin appeared to agree with this view, but insisted that Yukos 'stop financing the Communists'. Again, Khodorkovsky answered that it was not Yukos that was funding the KPRF but certain Yukos shareholders, again from personal resources. Khodorkovsky left the meeting with a good impression of Putin, although he was worried since 'the president was suspiciously benevolent'.[104] This was to be their last meeting alone.

Soon after, reports came to Putin that Khodorkovsky had met with the Communist leader, Zyuganov, to offer his support. Called in by Putin to explain himself, Khodorkovsky denied the accusation. Baker and Glasser recount the story as follows:

'Putin was furious', a well-connected government official said, 'because he already had the minutes from the conversation between Khodorkovsky and Zyuganov, and the minutes came not from the FSB [...] but from the Communist Party staff. And when someone lies to the president, it makes it personal.'

When Kasyanov and Voloshin tried to intervene on Khodorkovsky's behalf, arguing that Voloshin had authorised the financing, Putin responded negatively: 'That's Khodorkovsky. It's his game. He wants to buy parliament. I can't allow this.'[105] In evidence to the European Court of Human Rights (ECtHR) in July 2009 Kasyanov stressed that he believed that political motives were responsible for Khodorkovsky's persecution. He noted that he had pressed Putin several times to explain Lebedev's arrest, and in a private meeting later in July 2003 Putin told Kasyanov that Khodorkovsky had crossed a line by financing the Communists without his permission. 'He did not say any more.'[106]

From the Kremlin's perspective the promiscuous breadth of Khodorkovsky's support for political parties represented an attempt to buy influence in the new Duma. By contrast, Khodorkovsky asserted his right to participate in politics, although he agreed that corporations had no such prerogative. However, speaking in September 2003 he insisted that 'the heads of corporations have the right to lobby their economic interests and should be able to do this openly'. He warned that the events around Yukos could have negative consequences:

> The conflict is between autonomous citizens, giving birth to civil society in the country, and law enforcement organs, who consider that they have the right to dictate to citizens how they should live, and who believe that force is law.

He did not believe that a wholesale redistribution of property would take place. In his view, 'Civil society in Russia will be built only when every group can advance its view publicly and in detail.'[107]

The loss of Yukos support proved fatal for Yabloko and in December 2003 it failed to cross the 5% representation threshold: 'Not only was Yabloko's primary source of funding disrupted, but the arrest also called attention to the fact that the "anti-oligarch" Yabloko had in fact been financed by the largest of the oligarchs.'[108] The same applies to the KPRF, which was forced to explain placing millionaires on its list and accepting money from big business while condemning oligarch power.[109] Dubov was dropped from United Russia's electoral list, although by then he was no longer in the country. In the event, three Yukos people were elected to the Fourth

Duma on the KPRF list: Kondaurov, Muravlenko and Yuly Kvitsinsky, a former deputy foreign minister and former ambassador to Norway. However, the failure of Yabloko and SPS to enter deprived Yukos of its main support in parliament. If the goal of the Yukos affair was to reduce the company's influence on the electoral process and in parliament, then this was achieved, but the pressure on the company did not stop.

THE REORGANISATION OF POWER

Khodorkovsky did not limit his opinions to economic matters, and on behalf of the RSPP in early 2003 he put forward ideas for the reorganisation of government and administrative reform, suggesting a much slimmed-down 'mini-government' comprised of only 12 policy ministers responsible for managing the needs of the private sector.[110] This was similar to the administrative reform proposed by Dmitry Kozak and implemented, although not very effectively, in 2004. More contentiously, Khodorkovsky also advocated Russia's transformation into a parliamentary republic.[111] For the business community, the shift to a more controllable parliamentary system would be a way of reducing political risks, although the report 'The state and the oligarchs' emphasised more sinister motives. Some in the presidential administration, such as Voloshin, even sought 'to neutralise the growing influence of the Putinite cabal, including Sechin'.[112] Thus the shift from a presidential to a parliamentary, cabinet-based government headed by a more powerful prime minister was in the air, and this even influenced Putin's thinking. There had long been rumours that Surkov was working on plans to enhance the responsibilities of the parliamentary majority. In his annual address to the Federal Assembly on 16 May 2003 Putin warned against parliamentary populism in the forthcoming elections, while welcoming them as a new stage in the development of the country's multiparty system. Most significantly, he looked forward to a 'professional and efficient government relying on the parliamentary majority' being formed after the elections.[113] A decree had been drafted to start the process, and reports even suggested that an announcement to that effect had been prepared.[114] The move was suddenly stopped in its tracks, and Putin only returned to the issue to condemn the idea as premature.[115]

The reason for the volte-face remains intriguing, but one can assume that opponents of the idea had warned Putin that a strengthened parliament would be exploited by unfriendly forces. The idea came to be seen as a stratagem for Khodorkovsky to take power. Years later Khodorkovsky commented on this, noting that 'When the attack on Yukos started in 2003, some observers said that my partners and I were allegedly drafting secret plans for the Russian Federation's transformation into a parliamentary republic to limit the powers of Vladimir Putin.' He admitted that he and his associates 'really supported in 2002–2003 certain independent research institutions, which were considering a new design of the Russian political system'.[116] The plans did not stipulate a shift to a fully parliamentary system but advocated the creation of a presidential–parliamentary model, with a popularly elected president standing above the separation of powers as the guarantor of the constitution and holding the power to appoint certain key state officials, while parliament would have greater powers to conduct inquiries – ideas to which Khodorkovsky would return in 2011 (see Chapter 11).[117] According to Nevzlin, 'I learnt from Khodorkovsky himself that he informed the president of this concept. Putin heard him out and that was that.'[118] Khodorkovsky argues: 'The idea of a parliamentary republic has nothing whatsoever to do with the raiding attack on Yukos';[119] although commentary at the time suggested that he sought to reduce the powers of the presidency to little more than 'supreme arbitrator'.[120] This version was undoubtedly reported to Putin.

Limited to two successive terms, Putin would have to leave office in May 2008. This would leave the presidency vacant, and Khodorkovsky was touted as a possible successor. No other oligarch was considered in this light, and thus from the start of 'Operation Successor 2' (the first was in 1999) Khodorkovsky emerged as a potential rival to the existing Kremlin elite. According to Golubovich, discussions within Yukos began in 2001 about advancing Khodorkovsky to a high political position.[121] On several occasions Khodorkovsky spoke of handing over management of Yukos to others. In 2002 he announced to the board of directors that he would leave the company before 2008.[122] On 3 April 2003 he declared that he intended to resign as head of the Yukos management board in 2007, a post that he had held since 1998, and did not wish to do so after his 45th birthday.[123] In an interview with *Der Spiegel* later that month Khodorkovsky stated that he intended to retire as chair of the Yukos board of directors on his 45th birthday in 2008: 'When I'm 45 I no longer want to be a business manager. I may well go into politics.'[124] This was interpreted as a declaration that he planned to run for the presidency in that year, when he would reach that age. It is not clear how seriously these utterances were to be taken, but the authorities were not going to wait to find out. In late 1999 the full might of the Kremlin's propaganda and administrative apparatus had been unleashed against a potential contender, Primakov, and now a strengthened state would go even further in destroying a political opponent.

Khodorkovsky was not the only one of the Yukos team with an interest in politics. Nevzlin had been on the federal list of the Preobrazhenie ('Transformation') electoral bloc in 1993, and in the 1990s was active in various lobbying groups for entrepreneurs. In 1998 he worked as the first deputy head of the ITAR-TASS information agency while retaining his senior posts with Rosprom and Menatep, before in October 1998 becoming first deputy head of Yukos and from 1999 taking up the same post with Yukos-Moscow. He took over as president of the Russian Jewish Congress after Gusinsky went into exile in 2001. He was also the senator from the Republic of Mordovia from November 2001 to March 2003 and served as deputy head of the Federation Council's foreign-affairs committee. In March 2003 he became deputy head of Khodorkovsky's Open Russia Foundation (a post he held until January 2004), and at the same time between June and November 2003 he acted as rector of RGGU.

Although the scale and tone of Khodorkovsky's actions may have been distinctive, most of what he did was not unique to him. Other business leaders supported candidates in parliamentary elections, and not a few pursued a predatory business strategy. Nevertheless, as Baker and Glasser note, Khodorkovsky was going beyond anything attempted before: 'He was talking about virtually privatizing the two market-oriented parties, Yabloko and the Union of Right Forces, as well as placing sizable numbers of legislators in the Communist party and Putin's own newly renamed United Russia party.'[125] Political issues on their own do not explain the assault on Yukos, but they certainly played their part.

FOREIGN-POLICY STRUGGLES

As we have seen, Khodorkovsky had good relations with numerous American politicians;[126] this boosted his confidence in 2003 as his arrest approached. In turn, Khodorkovsky became 'the oil industry's most pro-United States advocate'.[127] In a number of spheres Khodorkovsky began to advance a parallel foreign policy. In particular, with 17% of Russian oil production at his disposal, Khodorkovsky rejected OPEC pleas in 2003 to allow the price of oil to rise, although other Russian companies such as Lukoil were in favour, while the government temporised.

One of the most insistent explanations for the attack is that Khodorkovsky backed the war in Iraq in 2003, arguing that it would allow a strategic partnership with America to be forged.[128] He found a ready ally in Voloshin, who in turn sought to protect Yukos. Khodorkovsky's logic in supporting the war was simple: he anticipated a long period in which Iraqi oil supplies would be disrupted (which in the event proved the case), thus pushing up the price; although publicly Khodorkovsky favoured a period of lower but stable oil prices. The liberals also supported the invasion, although for different reasons – the overthrow of a vicious dictator and the restoration of freedom to the Iraqi people. While the business logic for Yukos may have been impeccable, in terms of larger politics it was fundamentally misjudged. Putin on this issue refused to allow Russia to become a pawn in the intrigues of others. On the one hand, he was pushed by Washington to join the assault; while on the other, Germany, and even more so France, tried to bring Russia in as part of an 'old Europe' alliance in defence of state sovereignty against 'humanitarian intervention' and 'regime change'. Resistance to the neo-conservative attempt to remould the Middle East and with it the shape of world politics, by sanctioning an attack against a sovereign state without due cause, was a principle close to Putin's heart (if only out of the instinct of self-preservation), but while he endorsed Franco-German arguments, he feared that Russia would end up trapped if he became part of an informal anti-American alliance.

Caught in a delicate web of great power politics, the last thing Putin needed was an independent foreign-policy entrepreneur forcing his hand. Russia was often accused of speaking with multiple voices on foreign-policy issues, but under Putin, for good or ill, some sort of order in this sphere was imposed. Russian foreign policy became far more single-minded, yet Iraq proved to be a great test. Certainly, Putin feared being pushed into a war that he considered technically complicated and politically wrong, but there were also more immediate concerns. On the eve of war the Americans refused to recognise Russian economic interests in Iraq, and in particular its claim to the giant West Qurna oilfield. In 1979 alone Soviet engineers had sunk 300 wells, but the war with Iran halted the start of production. A PSA with Lukoil in the mid-1990s gave the company a 50% stake, the Iraqi state a quarter, and two other Russian government agencies the other quarter, intended to repay Iraq's $8 billion Cold War debt that was incurred when the country had been a Soviet client.[129] None of these concerns was recognised by the Anglo-American war coalition.[130]

Khodorkovsky enjoyed close relations with the neo-conservatives, and in particular with the unreconstructed 'cold warrior' Richard Perle, and contributed funds to support their activities. Yukos in America became part of the pro-war coalition, which included ExxonMobil, the *Washington Post* and the *Wall Street Journal*. Yukos and Khodorkovsky tried to shape the foreign-policy agenda in other spheres as well. His support for an oil pipeline to Daqing in Manchuria had enormous implications for Russian policy in the Far East, as did his plans for an independent pipeline to Murmansk. Even more ambitious was the purported suggestion made by Nevzlin in a meeting with the American secretary of state that if Khodorkovsky came to power he would push for Russian nuclear disarmament.[131]

CHAPTER 4

THE STATE STRIKES BACK

Under Putin the 'new bureaucracy' became an independent political force, allied with the security and enforcement agencies. Khodorkovsky later regretted that he had devoted himself to building up a business, when the time would have been better spent developing the country and society: in other words, an effective and democratic state.[1] He felt himself free in the business world, and left governmental intrigues to others: 'Byzantium was not for me.'[2] Instead, others occupied the power system. The regime did not dispute the value of the market or private property but, more dangerously, it entered the market as a player and manipulated the rules to its advantage.[3] Khodorkovsky engaged in numerous activities, each one of which may be considered legitimate but the attempt to pursue them all simultaneously was perceived as a challenge to the regime. Khodorkovsky insists that when he argued with Putin on 19 February 2003, 'I knew what I was risking';[4] but his actions, although courageous, were ill-judged. By the time he agreed to transfer Yukos to other managers at the end of the year, it was too late. The newly energised regime engineered the destruction of Yukos and undermined the independent power of big business.

THE ANTI-YUKOS 'POLITBURO'

After an initial period of relative liberalism, from 2003 there was a clear 'turn to statism' in energy and other policies.[5] By taking action against Khodorkovsky the Kremlin was not only reasserting control over economic policy, but warning others not to challenge the Kremlin's prerogatives. The case reflects the powerful current of dissatisfaction with the privatisations of the 1990s. Like most other Russian corporations, the Yukos empire emerged from the 'Wild East' 'piratisations' of the Yeltsin era, with Yukos assets purchased for around one thirtieth of their later market value.[6] While the Kremlin insisted that it was not engaged in a general roll-back of privatisation, it did seek to strengthen the position of state-owned assets in Russia's new marketplace.

This was made explicit in the energy strategy adopted by the government on 28 August 2003, which outlined the tasks through to 2020 and, while predicated on the use of market mechanisms, stressed the strategic importance of managing natural endowments. The first sentence argued: 'Russia possesses great energy resources and a powerful fuel and energy complex that provide the basis of economic development and are the instrument for carrying out domestic and foreign policy.' The next sentence made the point explicit: 'The country's role in world energy markets to a large extent defines its geopolitical standing.'[7] The core of the strategy, devised by the energy minister Igor Yusufov, was to increase oil production, and thus the political importance of the sector could only grow.[8] Alexander Temerko, then a Yukos vice president, noted that on reading the strategy 'we knew they'd go after some company' to give the state leverage over the whole sector.[9] By then, partially or largely foreign-owned corporations were producing a quarter of Russia's oil.[10] Companies such as Norilsk Nickel also came under pressure, with Onexim Bank allegedly underpaying $140 million for a 38% stake in 1995; but after Potanin apparently paid a symbolic 'windfall' levy, the tax hounds were called off. When it came to Yukos, however, far more was at stake, and no amount of Danegeld would save the company.

Rosneft played a central part in the assault against Yukos, and the company has a special place in the development of the Russian state and political economy. Rosneft was the legatee of the old state oil monopoly, and it was given its corporate status in 1995. At the time of the Yukos affair it was still 100% state-owned, although soon after 15% of shares were sold off through a controversial initial public offering on the London Stock Exchange in 2006. Sergei Bogdanchikov's appointment as chief executive in 1998 signalled a new stage in Rosneft's development, based on 'emphatic loyalty to the regime, that it has no ambitions to be independent in political matters, and indeed, does not strive to exercise political influence.'[11] Bogdanchikov had previously worked for five years as head of one of Rosneft's major subsidiaries, Sakhalinmorneftegaz, and he brought his former colleagues from the Far East to run the company. Unlike Yukos or TNK, Rosneft did not appoint any foreign directors.[12] In the late 1990s Rosneft had barely escaped incorporation into Sibneft and Yukos, and Bogdanchikov thereafter fought ferociously to defend the company's independence and interests. In late 1998 he was supported by Primakov, who ensured that Purneftegaz, producing at the time 70% of Rosneft's output, remained with the company, and also blocked Rosneft's privatisation. With the change of presidency Putin became Bogdanchikov's new patron and helped transform Rosneft into a major energy company. Bogdanchikov enjoyed direct access to Putin and was favoured by him since he was not one of the oligarchs and had no political ambitions.[13] Sechin later supported Bogdanchikov, and together they transformed the company's fortunes. Rosneft became a vehicle for Sechin's ambitions, with him becoming chair of the board in August 2004 and then returning as CEO in May 2012.

An informal 'politburo' took shape, ranged against Yukos. Already in late 2002 the working group headed by Zaostrovtsev, the deputy director of the FSB and head of the department of economic security, started investigating Yukos. He had already distinguished himself in the struggle against Gusinsky and Berezovsky, and he was clearly working closely with those who would later seize Yukos.[14] Bogdanchikov was reputed to be close friends with the head of Putin's personal bodyguard, Viktor Zolotov, and also to have good relations with another powerful figure at the heart of the Putin establishment, Sergei Pugachev, a banker and a senator.[15] Thus at the very time that Yukos was implementing grandiose plans, including the merger with Sibneft, sale in part to a Western company, pipelines in several directions and the development of a social and political agenda of its own, the moles were burrowing under the whole edifice, which in the end proved shockingly fragile. Khodorkovsky ultimately sought to challenge the arbitrary power of the administrative system, but the Yukos affair demonstrated that this system was not ready to relinquish its power.

In their behaviour and views the 'politburo' harked back to the Soviet era, although now operating in conditions of market capitalism. The politburo's key members were Sechin himself, along with his sub-faction, which included FSB deputy director Alexander Bortnikov, whom Sechin sponsored in 2004 to head the FSB's department of economic security, Putin's aide Viktor Ivanov, Vladimir Ustinov at the head of the PGO, deputy prosecutor general Yury Biryukov, and reportedly Gennady Timchenko, one of the key partners in the oil trader Gunvor.[16] Yukos had traded through its own Swiss subsidiary Petroval, but with its formal bankruptcy on 1 August 2006 its main assets were transferred to Rosneft, and its foreign trading activities to Gunvor. On the back of Rosneft's acquisition of the main Yukos assets, the Swiss-based Gunvor Group became one of the world's largest oil traders, posting profits of $8 billion on a turnover of $43 billion in 2007.[17] The appointment of Sechin to chair the Rosneft board in July 2004 confirmed the interlocking nature of interests. Political ties were reinforced by family alliances when in autumn 2003 Sechin's daughter Inga married Ustinov's son Dmitry.

On the eve of his arrest Khodorkovsky launched an unprecedented personal attack against the PGO, noting that Biryukov had spoken of 'a war between the procuracy and the Yukos oil company', and he called his opponents 'werewolves in epaulettes' (*oborotni v pogonakh*) who break the law and 'discredit their uniforms'. Khodorkovsky insisted that his company was not in conflict with the state but with 'unscrupulous officials'.[18] The turn to statism in 2003 was accompanied by the establishment of national 'energy champions', and while there was much hesitation over the form that this would take, one thing was clear: the independent Yukos oil company stood in the way of achieving the Kremlin's strategic goals. The courts were routinely used by one side or the other in the struggles of the energy majors, and also by the government. The dynamics of politics had changed. The 'politburo' was determined to achieve its goals at a time when Khodorkovsky also harboured ambitions to change Russia. He had a strong sense of his historical role but only too late understood the very different logic represented by Putin and his regime.

FIRST ARRESTS

The Yukos affair was long in the making but finally took shape in summer 2003. The Duma backbencher Vladimir Yudin suggested that Yukos's 20% stake in Apatit, worth $280 million, had been embezzled, even though only in April Ustinov had argued that there were no legal reasons to initiate an investigation. It was clear that the renewed investigation had a political motivation. Why was Apatit singled out of the 264 auctions conducted at the same time as Yukos's acquisition of the plant? On 19 June 2003 the head of the fourth department in the economic-security service of Yukos, Alexei Pichugin, a former KGB officer, was arrested and accused of organising at least three murders and two attempted murders, allegedly on the orders of Nevzlin, thus setting in train the attack on the company. The first criminal investigation concerning Yukos was opened on 20 June. Six days later the PGO conducted a search of the company's Moscow headquarters.

In a major escalation of the case, on 2 July Lebedev was arrested while in hospital in connection with the alleged fraudulent acquisition of the Apatit stake. The charges against him were of large-scale fraud and tax evasion. On the same day the PGO issued an international search warrant for Ramil Burganov, a former Yukos executive and general director of VNK.[19] On 4 July Nevzlin and Khodorkovsky were questioned as witnesses in the Lebedev case, with the investigator focusing on Apatit.[20] In an interview with a regional TV station three days later Khodorkovsky argued that the attack on Yukos was the outcome of a struggle among Kremlin factions for power before the presidential elections.[21] Lebedev's arrest was immediately followed by an extraordinary audit of Yukos's accounts by the tax ministry, which in the following year resulted in a $3.5 billion claim, an action repeated three times in subsequent months to result in a total claim of some $27 billion, ultimately bankrupting the company. Already on 5 July Brudno left Russia, followed shortly thereafter on 31 July by Nevzlin, even though at that time he was not employed directly by Yukos but headed the board of Menatep's international banking arm, which held the 61% of the Yukos shares held by its top managers. In July 2004 Nevzlin, who by then faced tax-evasion and misappropriation charges, was accused of being the mastermind behind the murder of Olga and Sergei Gorin, and the attempted murders of the Moscow government's PR director Olga Kostina and of Rosprom managing director Viktor Kolesov in 1998.

The RSPP met on 9 July and agreed to appeal directly to Putin to warn against a wholesale review of past privatisations, but no public statement was issued.[22] On 8 July Kasyanov declared that the arrest of people charged with economic crimes was excessive, but pressure continued throughout the summer. On 9 July Duma deputy Mikhail Bugera (the deputy head of the Russian Regions caucus) called on the PGO to investigate tax offences by Yukos, claiming that the company had paid only 90 million roubles ($3.3 million) in taxes in 2002, a figure completely at variance with Yukos's GAAP (Generally Accepted Accounting Principles) results, which showed that it had paid $445 million, and the company asserted that it paid a total of $3.4 billion.[23] On 14 July Putin declared that economic crimes should not be fought by the use of 'the prison cell', but he condemned businesspeople who sought to defend their interests through excessive parliamentary lobbying. On 18 July the PGO declared that it was investigating seven criminal cases connected with Yukos, and on 23 July Lebedev was charged with tax avoidance, above all through the use of promissory notes. Khodorkovsky tried to calm investors by asserting that the attack was restricted to certain Yukos shareholders and not aimed at the company itself, but this argument soon became unsustainable.

On 3 October heavy-handed searches were conducted of the company's business centre in Zhukovka (where several prominent Menatep shareholders lived) and the Koralovo orphanage. Although the search provoked harsh criticism, with Khodorkovsky calling the raids 'an attempt to intimidate us', it appears that a computer server of Bank Menatep was found, with material relating to the documents lost in a truck that mysteriously fell off a bridge in May 1999.[24] On that day Dubov's offices were searched. On 9 October Shakhnovsky, a former Moscow deputy mayor and Yukos-Moscow's chief executive with a 4.2% stake in the company, was arrested and on 17 October he was charged with fraud and tax evasion. In November his selection as senator representing the Evenk autonomous *okrug* legislature was annulled by the Krasnoyarsk Krai Supreme Court. A search of ASK, a Yukos-related public-relations company, on 23 October netted a haul of $700,000 in cash as well as five computer servers. The company also handled Yabloko's election account, and as a result the party was dealt a severe blow.[25] At this stage the attack was not limited to Yukos, with Sibneft (effectively merged with Yukos) in mid-October charged with evading taxes to the tune of $332 million. 29 December 2003 would prove fateful for Yukos. On that day it received notice of a full tax review, and it was accused of illegally exploiting tax advantages and minimising taxes through the use of shell companies.

As the election approached, the government launched an assault against corruption in state bodies, in particular against bribery and extortion by police and other security officials (the so-called 'werewolves in epaulettes' campaign). On 23 June 2003 some 40 simultaneous raids were conducted, leading to the arrest of about 15 suspects, including seven colonels of the MVD, an FSB officer and the head of the emergency ministries' security directorate, Lieutenant General Vladimir Ganeev. The arrests were given prominent media coverage, with the MVD officials charged with running a protection racket with the proceeds laundered through a veterans-association charity. The Russian government had been pressed by Western powers to crack down on corruption, with one author in particular noting the continuing 'operative links' between organised crime and the new oligarchs.[26] However, when the assault against prominent oligarchs began, the response in the West was less than enthusiastic – with some justification. This was less an attack on venal corruption than the intensification of meta-corruption.

Kasyanov on several occasions noted that it was inappropriate for arrests to take place if the key issue was the investigation of taxes, while the presidential adviser on the economy, Andrei Illarionov, was loud in his denunciation.[27] Voloshin circumspectly noted that 'There has been no revision of the results of privatization. There are simply some concrete cases that are being investigated. Our political position is that the results of privatization will not be revised.' He stressed, 'We need quietly to leave behind us the period of initial capital accumulation without undermining the foundations of our economy,' but how this would be done in a fair and legal manner was left uncertain.[28] Pavlovsky noted that the case reflected the exacerbation of the struggle between various groups within the hierarchy of power, notably regarding who would have the right to confiscate, and thus the arrests threatened all property owners in Russia. He compared the situation to 1928, on the eve of Stalin's 'great turn' against the New Economic Policy in favour of forced collectivisation and rapid industrialisation.[29] Russia was once again at a major turning point.

KHODORKOVSKY'S RESPONSE

On the evening of Lebedev's arrest Khodorkovsky met with Kasyanov, and the latter apparently passed on a message from Putin that Khodorkovsky had no need to worry; Lebedev's arrest apparently had not been a 'political order' but reflected conflicts between oligarchs.[30] Throughout, Putin was a master at dissimulation and false naivety. A week later Khodorkovsky threatened that he could deprive Russia of oil and heating, further alienating him from the administration.[31] His second response was to separate the personal attack from the work of the oil company. Addressing the managers of the Angarsk petrochemical plant in early September, Khodorkovsky stressed that his message to the Yukos board was that 'I am pleased that our security agencies and the political forces that can influence them have enough sense to realise that their political–bureaucratic games should not affect the work of Russia's largest company.'[32] He was to be disappointed in the 'good sense' of his opponents.

His third strategy sought to mobilise Western opinion – mainly policy-makers and the media – behind Yukos and, in so doing, to establish a defensive shield around the company that the Kremlin would breach at its own reputational cost. Thus Menatep hired various PR agencies, above all in Washington, to shape public opinion. To this end he travelled ceaselessly, including 17 trips abroad between Lebedev's arrest and his own, adopting the mantle of the 'defiant democrat'.[33] His fourth response was a more personal one. At a press conference on 6 October, Khodorkovsky condemned the aggressive tactics of the prosecutor's office and declared: 'If their intention is to get me to leave the country or put me in jail, then they should put me in jail. I'm not going to be a political exile.'[34] He had no intention of becoming another Berezovsky or Gusinsky, railing impotently against Putin's regime from abroad.

Khodorkovsky established close relations with many influential figures in the American elite. Already in July 2002 Khodorkovsky was greatly encouraged by a meeting he had with Vice President Dick Cheney at Jackson Hole in Wyoming, and he now intensified the American leg of his strategy, including a visit to Sun Valley, Idaho, in July 2003, where he met senior American business and government officials. His daughter at this time was placed in a summer camp in America, while on 16

July Khodorkovsky returned to Moscow.[35] In his meeting with Cheney he discussed ExxonMobil's plan to buy a stake in Yukos. Khodorkovsky visited America repeatedly in the summer and autumn of 2003, speaking at think tanks and lobbying bodies. Volsky noted that the authorities could misinterpret his American visits, but as usual Khodorkovsky pursued a resolutely independent (some would say provocative) course.[36] Speaking to journalists in Berlin in August, Khodorkovsky warned that presidential associates were trying to appropriate businesses, threatening Russia with becoming another Latin America.[37]

On 9 October he gave the keynote address to the US–Russia Business Council in Washington. He noted that Yukos had become the largest company in Russia in terms of capitalisation, and the world's fourth-largest oil company following the merger with Sibneft. Just ten years ago, he stressed, it would have been unthinkable for a Russian oil company to have a foreign chief financial officer, whereas Yukos had appointed the American, Bruce Misamore, to that post. The company also now applied GAAP and quarterly reporting, had appointed independent directors and held international audits. The question of property rights had been largely settled, but he noted that individual rights still lagged. He gave the example of Lebedev, who had already spent three months in detention on flimsy evidence. Presciently, he argued: 'There is no independent judiciary in Russia, and law-enforcement agencies use Soviet-style methods that are not appropriate for a modern, civilized country.'[38] 'In the next four years, the country must decide what direction its development will take, and resolve what kind of model will be followed in Russia: whether it will be authoritarian; follow a Mexico-style path; or a more modern, civilized model.'[39] In Washington, in a speech to the Carnegie Endowment for International Peace on the same day, Khodorkovsky defended his company's right to engage in public activity and once again stressed the alternatives: 'Are we going to become a democratic Russia for the first time in our thousand-year history, or are we going to continue along our thousand-year path of authoritarianism?'[40]

Listeners report that Khodorkovsky was brimming with confidence and gave little indication that he feared imminent arrest, although he was probably putting on a brave front for a Western audience.[41] His assurance was bolstered by a number of factors: the belief that his ties with the West would shield him from punitive actions, that his plans to tie up with one of the US oil majors would give him some security and, above all, that no rational government would attack one of Russia's most successful companies. Few expected that he would be let off as lightly as Gusinsky, and fears for the company's future were openly aired after the fateful February confrontation. Khodorkovsky was often warned that Putin could not be trusted, but, as he puts it, 'It was difficult for me to comprehend that the president of the country could lie so brazenly. I am now paying for that.'[42] 'We considered it quite likely that they would take Yukos from us, but we could not foresee the destruction of the company. Not only would it be illegal, but it was incompatible with the logic of pragmatic "statecraft".'[43]

Khodorkovsky's foreign interlocutors added to his self-confidence. Cheney was sympathetic to Khodorkovsky's cause, as were a number of leading politicians, including Tom Lantos, the Democratic Congressional representative from California's 13th district. Bruce Jackson, the pundit on foreign-policy issues who vociferously advocated the war on Iraq, supported Khodorkovsky. They informed him that at the Camp David summit on 27 September 2003 Bush had raised his case with Putin. In the context of such high-level representations, Khodorkovsky was led to believe that the Russian authorities would hardly risk jeopardising the relationship with the United States by arresting him. However, Khodorkovsky was misinformed, and his fate had not been raised at Camp David. Worse, some of the Texan oil people with whom Bush associated had been at the sharp end of Yukos's tough business practices (for example, Amoco lost its stake in YNG in 1998). Western oil companies were upset at Yukos's opposition to PSAs and whispered unpleasant words about the company to the president.[44]

Bush relied on Condoleezza Rice, national-security adviser, for much of his information about Russia, and she was no friend of the new business class. As a specialist in Russian affairs she had watched the oligarch antics in the 1990s with horror. The summit in any case had been designed to relaunch what had become a rather flagging 'strategic partnership', forged after the al-Qaeda attack of 9/11, and the affairs of one individual hardly rated as the priority. Bush stressed that in the context of 'expanding our cooperation in Iraq and Afghanistan [...] [o]ld suspicions are giving way to new understanding and respect. Our goal is to bring the U.S.–Russian relationship to a new level of partnership.'[45] Khodorkovsky and Yukos thus lacked the kind of Western support on which their supporters counted. In the event, the Russo-American relationship continued to stagnate, in part because of the fallout of the Yukos affair. Bush personally remained loyal to the sentiments he expressed at the press conference: 'Plus, I like him [Putin], he's a good fellow to spend quality time with.'[46] Despite the strong personal relationship that survived to the end of both their respective presidencies, Yukos joined Chechnya and Iraq as an issue that poisoned Russia's relations with the West.

Khodorkovsky also tried to rally domestic resistance to the imminent attack, the fourth prong of his survival strategy. He assumed that he had adequate protection

(a *krysha*, or 'roof') in the form of Voloshin at the head of the presidential administration and Kasyanov at the head of the government. Meeting with Western
journalists on 29 July 2003, Voloshin stressed that Putin did not know in advance
of the various Yukos searches and arrests and would not be able to influence the
course of the investigation.[47] Voloshin was convinced that Khodorkovsky would
not be arrested. Kasyanov's response to Lebedev's arrest was to warn of 'civil war'.[48]
Medvedev apparently joined with half a dozen like-minded Kremlin officials and
tried to block the arrest.[49] Putin always feared being manipulated by his entourage
and thus was deeply suspicious of the initiative. When Medvedev approached Putin
on behalf of the group to request an end to the Yukos affair, Putin is alleged to have
exclaimed: 'This is a conspiracy.'[50] However, the liberals were far from united. The
finance minister Alexei Kudrin supported the attack, declaring that 'tax transgres-
sions must be punished', noting that Yukos was not the only oil company in this
category, but it was in his view the worst.[51] Kudrin was particularly incensed by his
inability to close down the three 'onshore offshores', Mordovia (actively used by
Yukos), Chukotka and Kalmykia. Even Medvedev, although opposed to the attack
on principle, shared the *silovik* diagnosis that Russia was fighting for its survival
as a state, and hence the premium was on elite unity.[52] Putin feared being manipulated, yet a section of his entourage exaggerated Khodorkovsky's misdemeanours.
Khodorkovsky did nothing to allay these concerns.

In one of his last press conferences Khodorkovsky revealed that he had organised a
collective letter to Putin from the RSPP, not so much talking about a non-aggression
pact but to inform Putin about the lawlessness of the judiciary and the threat that this
posed to economic growth. He insisted that Yukos had not manifested any political
ambitions, but that its leaders had exercised their civic rights. All businesses lobbied
their interests, he insisted, but Yukos in parliament was the first to do this openly. If
it came to a choice between property and civic rights, Khodorkovsky declared, he
would choose rights, 'since without them it would be impossible to keep property'.[53] To
rally resistance among regional elites and the public sphere Khodorkovsky undertook
an extraordinary tour of the provinces, visiting Orel, Belgorod, Lipetsk, Tambov,
Voronezh, Saransk, Samara, Saratov and Nizhny Novgorod, and later he was due to
visit Irkutsk, Angarsk and Tomsk. Interviewed in Voronezh, Khodorkovsky noted
that he was facing 'werewolves in epaulettes', in this case from the prosecutor's office.
The president's position was 'perfectly understandable': 'The prosecutor general or
some other official comes to him and says that there is evidence that some company
or individual committed numerous murders, then the president cannot forbid the
investigation.'[54] Khodorkovsky never made it to Tomsk. Asked in 2011 why he did

not leave the country, he responded: 'If I had known there were so many years of jail ahead, returning would have been much more difficult. But I could not act in any other way and I would have returned in any case, to defend my honour.'[55]

Khodorkovsky pursued a strategy of personal resistance. He resolutely insisted that he would not go into exile. Although he visited the United States numerous times, he was adamant that he would return to confront whatever fate the Kremlin had in store for him. Indeed, for his October visit to Washington he travelled with his family, and they could have stayed together in exile. He was strongly urged by Nevzlin and others to take this step. Among other things, Nevzlin considered that this would be a way of saving the company. It is quite possible that the leaks about his imminent arrest were intended to provoke him into flight; however, as he noted, even if he did try he would have been arrested anyway and then accused of being a criminal who tried to escape.[56] Khodorkovsky was caught in an impossible dilemma. On the one hand, he fully appreciated the gravity of his situation and the dangers facing Yukos; on the other hand, he appeared unable to appreciate the viewpoint of his opponents. He was playing one game, while Sechin and the 'politburo' were playing another. Putin as usual temporised, but once he made up his mind he acted decisively. With 30–40 deputies considered to be aligned with Yukos, and with the perceived goal in the 2003 election to raise this to a blocking minority, irrespective of whether they were liberals or Communists, with clearly expressed political ambitions for 2008 and numerous policy disagreements, Khodorkovsky represented a political challenge to the regime. His actions also made the other oligarchs nervous. Thus Khodorkovsky was cast to his fate.

KHODORKOVSKY'S ARREST

In the months preceding his arrest Khodorkovsky delivered several programmatic speeches in Europe and America, and he also toured Russia's regions, meeting governors and giving a number of university lectures. In a press conference in Saratov on 23 October Khodorkovsky was open about the 'ordered subtext to these actions', referring to the pressure on his colleagues. Speaking to students in Samara on the theme of 'Oil, society and the development of the Russian economy', he condemned Putin's calls to double Russian GDP in a decade as unrealisable and a dead-end, and that the only way to escape from the 'energy vicious circle' was to invest in the talented minority, the intellectual elite of the country.[57] Khodorkovsky then addressed a civic forum of business and government leaders in Nizhny Novgorod, which, paradoxically, discussed the legal framework for a new social contract between the state and big business.[58] Right to the end Khodorkovsky did not really believe that he would be detained, although he was aware of the possibility. When Irina Yasina, head of Open Russia, warned him that he would be arrested, Khodorkovsky responded: 'They won't jail me. After all, they are not enemies of their own country.'[59] Eric Kraus, chief analyst at Sovlink, saw things rather differently: 'There is no rational reason why he [Khodorkovsky] did not back down. Khodorkovsky has foreign support and a good security service. Putin has a nuclear arsenal. In a collision course, Khodorkovsky was always going to come out the loser.'[60]

The authorities struck on 25 October in a dawn raid on Khodorkovsky's chartered TU-134 plane at Tolmachevo airport in Novosibirsk. He had made a refuelling stop there on his journey from Nizhny Novgorod to Irkutsk, where he was due to deliver a lecture on civil society to the local Open Russia-supported school for public politics before going on to inspect the Yukos oil refinery in Angarsk. At 5 a.m. the plane was stormed by some 20 black-uniformed, masked members of the FSB's anti-terror Alfa Unit, and all those on board, including flight attendants, were forced to the floor.[61] Khodorkovsky was reputed to travel with armed guards, which may explain the excessive use of force by Spetsnaz forces. Other FSB units also made heavy-handed interventions at his daughter's school. According to Belkovsky, the arrest was carried out in the dead of night to force Putin to accept a fait accompli. According to this account, Putin had not been able to make up his mind, and now Sechin seized the initiative to force Putin to accept the facts on the ground.[62] If he ordered Khodorkovsky's release he would look weak and an instrument in the hands of others; however, to accept the arrest and all that it entailed brought him into the *silovik* camp on this issue and set Russia and his presidency on a new path. A more credible version is that two days before the arrest the prosecutor general, Vladimir Ustinov, came to Putin with a folder outlining Khodorkovsky's alleged crimes. On reading the material Putin declared: 'Let the law do its work' – and the machine was set in motion.[63]

Khodorkovsky was arrested for not complying with a summons to present himself to the PGO the day before, even though it had been issued on that day only at 3 p.m. and his lawyers had made it clear that he was away. Russian law states that enforcement procedures are applied only when there is evidence of the wilful or malicious evasion of appearing as a witness. The use of FSB forces was inappropriate in the circumstances. A number of procedural rules were violated, including the fact that the arrest of a witness took place on a holiday, and that he was taken under armed escort to Moscow, which is not the usual way to behave with a witness. Later that day he was already being questioned by the PGO investigator Salavat Karimov. He had been specially brought in from Bashkortostan in 2000 to lead the attack on Gusinsky and the seizure of NTV; he also led the attack on Nikolai Aksenenko, a potential rival of Putin's, and shortly afterwards another on Berezovsky. Karimov would figure in many Yukos cases, confirming his reputation as the 'oligarch killer'. That evening judges in the Basmanny District Court denied bail and sanctioned Khodorkovsky's imprisonment for two months until 30 December, later extended for another three-month period and similar periods thereafter up to the end of his trial. Khodorkovsky considered this was intended to prevent him from dealing with the attack on Yukos.[64] The broader case against him involved seven charges, including personal income-tax evasion, avoiding corporate taxes, falsifying documents and theft.

FIRST REACTIONS

Khodorkovsky's arrest shocked the Russian and international business and political communities, but the reaction was remarkably muted. Khodorkovsky was a long-time member of the Rand US–Russia Business Leader Forum, and he was due to attend a session on his return from Siberia. Members had already gathered in Moscow when news came through of his arrest.[65] Various oligarchs such as Fridman were in attendance, but they issued little more than symbolic protests. Medvedev, however, was quite open about his opposition to the arrest.[66] Voloshin and Kasyanov, as well as Medvedev, were not opposed to subordinating Yukos to the state, but they all opposed criminalising the affair and arresting Khodorkovsky.[67] For others, such as Khlebnikov (the editor of the Russian *Forbes*), selective justice was better than no justice, and Khodorkovsky's arrest signalled the death agony of the Yeltsin-era kleptocracy.

On 25 October the RSPP met with two other business organisations (Delovaya Rossiya and OPORA) and signed a common declaration drafted by Chubais and some others, meeting in the Balchug hotel: 'The escalation of actions by the authorities and law-enforcement agencies against Russian business has severely damaged the atmosphere in society. Trust of business in the authorities has been undermined.' They stressed that society would only be calmed by 'a clear and unambiguous statement' from president Putin.[68] Although Chubais criticised Khodorkovsky's behaviour, he categorically opposed his arrest, fearing among other things that it would damage the investment climate. However, Chubais later tempered his condemnation, fearing (correctly as it turned out) that outspoken defence of the oligarch would have a negative effect on the vote for SPS in the forthcoming parliamentary elections. In an interview that evening he categorised Khodorkovsky's arrest as a 'mistake by the authorities', and went on to stress that 'a mistake by the authorities in response to mistakes by business is much graver'.[69]

Volsky twice spoke to Putin about the arrest and bravely left Khodorkovsky's name on the list of members of the RSPP's bureau. Most of the others remained silent.[70] The RSPP board met twice to discuss the case, and although initially it planned to protest, its response remained low-key. Only six of the 27 members of the RSPP board spoke against the arrest, and the others accepted that the business community had to shoulder its share of the blame. Not a single leading magnate stood up publicly to defend Khodorkovsky, including the architect of privatisation, Chubais. Igor Yurgens, the deputy head of the RSPP, noted how the case undermined the trust of business in the security services, that 'the selective application of law leads to it being undermined', and that the case strengthened the drift to a 'unipolar political model' in which 'parties and governors are totally dependent on the Kremlin'.[71] The RSPP's membership was also divided but acquiescent. A survey of the heads of 83 companies conducted by the business journal *Kompaniya* in the early stages of the Yukos affair found that they were split over whether it threatened private property, but an absolute majority did not think that the case would affect their business or their relations with state agencies.[72] Many business leaders agreed that Khodorkovsky had defected from the unwritten conventions of political behaviour.

Putin on 27 October responded to the calls of business organisations and politicians to comment on the Yukos affair. His response was implacable, insisting that there would be 'no meetings or deals over the work of the law enforcement agencies' and that if the courts held Khodorkovsky they must have a case (a typically Soviet circuitous exercise of logic), arguing that all were equal before the law, including 'a big businessman, irrespective of how many billions he had in his personal or corporate accounts'. However, he acknowledged the concerns of the business community, remembering how in the Soviet period specific cases turned into general campaigns. The charges laid against Khodorkovsky could have been preferred against any number of tycoons of the era, and the analogy was drawn with the trial against the Industrial Party in 1929 that signalled the beginning of the era of Stalinist repression.[73] Putin insisted that 'in connection with the case under discussion there would be no generalisation, analogies, precedents, in particular associated with the results of privatisation', but warned against 'speculation and hysterics' and forbade the government to 'get involved in this discussion'.[74] Putin affirmed that the fundamental principles of the 'equidistance' period would not be repudiated: the privatisations of the 1990s would not be revisited as long as business continued to pay informal rents to the regime, supported its socio-economic projects and kept out of politics. The inadequacies of the equidistance model were also perpetuated: notably, the failure to institutionalise stable business–politics relations, permanent uncertainty about where the limits lay, fostering a spirit of 'anticipatory obedience', the continued prevalence of informal rules and the Byzantine struggle of factions for power and property.

At an expanded meeting with 800 RSPP business leaders on 14 November, Putin was greeted by Soviet-style extended applause, rather surprisingly in the light of recent events. In his final address Putin noted that 'it is sometimes hard to tell where business ends and the state begins; and where the state ends and business begins', and condemned the use of security agencies in business conflicts, noting that in connection with a 'specific case' (obviously Yukos) 'one must apply a certain legal culture and not drift into extra-procedural decisions'.[75] Delegates carefully avoided the Yukos question, but Putin raised the issue himself, which was awarded an ovation. In comments that are not repeated in the official text, he asserted that the Yukos case was an isolated event and that there would be no return to the past, but that the law must be upheld.[76] He insisted that Russian business 'must develop a new system of social guarantees for the population in accordance with the changed demands of the time'.[77] Business responded to the calls and supported the government's various programmes, including resources for service personnel wounded in Chechnya. The RSPP bureau meeting soon after appointed Vekselberg to fulfil Khodorkovsky's functions at the head of its committee for international cooperation, but Khodorkovsky formally remained a member of the bureau.[78] Khodorkovsky finally resigned from the RSPP's bureau in November 2005, and Vekselberg was formally appointed head of the international section.[79]

The Soviet spirit was back with a vengeance. When asked on television in July 2004 who he thought was behind the attack on Yukos, Volsky refused to answer: 'I am very scared to name names now', he said. 'I am simply scared. I have six grandchildren, after all, and I want them to live.'[80] When 33 business representatives (including 22 from RSPP) met with Putin on 1 July 2004 they agreed in advance not to raise the Yukos question. Potanin, who had long worked closely with the Kremlin, was apparently the key figure in ensuring that the RSPP did not make much of the Khodorkovsky case. Potanin was instrumental in ensuring that in October 2005 Alexander Shokhin, Surkov's favoured candidate, replaced Volsky, who had displeased the Kremlin with his criticism of Khodorkovsky's arrest. Nevzlin's hopes that Yukos could use Surkov's old links with the company to help Khodorkovsky proved illusory.[81] Surkov by 2003 had become a loyal member of Putin's team and maintained a discreet silence over his relations with Khodorkovsky.

POLITICAL FALLOUT

In a disturbing echo of Stalinist practices, some 50 writers, scientists, cosmonauts and artists issued a public letter calling for an exemplary sentence to be imposed on the fallen oligarch.[82] Later one of the signatories, the ballerina Anastasia Volochkova, claimed that she had been tricked into signing.[83] Abramovich at this point made his bid to take over the Yukos–Sibneft company. The opposition parties restricted themselves to critical declarations, and even Yabloko and SPS, those most affected by Khodorkovsky's arrest, refused to take protest to the streets. Even the Yukos management was at a loss to think of an effective response. The use of pseudo-legal forms to pursue para-constitutional acts was typical of Putin's style, disarming his opponents and disconcerting even those loyal to the regime.

Those not entirely loyal to the Putinised regime fell on their swords or were purged. Just five days after Khodorkovsky's arrest Voloshin resigned as head of the presidential administration, the first major political casualty of the shifting balance of factional power. Voloshin's departure on 30 October represented a defeat for the old Yeltsin style of political management. In a meeting with journalists in late July 2003 Voloshin, as noted, conceded that the case represented a political campaign against Yukos, but insisted that Putin had not known about it in advance.[84] Following Voloshin's resignation it appears that Putin threw his weight behind the continued attack on Yukos and Khodorkovsky personally. Sechin's role in all of this appears consistent, with the political attack on Yukos permitting him to expand his economic fiefdom. Rosneft's development at Yukos's expense allowed the state to pursue its strategic priority of creating a national champion in the oil sector. However, to maintain a residue of factional balance Voloshin's replacement as head of the presidential administration was not a *silovik* but the relatively liberal Medvedev, and the economic liberals in the government remained in their posts. In addition, Voloshin remained chair of the board of directors of RAO UES, and thus the electricity monopoly remained a bastion of liberals to balance the *silovik* stronghold in Rosneft. Gazprom was torn between the two, and Medvedev engaged in an intense struggle to prevent a *silovik* takeover of the gas corporation, for which he called on the Petersburg liberals for help.[85] One manifestation of this struggle was the conflict over the merger with Rosneft.

Leading politicians, even at the highest level, were demoted if they criticised the affair. Kasyanov called the arrest of Lebedev 'excessive', and argued that the situation surrounding Yukos had a deleterious effect on Russia's image and alarmed potential investors. In late 2003 he again expressed concern about the freezing of Yukos shares. The 'politburo' had long agitated for his dismissal, as one of the few independent figures in the regime ready to question Putin's judgement. He criticised the handling of the Dubrovka theatre siege in October 2002, when nearly 50 Chechens took hostage an 850-strong audience watching the popular *Nord-Ost* musical. In the ensuing assault 130 members of the audience died, the majority from the effects of the gas pumped through the ventilation system by the special forces in their attempts to rescue the hostages. Kasyanov was summarily dismissed on 24 February 2004, a fortnight before the presidential election.[86] There are rumours that he was sacked because of his attempt to get involved in the distribution of Yukos assets.[87] In May 2005 he argued, 'This trial is a farce. The Khodorkovsky case has brought Russia to a turning point, while the verdict could mean that the point of no return will be passed.'[88]

Kasyanov's replacement, Mikhail Fradkov, was a compromise figure in factional terms, but he was clearly affiliated with the hardliners. In the cabinet reshuffle the Yukos-friendly energy minister Yusufov lost his post, and the ministry itself was merged with industry under a new minister, Viktor Khristenko, who had no special relationship with Yukos. The federal energy agency in the new ministry was headed by Sergei Oganesyan, who had previously worked as a vice president in Rosneft. Thus Yukos was systematically deprived of administrative cover. It also lost political cover with the failure of the two main liberal parties, Yabloko and the SPS, to enter the Fourth Duma (2003–7), which thus lacked a liberal caucus. Instead, the Rodina party surged ahead on a programme of militant nationalism and oligarch-bashing. It is still not clear why the liberals did not make more of the obvious issue that the justice system was being used for blatant political goals, and in general their response was remarkably mute. This paralysis of the liberal spirit may well have been provoked in part by fear, but probably more important was the lack of conviction that the property acquired in the 1990s was legitimate and the realisation that the oligarchs had abused their economic power. Such sentiments were taken to their extreme by Bill Browder, the head of Hermitage Capital, the largest portfolio investor in Russia, who had long been engaged in a crusade to improve corporate governance. For Browder, Khodorkovsky's arrest meant that Putin 'would stop at nothing to establish law and order'.[89] Browder would soon discover that the case had little to do with 'law and order'. In November 2005 he became a *persona non grata*, his business raided on 4 June 2007, and his associate Sergei Magnitsky died in custody in November 2009.[90]

The liberal parties hesitated to claim credit for having laid the foundations of a market economy, on which Putin's economic success was built. Yabloko of course could not do so, since it had criticised every step of the way in the 1990s, while SPS was dogged by the perception that it represented only the elite. As a perceptive commentary put it at the time:

> If a single leading party seriously depended on the views of its electorate, it would be banging every available bell over the Yukos case: it's not every day that there is such an opportunity to outline one's views and the interests of one's electorate – and this just before an election.[91]

Politicians in this election, however, sang to a very different tune. There was much talk at the time of the big energy companies having to pay a 'resource rent' (*prirodnaya renta*), effectively something akin to New Labour's 'windfall tax' imposed on companies in 1997. The liberals estimated that this could bring in about $3 billion, while Glazev talked of up to $40 billion. There was no agreement among political leaders on the issue, and in response, as one commentator put it: 'Not receiving a reply from the elites, the president will have to seek and find an answer himself, thus demonstrating the superfluity of the elite.'[92] As an interviewer put it to Medvedev, 'there are practically no parties actively defending freedom, private life and the associated property rights, and thus the presidential administration shapes political space in Russia.' Medvedev conceded, 'The absence of a normal rightist ideology gives rise to substitutes and prejudices.'[93] He insisted that 'Traditional state capitalism is a dead-end path for economic development', but he did recognise that 'state companies have far from exhausted their potential'.[94] As chair of the board at Gazprom, he was in a position to know.

Khodorkovsky's arrest provided a sharp boost to Putin's approval ratings, just as the Chechen war had done three years earlier.[95] Support for the pro-presidential party gave the attack on Yukos the patina of popular legitimacy. The scholar Konstantin Sonin noted:

> It is entirely possible that Khodorkovsky might be a free man today and Sibneft might still be in private hands if United Russia had garnered only 25 percent of the vote instead of the 40 percent that it actually polled in 2003. [...] The Putin administration can be accused of many sins, but there is no denying that its actions

and policies have more closely reflected the public mood than did President Boris Yeltsin's elitist, more progressive government.[96]

Putin's annual address to the Federal Assembly on 26 May 2004 was imbued with a paternalistic and bureaucratic approach with little sense of a confident and pluralistic democratic community of citizens. His comments on non-governmental organisations that are 'fed by an alien hand' harked back to the Soviet era.[97] The tone of Western commentators on Russia equally became more harshly reminiscent of Cold War times. An 'Open letter to the heads of state and government of the European Union and NATO' by some 50 public figures, published on 28 September 2004, castigated political developments under Putin and in particular the attack on Yukos.[98]

CHAPTER 5

BASMANNY JUSTICE

The Yukos affair was about the restructuring of political and economic relationships; hence the Khodorkovsky trials were politicised and judicial impartiality suborned. The affair represented a political struggle between the state (and subsections of the state) and a powerful business concern in which judicial proceedings were used to advance particular interests. The classic *siloviki* shared an 'anti-bourgeois' ideology, and it was this mindset that predisposed the regime to launch the Yukos affair. As for Khodorkovsky himself, he refused to go into exile, which would have meant his political annihilation and the repudiation of his expressed values of civic responsibility. Once arrested Khodorkovsky hoped for some sort of negotiated settlement with the Kremlin, resigning on 3 November 2003 as head of Yukos in an attempt to separate his fate from that of the company. He failed to understand the remorseless nature of the struggle. As his lawyer Yury Schmidt put it:

> We, old hands at Soviet and Russian justice, knew that the judges obeyed orders when the Kremlin took a personal interest in the case. But we were unable to convince our client, or we didn't go about it properly. We probably should have protested against the partiality of the investigation and the trial right from the start, refused to cooperate and accused the government of locking up a political prisoner.[1]

Khodorkovsky chose to refute the substance of the charges against him, rather than turning the trial into 'a political indictment of the Putin regime'.[2] Khodorkovsky mobilised a powerful team of lawyers to rebut the charges on the normal logic of evidence, but they understood that the defence was a political act and could only be conducted as such.[3]

PRE-TRIAL DETENTION

At the PGO's request, the Basmanny District Court repeatedly extended Khodorkovsky's pre-trial detention. In the end, Khodorkovsky spent nearly two years in Block 4 of the IZ-99/1 Matrosskaya Tishina pre-trial detention centre (SIZO), a special-purpose building known as the VIP prison, while Lebedev was held in the main section, IZ-77/1.[4] Block 4 is a relatively small detention centre for some 100 inmates located on the territory of the general prison but administratively separate and with its own rules, including frequent moves from cell to cell. It had previously been under the control of the KGB, and it was here that the members of the junta that had launched the attempted coup in August 1991 were held. As was the case for so many other political prisoners in the Putin era, 'What appeared at first to be tourism turned out to be emigration' as the months turned into years.[5]

There were repeated attempts to allow Khodorkovsky out on bail, with up to 40 Duma deputies ready to stand as guarantors.[6] An international group of defence lawyers called for his release. Karinna Moskalenko, at the appeal against the Basmanny District Court's bail decision heard in the Moscow City Court on 15 January 2004, argued that none of the points in Article 108 of the Criminal Procedure Code (UPK), which details reasons for refusing bail, applied to her client.[7] Moskalenko is the founder of the International Protection Centre, based in Moscow, specialising in cases to be heard at the ECtHR in Strasbourg, to which Russia is legally bound since joining the Council of Europe in 1996. At that hearing Khodorkovsky offered to surrender all of his passports (he apparently had three) and promised that he would not flee, noting that 'I travelled abroad several times during the investigation' and stressing 'that I will not hide from the proceedings'. His application for house arrest was rejected on the grounds that he could escape and would use his freedom to 'launder his ill-gotten gains'.[8] Back in 2000 Gusinsky had promised a court that if released he would not try to escape, but in the event he fled, first to Spain, then to Greece and Israel. However, Khodorkovsky was a very different character, and he had demonstrated that he had no intention of leaving.

During the investigation evidence is examined and collected into a folder that governs the trial. The procedures reflect Soviet traditions and remain in Russia's revised Criminal Code of 2001. The new code introduced some important innovations, yet ultimately retained its 'neo-inquisitorial' or 'investigatory' character whereby 'the state – objectively and on behalf of everyone concerned, including the accused – actively investigates the circumstances of a crime to determine what happened'.[9] The Russian system is firmly located in the civil-law tradition, where the state is considered to be an impartial investigator, and where an early role for defence lawyers or the defence of the procedural rights of the suspect are less prominent than in the Anglo-American adversarial common-law tradition, where the trial is everything. The 1993 constitution states that judicial proceedings should be 'conducted on adversarial principles and equality of the parties' (Article 123(3)), which Article 15(1) of the new UPK declares applies to criminal cases.[10] However, practical implementation remains disputed.[11]

A later part of the same Article (15(3)) asserts that 'The judge is not an agent for criminal prosecution, and sides neither with the prosecution nor the defence. The judge creates the necessary conditions for all sides to fulfil their procedural duties and the fulfilment of their rights.' This injunction, to put it mildly, was not fulfilled in the Yukos case. This prompted an appeal to the provisions of Articles 5 and 6 of the European Convention on Human Rights and Fundamental Freedoms (ECHR), which defends the procedural rights of suspects.[12] The long shadow of the pre-trial investigation and the pressure from the Russian authorities over the conduct of the trial revealed how much remained to be done to ensure that progressive legislation modified traditional juridical practices.

The number of inmates for much of the time was reduced from the normal four to three, and the whole institution was very small, with only 20 cells, each with four people, and rarely eight, and with only two of the six floors occupied by prisoners, and the rest by prison personnel. The official message issued to the criminal world was not to touch Khodorkovsky: 'Which once again only goes to show that the criminal world, big business and high politics are worlds not so alien to each other.'[13] In his first days in prison Khodorkovsky was in a state of shock. He was unable to eat, which in prison could be taken as a hunger strike and alarmed the authorities.[14] The journalist Yulia Latynina passed him a copy of Plutarch, so that 'he did not think that he was the first person on earth to be persecuted', and to help when fate turns sour.[15]

The reminiscences of four of Khodorkovsky's cellmates have been brought out in a small book, which, as the author notes, represents Russia in miniature.[16] Khodorkovsky's cellmates asked whether he regretted not escaping, to which he said no.[17] One introduced him to the works of Boris Akunin (the pen name of Grigory Chkhartishvili, an erudite stylist, Japanese translator and political activist, with whom he would later enter into dialogue), and he quickly read all the Erast Fandorin detective mysteries, which he greatly liked.[18] This is hardly surprising, since these novels speak precisely to the concerns of the nascent bourgeoisie, imbued as they are with a spirit of patriotism and individual freedom.[19] Khodorkovsky followed current events on television and daily received a thick package of newspapers and journals, and was very upset when Yabloko and SPS failed to enter parliament in December 2003. He spoke ironically about his business colleagues and politicians, with the exception of the independent liberal Vladimir Ryzhkov, and referred to Putin in sardonic terms as *vozhd* ('leader', a term historically applied to Stalin), and said that he, Khodorkovsky, would be willing to make compromises and negotiate with anybody. He noted that running a business and running the country were totally different things and apparently admitted that he had entertained notions of becoming prime minister.[20] He spent much of the time working at his desk, and when writing 'The crisis of liberalism in Russia' (see Chapter 9) he discussed the main points with his cellmates, and incorporated some of their suggestions.[21] The prisoners joked that cell 501 was probably the freest place in Russia.[22]

THE CRIMINAL CASE

The substance of the legal case against Khodorkovsky, Lebedev and Krainov (the last of whom was included because of Apatit) focused on fraud, tax evasion and money laundering, while that against Pichugin focused on criminal matters. Seven charges were levelled against Khodorkovsky personally: major fraudulent embezzlement by an organised group, failure to comply with an enforced court decision, inflicting damage on others' property through fraud, major tax evasion by collusion within a group, avoidance of private income tax and insurance payments to state extra-budgetary funds, repeated forgery of documents, and major embezzlement or laying false claim to others' property within an organised group. The charges were mainly financial and notably did not include illegal privatisation.

Lebedev had long been one of Khodorkovsky's core business associates, in control of the banking activities from which the whole Yukos empire was born. At the time of his arrest, Lebedev owned 7% of Menatep, giving him a 4.2% stake in Yukos, placing him at number 427 on the *Forbes* list of the world's richest people, with an estimated fortune of $1 billion.[23] He was charged with fraud relating to the privatisation of the Apatit fertiliser plant through Menatep and the Volna subsidiary. According to Dmitry Gololobov, the former deputy head of Yukos's legal department, an examination of the charges against Khodorkovsky and Lebedev 'provides some surprising results'. In his words, 'Yukos as a corporate group has generally complied not only with international business practice, but also with the practices of comparable Russian companies.' There was little that distinguished the corporate restructuring and business operations of Yukos from any other Russian oil company.[24] His testimony is all the weightier since he was no friend of Khodorkovsky's. In the Tuschi film (discussed in the Conclusion), he is unequivocal about his former boss: 'I despise him. He was one of the oligarchs who created the whole judicial system in which he now finds himself.'

Andrei Krainov, who won the investment competition for Apatit in 1994, is perhaps the most enigmatic of all the figures in Khodorkovsky's trial, and he tried to keep out of the limelight. At the head of Volna he bought 20% of Apatit's shares; he then sold them on in smaller blocks, but failed to invest the promised $283 million in the prescribed manner. He was charged as a co-defendant, with the accusation that Volna was no more than a front company for Khodorkovsky and Lebedev. Krainov admitted as much in court, although, as noted, the situation was rather more complex.

Pichugin is undoubtedly one of the main victims of the Yukos affair. Born on 25 July 1962, he considered himself a Don Cossack. After school he entered a military academy, from which he was posted to the KGB academy in Novosibirsk, and between 1987 and 1994 he worked in the KGB's military counter-intelligence unit. After countless reorganisations he left the KGB in 1994 with the rank of major and joined Menatep's security service. In 1998 he formally transferred to Yukos, with his section responsible for the prevention of criminal infiltration, including theft.[25] The head of the service was Kondaurov, a former KGB general and later a Communist member of parliament. Pichugin was first called in for questioning on 27 May 2003 but thought little of it at the time. In identifying Pichugin as a possible weak link who could incriminate Nevzlin, Khodorkovsky and other Yukos managers, the architects of the Yukos affair clearly misjudged their man. Testimony from friends and relations portray Pichugin as one of 'a dying breed':

> a military man, raised in the USSR and by no means the worst relic of those times. Patriotic, orderly, true to his word, demanding yet respectful of subordinates, honest, willing to sacrifice his civilian career when the call comes to 'Save the Homeland!', and true to his destiny – these are the distinguishing features of the breed.[26]

He had welcomed Putin's ascent to power, considering him just the sort of person the country needed to restore order.[27]

On 19 June 2003 his home and offices were searched, and on 21 June the Basmanny District Court issued an arrest warrant, even though there appeared to be no evidence against him.[28] On 26 June he was charged with the attempted murder of Kostina and organising the murder of the Gorins. Failing to gain a confession or to find any convincing evidence, especially since Nevzlin and Pichugin barely knew one another, a powerful truth serum was administered on 14 July. Knowing nothing of any crime, Pichugin could say nothing of use to the prosecution.[29] The various cases against Pichugin will be examined in the next chapter.

THE FIRST TRIAL

Khodorkovsky's trial has been described as a 'kangaroo court'.[30] Lawyers were subject to searches and other forms of harassment, provoking them to appeal to legal professional organisations to defend their rights. The case was accompanied by repeated breaches of advocacy rules.[31] For example, Anton Drel, the lead lawyer representing Khodorkovsky, was summoned for questioning by the PGO on 17 October 2003, in contravention of Article 8 of the Law on the Rights and Duties of Lawyers, which states that a defence attorney cannot be summoned for questioning or to give evidence in a current case, and also Article 56 of the Criminal Code. There were numerous searches of the law offices of companies associated with the Yukos case. On 9 October 2003 Drel's offices were searched and documents connected with the Yukos case confiscated, clearly violating attorney–client privilege. At the time of the search the FSB knew that Drel was at a court hearing representing Lebedev. The investigations were accompanied by improper searches, often executed with a show of force, without proper search warrants or complete records of the materials confiscated, and without the subjects of the search or their representatives being present, as stipulated by law. The Koralovo orphanage was raided by armed men allegedly looking for evidence.

While Pichugin was accused of murder and attempted murder, the charges against Khodorkovsky and Lebedev focused on economic crimes, covering 11 charges against 7 articles of the Russian Criminal Code.[32] Khodorkovsky was accused of organising a network of shell companies to achieve corporate tax evasion. In the second trial (see Chapter 7) the organisation and management of these companies were considered part of organised criminal activity intended to commit fraud and money laundering. The myriad shell companies were allegedly used not only to launder funds but also for corporate tax evasion. Yukos managers were accused of forming a 'criminal corporate group', which was a new category in Russian law but served clear political goals in identifying a threat to the Russian state. Others were charged with membership of an 'organised criminal group', a catch-all category typically used in raiding when the evidence is flimsy. Numerous other accusations were later made against Khodorkovsky, and some figured in the trials of his associates and form part of the penumbra surrounding the Yukos affair. They were aired in the media and thus served to discredit Khodorkovsky.[33] The complicity of Yukos executives in killings became a prominent meme (see Chapter 6). The authorities with increasing stridency sought to present the 'Yukos affair' as a strictly criminal matter.

The most important trial in the country's post-Soviet history, that of Khodorkovsky, Lebedev and Krainov, began on 11 July 2004 and lasted nearly a year. It took place in the Meshchansky District Court in Moscow, but the decision on whether bail should be given and other key procedural issues were decided by the Basmanny District Court. The reformed UPK gives the courts and not procurators this right, thus the Basmanny District Court became crucial to the work of the PGO.[34] This court specialises in 'political' cases and is closely associated with the procuracy. The prosecution team worked out of the investigative division of the PGO based in the Basmanny district of Moscow, hence the term 'Basmanny justice'. The judge who approved Khodorkovsky's arrest, Andrei Rasnovsky, was a former employee of the PGO. The term 'Basmanny justice' has entered the lexicon to denote politically arbitrary justice or justice serving the needs of authorities or powerful persons. Pavlovsky in this connection recalls the notorious slogan: 'For our friends, everything; for our enemies, the law'. This was a postulate that Putin allegedly endorsed: 'Many know that I have tried to put this into practice.'[35]

There are numerous criticisms of the whole process, including the keeping of defendants in pre-trial detention without due cause and the fact that prosecutors were allowed to confront the defendants without their lawyers being present. Pichugin up to September 2004 was held in the Lefortovo detention centre, run at the time by the FSB, in contravention of Russia's Council of Europe commitments. Pichugin was allegedly interrogated with the help of psychotropic drugs, in an attempt to glean evidence that could have turned him into a witness for the prosecution. Lebedev suffers from diabetes and a heart condition and alleges that he was not given adequate medical assistance. Indeed, he was arrested in hospital and taken initially to Lefortovo before being transferred to Matrosskaya Tishina.

The head of Khodorkovsky's legal team, Genrikh Padva, warned his client not to politicise the trial, but the trial could not be anything but political.[36] The opening day was attended by a moving public demonstration of support outside the courthouse, and throughout small groups picketed the building, condemning 'Basmanny justice'. Numerous witnesses were called to give evidence for the prosecution. Among them was Yevgeny Komarov, the governor of Murmansk oblast at the time of the partial privatisation of Apatit. He noted that the Apatit auction had been conducted correctly, but later the investment conditions for the purchase of the 20% stake had not been fulfilled. He conceded that the company's debts for transport and electricity had been repaid, although further investment had not taken place, hence the matter had been referred to the arbitration court.[37] Khodorkovsky vigorously rebutted the charge.[38] In the end, even though the whole affair had begun with Apatit, it was excluded from the sentencing because of the statute of limitations – time had simply run out on the case. On several occasions Khodorkovsky attacked the procuracy as a great danger to Russian justice, declaring on 13 January 2005 that 'Today's problems in the PGO will be dealt with when genuinely independent courts are established', which the state prosecutor Dmitry Shokhin interpreted as a threat.[39]

Giving evidence in February 2005, Khodorkovsky declared that he did not consider himself guilty on any of the charges: 'Everything they accuse me of was normal business practice.' Khodorkovsky was proud that for 15 years he ran a number of successful businesses, 'but I categorically object to the criminal–artistic presentation of normal business practices.' He argued that the prosecution had 'dreamt up accusations' in matters with which he had no connection: 'Since 1994 I have held over 3,000 meetings and signed over 10,000 documents, so I cannot remember every point and every paper, although I have a good memory.' Khodorkovsky's basic argument was that he was being charged for crimes that did not exist, about events that were torn out of context.[40] He was not cross-examined by Shokhin. The chief judge (of three), Irina Kolesnikova, asked Khodorkovsky to specify precisely what posts he had occupied in his various businesses, so that his personal responsibility could be established.[41] At issue was the freelance consulting work that Khodorkovsky had carried out in 1998–9, based on a licence issued on 24 December 1997.[42] Khodorkovsky refused to name the companies that he had advised, since they had not agreed to their names being publicised. Khodorkovsky pleaded the 51st – the article of the Russian constitution granting the right not to give evidence against oneself.

Khodorkovsky's legal team offered detailed rebuttals of the charges. For example, on 5 April 2005 Padva noted that the date on which Khodorkovsky was alleged to have created a 'criminal group' was sometimes stated to have been 1990, in other documents 1993, and elsewhere 1995 or 1997.[43] On 7 April Padva argued that Menatep had actually saved Apatit, and he stressed that the company's shareholders had suffered no loss and its directors had been fully aware of the sales plan.[44] The trial came to a close on 11 April 2005. While the full ten years was demanded for the other two, the prosecution recommended a five-and-a-half-year suspended sentence on Krainov because of his 'repentance and partial admission of guilt'.[45] Krainov argued that Volna's complete dependence on Menatep prevented him managing it as he would have liked. He claimed that when he demanded that the investment conditions in Apatit be fulfilled, he was sacked.[46] He was also involved in the Volgograd case, where the regional authority was allegedly defrauded.[47] Throughout the trial he sat separately on a bench with his lawyers away from the other two in the cage, and his lawyers did not try to coordinate their position with those of Khodorkovsky and Lebedev, and indeed his defence often was at cross-purposes with theirs. In the year-long trial Krainov barely exchanged a word or a glance with the other two defendants.

In his final statement on 11 April Khodorkovsky asserted his innocence and declared that he would not ask for leniency:

> I am a Russian patriot, and therefore I consider the events around Yukos, my part-ners and myself from the perspective of the interests and values of my country. [...] I behaved the way I did because I love Russia and believe in its future as a strong and legal state. [...] Certain influential people have undertaken the systematic destruction of Yukos so that they can take over a prosperous company, or rather its profits [...] these are mercenary bureaucrats. In contrast [...] I have no yachts, nor palaces, nor football clubs, or even property abroad. [...] I was the wrong sort of oligarch, therefore the authorities not only confiscated Yukos but are now holding me in prison for the second year running.

He insisted that he 'did not want to be president', and condemned the damage that the 'home-grown bureaucracy' had inflicted on the country. He was proud of his work, creating by 2004 the largest and most transparent oil corporation in Russia, arguing that he had sought to work for the good of the country. On no point had the prosecution been able to prove his guilt. He would not ask for leniency, but would 'strive for justice'.[48] He emotionally thanked his family and wife for their sup-port, movingly speaking of Inna as 'a real comrade-in-arms and Decembrist'.[49] At the end of his 39-minute speech the court burst into a spontaneous and prolonged standing ovation.

The reading of the verdict took from 16 to 31 May 2005, a fitting culmination to a trial that had lasted ten months. By then there were 227 volumes of material asso-ciated with the case. Kolesnikova read the document, 662 pages long, summarising the evidence. In Russia a trial verdict, which is read aloud, is not a straightforward declaration of whether a defendant is guilty but a full summation of prosecution and defence arguments.[50] In the event, it consisted of an almost verbatim summary of the prosecution case presented by Shokhin. Outside the court Khodorkovsky's supporters shouted 'Freedom! Freedom!', which turned to cries of 'Shame! Shame!' once the verdict was delivered.[51]

Khodorkovsky was found guilty of fraud, tax evasion and embezzlement, a total of nine out of the 11 offences with which he was charged against six articles of the Russian Criminal Code, with charges of repeated forgery of documents dropped; Lebedev was found guilty on eight charges, also against six articles of the code. Guilt was found on the following counts:[52]

i. Buying 20% of Apatit shares not at market but at nominal cost, and then failing to fulfil the investment conditions. Because of the statute of limitations the prosecution focused on the failure of the two to fulfil the court order to return shares to the state between 1998 and 2002 and that between 2000 and 2002 they sold the plant's output at low prices to intermediaries.

ii. In December 1995 Khodorkovsky and Lebedev bought 44% of the state's shares in the Samoilov Research Institute for Fertilisers and Insectofungicides (NIUIF) (through AOZT Walton), but, according to the prosecution, once again failed to provide the promised investment, instead purloining the land and buildings located in a desirable Moscow district. The pair was found guilty of failing to fulfil a November 1997 court order to return the shares of NIUIF.[53]

iii. Embezzling state funds in 1999–2000, at the time when Khodorkovsky was in charge of Yukos, by claiming refunds in cash based upon false payment of taxes in promissory notes, to the tune of 17 billion roubles, 395 million roubles and 444,000 roubles.

iv. Khodorkovsky transferred, in the form of promissory notes, money from the sale of oil and apatite concentrate to the accounts of the Media-Most bank owned by Gusinsky, against which security Gusinsky took out loans. The court found that in this way Khodorkovsky caused material harm to the company of some $100 million.[54]

v. Corporate tax evasion by Yukos through taking illegal advantage of onshore tax havens and paying taxes with promissory notes during 1998–9.

vi. Khodorkovsky (in 1998 and 1999) and Lebedev as well (in 2000) failed
to pay the appropriate personal income taxes by diverting company
resources to themselves for 'independent entrepreneurial activity' (for
alleged consulting services) and thus paid taxes on a lower level. The
losses amounted to 54.5 million roubles.[55]

The defence team insisted that the shares in Apatit and NIUIF were bought at a
fair price, set by the state itself, and, as for the failure to invest, the best evidence
was that appropriate support had been given and both enterprises were flourishing.
Khodorkovsky argued that he had never seen the institute's rector until they met
in court, when he declared that although the investment terms had changed, they
had been sensible and allowed the institute to make a profit in market conditions.
As for the problem of paying local government taxes with promissory notes, the
defence team noted that up to 29 December 1999 this had been legal and the law
did not forbid non-monetary forms of payment. In fact, the notes issued by Yukos
were interest-bearing and protected the Lesnoi ZATO (a tax haven in the Urals)
budget from inflation. The prosecution had not found any evidence of the transfer
of funds to Gusinsky's bank because they had been returned to Yukos, with interest. By signing consulting contracts with various foreign companies, Khodorkovsky
allegedly avoided paying $1 million dollars in personal income tax. According to
the prosecution, Khodorkovsky had provided no services. The charge is a bizarre
one, since Khodorkovsky had paid millions of his own funds for philanthropic and
political purposes, yet allegedly engaged in a complicated scheme to avoid paying
$1 million.[56]

Krainov received a five-year suspended sentence. Khodorkovsky received a
nine-year sentence to a general-regime penal colony, minus the 18 months he had
served in pre-trial detention, and Lebedev received the same term.[57] The sentence
was only one year short of that demanded by the prosecution, and its severity took
many observers aback. Their lawyers immediately announced that they would appeal.
Even before the verdict, on 13 May, the prosecutor general announced that further
charges could be laid against Khodorkovsky and Lebedev, and an international arrest
warrant was issued against Temerko.[58] On 31 May the PGO reiterated that there
would soon be new charges, probably for money laundering, although no details
were given. Appearing on NTV on 6 June 2005, Vladimir Kolesnikov, the deputy
prosecutor general, warned that other leading business figures could be in the
firing line: 'I can say one thing, [Khodorkovsky's] case will not be the last. We have
got plenty of cases in the cartridge clip.'[59] In response to the question of why other

oligarchs had not been arrested, he stated: 'Unfortunately some managed to run away. We were too humane at that time and they managed to hide.'[60] The vindictive spirit is unmistakable, and it explains the broad compass of Yukos-related prosecutions.

Asked whether he understood the ruling, Khodorkovsky from his prison cage in the courtroom answered: 'The sentence is clear: I consider it a testament to Basmanny justice,' using the term that the trial had made famous.[61] In a statement read out by Drel, he declared:

> I do not think of myself as guilty and consider my innocence proven. Judicial power in Russia has been turned into a dumb appendage, a blunt instrument of the executive branch of government; or not so much of the government, but of a few quasi-criminal economic groups. [...] I know that the verdict in my trial was decided in the Kremlin. [...] I have lost my place in the oligarchs' club, but I have gained a huge number of true and devoted friends. I have had my sentiment for the country returned. And now together with my people I will bear this, and victory will be ours together.[62]

REACTIONS

Khodorkovsky noted that he had expected no other outcome, but in due course the sentence 'would not just be reduced but abrogated by the Supreme Court', and he gave it 'some 3–4 years'. In the meantime, he would have to sit it out. He stressed that the PGO had worked closely with the Kremlin, and he reserved his sympathy for the judge, Kolesnikova, having to bear the burden of what she had done at the request of the authorities. He warned that the only way to avoid another case like his was to 'create a state based on justice and the law', but he did not think that there would be another Yukos affair since one was enough for Putin. Meanwhile, 'Privatisation has not been legitimised, and the struggle for property in our country continues,' with the courts, security agencies and procuracy involved, and with no one safe. 'The Kremlin is not the only player: Those who like the present rules of the game are forced to play by them and at any moment can become their victim.' Raiding had indeed become a mass phenomenon. In response to the question about what some considered the positive aspects of the affair – the end to tax minimisation and that 'oligarchs no longer consider themselves masters of the country' – he insisted that he had long ago stopped his own personal tax-minimisation schemes and that he had never considered himself the country's manager: 'I am convinced that business should be separate from power, but this does not mean that business does not have the right to defend its political interests.' He noted that the authorities were no less engaged in individual business matters than they were in the 1990s.

He questioned Nevzlin's view that Abramovich had been behind the case, and stated: 'Roma [sic] Abramovich, to put it mildly, is not St Peter. But the organizer and the motor behind the Yukos affair was in fact Igor Sechin, one of his competitors in the fight for influence over Putin.' Khodorkovsky noted: 'Abramovich of course didn't do anything to help me or my partners, but after all he is Putin's friend and not mine.' He also argued that little had changed and that the Yukos case showed that Kremlin officials were still pursuing their own business interests, as they had done in the 1990s: 'On the contrary, the level of cynicism has grown and it has become clear that the foundation of contemporary Russian capitalism is the rule of crude force.'[63] Khodorkovsky acknowledged the factional nature of Russian politics and accepted that Putin had been influenced by the hardliners. Asked about the level of support from society, he wryly noted that 'a rich person of Jewish background cannot be popular in Russia', but he had been struck by the high level of individual support from all over the country. As for his hopes for the future, he stated, first, that he would devote himself to social activity, including his foundation to support Russian art and to help Russian prisoners. 'In this work I am absolutely free of any external obligations and thus full of optimism. Now I know how one can feel free, even in jail.' His second hope lay 'with those generations, in a few years, who will have passed through the grey monolithic ranks of bureaucratic incompetence. At that time we will all leave "jail".'[64]

With the opposition lacking a generally recognised leader there was intense pressure for Khodorkovsky to become 'the conscience of the nation'. An article in the Yukos-affiliated *Moscow News* argued that only Khodorkovsky could unite the left and right to become a national leader, and likened him to Nelson Mandela, who spent 26 years in jail:

> Today Russia needs to change its socio-political climate, it needs freedom. For Khodorkovsky, like for all of us, there will be no easy walk to freedom. But, having endured the destruction of his company, the loss of friends, imprisonment, he could become the best president in modern Russian history.[65]

This was not something that the Kremlin wanted to hear.

Most immediate reaction stressed the political nature of the case. There was a general consensus that the severe sentence represented the victory of presidential officialdom working with law-enforcement and security agencies over the business tycoons who had come to prominence in the 1990s. A press release by Sabine Leutheusser-Schnarrenberger, the German MP and the Parliamentary Assembly of the Council of Europe (PACE) rapporteur appointed to investigate the Yukos affair, argued:

> The enemies of the rule of law and an independent judiciary in Russia have won in the trial against the former Yukos chief executive. [...] The trial was afflicted with numerous shortcomings for the rule of law and the sentence is an implacable act of revenge against a man who dared to stand up openly against the policy of Russia's President Vladimir Putin. [...] The verdict shows that legal security does not exist in Russia.[66]

Amnesty International was unequivocal in its view that the Yukos case was politically motivated. In a statement not long before the verdict it noted:

> Amnesty International takes the view that there is a significant political context to the arrest and prosecution of Mikhail Khodorkovsky [...] the case [...] has been accompanied by numerous reports of violations of international fair trial standards and health concerns with regard to some of the accused.[67]

However, Amnesty did not declare Khodorkovsky a political prisoner. Freedom House argued: 'The conviction and sentencing to jail of Russian businessman Mikhail Khodorkovsky underscores the serious erosion of the rule of law and growing intolerance for political dissent in Russia.'[68]

On hearing the verdict, Bush noted that he 'monitored' the Yukos case and would be watching the appeal process. He stressed that he had spoken with Putin about his concern that 'it looked like he [Khodorkovsky] had been judged guilty prior to having a fair trial'.[69] In a news briefing, Ambassador Richard Boucher, spokesman for the Department of State, reiterated his view

> that this case has raised some very serious questions about the rule of law in Russia [...] about the independence of courts, about the right of due process, about the sanctity of contracts and property rights, lack of a predictable tax regime. [...] this case and the verdict continue to erode Russia's reputation and public confidence in the Russian legal and judicial institutions.[70]

Lantos, part of a delegation observing the trial, noted that Khodorkovsky was 'being tried for things that others have not been tried for, and could have had a civilised trial rather than being behind bars like an animal'. He stressed that the verdict was political.[71] Together with Senator John McCain, he called for Russia to be expelled from the G8, or at least for its membership to be temporarily suspended.

In Russia there was no unanimity in response, since oligarch-bashing had a popular constituency. Russian public opinion clearly viewed the case as political. The Yuri Levada sociological-survey agency regularly tracked public opinion on the case. A poll in late November 2004 found that respondents were of the view that 'bureaucrats were pursuing their own financial interests' in destroying the country's largest oil company. According to the poll,

> 41 per cent of Russians believe that the *chinovniki* [bureaucrats] are deliberately hampering Yukos' tax debt repayment and forcing the company to the verge of bankruptcy, and 69 per cent of respondents were convinced that Yukos' bankruptcy and sale of its assets would be conducted for the benefit of the bureaucracy and businessmen close to the authorities.

The general view was that the country would only lose from the whole affair, with 48% believing that the authorities pressured court officials to pass a guilty verdict. A remarkably small number (10%) considered that the case was prompted by strictly judicial considerations, while 36% considered the aim was to wrest control of assets owned by Khodorkovsky. 29% said the situation was provoked by the authorities' desire to limit Khodorkovsky's political influence, while 57% foresaw similar legal moves against other businessmen in Russia.[72] A film by Vladimir Grechkov called *Reaktsiya* (*Reaction*) was premiered in November 2005 and covered popular reactions to the case. It revealed a deep current of hostility to Khodorkovsky, although this was explained as having nothing to do with him personally, but as a 'reaction to all that happened to Russia in the twentieth and even the nineteenth centuries'.[73] The film failed to make it to television or to achieve general release in cinemas.

APPEAL

In an outspoken interview with *Süddeutsche Zeitung* in September 2005, Khodorkovsky insisted that his persecution was a sign not of the state's strength but its weakness: 'I was thrown into prison because the Kremlin is too weak and not willing to conduct an open and honest fight with an independent political opposition.' He once again identified those he thought responsible:

> The breaking up of Yukos was initiated by Putin aide Igor Sechin with the help of Kremlin-loyal businessmen. The result is apparent: the discrediting of the Russian leadership, the Russian state and Putin himself. Putin can thank his vassals for this.

Questioned about the relative lack of Western response to his incarceration, he noted that 'Russia as an independent state with a 1,200-year-old history will resolve its problems by itself', although he stressed the need for 'common values'. As for his future as a politician, he declared, 'I became de facto a politician when the Kremlin put me in prison.'[74]

This now appeared to take concrete form. Constituencies lined up to offer Khodorkovsky a parliamentary seat and the accompanying immunity. On 31 August 2005 Khodorkovsky announced that he would stand in a by-election in Moscow's 201st district (the University constituency) for a seat in the State Duma, a traditionally liberal area whose previous incumbent had been Mikhail Zadornov, a close ally of Yabloko. In his 'Appeal to electors and all citizens of Russia' on 31 August Khodorkovsky thanked those who had proposed him as a candidate and promised that 'as soon as I am released from jail my first trips will be to Tomsk, Novosibirsk and Ulyanovsk. Brothers and sisters, thank you. Together we are advancing to victory and together we will win.'[75] While Khodorkovsky's appeal was pending he had the right to stand in the election due to be held on 4 December. Polls predicted that he would win at least a third of the vote,[76] more than the 27% won by Zadornov in 2003.[77]

In the event the appeal was rushed forward to 14 September 2005, but then postponed because of the hospitalisation of the only lawyer capable of dealing with it, Padva. When the appeal was heard on 22 September the deliberations lasted just eight hours. Khodorkovsky's lawyers insisted that the accelerated proceedings represented a travesty of justice and pledged to take the case to the Supreme Court and Strasbourg. In his detailed refutation Khodorkovsky commented:

> It is not the courts who have found me guilty but a group of bureaucrats who convinced the authorities that I should not fund the opposition [...] These people have no honour or conscience. The motherland and its future mean nothing for them.[78]

The verdict was upheld, with the sentence reduced by one year. Khodorkovsky's right to stand as an official parliamentary candidate ended, although informal attempts continued for him to stand as a 'people's candidate'. On 3 May 2006 the Moscow City Court upheld the eight-year sentence on Khodorkovsky, insisting that there was no reason to review the verdict. Once the Criminal Collegium of the Supreme Court and the Presidium of the Supreme Court had given their verdicts, all avenues within the country were exhausted and the case could go to the ECtHR in Strasbourg.

IN THE PENAL COLONY

On 9 October 2005 Khodorkovsky undertook the long journey into internal exile. He penned a sarcastic birthday message for Putin, regretting that he would not be able to greet him personally 'for reasons that you know', and he commented that Putin was 'an excellent friend and partner: you did not regret ruining your reputation for your colleagues who destroyed Yukos, not long ago the country's biggest oil company'.[79] Khodorkovsky travelled in a 'Stolypin' wagon attached to a normal train, and on 16 October, nearly two years after his arrest, he arrived at his place of incarceration in Chita oblast. He remained defiant. Lebedev also left Matrosskaya Tishina on 9 October to serve his eight-year sentence in Kharp Corrective Colony No. 3[80] in the Yamalo-Nenets autonomous *okrug*, 60 kilometres from Salekhard and well into the Arctic Circle.

A few days after his arrival Khodorkovsky issued a ringing declaration:

> As of October 16, 2005, I have been in the land of the Decembrists, political prisoners subjected to hard labour and uranium mines. [...] The Kremlin tried to isolate me completely from my country and its people; they sought to destroy me physically. [...] They hope Khodorkovsky will soon be forgotten. They are trying to convince you, my friends, that the fight is over, that we must resign ourselves to the supremacy of self-serving bureaucrats. That's not true – the fight is just beginning.

The main challenge was 'to formulate Russia's development for the twenty-first century', to '[c]reate from scratch a new breed of officials – those interested in the fate of the country and its people, not their own unbridled personal enrichment', and to 'preserve the Far East and Siberia as part of Russia'. He ended with the rousing exhortation: 'The time of mediocrity is past – the era of heroes dawns.'[81]

The 1996 Russian penal code stipulates that prisoners serve their sentences in the region where they are convicted unless exempted. In the case of Moscow this is often not possible since all the penal establishments in the region are overflowing, hence Ministry of Justice resolution No. 71 of 2004, Article 6, allows a neighbouring region also to be used. Some 12% of the total Russian prison population traditionally serve outside their home or sentencing region. However, there are plenty of camps in the regions bordering Moscow, such as Tver, Vladimir or Yaroslavl. In the event, the Federal Penitentiary Service (FSIN) sent Khodorkovsky to colony YaG 14/10 (IK-10) near the town of Krasnokamensk in the Trans-Baikal steppe, 550 kilometres south-east of Chita, 6,500 kilometres from Moscow and only 90 kilometres from the border with China. It is extremely unusual for Moscow prisoners to be sent to Siberia without their agreement.[82] The colony is located a six-hour flight from Moscow to Chita, followed by 15 hours by train and then a 40-minute car journey.[83]

Not for the first time in Russian history, space was used as a form of punishment. Its distance from Moscow made this an ideal location for political exiles, including archpriest Avvakum, the Decembrists, the Polish insurrectionists of 1830 and 1863, Nikolai Chernyshevsky, the Populists and even Marshal Konstantin Rokossovsky during Stalin's purge of the Soviet High Command in the late 1930s.[84] It is still not clear why the FSIN chose precisely this colony out of the 762 in Russia.[85] There is nothing special about it, with most inmates serving 3–5 years, 40% for theft, and this could well have been the reason.[86] Krasnokamensk's distinguishing feature is its lack of 'social status', to use criminal jargon. Prisons in Russia are divided into 'red' and 'black', depending on relations between the prison administration and the criminal bosses. Where the guards are in control, a prison is known as 'red' (*krasnaya zona*), but where the criminal elite dominates the prison is known as 'black' (*chernaya zona*), which is the usual situation in Siberia. As far as normal prisoners are concerned, both are equally undesirable. In 'black' institutions prisoners are forced to live by the code of the underworld 'bosses' (*avtoritety*), having to pay a share of all food parcels and money as a 'tax' to the criminals. They have to participate in various criminal rituals that establish a whole set of counter-norms that are ignored by prisoners at their peril. In 'red' prisons informing is encouraged, and the regime can often be draconian. The power of warders is typically unrestrained by criminal organisations, and they then act as oppressors in their own right, stealing wages from prisoners and extorting bribes to allow what should be due by right. YaG 14/10 is one of the few prisons in Russia without a colour code because its management and regional criminal structures worked out a modus vivendi. The regional nature of the colony helped, with administrative staff recruited locally and about a third of its 1,200 inmates coming from Krasnokamensk and the rest from the region.[87]

This is not a labour camp in any traditional 'Gulag' sense, hence the correct word to describe it is 'colony'. Prisoners work in a reinforced concrete plant for the mining and building industries, in a timber-working plant, or in a sewing unit, making uniforms for the police. Khodorkovsky was assigned to the sewing unit, making shirts and gloves. Additional meetings with family members can also be bought, over and above the permitted number. Wealthy inmates can also buy favours for other prisoners, and thus make life rather easier for themselves. As for financial support for prison officials, this is a matter about which all sides keep quiet. It came out during parole hearings that Moscow had instructed the colony's director to place Khodorkovsky on a strict regime, and as a result he spent a disproportionate time in detention cells. No one suspected him of informing, and equally, although he was forced to spend a lot of time with the *blatkomitet* ('criminals' committee'), he retained his independence from the *blatnoi* ('criminal') world.[88]

Distance made visiting very difficult. Inna had been able to see Khodorkovsky in Matrosskaya Tishina once a month for 45 minutes, talking by telephone through a partition made of glass and wire netting. Visiting rights in the Krasnokamensk colony were more extensive, with four three-day visits a year and six visits of three hours each. Having arrived in Chita, the hardy traveller negotiates the final miles to the colony in one of three ways: a slow passenger train to Krasnokamensk and then a taxi; a minibus along a road that peters out about 200 kilometres out of Chita, and which starts again not far from Krasnokamensk; or a taxi. During the longer visits prisoners and their families are accommodated in a small hut with a communal bathroom and kitchen. On arrival in the colony in late 2005 Khodorkovsky forbade his children to visit: his daughter Anastasia was then 14 years old, while their twin boys Ilya and Gleb were six years old. By June 2008 his mother had visited him eight times, and Anastasia had also been allowed to travel to what had become the Zabaikal region.

After meeting with her husband for the first time in the colony, Inna Khodorkovskaya stressed that his spirit was far from broken and that Khodorkovsky would dedicate his life to achieving political reform. The meeting came at a time when Khodorkovsky released another in his series of political missives on how to reform Russia ('Left turn 2', see Chapter 10), accompanied a week earlier by the full-page advertisements in which he called for a new breed of official. Inna noted after her first three-day visit starting on 26 October, accompanied by Khodorkovsky's mother:

He's changed a lot but I recognised the man I knew before his arrest. […] He is not
consumed by anger. Instead he is a man with a clear vision. He is feeling combative.
He has no regrets. Nor do I.

Inna continued, 'Neither of us would have wanted to flee abroad. Russia is our country.
They will never break him.'[89] Only in September 2006 did he meet with his daughter, whom he had not seen for a year and half, together with his wife and mother,[90]
and another three-day visit followed in December.[91] In a communication with his
wife Khodorkovsky described life in his prison colony as an 'anti-world'.[92] He spent
much of his time reading religious literature, which Inna noted was analytical: 'He
doesn't push faith away, but he has begun to experience it in a new way. If before he
approached the subject from a sort of historical point of view, now he feels closer
to it.' She noted that they had long feared that the state would attack them, but they
had decided together to stay in Russia.[93]

On numerous occasions Khodorkovsky was placed in the punishment block
for minor infractions of prison rules: on 14 December 2005, for leaving his sewing
machine without permission when it had jammed, which on 9 February 2006
was judged illegal by Krasnokamensk City Court; on 24 January 2006 for alleged
unsanctioned possession of documents (a copy of the prison rules), for which he
received five days in solitary confinement; on 17 March, when he was punished for
drinking tea in an unsanctioned place, after he had missed his supper because he was
preparing his appeal to the ECtHR;[94] in April, for eating in an unsanctioned place;
and in June 2006 for possession of two unsanctioned lemons.[95] The appeal against
the January 2006 incident once again ended in victory when the Krasnokamensk
City Court on 18 April 2006 found that his punishment had been illegal.[96] These
punishments exposed Khodorkovsky to new dangers. In the early hours of 14 April
2006 his nose was slashed with a knife by a fellow inmate, the 22-year-old Alexander
Kuchma.[97] The two had initially got on well in the punishment block but then had
fallen out.[98] The FSIN was in a quandary: Khodorkovsky had to be seen to be obey-
ing the rules, just as any other prisoner; but the politically sensitive nature of the
case meant that the authorities had to guarantee his safety. As one commentary put
it: 'Khodorkovsky the prison inmate poses a greater danger to the authorities than
Khodorkovsky the oligarch ever did.'[99]

Khodorkovsky announced that he would work on a doctoral (*kandidat*) dissertation, and he brought two suitcases of material with him. He cast around for
a topic, with the possibilities including a study of the development of Russia's oil
industry, local self-government or the fate of the region in which he found himself,

including relations with its neighbours China and Mongolia.[100] In February 2006 he requested the prison administration to allow him to take up scholarly activity instead of working in the sewing shop, planning in the first instance to write an article for the journal *Khimiya i zhizn'* (*Chemistry and Life*). His request could not be satisfied, in the FSIN's view, since academic exchanges would be subject to restrictions, with all letters censored and any meetings with academic colleagues would have to be at the expense of meetings with family and friends. In the end Khodorkovsky gave up on the idea, and continued to work at packing gloves, since he had failed to pass the sewing exams;[101] with two higher-education degrees, Khodorkovsky in February 2005 once again tried to improve his professional qualifications.[102] If he had passed the test his wages would have gone up from 27 to 50 roubles a month (under $2); rather less than the millions in which he used to count.

CHAPTER 6

COLLATERAL DAMAGE

In parallel to the criminal trials of the principals in the Yukos affair, a number of other cases were also pursued, accompanied by attempts to portray the Yukos affair as no more than legitimate criminal proceedings. This was balanced by Medvedev's more liberal tone. His election as president in 2008 changed the balance of power and appeared to represent a defeat for the 'politburo' sub-faction among the *siloviki* and its allies. In May Putin moved out of the Kremlin to take up his duties as prime minister in the Russian White House, while Medvedev, Putin's nominated successor, moved into the Kremlin. A law of 7 April 2010 amended Article 108 of the Criminal Procedure Code to exclude those suspected or accused of certain crimes (including those under which Khodorkovsky and Lebedev were tried) from the more severe confinement conditions of pre-trial detention. Hopes were raised that there would be an end to the Yukos affair, including parole for those in jail. Khodorkovsky was one of those who shared this cautious optimism. In the event, the 'tandem' form of rule stymied a turn towards significant liberalisation. Khodorkovsky's second trial began in March 2009 (see Chapter 7), and despite endless speculation there was no parole or pardon. In his 'talk with the people' in December 2009 Putin stressed the alleged financial damage caused by Yukos, but he also referred to the various murders: 'Unfortunately, no one recalls that one of the Yukos security chiefs is in jail too. Do you think he acted on his initiative and at his own risk?' He also mentioned the killing of the tea-shop owner Valentina Korneeva and the mayor of Nefteyugansk.[1] Putin was clearly trying to reshape the Yukos narrative as less a political trial than a tawdry criminal case.

PICHUGIN: THE TAMBOV CASES AND VALENTINA KORNEEVA

Some 200 criminal prosecutions were launched against company managers, accountants, lawyers and others connected with Yukos. In 2007 alone a total of over three-dozen cases were in progress. These subsidiary cases were launched for a variety of reasons: to undermine the financial viability of the defence, to intimidate witnesses into giving evidence against Khodorkovsky and his associates, to weaken the will of defence lawyers and, possibly as a demonstration effect, to warn people not to step forward or even to speak in Khodorkovsky's defence. There were occasions when courts resisted the procuracy's line, as when on 30 January 2004 a regional court dismissed the charges against the Yukos executive Rafail Zainullin for lack of evidence, but this was an unusual occurrence.

Shiryaev argues that Pichugin was the first victim of the Yukos affair and insists that his case is unfairly neglected.[2] Investigating a number of horrible crimes in Tambov, the police arrested Igor Korovnikov, a member of a criminal gang convicted of eight murders and five particularly horrific rapes. Under interrogation, he and his colleagues described a bombing that they had organised. In autumn 1998 they had met 'a man in a jeep' in Moscow, who ordered them to take Olga Kostina out of town and kill her, for which they were to be paid $15,000. As we have seen, Kostina had been an adviser to Khodorkovsky and deputy head of Yukos's analytical service before moving on to become head of the press service in the Moscow mayor's office. The murderers discovered that Kostina was never alone, hence they changed tack and organised an explosion, which they argued could always be ascribed to 'Chechens'. On 28 November 1998 a small bomb exploded on the landing near to Kostina's parents' residence. Once this evidence came out the case was immediately transferred to Moscow. Before Pichugin's arrest in 2003, no link had been made between Yukos and the attack on Kostina.[3] She later worked for the MVD's press service and became head of the Soprotivlenie ('Resistance') human-rights organisation and a member of the Public Chamber. She was a prosecution witness in Khodorkovsky's second trial and became head of the MVD's advisory council in 2012. Her husband Konstantin Kostin also testified against Pichugin (and later Nevzlin) and was appointed to head a section in the presidential administration.[4]

The investigators found a lead to Sergei Gorin, Korovnikov's friend from Tambov. However, they were not able to arrest Gorin, since on the night of 20–1 November 2002 he and his wife Olga disappeared. Masked men forced entry to their house and took them away. Although their bodies were never found, they are thought to have been murdered, since traces of Sergei Gorin's blood and brains were found in his garage and also in the car in which their bodies are thought to have been transported.[5] Sergei Gorin was a well-known businessman in Tambov, who in 1993 established the Algoritm financial–construction company. After having attracted major investment in what appears to have been a pyramid scheme, the company went broke in 1997, leaving half of Tambov out of pocket. Later Gorin was employed by the local branch of Menatep, but was soon sacked. In the three years before his disappearance Gorin was unemployed, but had considerable sums of cash at his disposal. He may well have been associated with the St Petersburg Kumarin gang, which dominated criminal life in Tambov at that time. Gorin in his final year tried to use his Yukos contacts to break into the oil-distribution business, but the company by then was so effectively vertically integrated, with a single chain from pumping the crude to petrol sales, that he could find no foothold. The investigation into the Gorins' disappearance went cold, but there is evidence to suggest Korovnikov's involvement.

Pichugin was arrested on 19 June 2003 and accused of organising the attack on Kostina and the murder of the Gorins. According to the prosecutors, there was a clear link between the Gorins and Pichugin since the latter was the godfather of the Gorins' youngest son. Pichugin allegedly asked Sergei Gorin to find someone to organise the attack on Kostina. Gorin asked his friend Alexei Peshkun to arrange this, who in turn contacted Korovnikov. Shiryaev notes that the case against him as the alleged mastermind behind the murder of the Gorins is based on flimsy evidence; an alleged conversation with killers three years before the assassinations took place, by people who were never found and in a location that was never established.[6] In the Lefortovo SIZO Korovnikov alleged that not long before his disappearance Sergei Gorin had given him documents that included a photograph of those who had ordered the attack on Kostina. The documents disappeared, but Korovnikov claimed to recognise Pichugin and Nevzlin. The trial was held in camera and the defence was unable effectively to challenge what was clearly highly dubious evidence. The stains found at the Gorins' house were initially not matched to their blood type, and only at the second attempt and under considerable pressure were they found to match.

In pre-trial detention Pichugin was apparently made an offer: in exchange for admitting that he had acted on the orders of Nevzlin, he would be offered clemency.[7] He refused, and on 14 July 2003 he was administered some psychotropic substance in his coffee to get him to talk. He lost consciousness for six hours, but even under the influence of the truth serum he incriminated neither himself nor his Yukos colleagues.[8] The substance had long-term health effects, and Pichugin lost weight and developed lumps on his head.[9] The use of such drugs during questioning clearly violates international law and Russia's treaty obligations. Throughout Pichugin refused to give evidence against his former colleagues or to accept guilt in any way. In one of the first major trials to be heard by a jury in Russia, on 24 March 2005 Pichugin was found guilty, by a majority of eight votes to four, on all counts: for complicity in the murder of the Gorins, for organising the attempted murder of Kostina, and for the assault on Kolesov, the managing director of Rosprom. On 30 March he was sentenced to 20 years in a strict-regime penal colony. No link with Khodorkovsky was established in any of these cases. Of all the Yukos-related trials this one was presented to the media as being the most clear-cut, based on convictions for criminal offences; however, it turns out that this is perhaps the weakest of all, with exonerating evidence ignored.[10] When the first convocation of jurors seemed inclined to acquit him it was discharged, and new jurors were selected.

New charges for murder and attempted murder were almost immediately preferred, on 14 April, and ultimately Pichugin endured three trials with increasingly severe sentences, with the second criminal case heard twice. In his second trial from March 2006 Pichugin was charged with the attempted murder of Yevgeny Rybin, the managing director of the Austrian company East Petroleum Handels, and the murder of Nefteyugansk mayor Vladimir Petukhov (see below). One of the co-accused was Yevgeny Reshetnikov, who in November 2000 had been found guilty of the attack on Rybin. Reshetnikov admitted culpability for the murder of Petukhov, as well for the attack (with Gennady Tsigelnik) on Kolesov on 5 October 1998. The aim according to the prosecution was to kill Kolesov, since his ambitions had begun to alarm Yukos leaders, and they entrusted Pichugin to deal with the matter. Kolesov himself doubted whether Yukos leaders had anything to do with the attack, in which his wallet with $2,000 was stolen. Reshetnikov accused Nevzlin, Khodorkovsky and Pichugin of ordering the attacks, although no direct evidence was produced. The case relied on the alleged confessions of Reshetnikov and Tsigelnik.

Pichugin was also accused of killing Valentina Korneeva on 21 January 1998, after allegedly refusing to sell office space in central Moscow to Menatep. Korneeva had been the director of a shop serving the Western Group of Forces in East Germany and after the withdrawal of Soviet forces had opened a shop in Moscow called Feniks. In summer 2006 during Pichugin's second trial the former militia officer Vladimir Shapiro admitted to killing her; he was found guilty on 17 August 2006. Her husband, Dmitry Korneev, had been convinced that his wife was killed as part of the conflict with one of the co-founders of Feniks, Valentin Taraktelyuk, who had lost all his money in Mavrodi's MMM pyramid scheme and was thus unable to repay his debts to Korneeva. Instead, the prosecution stressed the alleged conflict with Menatep about the sale of the Chai tea shop (part of the Feniks group) at 8 Ulitsa

Pokrovka in Moscow, next door to a Menatep office.[11] She was allegedly offered $300,000 for a property worth at least $500,000.[12] Another of the key characters in this case is Mikhail Ovsyannikov, who allegedly drove Vladimir Shapiro, Tsigelnik and Reshetnikov to Korneeva's apartment when Shapiro committed the murder. Dmitry Korneev was acquainted with Sergei Gorin; according to the prosecution, Pichugin ordered Gorin to organise Korneeva's murder, paying the 35-year-old Ovsyannikov and the 41-year-old Shapiro to do the deed.[13] At first Ovsyannikov agreed that the murder had been committed at Yukos's behest, but on 17 July 2006 he withdrew this allegation, stating that 'All the evidence against Khodorkovsky, Nevzlin and Pichugin was given by me under pressure from the investigators.' He stated that he had only occasionally glimpsed Pichugin, notably when he drove Sergei Gorin to Pichugin's for a wedding, and had barely had contact with Gorin since 1998.

Kondaurov testified that Pichugin could not have received orders directly from Nevzlin, since Pichugin was subordinate to the head of the Yukos security department, Mikhail Shestopalov.[14] All the counter-evidence was ignored, and on 17 August 2006 Pichugin and Reshetnikov were found guilty, with the latter sentenced to 18 years in jail while Pichugin was sentenced to an additional four years to make a total of 24 years for all the crimes, including the two murders of which he was convicted the previous year.[15] In the second hearing of the second case Reshetnikov was now one of the witnesses, testifying against the leaders of Yukos.[16] Ovsyannikov was brought in as a witness, but refused to testify beyond his statement of July 2006.[17] The inconsistencies in Shapiro's evidence were revealed on 24 May 2007, when he admitted that he had never seen Pichugin or Nevzlin and that the order to kill Korneeva had come from Sergei Gorin.[18] At the end of the 'third' trial on 6 August 2007 Pichugin was given a life sentence in a strict-regime camp. On 23 April 2008 he was called upon to give evidence against Nevzlin in his trial *in absentia*, and once again investigators put pressure on him to incriminate Nevzlin.[19] As Khodorkovsky put it in his closing speech in the second trial (see Chapter 7) on 2 November 2010, 'I am proud that in seven years of persecution out of the thousands of Yukos employees none could be found to bear false witness, to sell their souls and conscience.' This was not for want of trying, with investigators pressuring Pichugin, Aleksanyan, Pereverzin, Bakhmina, and many more.[20]

Pichugin is undoubtedly one of the main victims of the Yukos affair. Despite the injustices heaped upon him, Pichugin maintained a stoic calm and dignity. Putin referred to Korneeva's murder in his notorious 'a thief should sit in jail' dialogue on 16 December 2010 (see Chapter 7). Sechin amplified the Putin line in a rare interview in February 2011, when he insisted that there had been no 'expropriation' of

Yukos and that indeed its bankruptcy 'was initiated by a group of foreign investors, headed by the French bank Société Générale'. He then went on to state: 'Let me remind you that Yukos leaves a trail of not just simple violations, but of very grave criminal offences, such as murders, torture and extortion.' He argued that Pichugin was 'up to his elbows in blood', and he listed the murders of Petukhov and Korneeva and the attacks on Olga Kostina and Yevgeny Rybin.[21] Khodorkovsky himself in an interview of 5 April 2011 insisted that Yukos never resorted to violence to achieve its goals. Responding to a question put to him by *Snob* magazine whether it was true the company had killed the woman to get hold of the café, he argued:

> Not I, nor other Yukos shareholders, nor top managers used such methods. First of all, it wouldn't even have occurred to anyone to try to resolve some problems by resorting to murder. We were brought up somewhat differently. And second, businessmen are driven by calculation, and violence harms business, it is unprofitable. For a businessman it is easier to pay double than to commit a crime.

More specifically:

> One can't honestly believe that the Yukos business would have collapsed without this café and that Yukos could have killed a person to get hold of it. Moreover, as far as I know, the café went to the heirs of the deceased and not to Yukos.[22]

NEFTEYUGANSK AND THE MURDER OF PETUKHOV

On 26 June 1998 (Khodorkovsky's birthday; he turned 35 that day) the mayor of Nefteyugansk, Vladimir Petukhov, died in a hail of bullets from a machine pistol as he walked to work.[23] Residents immediately blamed Yukos for his death. The company provided 70% of the town's budget and allegedly sought influence over local affairs commensurate with its tax contribution, whereas the mayor sought to defend the autonomy of the local authorities. Petukhov fought tenaciously to get Yukos to pay its debts to the city, including writing open letters to Yeltsin and prime minister Sergei Kirienko accusing Yukos of failing to pay its taxes and engaging in criminal acts by 'concealing taxes in large volumes from 1996 to 1998'.[24] Khodorkovsky by contrast did not trust the city authorities and considered it a mistake to build housing in what was effectively a marsh.[25] This stand-off continued for some time, with the mayor's stance backed by the overwhelming majority of the local population. Hence Yukos tried new tactics. This included on 28 May 1998 bringing money, which should have been paid to the town's exchequer, in cash and being paid directly to municipal agencies. On a flying visit to the town on 3 June Khodorkovsky alleged that the town authorities had misused the tax revenues. A national media campaign was launched against the municipality, accompanied by personal accusations against Petukhov. In response, in his letter of 15 June to Yeltsin and nine top government officials, Petukhov announced an indefinite hunger strike and assailed the 'murderous policies' of Yukos, demanded a tax and criminal investigation into the company and related shell organisations for 'large-scale under-payment of taxes by Rosprom-YUKOS in the years 1996–1998', and called for the restoration of the economic independence of YNG.[26] Demonstrations attended by up to 25,000 people, the bulk of the able-bodied population, gathered in his support.

Petukhov was born on 16 December 1949 and in 1978 moved to Nefteyugansk to work on the drills and later as a technical foreman before joining management. In 1990 he became head of Debet, a company servicing the drilling and capital repairs department of YNG. By 1995 the company had become a major creditor of Yukos, and Debet launched a court case. Yukos responded with counter-charges of financial irregularities, including concealing half of its profits, and at the same time the tax police began to harass Petukhov. To get Yukos to pay him, Petukhov in 1996 ran in the first elections for mayor of Nefteyugansk on an avowedly anti-Yukos platform. The former mayor had allowed Yukos to pay its local taxes with non-convertible promissory notes, some issued by shady companies, a practice condemned by Petukhov. Riding a wave of anti-Yukos sentiment, Petukhov unexpectedly won the election, setting the stage for a prolonged confrontation. Petukhov demanded that Yukos pay its taxes with money and not promissory notes or property – Yukos had transferred the airport, agricultural installations and an asphalt plant to the city. With the price of oil falling to $10 per barrel in 1998, as we have seen, the company faced severe liquidity problems. It paid even less of a proportion of its local taxes in cash than it had done the previous year, and the city ran out of money to pay its teachers, doctors and police.[27]

At the same time, the oil workers of YNG, who for so long had prospered in a successful industry, endured wage cuts and significant wage arrears. In April 1998, with the oil price falling, Yukos announced drastic pay cuts of about two-thirds, accompanied by a restructuring programme that saw 26,000 of the company's 38,000-strong workforce hived off to 51 service companies, which were then forced to negotiate directly with the main YNG enterprise. Itself facing liquidity problems, and as the monopoly employer in the town, YNG imposed harsh conditions on the nominally independent companies. In less than a year the oil workers of Nefteyugansk had fallen from relative affluence to poverty, provoking an enduring hatred of Yukos. The best specialists went to work in Surgut and Kogalym, where wages and conditions provided by Surgutneftegaz and Lukoil, respectively, were much better. Surgut, just an hour's drive away over the river Ob, the base for the Kremlin-friendly Surgutneftegaz, 'was an oasis of tranquility and well-being in comparison. Taxes were paid and workers' salaries did not suffer.' Visiting Surgut in early 2004 Putin stressed the difference: 'Surgut and Nefteyugansk are as different as day and night. Here is an example of the businesses' attitudes towards the areas where they work.' He commented that some companies like Surgutneftegaz are good corporate citizens, while others, like Yukos, are irresponsible.[28] Putin drew on an article in the *Financial Times* by Arkady Ostrovsky, who later expressed disgust at the way his material had been used.[29]

Nefteyugansk is set in a vast marsh, which in the summer releases swamp gas, while the winters are bitterly cold. Yet out of this the Soviet Union since the mid-1960s had created one of the world's largest production fields. The pioneering Soviet spirit was now affronted by a parvenu entrepreneur who was felt to have no respect for what had been achieved in such difficult conditions. Indeed, according to his wife Fatima Islamova, Petukhov, an oilman to his fingertips, had been appalled to discover on Khodorkovsky's first visit to inspect his newly acquired oilfields that he had never 'seen a well and how oil was extracted. This was a real eye-opener for the oilmen here.'[30] The official trade union collaborated with the employers, so an independent trade union called Nefteyugansk Solidarity was created to defend the workers' interests. On 27 May 1998, the day of the YNG shareholders' meeting, the union staged a massive demonstration in front of the company's headquarters. Addressing the crowd, Petukhov called Yukos 'a criminal organisation that was growing fat on the sale of oil produced by the people of Nefteyugansk.'[31] A second demonstration on 2 June with 25,000 people saw the YNG building blockaded, locking in Muravlenko, who was forced to promise a partial payment of Yukos's debt. Dubov, the deputy head of Rosprom–Yukos, then arrived in the city to negotiate with the tax authorities, which announced that Yukos and YNG owed the city about 80 million roubles, whereas the city owed Yukos nearly 228 million roubles. Petukhov now staged an eight-day hunger strike, demanding the dismissal of the heads of the city and *okrug* tax offices. At this point Alexander Filippenko, the governor of the Khanty-Mansi autonomous *okrug*, intervened and established a budget commission to verify the earlier audit. Petukhov had thus been able to take the matter to arbitration, and he ended his hunger strike just four days before his murder.

On the afternoon of his death a crowd of over 30,000 gathered in the central square, at one end of which was the mayor's office and at the other the headquarters of YNG flying the Yukos colours: 'The people in the square had only one explanation for the mayor's death. He had been murdered by Yukos.'[32] The demonstration nearly turned into an assault on the Yukos building, and the passions aroused at the time have still not subsided.[33] Petukhov's funeral on 30 June was attended by 70,000 people, accompanied by a massive outpouring of grief, lamenting the death of a man and an era. However, at least three other versions of the tragedy are in circulation: the 'family' and least likely one – following his death Petukhov's widow apparently came into over half a million dollars; the 'Chechen' version, since Petukhov closed the city market dominated by Chechen groups;[34] and the Kamyshinsky criminal gang version, dating from 1999, with the murder actually committed by two gangsters who better met the description of witnesses than Tsigelnik and Reshetnikov (who are dark-haired, whereas the killers were described as blond), but who died before they could be questioned.[35]

The case was later revived as part of the charges against Yukos associates. The weapons were taken with them by the killers, but in the end Tsigelnik (on 11 July 2006) and Reshetnikov confessed to the murder, accusing Pichugin and Nevzlin of having ordered the killing.[36] Even though eyewitnesses described totally different people as the murderers, the court accepted the confession. The prosecutors in the Pichugin case refused to accept any evidence that could prove that Pichugin had nothing to do with the killing. Pichugin's defence, led by Kseniya Kostromina, on the other hand, minimised the conflict between Petukhov and Yukos and took the initial tax inspectors' report at face value; it stressed the conflict between the mayor and the city duma, charging Petukhov with unsanctioned budgetary expenditures. The defence, however, was on more solid ground when it argued that Petukhov's murder was ultimately not in Yukos's interest, since it disrupted the work of Filippenko's arbitration efforts, quite apart from inflicting huge reputational damage on the company.[37] Yukos certainly was not popular in the region, especially when other companies were able to pay their workers double what Yukos offered, and there were few regrets when Khodorkovsky was arrested and YNG once again returned to the state through Rosneft.[38]

In early 2008 the trial *in absentia* of Nevzlin began, in which he was charged with organising multiple murders. Although he was in exile in Israel, the court heard a considerable body of evidence. In mid-March Rybin, the director of the Vienna-based East Petroleum Handels (see below) asserted that he believed that Khodorkovsky had been behind the two attempts on his life. On 26 March the widow of Nefteyugansk mayor Petukhov testified that Khodorkovsky had been behind her husband's death: 'I can think of no one else but Khodorkovsky who could have done it. There was no one else.'[39] As we have seen, there are a number of other possibilities, although Pichugin was convicted of Petukhov's murder in a rather strange trial. Nevzlin insisted that the trial was politically motivated, and his spokesman Eric Wolf noted that the charges had been framed in such a way as to allow for the prosecution of other Yukos people, including Khodorkovsky.[40] In August 2008 the Moscow City Court found Nevzlin guilty of organising the murders of Petukhov, Korneeva, Olga and Sergei Gorin, and for the attack on Kostina and Rybin, and was sentenced to life imprisonment.[41]

THE EAST PETROLEUM HANDELS CASE (YEVGENY RYBIN)

In 1998 and 1999 two assassination attempts were made against Yevgeny Rybin, who had worked for 20 years in the Soviet and then Russian Ministry of Fuel and Energy. In 1994 he joined the management of the Austrian company East Petroleum Handels, and under his leadership the company's Russian activities thrived. However, when in 1997 Yukos took over 60% of VNK as part of the Tomskneft deal, East Petroleum Handels found itself cut off from its oil supplies, and neither its shares nor investments were returned. Rybin led the charge on the behalf of minority shareholders and claimed $100 million in compensation, but Yukos offered only $25 million. Various attempts to resolve the conflict failed.[42] Yukos considered itself the target of a raiding attack and, to defend itself, organised a share swap between Yukos and its TNK subsidiary.[43] Finally, in summer 1998 East Petroleum Handels applied to the arbitration court in Vienna for $83 million. East Petroleum Handels also referred the case to the International Arbitration and Hague courts. The first judgment in his favour was soon followed by an attempt on Rybin's life (by our now-familiar Reshetnikov) on 24 November 1998, but the bullets passed harmlessly over his head. The evidence at first was concealed, but a second investigation found a number of bullets. Forensic tests allegedly identified them as coming from the same weapon as had been used in Petukhov's murder. A second attempt was made on Rybin's life on 9 March 1999, this time by blowing up his car as it passed over a device laid in the road. The putative killers then fired into the blazing car, killing the driver and bodyguard, and seriously wounding a militia officer. At the last moment Rybin had decided not to travel in the vehicle, staying to celebrate a relative's birthday. Rybin was convinced that Yukos was responsible and declared that its security service had broken into his apartment and had him under observation.[44] In numerous letters to the MVD and the procuracy Rybin argued that Yukos had laundered some $24 billion.[45]

All these cases received widespread media attention. The PGO conducted further investigations into Pichugin's activities and alleged that he was operating on Nevzlin's orders. Nevzlin at the time was a member of the Yukos board of directors and first deputy director of Yukos-Moscow. The allegation was that he ordered Pichugin to kill individuals who in one way or another were a hindrance to Yukos. Kostromina argued that there was no evidence to demonstrate that Rybin's murder would be to Yukos's advantage. The Vienna court had decided 10% in Rybin's favour and entirely refused the second appeal. In November 2000 Reshetnikov was found guilty of the murder attempt, and the involvement of Yukos was not even mentioned. In July 2004 Nevzlin, in a letter to prosecutor general Ustinov, accused Rybin of extortion and of colluding with the authorities to provide false evidence against Yukos and in particular against Pichugin, at that time in the Lefortovo SIZO. Two days later the Basmanny District Court issued an arrest warrant against Nevzlin, who by that time had already long been in Israel. During Pichugin's second trial in July 2006 Reshetnikov suddenly remembered that the assassination attempt against Rybin had indeed been ordered by Pichugin and Nevzlin.[46]

THE TEMERKO CASE

On 13 May 2005 Alexander Temerko was charged with fraud. Temerko at the time was in the UK and an international arrest warrant was issued against him. Russia's extradition request, as with so many others, was refused. Prosecutors named lawyer Ivan Kolesnikov an accomplice in this case. Kolesnikov at the time was in Cyprus, and Russia also requested his extradition. Kolesnikov was employed by the Moscow-based law firm ALM Feldmans from the time of its establishment in 1995. One of the firm's most important clients was the Yukos Group, and both Khodorkovsky and Lebedev personally used the services of the firm. In time, Yukos became the firm's major client. One of the lawyers at the firm, Anton Drel, became Khodorkovsky's personal lawyer. Two more of the firm's lawyers, Yelena Agranovskaya (the managing partner) and Pavel Ivlev (the deputy managing partner) feature in the case.

Temerko is one of the most senior Yukos executives to be charged with criminal offences. Temerko and Khodorkovsky got to know each other in the late 1980s when they were both involved in the Moscow Komsomol organisation. As we have seen, Khodorkovsky used his leadership of the Scientific and Youth Union to transform it into what was later to become Bank Menatep. Many of the individuals with whom he worked at the time later took prominent positions in the Menatep–Yukos organisation. Temerko's career took a rather different trajectory, although he maintained contact with Khodorkovsky. By 1999–2000 Temerko was president of the Russian Armoury Corporation and then was involved in the creation of Rosvooruzhenie. On 5 June 2000 Temerko joined the Yukos board of directors as part of its corporate transformation. Temerko was responsible for relations with the Russian government and other oil companies, and he was involved in top-level negotiations with the Chinese government, and in particular CNPC, regarding the Daqing pipeline plan. In June 2003 Temerko left the Yukos board to focus on Open Russia.

As the crisis developed, on 20 October 2003 Temerko was appointed senior vice president of Yukos-Moscow; at this time a management board was created consisting of the senior vice presidents, and Temerko was one of these. Following Khodorkovsky's arrest Temerko was elected to the board of Yukos-Moscow, with Khodorkovsky's prior agreement, and on 3 November he was elected chair of the board, a post he held until 15 March 2004, and two months later he was replaced by Gerashchenko. The attack on Temerko was intended to weaken the defence of Yukos. Temerko is convinced that Bogdanchikov was the driving force behind the whole business.[47] Temerko's involvement in the Murmansk project as well as the planned pipeline to Daqing placed him at the centre of the challenge to the government's strategic control of pipelines. The case was accompanied by numerous acts of petty and not so petty harassment to encourage him to go into exile. On 6 May 2004 the PGO once again seized documents from Yukos's headquarters in Moscow, in particular from Temerko's office.[48] After Temerko left in November 2004 to live in London, his family in Moscow were subject to a string of complications.

The Temerko and Kolesnikov cases can be seen as part of the broader pattern of collateral attacks against Yukos employees and associated legal firms. The offices of ALM Feldmans were raided by the PGO on 9 November 2004, followed on 15 November by the questioning of its employees. Yukos personnel caught up in the action included Gololobov, the former head of Yukos's legal department, with an arrest warrant issued against him on 18 November 2004, and Ivlev, who was interrogated on 16 November and pressed to provide incriminating evidence against Yukos officials, including Khodorkovsky. Gololobov ended up in London, while Ivlev went to New York. On 8 December Agranovskaya was questioned and then detained, with charges of fraud, money laundering and tax evasion preferred against her on 17 December, although she was released from pre-trial detention on that day because of poor health. As the *Wall Street Journal* put it, 'the arrests and interrogations of

Yukos lawyers have fuelled fears that those who defend politically unpopular clients could themselves become targets.'[49]

THE BAKHMINA CASE

The case of Svetlana Bakhmina, deputy head of Yukos's legal department, graphically illustrates the human cost of the Yukos affair. On 7 December 2004 she was imprisoned in connection with the Gololobov case, following a series of punitive nocturnal interrogations. Refusing to give the answers sought by the authorities, her status changed from witness to defendant. She was charged with crimes committed seven years earlier, when she was 28 and new to Yukos, and just back from maternity leave.[50] Bakhmina's prosecution was designed to put pressure on Gololobov, her former boss at Yukos, to return from London.

The case relates to the time when Yukos launched its bid to take over VNK, and she was accused of damaging the interests of shareholders by transferring assets out of Tomskneft. The latter resisted and, as was common practice in the late 1990s, claimed to have debts of $440 million to deter the bid. Yukos went ahead anyway and gained control of the company, but refused to pay the debt and instead transferred Tomskneft's assets offshore. When the state, as a minority shareholder, requested Yukos to explain why the transfer was made, Yukos asserted that it was a way of defending itself against fictitious claimants, a standard practice at the time. In the event, all the enterprises were returned to Tomskneft a year before Yukos bought out the state's remaining share.[51] There was thus no crime and no victim. However, in the Bakhmina trial, the temporary transfer was classified as theft, and Bakhmina, the lawyer who carried out the orders of Yukos management, was cited as the mastermind behind the operation.[52] She was refused bail, and in pre-trial detention she was not allowed to talk via telephone with her young children, aged six and three at the time of her arrest.

Her trial began in October 2005 in Moscow's Simonovsky Court on charges of tax evasion and embezzlement. The prosecutor on 23 March 2006 called for a nine-year sentence. The selective nature of the case was reinforced by Tomskneft's insistence that the assets in question had been returned and were still on the company's books. In the event, in April 2006 she received a harsh sentence – seven years in prison – which made her ineligible for amnesty. She received a two-year sentence for large-scale tax evasion, but the main charge, which increased the sentence, was conspiracy to commit major fraud against Tomskneft and to transfer the company's financial assets abroad, even though Tomskneft had not filed complaints in relation to any of these charges. In August the Moscow City Court overturned the tax-evasion conviction but confirmed the embezzlement charges, and reduced her sentence by six months. In September her lawyers requested that the court postpone the imposition of her sentence until her younger boy turned 14, since this lies in the powers of the court. On 2 October 2006 the Simonovsky Court rejected the request and Bakhmina was sent to a women's penal colony in Mordovia. On 27 December 2006 the Moscow City Court conclusively rejected the request to postpone the sentence.

It is not clear what the government achieved by jailing Bakhmina. Already there had been much criticism in the press, and even by some senior United Russia officials, that Bakhmina had been refused bail and spent two years in pre-trial detention, and that this was enough for someone who was no more than a relatively junior Yukos official. What could the state possibly gain by jailing her? Mikhail Fishman, later editor of Russian *Newsweek*, argues that

> everyone understands that Bakhmina's sentence is politically motivated. It's an object lesson, precisely due to its excessive severity – intended to show that justice is unconditional, taking no notice of titles or merit. The sentence seems to assert that the Yukos case is nothing personal, and that Khodorkovsky, with his billions, is neither a victim nor a target, but a participant in an extensive crime ring.[53]

Although she was pregnant, her application for parole was twice rejected, in May and September 2008, by the Saransk courts and she continued to serve time. This provoked a mass campaign, including a letter to the president calling for her release signed by over 100,000 people. In October 2008 she requested a pardon but withdrew it five days later. Following the birth of her daughter on 28 November she was hospitalised in Moscow because of complications. She was paroled (and not pardoned) by a Moscow court in April 2009 and released on 1 May 2009 amid speculation that she would be called as a witness at the second Khodorkovsky trial.[54]

VASILY ALEKSANYAN

On 3 April 2006 the Simonovsky Court began consideration of the procuracy's request to consider embezzlement and tax-evasion charges against Vasily Aleksanyan, a Yukos vice president. He was born into a highly educated family in Moscow in 1971, with an Armenian father, a physicist, and a Russian mother. He studied law at Moscow State University and then Harvard, and joined Yukos in 1996, going on to head Yukos's legal department until 2003. Aleksanyan refused to emigrate; like Khodorkovsky, he considered it part of his 'civic position' to face his persecutors head on. He was known for his sharp legal mind, courage and loyalty. On resigning from his corporate positions in 2003, he worked as a personal lawyer for Khodorkovsky and Lebedev. By early 2006 Steven Theede, Yukos's new managing director, was in London to avoid a Russian criminal investigation, warning that what was left of Yukos in Moscow was answering to Rosneft rather than to him. Nevertheless, Aleksanyan in March 2006 agreed to return to Yukos as an executive vice president to negotiate with the court-appointed bankruptcy manager, Eduard Rebgun. He was repeatedly called in for questioning by the PGO and followed by the same four cars. Despite the intimidation, he refused to resign: 'After I said I would not leave Yukos, they told me with a smile that it was the first time they had seen a person voluntarily asking to go to jail.'[55]

He was arrested on 6 April 2006 on charges related to VNK–Tomskneft. He was accused, along with three other Yukos managers, of spiriting $10 billion of assets out of the country through a Dutch-based foundation. He was charged with embezzlement and laundering $433 million and detained in our now-familiar SIZO No. 1, Matrosskaya Tishina. On 15 September he learnt that he was HIV-positive, which by October 2007 had developed into Aids. He began to lose the sight of his one good eye, having become blind in the other following a childhood accident. By 2008, aged 36, he had become gravely ill, contracting tuberculosis in addition to other illnesses. He accused the authorities of trying to blackmail him to testify against the two principal defendants in exchange for the necessary medical treatment and freedom.[56] He alleged that Karimov personally offered him medical treatment, possibly even abroad, in exchange for giving evidence. At issue was the East Petroleum Handels case, which we have discussed earlier; the aim was to provide the first evidence of Khodorkovsky's direct involvement in fraud.[57] Aleksanyan refused, and in the absence of the appropriate medical treatment his condition rapidly deteriorated.[58] The ECtHR three times between November 2007 and January 2008 requested Aleksanyan's transfer to a specialist hospital, but this was refused.

Khodorkovsky on 30 January 2008 declared a hunger strike to win improved conditions for his former colleague.[59] In his letter to the new prosecutor general, Yury Chaika, he accused Karimov of acting in concert with Sechin to lay charges against totally innocent people as part of their campaign against Yukos and noted that a 'direct threat' had been made by Karimov that Aleksanyan would not receive the needed medical help unless he testified against Khodorkovsky. As long as the issue was procedural Khodorkovsky could play the game, but with a life at stake he was faced by 'an impossible moral choice' and decided to act directly to save his colleague's life.[60] The government responded with surprising speed, and from 30 January Aleksanyan enjoyed much improved facilities: 'My cell was cleaned [...] I returned from yesterday's hearing and thought I was in the wrong place.'[61] With the improvement in Aleksanyan's conditions, Khodorkovsky ended his 'dry' hunger strike, but kept up his refusal to take food.[62] On 1 February 2008, despite having now been publicly identified as suffering from Aids, which manifested itself as terminal lymphoma, the Simonovsky District Court, in the person of judge Irina Oreshkina, ordered Aleksanyan to remain in custody while awaiting trial, even though the head of the detention centre had argued that he needed to be moved.[63] She also refused the defence request for Aleksanyan's case to be joined with that of Nevzlin and Gololobov.[64] Finally, on 8 February Aleksanyan's trial was suspended and on 11 February he was moved to a specialist treatment centre, and Khodorkovsky, after 14 days, ended his hunger strike, noting that 'we have many people in this country who are not indifferent: it is the beginning of civil society. This inspires us with optimism.'[65]

The Bakhmina case and that of Aleksanyan, who had a six-year-old son, drew the criticism of even the Kremlin's own human-rights officials. Ella Pamfilova, head of the Presidential Council for Civil Society and Human Rights, called Aleksanyan's situation 'simply monstrous', calling on the authorities to transfer him to a civilian hospital for treatment and urging the Supreme Court and the PGO to 'find the means, on the basis of their authority [and] the spirit and letter of the Constitution, to resolve the problems of this person on the basis of the principles of humanism and mercy'.[66] Even the prison director argued that Aleksanyan needed to be moved into a special treatment centre. However, Aleksanyan's tribulations continued at Moscow City Hospital No. 60, where he was handcuffed to his bed, and prevented from taking showers.[67] He was visited in hospital by a special commission created by the Public Chamber to look into his conditions of detention.[68]

On 22 December 2008 the ECtHR issued its full opinion of the case, in a judgment that was supported unanimously by all seven judges, including the Russian judge Anatoly Kovler. The court found that there had been violations of Articles 3, 5(3) and 8 of the ECHR. It also held that Russia had failed to meet its obligations under Article 34, by refusing to implement the court's recommendations, stating that 'what is clear is that for over two months the Government continuously refused to implement the interim measure, this putting the applicant's health and even life in danger' (para. 230).[69] Instead, the courts continued to approve extensions of Aleksanyan's pre-trial detention. In January 2009 he was finally released on bail (having posted an enormous security of 50 million roubles), by which time his health had seriously deteriorated. The PGO still pursued the proceedings until the case was finally discontinued in 2010, after the statute of limitations expired. On 5 October 2011 Aleksanyan died.

ANTONIO VALDÉS-GARCÍA (SEIBATDALOV)

In 2005 an extradition request was issued for Antonio Valdés-García (Seibatdalov), born in Russia in 1971 and a Spanish–Russian dual national (he was granted Spanish citizenship in 1997): his father was a Spanish Civil War refugee and his mother Russian. Valdés-García was the former president of Fargoil, the Yukos-affiliated company located in Mordovia, which played a central role in the second trial. Fargoil was accused of being involved in a scheme to launder $10 billion in oil revenues on behalf of Yukos. The case was the counterpart of that against Ratibor, headed by Malakhovsky.

Valdés-García left Russia in December 2003, soon after Khodorkovsky's arrest, but following a series of telephone calls from the Russian authorities he agreed to return as a witness concerning his activities as a Yukos associate. In June 2005 Valdés-Garcia flew to Moscow after assurances that he would not be prosecuted. Instead, he was held under 24-hour guard in a former-KGB facility in Istra, near Moscow, and was denied his right to legal counsel. In what is one of the most grisly cases in the whole Yukos affair, months of detention and severe interrogation culminated in torture. He was relentlessly pressured to give evidence against former Yukos executives, including Khodorkovsky, Nevzlin and Brudno. On 7 August 2005 he was admitted to hospital with head and facial injuries and multiple fractures to his legs, accompanied by conflicting official stories that he had suffered a car accident or jumped out of a second-storey window. In his own account he states that during an interrogation session he suddenly felt a blow that knocked him unconscious. He awoke in hospital with his face and teeth shattered, his jaw wired shut, and his leg and hip broken. He remained in intensive care for months and to this day requires regular treatment. While in hospital, the same prosecutor who led the interrogations coerced him into signing a false statement that his injuries had been caused by an accidental 'fall'.

On release from hospital Valdés-García changed from witness to defendant, and his trial began in April 2006 for his purported role in the Yukos-related embezzlement scheme. Rather than being held in detention, he was allowed to live in a flat under police surveillance. On 2 January 2007 he escaped and made his way to Spain.[70] On 2 February 2007 the Basmanny District Court issued an international arrest warrant against him under embezzlement and money-laundering charges. In 2009 the Russian authorities began a trial *in absentia* on charges similar to those against the Yukos principals in the second trial, in effect criminalising what was the normal conduct of a vertically integrated oil company. At the same time the Russian authorities issued an extradition request. On 18 July 2011 Valdés-García was convicted *in absentia* by the Basmanny District Court and sentenced to eight years in prison.[71]

The Audiencia National granted Valdés-García bail and he remained free as he fought the extradition request on the grounds that it was politically motivated, that he would not receive a fair trial in Russia, and that if he returned he would no doubt suffer more abuse of the sort that he had endured earlier. In April 2009 Valdés-García issued a statement through his lawyer, stating that he had been pressured into making false statements against other Yukos directors, including Khodorkovsky and Lebedev, through the use of violence and maltreatment.[72] On 26 June 2009 the Spanish Council of Ministers resolved that Spain would deny the Russian extradition request, and on 6 July 2009 the Central Criminal Investigation Court No. 1 in Madrid dismissed the extradition proceedings.[73]

OTHER CASES

The 'Yukos affair' multiplied and mutated, and as in the era of Stalinist repressions weaved multiple webs. Already by early 2007, according to Gololobov,

> the total number of exclusively personal criminal cases launched against managers, employees, or affiliated persons of the Company has exceeded one hundred; the overall number of the individuals charged or prosecuted totalled more than sixty; the number of court cases in different jurisdictions, including Russia, has already exceeded five hundred; the number of individuals on the Interpol search list is fifteen.[74]

Gololobov himself, a former Yukos lawyer, was one of the victims. On 12 November 2004 an arrest warrant was issued, although by then he was living in Britain. He was accused of fraud in connection with Yukos's takeover of a VNK subsidiary. Numerous Yukos-related cases continue to this day in various jurisdictions.[75]

In January 2004 an arrest warrant was issued against Vladimir Dubov, the former State Duma deputy. He was accused of participating in allegedly illegal Yukos transactions intended to avoid tax payments. He did not wait for his term as deputy to expire, but as soon as he heard of Khodorkovsky's arrest he had fled to Israel. Following his arrest in October 2003 the former Yukos-Moscow CEO Vasily Shakhnovsky was selected by the regional legislature of the Evenk autonomous *okrug* on 27 October to act as their representative in the Federation Council, giving him immunity from prosecution. The PGO managed to have this rescinded, and on 5 February 2004 Moscow's Meshchansky District Court convicted him of tax evasion and sentenced him to a one-year suspended sentence. Shakhnovsky recanted, hence the light sentence. The court ruled that since Shakhnovsky no longer worked for Yukos he presented no danger to society and that he had compensated the government for all losses incurred. On 11 March 2004 an arrest warrant was issued for Menatep shareholder Brudno on tax-evasion charges. On 4 March 2005, an additional warrant for Brudno was issued on charges of fraud and money laundering. Brudno currently lives abroad.

On 18 November 2004 Yukos-Moscow manager Alexei Kurtsin was arrested and charged with large-scale embezzlement and money laundering through alleged charitable donations. On 1 December 2005 he was convicted and sentenced to a 14-year term in a hard-labour camp. All appeals against this harsh sentence failed, and instead in a third trial he was given a further 15 years in January 2010 when he was found guilty of embezzling Yukos funds. On 8 December, the day after the arrest of Bakhmina, another Yukos lawyer, Yelena Agranovskaya, was also arrested in connection with the Gololobov case. She was released, as noted, from pre-trial detention on 17 December because of poor health. On 16 December 2004 Yukos personnel manager Anton Zakharov was detained and questioned by prosecutors for two hours in connection with the case against Gololobov, Bakhmina and Agranovskaya.

On 10 December 2004 Vladimir Malakhovsky, general director of Ratibor, was arrested. Prosecutors allege that Ratibor was a shell company created by Yukos to commit fraud and launder money. Following a secret trial, on 5 March 2007 the Basmanny District Court convicted Malakhovsky and Vladimir Pereverzin, a former deputy director of Yukos and head of its external debt division who had been arrested on 18 December 2004, of having stolen and laundered $13 billion from Yukos; they were sentenced to 11 and 12 years, respectively.[76] The charges against Malakhovsky largely coincided with those in the second case against Khodorkovsky and Lebedev, dealing with transfer pricing. In August 2010 Pereverzin appeared as a defence witness in the Khamovnichesky District Court and claimed that the prosecutors had offered him a suspended sentence in exchange for testifying against Khodorkovsky and Lebedev, 'since my innocence was obvious'. Judge Viktor Danilkin made as if nothing out of the ordinary was being said, and it appeared to be a matter of little import that an innocent person had spent years in a hard-labour camp. In February 2012 Pereverzin was released, after spending seven years and two months in prison, as a result of Medvedev's laws softening the penalties for economic crimes, including Articles 160 and 174 of the Criminal Code under which he had been convicted.[77] The same articles had been used to convict Khodorkovsky and Lebedev, and it was on this basis that they appealed to the Supreme Court in early 2012.[78]

On 28 December 2004, charges were filed against lawyer Pavel Ivlev, but a Moscow court dismissed the case against him on 15 February 2005. By then he was in the United States, and he went on to collaborate with Khodorkovsky's son Pavel to create in February 2010 the Institute of Modern Russia, a mix of a public-policy and an academic think tank, which issues numerous papers on current affairs in Russia.[79] In January 2005 Dmitry Velichko, president of the financial group Rosinkor, was arrested and charged with participating in a criminal group allegedly organised by Khodorkovsky to commit large-scale embezzlement. In February 2005 an arrest warrant was issued for Yukos-Moscow first vice president Mikhail Trushin on charges of embezzlement in connection with the case against Kurtsin. On 25 February 2005 an arrest warrant was issued for Yukos acting president Mikhail Yelfimov. Thus the affair continued.

CHAPTER 7

THE TRIAL OF
THE CENTURY

When the first verdict was delivered in May 2005 the prosecutors warned that further charges would follow, and in late 2006 the machine once again creaked into action. The Yukos affair closely followed the electoral cycle, and with parliamentary elections due on 2 December 2007 and presidential elections on 2 March 2008 the regime wanted to keep Khodorkovsky out of the way. A replacement would have to be found for Putin, at the end of the two successive presidential terms allowed him by the constitution. The elections were accompanied by factional conflict, in part over the attempt to control the succession as well as over the property settlement of the Putin and Yeltsin years. The creation of the 'tandem', with Medvedev as president and Putin as prime minister, raised expectations that the opportunity would be taken to end the Yukos affair. In the event, 'the system' prevailed. At least 80 investigators worked to prepare the 'trial of the century'.[1] Despite attempts by the regime to portray the trial as purely criminal, it has all the characteristics of a 'political trial', intended above all to destroy a political opponent. It entailed the judicialisation of politics, accompanied by the corollary of the politicisation of the courts.[2]

FURTHER CHARGES

On 3 February 2007 Khodorkovsky left the relative comfort of the Krasnokamensk colony and was transferred to pre-trial investigative prison (SIZO No. 1) in Chita, where Lebedev soon joined him. Khodorkovsky spent only 15 months in the camp, where there was the possibility of extended walks in the open air, and now he once again found himself incarcerated. Khodorkovsky complained later how much harder it was to be confined in a cell than in the corrective colony.[3] Although sentenced earlier primarily for tax evasion, the new charges announced on 5 February 2007 focused on embezzlement and money laundering. Prosecutors alleged the theft of approximately 350 million tonnes of oil worth over $25.4 billion, laundering over $21.4 billion, embezzling $102 million in shares held by Tomskneft (VNK), and laundering the proceeds of their sale.[4] The defendants faced additional sentences of 10 to 15 years.

The basic charge was that between 1998 and 2003 Khodorkovsky and Lebedev bought the oil (in the end the prosecution settled on 218 million tonnes) from its YNG, Samaraneftegaz and Tomskneft subsidiaries at transfer prices and pocketed the difference when the oil was finally sold at retail prices in the Amsterdam terminals.[5] The prosecution alleged that between 2000 and 2003 Yukos officials illegally transferred billions in crude sales from its production subsidiaries through Fargoil and Ratibor, two trading companies registered in tax havens, with sales from the refined product then transferred back to Yukos and the profits siphoned off by Khodorkovsky and his associates.[6] Once again transfer-pricing schemes came under scrutiny. Crude oil was allegedly delivered on paper at reduced prices to companies registered in tax-benefit zones in Mordovia, Evenkia and other regions, and then sold on at market prices, thus severely reducing tax liabilities. Such tax optimisation schemes, according to Ivlev, who had earlier represented Yukos, continued to be practised by Rosneft.[7] The money was allegedly laundered through offshore trading companies and philanthropic contributions to Open Russia. Yury Schmidt pointed out the contradictions of the new charges, which suggested that Khodorkovsky and Lebedev stole their own oil and then tried to launder the profit of what had been normal cash flows from the sale of a product that was at the core of the company's business.[8] If the accusations in the first case had been true, then why were the tax officials who had signed off the Yukos accounts not punished?

Khodorkovsky insisted that the charges were 'absurd' and called the whole process a 'farce', based on false evidence provided by 'frightened or fooled false witnesses'. It was clear why the second case was started: 'Those people who had invented the "Khodorkovsky affair", to steal one of Russia's most flourishing oil companies, Yukos, are very frightened of seeing me free and want to insure against my release on parole.' Khodorkovsky considered the forthcoming trial an opportunity to demonstrate 'that in Russia justice is dependent [on the authorities]'. Khodorkovsky was given a limited time, until 22 December 2007, to acquaint himself with the 70 volumes of evidence gathered for the second trial.[9] Once again, repeated attempts to allow the accused out on bail were refused.[10] Khodorkovsky was not intimidated by a new sentence, since it made little difference to have yet more patently absurd charges preferred against him: 'Platon Lebedev's and my fate will be entirely decided by the fate of our motherland, after the change of power in 2008.'[11]

Karimov was once again the chief investigator and, characteristically, hampered defence-counsel preparations. For example, on 29 December 2006 Lebedev filed a motion requesting information about his international travels from the beginning of 1994 to 2 July 2003 in order to establish his whereabouts and thus to confirm his alibi, but on 11 January 2007 Karimov refused this request. On 18 May the Ingodinsky District Court in Chita censured Karimov's decision, arguing that it was incumbent for an investigator to prove 'the time, the venue and other circumstances' in a case.[12] Equally, Russian law states that defendants should be tried either in their place of residence or where the crime was allegedly committed. Chita met neither of these conditions, and there were numerous appeals and counter-appeals over the issue, demonstrating the lack of finality in Russian judicial decisions. With the establishment of the Investigative Committee (IC) within but not subordinate to the PGO in September 2007, the case was transferred to the new agency headed by Alexander Bastrykin. Karimov was relieved of responsibility for the case, and Alexander Drymanov took over. One of his first acts was to refuse to transfer the case to Moscow. This made the work of the defence team much harder since they had to keep a team in Chita and another in Moscow to research the relevant material and prepare the appropriate documents. Throughout Khodorkovsky insisted that he would continue to seek justice in Russia.[13] With the uncertainty surrounding the succession, the new trial was repeatedly postponed.

In an extensive submission to the IC in December 2007, Khodorkovsky's lawyers provided a forensic and devastating critique of the new case. They insisted that the charges were political, 'as part of the deliberate attempt to destroy the Yukos oil company'. In addition to quoting the various relevant foreign judgments against Russia, the letter cited the Russian Constitutional Court decision of 22 March 2005 that condemned the extension of pre-trial detention by judges without a court hearing. A whole range of infringements of the UPK was cited. They noted that the PGO, and now the IC, had ignored court decisions, notably the decision of the Ingodinsky District Court of 14 February and 18 May 2007 to allow Lebedev to prove his alibi. The various searches of the defence lawyers' offices, notably of ALM Feldmans on 15 December 2004, without the sanction of a judge, were condemned. The search of Drel's offices on 9 October 2003 was conducted without him being present; indeed, his absence had been forced. Evidence gathered by illegal means is not admissible. The notion of an 'organised criminal group' as applied in the Yukos case was condemned, as was the charge of money laundering through the various Yukos subsidiaries, notably involving VNK. They concluded by arguing that a whole range of legal guarantees and standards enshrined in Article 6 of the ECHR had been disregarded, and that there had been procedural violations of a number of other articles as well. The presumption of innocence had been ignored, and the equality of all parties in a trial had not been respected.[14]

The delay in the second trial was connected not only with technical preparations but also with the succession operation. In the event, the Sechin group lost out. The *siloviki*, with no candidate of their own, hoped that Putin would take up a third term, but instead the candidate least sympathetic to the interests of the security establishment was advanced to the presidency. In his first major programmatic speech, delivered to the Civic Forum in Moscow on 22 January 2008, Medvedev stressed: 'We shall pursue a firm policy of free development for private enterprise, protecting property rights and reinforcing the common principles of a market economy', accompanied by the need to turn the struggle against corruption into a national campaign. This was hampered by the fact that

> Russia is still suffering from legal nihilism. No European country can boast of this degree of contempt for the law. This phenomenon is rooted in our country's distant past. The state cannot be a law-based state, or a just state, unless the authorities and citizens know and respect its laws, and citizens have sufficient awareness of the law to monitor the actions of state officials effectively.[15]

The tone of the speech suggested that the Yukos case would be seen in a very different light under the new presidency.

Even some seasoned lawyers began to believe that Russia was entering a more liberal era. Schmidt argued: 'If the courts can at least regain the level of independence that they enjoyed before Putin came to power, we can win the case in Russia.'[16] Instead, on 1 July 2008 the IC brought revised charges against Khodorkovsky that threatened to add another 15 years to his sentence. The charges were essentially a rehash of those preferred in February 2007, accusing Khodorkovsky and Lebedev of embezzling 350 million tonnes of oil, of laundering 487 billion roubles ($20.7 billion) and of breaching Articles 160 and 170 of the Criminal Code, the same ones mentioned earlier.[17] It appeared that the reformulated charges were little more than a holding action, designed not to advance the case but to keep it alive while the political authorities decided what to do. Just a few days earlier, on 26 June, Khodorkovsky celebrated his 45th birthday, and his mother, Marina, feared for his well-being: 'At our last meeting, he looked bad. Blotches have appeared on his face.'[18] There were also petty sanctions against his wife. The ten-year-old twins Ilya and Gleb were due to start secondary school in September 2009, but the designated school at the last minute withdrew permission and no other would take them. In the end the matter was swiftly resolved after Inna in desperation asked Surkov for help.[19]

'A THIEF SHOULD SIT IN JAIL'

The pair spent two years in Chita, before being returned to Moscow in February 2009, to the now familiar Matrosskaya Tishina. Khodorkovsky observed how the inmates had changed, with fewer 'maniacs and street criminals' and more of those 'whose property had been stolen by raiders in uniform':[20] in other words, people like Khodorkovsky and Lebedev. The second trial began on 3 March 2009 in the Khamovnichesky District Court in Moscow and ended on 30 December 2010. Putin professed to be astonished to discover that a second trial was being held:

> When I learnt about the second trial, I was surprised and asked, what trial, he is already serving his sentence. What second trial? But if such a trial is being held, then it is necessary according to the law. It's not me who leads the case.[21]

Either Putin was being disingenuous or he had created a machine that was out of control. This time, instead of a cage, Khodorkovsky and Lebedev were kept in a glass box, known as the 'aquarium', and were forced to stoop to speak to their lawyers through a small letter box-sized opening. The summer of 2010 was especially hard, with sessions held despite temperatures of over 40°C and a suffocating blanket of smoke from the peat fires surrounding Moscow. Khodorkovsky and Lebedev were repeatedly ordered to remain in detention, apparently on the direct orders of Olga Yegorova's Moscow City Court.[22] For example, in May and again on 16 August 2010 Judge Danilkin ruled for the prosecution in denying bail for the defendants, even though Medvedev's law of 7 April 2010 allowed entrepreneurs accused of economic crimes to be released on bail. These extensions were to be condemned later by the Supreme Court. From the outset one of the lead prosecutors, Gulchekhra Ibragimova, openly stated: 'Don't raise your hopes. We will do everything that we set out to do.'[23] In other words, whatever the evidence, the outcome of the case was a foregone conclusion.

Over the course of 19 months the court sat 280 times and examined hundreds of volumes of evidence, as well as numerous other documents, such as minutes of shareholder meetings. A total of 81 witnesses testified in court: 52 for the prosecution and 29 for the defence. Given the seriousness of the case and the background, it would have been reasonable to expect the case to have been heard at a higher instance, that is, by the Collegium for Criminal Cases of the Moscow City Court, where the trial would have been heard by a panel of three judges or by a jury.[24] Instead, the case took place before a single judge, Viktor Danilkin, in a district court. The double-jeopardy issue was frequently raised, since the previous case had dealt with associated issues.[25] Article 50(1) of the Russian constitution prohibits a repeat conviction of someone already found guilty on charges related to circumstances of another crime. The logical incompatibility of the two trials soon became clear.

The first trial found the two guilty of fraud and tax evasion, but the legality of the extraction and sale of the oil was not questioned, the proceeds of which were part reinvested in the company and part distributed to shareholders. The new trial accused the defendants of embezzling much of the oil produced by the three main Yukos production subsidiaries for a period of six years, embezzling the shares held by a Yukos subsidiary in one of the production companies and in five other companies, and laundering the proceeds of the allegedly embezzled oil and the shares in the indirect subsidiaries. The investigative material originally ran to 188 volumes, but during the trial new materials were constantly added, and by the end comprised 275 volumes running to over 69,000 pages. The indictment was confused and contradictory but essentially boiled down to charges focused on embezzlement associated with the swapping of shares between Yukos and Tomskneft, the laundering of Tomskneft shares, the embezzlement of crude oil and/or the proceeds from the sale of that crude oil, and the laundering of that immense quantity of crude oil and/or proceeds from its sale. The functions of numerous 'special purpose entities' was the subject of particular attention.[26] The prosecution adopted a very simplistic approach to complex business transactions, within and beyond the legitimate 'consolidation perimeter' of the business.

As in the first trial, procedural obstacles were placed in the way of the defence counsel. For example, the judge rejected a request for adequate access to their clients. The defence motion to summon Misamore, the former chief financial officer of Yukos with crucial insider knowledge, was refused. A large part of the early stage of the trial was limited to the prosecution simply reading out parts of the charges, in what appears to have been a deliberate attempt to drag out proceedings and to deaden external interest. With a list of prosecution and defence witnesses running into the hundreds, the trial was even longer than the first. In the event, between 28 September 2009 and 29 March 2010 the prosecution presented its witnesses either in person or via interrogatory transcripts read into the record. Khodorkovsky and Lebedev maintained a stoical and even cheerful demeanour, with the former taking a close interest in proceedings, constantly passing notes and discussing issues with his team.

Khodorkovsky exposed the contradictory nature of the charges in what soon became the most notorious trial of the twenty-first century. On the first day he announced: 'Your Honour, my slogan in this trial is taken from the Soviet political dissidents of the 1970s: "Authorities, obey your own laws" ["*Vlast', vypolnyai svoi zakony*"].'[27] He provided a detailed rebuttal of the charges. The amount of oil that was allegedly embezzled was greater than Yukos's entire production for the relevant period. They were supposed, moreover, to have done this without alerting the attention of the company's independent auditors PricewaterhouseCoopers or the Russian authorities, or indeed the prosecutors in the first trial. The charges were essentially in contradiction to those of which the men were convicted in their first trial; they had been convicted of failing to pay taxes on output that was now alleged to have been stolen, although this issue was not even raised earlier. If the charges presented in the second trial were correct, then there would not have been any revenue to be taxed, thus rendering the first trial void.

Following the many months in which the prosecution drearily read out the charges and made its case, the defence presented its arguments between 6 April and 24 September 2010. They requested a number of leading politicians to take the stand, including former president Putin, although of course he was not called. Attempts by the defence to summon the finance minister Kudrin and Sechin, who by now was a deputy prime minister in Putin's government, were also declined, arguing that there were no legal grounds on which to call them. However, a number of leading politicians did testify. The first, on 24 May 2010, was Kasyanov, who had survived as prime minister far longer than anticipated. He tried to thwart the attack on Yukos, fearing the damage that such an assault would inflict on the Russian economy, liberal reforms and the country's reputation. As a result, he was dismissed in February 2004 and went on to become one of the most consistent critics of the Putin regime. Kasyanov insisted that the new charges against Khodorkovsky were absurd and politically motivated. Yukos's behaviour in his view was little different from that of the other eight oil companies, and he was unequivocal that theft on such a grand scale simply could not have taken place. The company's activities had been conducted in permanent interaction with the government, and as prime minister he had never received any information about violations of the law by Yukos. The company had been the country's largest taxpayer, with 'all revenues and tax flows controlled by the government'. He considered that the political motivation for the criminal case against Khodorkovsky lay in his funding of the opposition: not only the Union of Right Forces and Yabloko, but also the Communists.[28]

On 1 June Gerashchenko, who headed Yukos in its time of greatest difficulty in 2004, asserted in no uncertain terms that the new charges were utter nonsense. Two other leading politicians were subpoenaed by the court and agreed to testify. On 21 June the Sberbank director German Gref, who had previously headed the Ministry of Economic Development and Trade (MERT), took the stand. He argued that he would have been aware of embezzlement at Yukos if it had been taking place on anything like the scale alleged by the prosecution, although he acknowledged that he had not been directly responsible for oil transport. He conceded that transfer pricing was a problem, but not illegal. He spent over two hours hesitantly answering questions posed by Khodorkovsky and then rushed out of the courtroom, leaving his glasses on the stand. Speaking to reporters later, he refused to express his personal opinion of the case and argued that he was testifying to the court, not in anyone's favour. As a member of the St Petersburg team of economic liberals, he owed his entire career to Putin. His appearance and the substance of his points clearly worked in favour of the defence and were taken as an act of civic courage in such a politicised trial. This was equally the case when the Minister for Industry and Trade, Viktor Khristenko, took the stand the following day. He insisted that he knew nothing about the alleged theft of millions of tonnes of oil, even though between 1999 and 2008 he had been the minister responsible for the Russian fuel and energy sector. Presenting his testimony in a confident and convincing tone, he essentially absolved the two defendants of criminal activity. Coming from one of the longest-serving ministers in the Russian government, having been in office continuously since 1993, his evidence carried particular weight. However, in conditions of 'legal nihilism' these words appeared weightless, and the prosecution ploughed on regardless.

'The charges are so absurd that even government ministers have rejected them in court,' Khodorkovsky stressed in an interview in October 2010. He noted the unresponsiveness of government: 'They accept corruption, embrace archaic ideas and are united in their desire to keep talented, creative people off the public stage. […] It is precisely these kinds of mistakes that led to the death of the Soviet Union.'[29] On 2 November, seven years after his arrest, Khodorkovsky delivered a powerful final speech to the court. He noted with pride that Yukos employees had not given false testimony (quoted above), and as for the broader situation:

> Stability became something like stagnation, society froze. [...] A country that tolerates a situation where the siloviki bureaucracy holds tens and even hundreds of thousands of talented entrepreneurs, managers, and ordinary people in jail in its own interests [...] is a sick country. A government that destroys its best companies, which are becoming world champions, a government that is suspicious of its people, which only trusts bureaucrats and special services, is a sick government.

He insisted:

> I am far from an idealist, but I am a person with ideals. It is hard for me, as for all, to live in jail and I do not want to die there. But if necessary, I would not hesitate. My faith is my life, which I think I have proved.

He condemned the lawless system (*bezzakonie*) that prevailed in Russia and spoke of the epochal nature of the events: 'Everybody understands that your verdict in this case [...] will become part of the history of Russia.'[30]

The verdict was scheduled to be delivered on 15 December 2010, but was postponed to 27 December. This meant that Putin's 'direct line' phone-in on 16 December was not overshadowed. Putin veered between disclaiming any detailed knowledge about the Yukos affair and surprisingly intimate familiarity. In response to the question, 'Do you think it fair that Mikhail Khodorkovsky is still in prison?', Putin let rip:

> As for Khodorkovsky, I have expressed my opinion on this on many occasions. But if you want me to repeat myself again now, I will. It is my conviction that 'a thief should sit in jail' [a quotation from the 1979 Soviet film *The Place of the Meeting Cannot Be Changed*, starring Vladimir Vysotsky]. Khodorkovsky has been convicted, by court, for embezzlement, pretty major embezzlement. We are talking about tax evasion and fraud involving billions of roubles. Then, very importantly, there is also the matter of his personal tax evasion.
>
> But the new embezzlement charges he now faces run to sums of 900 billion roubles in one case and 800 billion roubles in another. If we look at other countries' legal practices, in the United States Bernard Madoff got 150 years behind bars

1   Mikhail Khodorkovsky as CEO of the Yukos oil company.

2 Mikhail Khodorkovsky before the trial.

3 Russian President Vladimir Putin talks with Khodorkovsky.

4 Khodorkovsky in a meeting with President Putin.

5 Khodorkovsky behind bars during the Meshchansky trial.

6 Khodorkovsky and Platon Lebedev during the Khamovnichesky trial.

7 Vasily Aleksanyan, former vice president of Yukos.

8 Svetlana Bakhmina, who served as deputy head of the Yukos legal department.

9 The pre-trial detention centre in Chita, where Khodorkovsky was held.

10 Krasnokamensk penal colony.

11 Khodorkovsky's parents, Marina Filippovna and Boris Moiseevich.

12 The Koralovo orphanage, supported by the Khodorkovsky Foundation.

13 Pavel Khodorkovsky, son of the former Yukos oil company chief.

14 On the day of Vladimir Putin's inauguration to his third term as Russia's president, 7 May 2012, the two men in this photo take a bus to work in the Republic of Karelia. Their place of employment, seen in the background, is the Segezha penal colony, where Mikhail Khodorkovsky spent the last two years of his incarceration, until his release on 20 December 2013.

for a similar fraud scheme involving similar sums of money. Russia, by comparison, I believe, seems a lot more liberal. Anyway, we must start from the fact that Khodorkovsky's guilt has been proven in court.

In addition, as you are probably aware, and now I am talking about Khodorkovsky directly, but I note that the Yukos security chief is currently serving time for murder. The mayor of Nefteyugansk, Vladimir Petukhov, got in their way and so they killed him. One woman in Moscow refused to hand over her small property, and they killed her, too. And then killed the assassin they hired to carry out these killings. All they found was his brains, splattered all over his garage. Do you think the security chief decided to carry out these crimes all by himself?[31]

Putin drew a rather too vivid picture of the fate of the Gorins. Khodorkovsky had never been charged with these crimes – although this was possibly material for a third trial.

Putin would later claim that he was not referring to the current trial, but to the facts of the first one. However, even Medvedev was not convinced; on 24 December, in his annual end-of-year interview live on air, he rebuked his premier when he argued: 'Neither the president, nor any other official in state service, has any right to express a position about this matter or any other matter before the moment the sentence is delivered.'[32] Medvedev's pedantic legalism now crossed with Putin's emotional rhetoric. Putin had violated rules on the presumption of innocence, but this was about as far that Medvedev would go in asserting himself in the Yukos affair. Nevertheless, it marked the beginning of a breach between the two men, reinforced by disagreement over UN Resolution 1973 of 17 March 2011 imposing a no-fly zone on Libya (Medvedev ordered Russia to abstain, allowing the West to use military force to overthrow Muammar Gaddafi). These events ended any doubts that Putin may have had about returning to the presidency, and Medvedev's second run was not endorsed.

Putin's comments clearly signalled that no mercy was to be shown. Khodorkovsky threw oil on the fire in an article also published on 24 December, responding to the nationalist riot at the gates of the Kremlin on 11 December (following the murder of a Slavic football fan and the release of his alleged Caucasian killers) and Putin's outburst on 16 December. Khodorkovsky noted that 'initial frustration soon gave way to a different emotion. I suddenly realised that I was sorry for this man [Putin]: not young anymore, but brisk and horribly lonely before this vast and ruthless country.' As for the riots, he noted: 'Our children see no future for themselves.' 'Do we need Russia to be built once again through brutality?' Referring to Putin's liking for dogs, Khodorkovsky described it as 'the only sincere feeling within the icy armour of the "national symbol" of the 2000s'. He ended by wishing Putin 'compassion and tolerance. […] Better be loved than feared.'[33]

On 27 December Danilkin began by pronouncing Khodorkovsky and Lebedev guilty of stealing approximately two-thirds of the total petroleum output of Yukos (some 200 million tonnes) and of laundering the proceeds in excess of $16 billion. Danilkin then raced through his 350-page summary, which repeated almost verbatim the prosecution case – and in certain instances even exceeded prosecution claims.[34] The full verdict is 878 pages long, and contains some extraordinary statements. For example, the mercenary intent of Khodorkovsky and his colleagues was directed 'towards increasing profit due to increasing production, and also to increase the value of his Yukos shares'. Criminal behaviour indeed for the chief executive of a large corporation! Khodorkovsky and Lebedev were convicted of embezzlement and money laundering (Articles 160(3)(a) and (b) and 174.1(3) of the RF Criminal Code). On 30 December Danilkin sentenced the two to jail for thirteen and a half years each in a penal colony. This included time already served, which meant that the two would not be free for seven more years, extending their incarceration to 2017. In a separate judgment on the same day, Danilkin convicted the two men of a further charge of embezzlement, contrary to Article 160(3)(a) and (b) of the RF Criminal Code. This related to the alleged criminal acquisition of a majority shareholding in VNK. Because of the expiry of the statute of limitation, no further punishment was applied.

The verdict has been condemned on the grounds that it grossly violates basic legal principles of a rule-of-law state (Article 1 of the Russian constitution). The court's own records appear to show that the actions of the defendants did not constitute a crime, hence the verdict was unlawful. The proceedings and the verdict appeared to disregard the principles of a fair trial and have been criticised on three main grounds. First, defence requests for disclosure of papers from related cases, to call experts to challenge the prosecution calculations, and to summon witnesses were refused. This meant that much of the evidence that the defence wished to provide was not admitted or disclosed by the judge. Second, evidence admitted that was favourable to the defence was dismissed by the judge on questionable grounds. Third, Putin's comments on 16 December that 'a thief should sit in jail', that 'Khodorkovsky's crimes have been proven in court', and the intimation that Khodorkovsky was also guilty of murder, even though there was no reference to this in any court or investigative document, constituted political interference.

Khodorkovsky's lawyers filed an appeal on 31 December.[35] The sentence attracted widespread international criticism. It undermined Medvedev's intention to establish a rule-of-law state and seemed to confirm Putin's predominance in the tandem. Even worse, the trial prosecutors Valery Lakhtin and Gulchekhra Ibragimova even suggested that there could be a third trial, 'as long as 18 of Khodorkovsky's and Lebedev's accomplices are arrested'.[36] At issue was the use of dummy companies to allow Khodorkovsky to take control of Yukos subsidiaries, notably VNK, followed by the use of intermediaries to manage the huge cash flows, while the producers allegedly teetered on the brink of insolvency. Continued persecution seemed beyond the bounds of political reason, and the harsh extra sentence appeared gratuitous. The demonstration effect had already been achieved concerning the oligarchs as a class; since the first trial the 'robber barons' had become subservient to the regime and learnt the rules of fealty to the new order. Although no one expected an outright acquittal, the severity of the new penalty smacked of vindictiveness.

THE SYSTEM EXPOSED

There were persistent rumours that on 25 December Danilkin had been escorted to the Moscow City Court, with the imputation that he was then instructed on the sentence, a gross infringement of all the rules.[37] Khodorkovsky soon after wrote that although he considered Danilkin a decent man, professional and with a conscience, he had been 'broken, badly broken' by the system. Like other judges in Yukos trials (notably Kolesnikova in the first trial), outcomes favourable to the authorities were delivered despite evident distaste. As for the verdict, 'That it was not Danilkin himself who wrote the verdict is clear. It was written by several people who never attended the trial.' Concerning the accusations of murder, Khodorkovsky denied outright that Yukos had ever engaged in such behaviour, insisting: 'We handled all problems and all individuals in the courts.'[38] Khodorkovsky noted how the affair had now become deeply personal, with Putin considering him his mortal enemy.[39] As for why Putin insisted that Khodorkovsky had 'blood on his hands', Khodorkovsky argued that he was trying 'to convince his constituents that he is right, correctly assuming that they trust him more than they trust his Basmanny justice'. When asked: 'Why is Putin so afraid of you? Do you know something that makes him nervous or is he afraid that you could become the leader of the dissatisfied? Or that you would demand the return of your money?', Khodorkovsky responded that Putin's fears were not pragmatic but irrational.[40] The case demonstrated Medvedev's powerlessness in the face of the *silovik* faction and his own prime minister, and exposed the isolation of the regime as a whole. As Khodorkovsky put it at the time in an open letter to the president, 'When courts openly defy the law and the president cannot do anything about it, this is nothing short of a constitutional crisis.'[41]

It was also a major scandal. The court's press secretary and aide to the presiding judge, Natalya Vasileva, confirmed on 14 February 2011 that the judge had not written the verdict himself, as prescribed by law, but had been influenced by unnamed figures in the Moscow City Court.[42] The latter is ruled with a heavy hand by Yegorova, and had been involved in a number of scandals when reformist judges were dismissed and those who acquitted too many defendants censured. Vasileva's account was later supported by a former court administrator, Igor Kravchenko. He declared that Danilkin had not wanted to take on the Yukos case, but had been forced to do it by Yegorova, with whom he regularly consulted during the trial.[43] On 14 June Vasileva, who had left her job in the Khamovnichesky District Court in March, revealed that Danilkin intended to give a lighter sentence before changing his mind under pressure from above. The Agora human-rights organisation published a three-page document, which had come into Vasileva's possession by accident along with some other signed papers, showing that Danilkin had written in a ten-year sentence (scored with three exclamation marks) as opposed to the thirteen and a half years actually given.[44] It appeared that the lid was now coming off to reveal how the Khodorkovsky trial had been manipulated by outside forces.[45] Danilkin himself denied that any pressure had been placed on him.

On 24 May 2011 the Moscow City Court rejected Khodorkovsky's and Lebedev's cassation appeal, while reducing their sentences to a total of 13 years each.[46] In his speech Khodorkovsky declared: 'I am not seeking justice here. The experience of interacting with your colleagues has freed me of any such illusions [...] The system of the courts of general jurisdiction is dependent and does not protect citizens from the arbitrariness of officials; the number of acquittals is vanishingly small.'[47] He was convinced that 'the verdict was written not by judge Danilkin, but by a collective of authors personally not having taken part in the trial'. He noted that Danilkin had been summoned to the Moscow City Court on numerous occasions 'not only in the course of the trial (this is a universally known fact), but also during the preparation of the verdict'.[48] The whole case was then subjected to a forensic critique, including numerous appendices with such titles as 'Examples of mutually exclusive conclusions' and an analytical report on 'Problems of taxation in the Russian oil industry'. In particular, he reiterated: 'When the political decision to destroy Yukos was taken in 2004, they chose unfair tax claims as the mechanism.'[49] He argued that Yukos was one of the best taxpayers, as well as being a transparent and well-run company. The main Yukos operation comprised over 100 legal entities employing over 90,000 people, while the production subsidiaries employed 18,300.[50] Khodorkovsky mocked the notion that the company had been driven by 'mercenary aspirations' to increase profit: 'In what dusty cellar did they dig up the poisonous Stalinist spider who wrote this drivel? No modernisation will succeed without a purging of these cellars.'[51] He argued: 'The president will have to decide what he and Russia need: a state governed by the rule of law or one in which there is the possibility of unlawful reprisals. You cannot have both.'[52] He used Medvedev's words to condemn 'selective justice' and the absurdity of the charges against him. He warned that Medvedev's law on prohibiting the arrest of entrepreneurs would be sabotaged, in the context where 'Fifteen per cent of entrepreneurs are subjected to criminal repressions, as during the time at the end of NEP'.[53]

Lebedev's first term ended on 2 July and Khodorkovsky's on 25 October 2011, but they were now due to stay in jail, respectively, until July and October 2016. On 10 June the two left Moscow, arriving at their penal facilities a week later. Khodorkovsky was assigned to a Corrective Colony (FKU IK-7 UFSIN) in Segezha, Karelia, while Lebedev was sent to a Prison Colony (IK-14) in Velsk, Arkhangelsk oblast. The Segezha colony is an ordinary 'red' penal colony, a general regime camp where the administration is in control, with some 1,300 inmates. The camp is furnished with a library, a vocational school and since 2007 a church. Mobile phones are not allowed, but pay phones can be used to call home. From Segezha Khodorkovsky continued to comment on developments, above all stressing the need for political change as the country entered a new succession struggle.

Pressure for reform was building up, and this was reflected in some judicial decisions. On 15 April and then again on 13 September 2011 the Supreme Court ruled that the law was violated when bail was refused for Khodorkovsky and Lebedev. The court on the second occasion upheld the complaint by the two and issued a special statement to Yegorova. The court ruled that the decision in 2010 to extend their pre-trial detention by three months was made with 'violations of procedural requirements'.[54] Yegorova had long been condemned for ignoring the law and discrediting the judiciary in the way that she conducted affairs in the Moscow City Court. This balanced the decision of the Supreme Court on 15 May 2012 to reject the final appeal against the second conviction. The decision flouted procedural rules and deadlines, but not accidentally came a week after Putin was inaugurated for his third term.

PARDON AND PAROLE

In a move lobbied for by the *siloviki*, Presidential Decree No. 1500 of 28 December 2001 reformed the legal structure of pardon-review committees. Putin abolished the single Committee on Pardons that had existed since 1992 and in its place created a system of regional committees. Applications are first lodged with the regional commission and then referred to the governor, and only after these filters is the plea allowed to proceed to the president. The central commission under the writer Anatoly Pristavkin had released up to 12,000 a year, but the new system had the desired effect and the number of pardons fell sharply: in 2003 there were 187, in 2004 72, in 2005 42, in 2006 9, and in 2007, astonishingly, none. This was accompanied by a change in procedures, with Article 3 of the decree stating bluntly: 'A convicted person must petition the president in writing'; although it does not directly state that the petitioner must recognise guilt. Any petition could undoubtedly be construed as a confession of guilt, and this was something that Khodorkovsky and Lebedev repeatedly vowed they would not do. Indeed, Reznik argued that insistence on admission of guilt was unconstitutional, since Article 51(1) bans forcing someone to testify against themselves. It was purely up to the president's mercy to grant a pardon.[55] Despite expert analysis to the contrary, Medvedev stuck to a distorted view of Article 50(3), which states that prisoners have 'the right to appeal for pardon or a reduction of sentence'; but instead of a 'right', he turned it into an obligation. Article 89(c) baldly states: 'The president of the Russian Federation [...] grants pardons,' with no qualifications whatsoever. A pardon is thus technically possible even if a prisoner does not accept guilt.

Once half a sentence is served a prisoner may be released early on the basis of the 'conditional early release' (UDO) scheme envisaged by Russian law – in other words, parole. However, at the halfway mark of his eight-year incarceration in October 2007 Khodorkovsky was not considered for parole because of a reprimand that he had received over the alleged violation of prison rules.[56] Khodorkovsky apparently had not had his hands behind his back during a walk on 15 October but down his sides, like an ordinary person. Later another inmate, Igor Gnezdilov, who shared a cell with Khodorkovsky for a year in Chita, revealed that he had been forced to sign a statement accusing Khodorkovsky of walking in the unsanctioned manner: 'It wasn't true but I was told that if I didn't sign the statement they would make sure I wasn't released early. So I signed, but later told Khodorkovsky.'[57] With the infringement logged in Khodorkovsky's file, the case for parole was refused.[58]

Interviewed shortly after Medvedev's election as president, Khodorkovsky once again voiced his conviction that Sechin had been responsible: 'He orchestrated the first case against me out of greed and the second out of cowardice.' Khodorkovsky expressed bewilderment:

> Exactly how he managed to convince his boss is hard to say. Maybe Putin really thought I was plotting some political coup, which is ridiculous, since at the time I was publicly supporting two opposition parties, which at best could have won 15% in parliamentary elections. More likely they didn't need any reason, just an excuse to raid Yukos, Russia's most successful oil company.

Khodorkovsky voiced cautious optimism about the new presidency, and stressed that Medvedev was not his enemy.[59] Medvedev, as noted, had voiced cautious opposition to the Yukos affair from the start. However, Khodorkovsky stressed that Medvedev would need time to grow into the job: 'For a while Medvedev will be held back by his personal obligation to Putin':

> The outcome of my case depends on the speed with which reform to the judicial system, which Medvedev has said he wants, takes place. In an independent court only a complete idiot would swallow the kind of case brought against me. Unfortunately reforms don't happen overnight, but some steps taken by Medvedev's team are cause for cautious optimism.[60]

Khodorkovsky continued to read a lot, but admitted that 'The years in prison, the isolation, isn't [*sic*] easy but it's bearable. [...] Education and reflection are prison's great bonuses.'[61] There was no change of elites with Medvedev's accession and those who had put Khodorkovsky in jail remained in power, and therefore he would continue to have plenty of time for reflection.

Asked directly during Chancellor Angela Merkel's visit to Russia to meet with president-elect Medvedev on 8 March 2008 about the possibility of an amnesty for Khodorkovsky, Putin left it to his successor: 'The decision to grant an amnesty is one of the powers of the head of state, the president of the Russian Federation.'[62] The option was endorsed by Merkel: 'if the possibility of amnesty exists, this is something we would welcome.' This was both confirmed and tempered by Putin's comments to *Le Monde* on 31 May 2008 that any decision on relaxing the conditions of Khodorkovsky's imprisonment or reducing his term was one that the president would have to make 'on his own'. He stressed that Khodorkovsky had broken the law 'repeatedly and grossly', and that he had been part of a group accused not only of economic crimes but also murders. 'This kind of "competition", he insisted, is not admissible, and we will do our best to stop it.'[63]

Medvedev, however, took a rather different tack. In a press conference with Merkel on 5 June 2008 he was once again asked about the 'pardoning or freeing' of Khodorkovsky. His answer opened the door a little:

> There is a procedure for pardoning someone, to which any citizen convicted of a crime (including Khodorkovsky) can resort, as well as other procedures that exist in regard to criminal law enforcement. But such issues cannot be resolved in discussions at the intergovernmental level or by decisions taken by politicians.[64]

In other words, the possibility of freeing Khodorkovsky existed, but it would be done at a time of Russia's choosing and in a manner that observed established procedures. When on 16 July 2008 Khodorkovsky formally applied for parole, his lawyers invoked Medvedev's slogan of ending 'legal nihilism'.[65] His application was rejected by Ingodinsky District Court on 22 August 2008. With the infringement logged in his file (walking in an unsanctioned manner), parole was refused. Pre-trial custody was extended to 2 November 2008.

Khodorkovsky's release was a persistent theme of Medvedev's presidency and became an important issue in the 2011–12 elections. Discussions were accompanied by two main concerns. First, any amnesty raised the prospect of litigation by shareholders who had lost out as Yukos stock became devalued, and thus a 'zero-option' deal would have to be struck: Khodorkovsky's release and the end of associated prosecutions in exchange for a moratorium on economic claims. Second, Khodorkovsky's release would signal the lack of continuity in the succession from Putin to Medvedev, so his release would have to take an extremely legalistic form to obscure its political implications. Any deal would have to include the renunciation of political activity by Khodorkovsky.

The Khodorkovsky case was raised in almost every major interview given by Medvedev in 2011. At Davos on 26 January he was cagey, insisting that the president of any country, including Russia, should not talk about individual cases because that would be 'interference in the judicial system. [...] Let the judicial and legal systems develop independently, otherwise there will be problems'. Instead, as Putin had done in December 2010, he compared Khodorkovsky to Bernard Madoff, the mastermind of a Ponzi scheme who was sentenced to 150 years in prison in 2009.[66] Later he was more expansive. During Medvedev's much-anticipated 18 May 2011 press conference at the Skolkovo School of Management, the only such occasion of his presidency, there were expectations that he would make a major announcement as time ran out on his leadership. Medvedev was asked what danger Khodorkovsky posed if freed: 'You asked a short question and the answer will be brief as well: absolutely none.'[67] This raised hopes that parole was on the cards, especially when rumours circulated that the Kremlin was planning an economic amnesty. This was accompanied by remarkably favourable coverage of the case on both the NTV and Rossiya channels on 29 May, including a broadcast of Khodorkovsky's final statement to the court stressing the absurdity of the charges against him, the first time he had been shown in this way since 2003.[68] In an interview with the *Financial Times* after the St Petersburg Economic Forum, Medvedev cryptically insisted that 'Khodorkovsky enjoys all of the rights set by the Criminal Procedural Code, including the right to early release on parole. As far as I can see, he is going to exercise that right. He also has the right to appeal for a pardon.' He also repeated his view regarding Khodorkovsky's release: 'As for danger, what danger can he pose?'[69] It seemed that Medvedev's 'thaw' was finally going to have an effect as he dropped broad hints that he would like another try at the presidency. At his Skolkovo press conference Medvedev noted that despite their similarities, he and Putin did not coincide in every way.

Following the rejection of their appeal, Lebedev and Khodorkovsky once again applied for parole in May 2011, provoking a wave of press commentary that their release would demonstrate Medvedev's 'evolution into a bona fide politician' and 'put an end to the absurd saga that has been doing so much harm to the image of Russia'.[70] Soon after, Khodorkovsky's application was summarily rejected on 7 June, on the grounds that his lawyers had not supplied the proper documents showing that he was in prison.[71] In an interview shortly before his hearing, Lebedev insisted that he was a hostage of the political battle between the Kremlin and Khodorkovsky. Asked what kept him going during eight years in jail, he replied: 'my beloved wife, children, grandchildren, brothers, and lawyers, as well as a huge number of people both in Russia and abroad'.[72] Lebedev admitted that he was still shocked at how events had developed:

> I could not foresee even in my worst nightmare that it was possible to annihilate the best company in the country, brazenly vandalise its assets and commit repressions in relation to its employees and shareholders while the whole world watches. I had thought that Russia was capable of going into the third millennium without dragging its ulcerating sores from the second millennium with it.

Asked about his parole, Lebedev turned out to be remarkably positive about the president. He believed that 'Medvedev is genuinely trying to improve the rule of law and to boost the independence of the courts. He has the chance to do so.' A note of doubt did creep in: 'But will he be able to make use of it and will he be allowed to make use of it – that is the question.'[73]

In the event, these hopes were dashed, as were so many during Medvedev's presidency, and after a two-day hearing on 27 July the Velsk District Court rejected Lebedev's parole application. The prison authorities contested his application on the grounds that he had been repeatedly reprimanded for infractions during his time in prison. He had been issued 20 reprimands in eight years, but all turned out to be minor, bordering on the risible. These included 'violations of the fire safety rules' and the fact that Lebedev had not always followed the correct procedure in communication with the prison authorities. Lebedev had picked up two reprimands in Velsk: for allegedly losing a set of clothes and for being impolite to a warder. These nit-picking charges were contested by his lawyers.[74] The judge, Nikolai Raspopov, justified the decision on the grounds that Lebedev 'does not take measures for the voluntary repayment of claims, believing the reprimands to be unlawful'; he 'has not admitted his guilt in the committed crimes' and 'has no remorse for what he has done'.[75] Rather defensively, Raspopov denied that pressure had been exerted on him, insisting: 'This is an absolutely objective decision and [it was] made by my conviction.'[76] The refusal evoked considerable adverse commentary in Russia, including that by Russia's human-rights ombudsman, Vladimir Lukin, who suggested that the decision 'lends itself to the conclusion that the court had some other reasons besides those named', noting that 'the grounds behind the rejection of Lebedev's parole application are ludicrous'. This view was reiterated by the Presidential Council for Civil Society and Human Rights, insisting that the refusal was 'an arbitrary act. The grounds on which this decision was made appear to be not only laughable, but also derisory.'[77]

Asked whether Putin was the main obstacle to his release, Khodorkovsky answered:

> Vladimir Putin has designated me his personal enemy. As can be seen, he shares with Stalin a vision of the role of the judiciary that is incompatible with international standards. And still, he is not the only one like this in Russia. There is a whole group of people who have become billionaires and multi-millionaires on the rout of Yukos who are impeding my release. And who are going to impede it, irrespective of the degree of Vladimir Putin's personal involvement in the process.[78]

Several questions remained on the agenda. In what form could Khodorkovsky's exoneration take place; would he receive compensation for his losses, and to what extent, since it was highly improbable that he would get Yukos back? And what about the associated cases, notably Lebedev, Pichugin and all the others serving prison sentences as part of the Yukos affair? One of the leaders of the protest movement following the flawed 4 December 2011 parliamentary elections, Alexei Navalny, argued that the issue of pardoning Khodorkovsky 'seems ridiculous to me [...] it is obvious that he does not need pardoning in the second trial. The second Khodorkovsky case was quite simply an insult to justice [...] absolute fiction.' Navalny insisted that the fundamental question was who was responsible:

> There is a need to conduct an investigation of how these proceedings were carried out, punish the guilty and release him [Khodorkovsky] as an unjustly convicted person. And then, as regards Yukos – we need to deal separately with that, this is an issue for the government of the future.[79]

Navalny's caution was reflected in the self-limitation imposed by the Yukos defence team and the main actors themselves. The question has often been raised, as Paul Goble puts it, 'why the defendant and his lawyers have not tried to turn the tables on his accusers the way Vera Zasulich or Nikolai Bukharin did'.[80] He quotes Irina Pavlova, who asks precisely this question:

> As for the show trial of our time, it is legitimate to ask why neither Khodorkovsky himself nor his lawyers attempted to turn this trial into a trial of the specific crimes of the Russian authorities, which make a not guilty verdict inevitable.

Instead, no one involved 'revealed a single secret of the ruling mafia'. By placing hopes on mercy from above, the Yukos defendants only reinforced the authority of the system that they ostensibly condemned and were thus 'unable to go beyond the borders of the space and the rules set by the Kremlin'. She even suggested that Khodorkovsky turned out to be 'morally unfree of obligations before the Kremlin' and, even worse in her view, admitted that the authorities had the right to dictate the rules of the game, as in Khodorkovsky's 2008 *Esquire* discussion with Akunin (see Chapter 10). 'Khodorkovsky remains loyal to the ideas according to which the Russian authorities acted and continue to act.' The personal conflict between Khodorkovsky and Putin was accentuated and not the systemic defects that made such a trial possible.[81] Khodorkovsky placed his hopes on the distinction between mafia power and the legal state (what we have called the dual state), but the puzzle according to Goble remains. Three possible answers suggest themselves: that the Yukos people had no secrets to unleash against the 'mafia power'; that the authorities had far worse secrets with which to attack the Yukos group; or that the *Yukovtsy* ultimately shared many of the patriotic ambitions of the Putin regime. They were disarmed by the apparently senseless attack against them, continuing to believe (as they did with Medvedev) that they should be natural allies.

All candidates running in the 4 March 2012 presidential ballot promised to free Khodorkovsky if elected, with the signal exception of Putin. In his question-and-answer session of 15 December 2011, asked whether he would be ready to pardon Khodorkovsky, Putin laconically answered: 'If he [Khodorkovsky] files this appeal, I will review it, but before that I need to become president.'[82] In other words, Putin insisted that the quondam oligarch would have to recognise his guilt, something that Khodorkovsky vowed he would never do. Popular sympathies now turned in favour of the victims of the Yukos affair, and thus candidates saw this as a useful way of broadening their support. If in 2007 only 19% favoured Khodorkovsky's release, by October 2011 this had risen to 31%. Only 20% said that they would keep him behind bars, a drop from 44% in 2007. By late 2011 only 10% of Russians considered that the second trial had been fair, compared with 19% a year earlier. Over a quarter believed that the oligarch's second prison sentence had been ordered by the authorities, up 5% on the previous poll.[83] It is hardly surprising that the liberal candidate Mikhail Prokhorov and Sergei Mironov (running on behalf of Just Russia) called for Khodorkovsky's release. More unexpectedly, they were joined by Zyuganov, still the Communist candidate: 'I think humanity and mercy should be shown. Khodorkovsky has already served quite a long sentence,' Zyuganov told journalists on 11 January. However, he insisted that the 'illegal and criminal' privatisation of the 1990s should be reviewed first and those found guilty should be punished commensurate with the term served by Khodorkovsky.[84]

CHAPTER 8

RUSSIA ON TRIAL

The 'Yukos affair', as it is now customarily called, has been the subject of considerable comment by international media, NGOs and international organisations. Discussion of aspects centring on the Yukos oil company have given way in recent years to focus on the personal aspects of the various trials, above all the fate of Khodorkovsky and Lebedev, the focus of this book. The regime's attempts to portray the matter as purely criminal only highlighted the political nature of the case and the weakness of the constitutional state. Andrew Jack argues, 'The Yukos case is important in Putin's Russia not for the details so much as the broader picture it paints of the continued failings in the country's law enforcement system.'[1] This chapter will consider some of the more salient critiques of the Yukos affair.

INTERNATIONAL COMMENTARY AND RESOLUTIONS

Leandro Despouy, the UN Special Rapporteur on the Independence of Judges and Lawyers, conducted a fact-finding trip to Russia from 19 to 29 May 2008. His full report was published in March 2009 and makes a balanced assessment of the achievements and failings of political reform and the workings of the judicial system.[2] A matter of particular concern was the high number of judgments against Russia since 2002 by the ECtHR because of the authorities' failure to comply with decisions by the domestic courts: 'This shortcoming reflects negatively on the entire justice system and diminishes significantly public confidence' (para. 50). The report makes reference to the Yukos case as an example when defence lawyers 'have been limited in their ability to exercise their profession' because of intimidation by public officials and in which there have been 'important procedural and other shortcomings, mainly obstructing the right [to] adequate defense' (para. 80). The conclusion was clear: 'Political and other interference has damaged the image of the justice system in the eyes of the population' (para. 94), and while praising the achievements in terms of institutional reform this should be accompanied by 'a change in attitude' (para. 95).

Sabine Leutheusser-Schnarrenberger was first appointed rapporteur on behalf of the Council of Europe on judicial matters in Russia, and in particular the Yukos affair, on 15 March 2004. She is a member of the German parliament and was the German justice minister in the cabinet of Helmut Kohl and in Angela Merkel's second cabinet from 2009 to 2013. She was also a member of the Alliance of Democrats and Liberals for Europe in PACE. Her first report of November 2004 argued that the Yukos case was a serious threat to democracy and the rule of law in Russia. The detailed abuse of legal norms in the Yukos affair was described, raising the following concerns: despite repeated requests, Pichugin was not promptly examined after the alleged administration of a drug, so as to assess his complaint; Lebedev (who has chronic hepatitis) was refused access to treatment from independent doctors for one year; lawyers could not make use of their right to defend Lebedev when he was arrested as they were barred from entering the court chamber; access to the three detained prisoners by the lawyers was obstructed and delayed by the practice of having to present a general letter of permission by the public prosecution when visiting their clients in prison, something not required by Russian law; defending the accused was made more difficult by a confusing 'game' by the public prosecution regarding file references in the various pending proceedings against the defendants and Yukos, in particular due to the identical or closely related facts of the case in which the persons involved alternated as witnesses or defendants; the chambers of several lawyers were searched, files seized, lawyers summoned to give statements in the trial of their clients and several proceedings were launched to withdraw their registration as lawyers; lawyers voiced the justified suspicion that their conversations with their clients in prison had been tapped, as they were only allowed to speak in the same room in prison, even if others were free; the defence was made very difficult in court because lawyers were not allowed to speak to their clients and pass on written notes to them while witnesses were being heard without the court having read and approved them.[3]

The PACE resolution of 25 January 2005 argued that Khodorkovsky, Pichugin and Lebedev had been 'arbitrarily singled out' by the Russian authorities. The assembly, approving Leutheusser-Schnarrenberger's report, noted that intimidating action by law-enforcement agencies and careful preparation of this action in terms of public relations, taken together 'give a picture of a coordinated attack by the state', calling 'into question the fairness, impartiality and objectivity of the authorities'. The prosecutions went 'beyond the mere pursuit of criminal justice and includes elements such as the weakening of an outspoken political opponent, the intimidation of other wealthy individuals and the regaining of control of strategic economic assets'. Assembly members noted their concern over human rights and the judicial process in Russia revealed by the cases.[4] This was accompanied by a Recommendation with a number of suggestions, including 'the principle that detention on remand shall be an exceptional measure, and ensure that this principle is also applied in the case of Mr Khodorkovsky.'[5]

Visiting Moscow on a fact-finding visit in March 2009 in her new role as PACE rapporteur to the Committee on Legal Affairs and Human Rights on politically motivated abuses of criminal-justice systems, Leutheusser-Schnarrenberger attended the opening of the second Yukos trial. In a formal PACE press release, she made her feelings clear:

> Whilst I do not wish to interfere in pending judicial proceedings, I cannot help feeling bewildered by the fact that the two men are being tried for facts which appear to be essentially the same as those for which they were condemned in 2005.[6]

In other words, this was a spectacular case of double jeopardy. On 7 August 2009 she issued a new report which came to the same conclusions as Despouy. The report observed that 'the fight against "legal nihilism" launched by President Medvedev is still far from won' (para. 4.3.7). Turning to Yukos, she states: 'The legal justification of the new criminal cases against Mr Khodorkovsky and Mr Lebedev has me perplexed,' although 'as a matter of fair trial, any accusation must fulfil minimum standards of logic in order for a meaningful defence to be at all possible' (para. 99). Her description of the trial casts serious doubts upon the nature of the prosecution: 'the trial itself, so far, consists in reading out, apparently at random, short passages of corporate and other documents without any discussion of their significance, even from the point of view of the accusation' (para. 99). The section on 'Pressures on judges – pressure for conviction' (paras 69–76) provides a detailed account of abuses in this sphere as part of the drive to ensure convictions. She describes several instances of pressure against judges up to dismissal, including the notorious Sergei Pashin case. Leutheusser-Schnarrenberger met several Russian judges, including Olga Kudeshkina (para. 71), who recounted their experiences of being pressured and intimidated by government and judicial officials.[7]

In a section called 'Defence lawyers – a high risk profession?' (paras 85 and after), Leutheusser-Schnarrenberger details the travails of the Khodorkovsky and Lebedev defence team, upon whom the pressure is 'continuing unabated' in the second trial (para. 86). Attacks, including that on Lev Ponomarev, a veteran human-rights activist and lawyer, are

> perceived by those concerned as warnings and acts of intimidation aimed at weakening their resolve to defend their clients. I cannot help sharing their interpretation and I am shocked that the authorities are either unwilling or incapable to protect these courageous lawyers and their relatives [para. 86].

Schnarrenberger describes the atmosphere for judges as 'akin to that of a life-long "probation period"', so that judges who 'in this climate play their role in full independence still run a serious risk of losing their jobs' (para. 83). In the context of ECtHR decisions in Kudeshkina's favour and the reports of Despouy and Leutheusser-Schnarrenberger it is clear that there are questions to be asked about the validity of decisions taken by the Russian courts against Yukos and Khodorkovsky.

The International Bar Association Human Rights Institute (IBAHRI) issued an important 46-page report in September 2011, which subjected the second Khodorkovsky–Lebedev trial to forensic analysis. The report identified numerous legal failings and violations and concluded that the proceedings were 'incapable of providing clear proof' for a sound conviction, and affirmed that 'this trial was not fair'. The IBAHRI was the only organisation to retain a permanent observer throughout the second trial. The report argued that the indictments were unclear as to the precise charges, noting that they were 'long, chaotic, mistake-ridden and self-contradictory'. The indictments breached Article 202(2) of the UPK since they lacked 'references to the volumes and pages of the criminal case file', and instead there were multiple and contradictory allegations, confusing the whole process. The indictments moreover were constantly amended throughout the trial. There was also a lack of 'equality of arms', since the defence was not given a list of approved witnesses at the beginning of the trial, while the prosecution list was accepted from the start. The detention of the accused impeded their ability to mount a defence, hindering access to legal counsel. The absence of daily courtroom protocols was singled out as particularly deleterious to the defence, since they were unable to ascertain the basis of the court's rulings on the admissibility of evidence. Protocols in Russia are the equivalent to trial transcripts, but were not available until Danilkin finally completed them several months after the trial.[8]

APPEALS TO THE EUROPEAN COURT OF HUMAN RIGHTS

Russia joined the Council of Europe on 28 February 1996 and thereupon assumed the obligation to observe the rules that had been devised in the postwar era to regulate the normative world of the West European states. These included above all the ECHR, adopted on 4 November 1950, and its five Protocols, as well as the supranational jurisdiction of the ECtHR sitting in Strasbourg. A recent study of the four judgments so far issued by the court in the Yukos affair suggests that Russia has been in breach of Articles 5 (right to liberty and security) and 6 (right to a fair trial) of the ECHR, and in the case of Article 18 (permissible restrictions to the rights guaranteed) 'a certain suspicion as to the real intent of the Russian authorities existed in respect of his prosecution.'[9]

Khodorkovsky's first application to the ECtHR dealt with his arrest, pre-trial detention and first prosecution. It was submitted in 2004, before the outcome of the first trial was known, and was ruled partly admissible on 7 May 2009.[10] The court held that the case raised 'serious issues of fact and law' under the ECHR, rejecting arguments put forward by Russia that it had no proper basis. On 31 May 2011 the court issued its full judgment. In a detailed assessment of the very early stages of the Khodorkovsky trial, the court rejected some of the claims by the defence lawyers (for example, concerning the length of pre-trial detention and the conditions in which the defendant was detained), yet held that there had been some serious violations of Khodorkovsky's fundamental human rights and awarded Khodorkovsky €24,543 in damages and costs.[11]

The ECtHR made it clear that the Russian authorities had restricted Khodorkovsky's rights for political purposes: 'The Court *reiterates that it has already found that, at least in one respect, the authorities were driven by improper reasons.* Thus, the Court found that the applicant had been arrested in Novosibirsk not as a witness but rather as a suspect' (para. 254). The court accepted that it was 'reasonable to suspect that there was a political motivation in prosecuting MBK, and that this suspicion might be a sufficient basis for domestic courts to refuse extradition and deny legal assistance to the Russian Federation' (para. 260). The court found that there had been violations of Articles 3 (the prohibition against torture and inhumane treatment) and 5 (the right to liberty and security of the person) of the ECHR by Russia. The violations comprised:

i. The method of restraint employed against Khodorkovsky was degrading and violated Article 3 [paras 125–8];

ii. The conditions in the remand centre where Khodorkovsky was detained during the appeal hearing between 8 August and 9 October 2005 violated Article 3 [paras 117–18];

iii. Khodorkovsky's arrest at gunpoint in Novosibirsk in October 2003 violated Article 5(1)(b) [para. 142];

iv. The proceedings whereby Khodorkovsky's detention had repeatedly been extended were 'flawed in many respects', giving rise to a violation of Article 5(3) [para. 202];

v. Khodorkovsky had been denied a fair hearing at detention proceedings in December 2003, May 2004 and June 2004, which violated Article 5(4) [paras 234 and 242];

vi. The review of Khodorkovsky's detention order in March 2004 involved excessive delay, which violated Article 5(4) [para. 248].

The court did not support Khodorkovsky's application regarding Article 18, which provides that 'the restrictions permitted under [the] Convention to the said rights and freedoms shall not be applied for any purpose other than those for which they have been prescribed' (in other words, political motives). The court imposes a very high threshold before a positive finding can be made on Article 18 issues, setting standards of proof that are much higher than those that would be applied in a domestic extradition case. The court noted that it would need

> 'incontrovertible and direct proof' that would enable it to conclude that 'the whole legal machinery of the respondent State in the present case was *ab initio* misused, that from the beginning to the end the authorities were acting with bad faith and in blatant disregard for the Convention [para. 260].

It is extremely difficult, if not almost impossible, for an applicant to meet such standards. There have only been two cases in the ECtHR's history in which violations of Article 18 have been found. One of these involved what was effectively a signed confession, in that a Russian minister had signed an agreement making an improper motive plain.[12] In the Yukos affair, the reopening of the criminal case after the PGO had decided that there were no grounds to prosecute comes close to this level of proof.

On 14 December 2011 the Grand Chamber rejected a re-examination of the 31 May judgment, which as we have just seen ruled that 'incontestable proof' to sustain allegations that Khodorkovsky's prosecution had been politically motivated 'had not been presented', although it had found that Khodorkovsky's rights during his arrest in 2003 and detention had been violated. The court's decision was now final, giving Russia three months to pay Khodorkovsky's compensation. It also meant, as Klyugvant noted, that the decisions of the Russian courts that had authorised Khodorkovsky's detention could now be re-examined.[13] Khodorkovsky was satisfied with the decision:

> I consider the Court's judgment concerning my arrest on 25 October 2003 and subsequent detention throughout the duration of the first trial to be a significant success. The Court found that the conditions in which I was held in the SIZO cell and in the courtroom throughout the entire trial in 2004 and 2005 were inhuman and degrading, contrary to Article 3 of the Convention. The Court also found that, in violation of Article 5 of the Convention, my initial arrest in Novosibirsk was unlawful and that my subsequent pre-trial detention in SIZO conditions concerns a violation of a fundamental human right, which no State is ever permitted to derogate from, even in times of war or public emergency. The Court's overarching finding in relation to the serious violations of those Articles of the Convention is that my fundamental human rights were violated by the authorities from the moment of my arrest and throughout the duration of my first trial. Eight violations of the Convention in one application is some sort of record! And the application concerning the unfairness of the first trial has not been even considered on the merits yet.[14]

Khodorkovsky's second application to the ECtHR was declared partly admissible on 8 November 2011. The ECtHR held that the complaint raised serious issues of fact and law under the ECHR, the determination of which requires an examination of the merits. Khodorkovsky's complaint that the first trial was fundamentally unfair (contrary to Article 6), that he was subject to the imposition of a retrospective criminal penalty (contrary to Article 7), and that hindrance and pressure has been placed on his lawyers by the Russian Federation in connection with the Strasbourg proceedings (contrary to Article 34) were all found to be admissible. Of particular note is the fact that, despite the finding on Article 18 in Khodorkovsky's first application to the ECtHR, a complaint that the Russian Federation breached Article 18 due to the political motivation behind his prosecution and punishment was found to be admissible. An admissibility decision on a third application to the ECtHR, which is a complaint that Khodorkovsky's second trial should have been stopped, as it represented an abuse of process, is pending. The Khodorkovsky defence team made a fourth complaint to the ECtHR seeking a determination on whether Putin's comments on 16 December 2010 – 'A thief should sit in jail' – on Khodorkovsky's guilt in the second trial, just before the verdict was delivered, represented a breach of the presumption of innocence (contrary to Article 6(2)).

Lebedev also filed a number of complaints with the ECtHR, two of which were granted. On 25 November 2004 the First Section of the ECtHR rendered a partial decision regarding the admissibility of the first case, with a final decision on admissibility made on 18 May 2006. In the light of his serious illness, the case revolved around whether he had been subject to inhumane and degrading treatment. On 25 October 2007 the ECtHR recorded five specific cases of violations of Lebedev's right to liberty and security. It ruled that there had been a number of procedural violations during the investigation and his detention violated rights to freedom and security under Article 5 of the ECHR. These violations included his illegal pre-trial detention between July and August 2003, and March to April 2004, as well as the restrictions placed on Lebedev and his lawyers to attend court hearings. Lebedev was awarded €10,000 in compensation. Three of the court's seven judges voted against the judgment, arguing that Lebedev's rights had not been violated.[15]

As noted, on 22 December 2008 the court partially satisfied Aleksanyan's appeal and urged less severe detention conditions. In another milestone, on 23 October 2012 the ECtHR resolved in the Pichugin case that Russia had contravened Article 6 of the ECHR, the right to a fair trial, and awarded him €9,500 in damages. The judgment related to the first trial, in which Pichugin was charged with the murder of the Gorins and the attacks on Kolesov and Olga Kostina. In 2005 a jury trial had found him guilty and imposed a 20-year sentence. The court condemned two abuses. First, that the case had been held in camera, hidden from the public gaze on the grounds that secret materials would be presented, although in the event none were. Second, the defence never had the opportunity to question Korovnikov's key evidence, or to raise the issue of his criminal past. The court rejected the complaint about the way that the jurors had been chosen; it refused to examine the appeal to Article 3, the prohibition on torture, on the grounds that on 14 July 2003 in Lefortovo Pichugin had apparently been given a 'truth serum'; it also refused to examine the appeal to Article 5, the right to freedom and personal inviolability, alleging that

Pichugin's pre-trial detention had been unjustifiably long. Pichugin's defence team also filed a second complaint concerning the second trial, in which he was found guilty of organising Petukhov's murder and that of Valentina Korneeva, as well as the attack on the head of East Petroleum Handels, Yevgeny Rybin, and given a life sentence.[16] As Groen puts it, 'These elements taken together – unfortunately – raise serious questions about the degree of judicial independence in Russia nowadays, in particular where state interests are at stake.'[17]

CHAPTER 9

FROM OLIGARCH
TO DISSIDENT

As Khodorkovsky began his second year in jail in December 2004, he wrote: 'I, like so many other captives, known and unknown, must say thank you to prison. It has given me months of concentrated thinking, time to rethink many facets of life.' He now understood that 'money does not buy happiness'. Not so long ago he had been one of Russia's richest individuals, and he had sacrificed so much to gain and defend his property, but now he had no regrets about losing it. He promised that 'he would not seek revenge against the authorities and that he placed freedom above property'. He had 'no intention of becoming a Count of Monte Cristo'.[1] As a prisoner, Khodorkovsky engaged in a personal and political odyssey. He had always been distinguished by his awareness of spiritual issues and concern with Russia's development.[2] Relieved of the burden of running Yukos, he turned his attention to broader questions of public policy and political development. He refused to be trapped into a single identity, as a victim of an unjust regime or as a fallen oligarch, and asserted his right to find his own solutions to personal and social questions. He distanced himself from Yukos's managerial issues and instead focused on the fate of the country.

BUSINESS AND THE STATE

In an interview of June 2002, though only published after his sentencing in June 2005, Khodorkovsky proved highly prescient.[3] Publication had been delayed because he considered it too bold. His views on the perilous predicament of business in Russia and the lack of security from a predatory state were certainly hard-hitting. When asked about the risks facing big business in Russia, Khodorkovsky answered: 'There is no doubt that the state can easily destroy us, but this will denote a change in the social structure.' Although he did not believe that it would be rational for the state to launch such an attack, he did not discount it. He admitted that at the time when business began it was impossible to observe the law since there was no relevant legislation:

> So people did what they wanted. These were the conditions under which the original accumulation of capital took place. We did shape some moral requirements to ourselves, but those were our moral requirements so we should not even mention them today. They corresponded to the society we lived in. Then, gradually, the legislative field began taking shape; we continued functioning in its boundaries but it was still quite wide, a situation which remains to this day.

The flawed business ethic of the early oligarchs dogged the first generation of Russian capitalists. The claim that laws were weak or non-existent is true but can hardly been taken as long-term justification. By this time Khodorkovsky had changed his image from rapacious oligarch to benevolent businessman. Yukos had set up various philanthropic foundations, and shortly before the interview Khodorkovsky met the UN secretary general, Kofi Annan. Khodorkovsky admitted that the original accumulation of capital from the late 1980s had been a wild affair, but now insisted that his generation was performing a 'stabilising role'; the business atmosphere in Russia had changed, and 'we are trying to embrace the norms advanced by Western society'. Asked to be more specific, he answered:

> Democracy, transparency, social responsibility of business, corporate citizenship – these are quite clear things. Of course, to some extent our struggle for a business ethic is of a mercenary character. Yes, we do profit from that. Yes, this is unprofitable for some our rivals who have failed to break through so far. I will repeat though that in general today all of society benefits from our position […] Someone should be looking further than the others demonstrating with their own example that it is not only possible but even better to live normally.

He was explicit about the need to construct a positive image. His interlocutor asked him about a recent interview in the West in which Khodorkovsky had mentioned

Rockefeller as a role model. Gevorkyan noted that Rockefeller, however, "'got laundered" only in the third generation – it was only his grandson that became "clean". There were 100 years separating him from his grandfather. And it seems as though you would like to race through these 100 years during your lifetime.'

> I sure would. This is an objective requirement in business – the one who is fastest will win. You are not surprised by the fact that the path from horse to railway took thousands of years, whereas from a railway to spaceship – only a hundred years. The same applies to the Rockefeller issue. I was in Harvard and heard the director of their business school speak. He said that Khodorkovsky was Rockefeller, Rockefeller's son and Rockefeller's grandson in one person. Rockefeller had it much harder. Back then there were no ready rules. It took a hundred years to create a business ethic. It took them three generations. It is easier for us.

Khodorkovsky clearly liked the idea that he combined three generations in one and what had taken a century in America would have to be achieved in half a lifetime in Russia. By then Yukos was undergoing one of the most rapid corporate transformations in history. A similar process taking place in the country as a whole: 'During the past year and especially after September 11 [9/11] they [the West] began perceiving Russia as a normal country. This, incidentally, was the time when I strongly identified with Putin. It does not happen often with me.'

However, the country was not quite normal. The next question was 'Do you feel safe in your country?', to which Khodorkovsky responded: 'Of course not. As an individual – absolutely not. I think that the country's present judicial system and the contemporary law-enforcement system fail to protect an individual.' 'How about property?': 'No. The present generation is not prepared to treat private property as an absolute basic value.' Nevertheless, Khodorkovsky was not ready to believe that the state would launch an assault against him, as it had done in January 2002 against Nikolai Aksenenko, the 'Yeltsinite' who was dismissed as railways minister and whose affairs were investigated. As the questioner put it, Aksenenko was 'Quite an oligarch. In power into the bargain, a former candidate for the presidency as well, and he was gone in just a moment. The risk that in just a moment there will be no...'

> ... Khodorkovsky? I think that the probability that Khodorkovsky will disappear in just a moment is less than in the case of Aksenenko. The nature of property is different. In that case everything was too simple and clear. The situation has changed, hasn't it? Earlier it was like this (snaps his fingers, – NG) and there was no Yukos.

> Today (snaps his fingers again, – NG) – and there is no Khodorkovsky is still pos-
> sible. However, not in regards to Yukos. […] No, it is unlikely. Society has become
> too pragmatic and understands that the loss of a major business is a big loss for
> every person. After all it is three percent of the GDP, isn't it?

The fact that over 100,000 people depended on Yukos, one of the largest companies
in the country and a major budget contributor, acted as a type of insurance policy
for Khodorkovsky: 'That is why even if he [Putin] does not really like our company
he meets with us and enquires what impedes our work.' There was also the foreign
aspect: 'What about the shaping of your image (in the West as well). Is that also a
kind of a safety net for you inside the country?', to which Khodorkovsky responded:
'I would put it differently. This is an additional measure of freedom.'

Discussion then moved on to the events of 1996, one of the perennial issues in
Khodorkovsky's writings, which we discussed in Chapter 1. Khodorkovsky insisted
that he would act again as he had then.

> I well remember that situation. I was a witness to the conversation between Soros
> and Berezovsky. In Davos there is a restaurant in the basement. They were sitting
> at the next table. I turned to them. I actually heard Soros say: 'Many of my friends
> lost everything – and sometimes their lives – because they did not leave everything
> behind and depart. You've had a good time, guys, but it's now time to push off. A
> communist will win.' Zyuganov had a room next to mine, and we talked a lot. And
> afterwards I said: everything is fine, he represents the outlook of millions of people
> in the country, my fellow citizens whom I treat with respect as I do Zyuganov, but
> I do not want him to be in power in the country.

Later in the interview Khodorkovsky admitted funding the SPS and forces promot-
ing a 'liberal economy, democracy and stability'. Still relatively young, he was asked
whether he would consider doing something else, 'For example politics?':

> You should always do what you are better than others at. I have achieved much
> in business. I am an effective head of a company and my activity is quite highly
> evaluated. I will not go into a sphere where the assessment of my activity might be
> worse. In any case, this is a question of inner conviction. If I sense that I can be up
> to the mark, for example in international business, I will go for it. The same is true
> about politics. Why not? Indeed, I am 38 […] I still have time. Let alone the fact
> that I have said that I will withdraw from business at 45.

As for the role of money in his life, Khodorkovsky answered:

> Leonid Nevzlin and I once decided: we have enough personal money to keep us
> happy. From this point of view it plays absolutely no role. And there is money
> left over for the game, an instrument. This instrument is like ammunition for the
> military – you barely have time to replenish it.

With broad ambitions and the money to fund them, Khodorkovsky may well indeed
have been perceived as a challenge to the regime.

THE CRISIS OF RUSSIAN LIBERALISM

The fall of Yukos coincided with the debacle of organised liberalism in the December
2003 parliamentary election, when neither of the major opposition parties (SPS and
Yabloko) crossed what was then the 5% representation threshold. Beginning with the
resounding phrase 'Liberalism in Russia is experiencing a crisis – this is now almost
indisputable', Khodorkovsky launched into a sustained critique.[4] Both the content and
also the provenance of the 2,000-word epistle called 'The crisis of Russian liberalism',
published on 29 March 2004, were controversial.[5] The purpose of the letter was no
less contested, with some seeing it as a mea culpa before the regime with which he
was now suing for peace, while others saw it as a sign of conflict within the Yukos
camp.[6] Further confusion is added by Khodorkovsky's studiously ambiguous comments about his authorship, refusing to confirm that he had written it or turned
over anything to his lawyers. The deputy justice minister, Yury Kalinin, announced
that Khodorkovsky declared that he had not written any article or passed anything
through his lawyers, but he was 'fully in agreement with its contents'.[7] If, however,
the lawyers had in fact smuggled the text out of Matrosskaya Tishina, then the aim
of this statement was clearly to protect them. The law demands that all written materials, except complaints and applications relating to the case, have to be censored
by the prison administration. The letter may have been taken out in fragments and
then reconstituted.[8] Earlier two of Khodorkovsky's lawyers, Olga Artyukhova and
Yevgeny Baru, had been punished for carrying unsanctioned materials. According
to Moskalenko, Khodorkovsky had simply shared his thoughts, which were then
written down,[9] while Padva stated that his client 'categorically accepted authorship'.[10]

The letter was not like those of Grigory Zinoviev and Lev Kamenev, who even as
they waited to be shot in August 1936 sent Stalin letters of repentance, but of a man

convinced of his civic virtue. Khodorkovsky observed the failure of Russia's liberal parties, and he was also less than impressed by Irina Khakamada's performance in the presidential election of 14 March 2004, when she gained 3.84% of the vote compared to Putin's resounding 71.31%, arguing that 'she did her best to discard her own liberal past', and described Ivan Rybkin's candidature, sponsored by Berezovsky, as a 'vulgar farce'.[11] As Khodorkovsky stressed, liberalism in Russia is associated with the failures and hardships of the 1990s, when the country underwent not so much a reform as a socio-political revolution. In a cruel Bolshevik inflection, the ends once again justified the means. Khodorkovsky in the 2000s precisely sought to disprove Polanyi's maxim: 'If the immediate effect of a change is deleterious, then, until proof to the contrary, the final effect is deleterious.'[12] He sought to ensure that the 'final effect' of the democratic capitalist transformation was beneficial – as did Putin, although in a very different way.

Caught between the failing liberals and the party of national revenge (the reactionary nationalists and Communists), Khodorkovsky insisted that 'Against this backdrop President Vladimir Putin seems to be Liberal No. 1', far preferable to the 'nationalists' Vladimir Zhirinovsky and Dmitry Rogozin, the latter at the head of the Rodina party which had done exceptionally well in the 2003 elections, winning 9% of the vote. On this basis he argued: 'Probably Putin is neither a liberal nor a democrat, but he is more liberal and democratic than 70% of the population of our country.' He insisted that 'the cause of the crisis of Russian liberalism is not about ideals of freedom' but the inadequacies of the practitioners of the ideal, accompanied by the failure of the Kremlin to give them adequate support, the departure of the oligarchs from the political arena, and the 'standard lobbying mechanisms [having] ceased to work'. He placed himself in the ranks of 'Socially active people of liberal views', who were 'responsible for keeping Russia on the path to freedom'; however, Russian liberals now had to 'analyse our tragic errors and confess our guilt'. The reason was straightforward:

> Russian liberalism has suffered a defeat because it tried to ignore, first, some significant national–historic peculiarities of Russia's development, and second, the vital interests of the majority of the Russian people. Above all, it was fatally afraid of telling the truth.

It was not that liberals such as Chubais, Gaidar and their associates consciously set out to deceive the Russian people, but once in power they 'approached this whole revolution in a supercilious if not outright frivolous manner'. They worked on behalf of the 10% of Russians ready to adapt to the new conditions 'without state paternalism, and forgot about the other 90 per cent', and then 'concealed their failures with deception'. In particular, he condemned the loss of savings, the voucher privatisation and the loans-for-shares privatisation. He criticised the lack of attention in the 1990s to education, health care, public utilities and support for the poor, and in general 'Russian liberals ignored issues of social stability and social peace, which alone could establish the basis for long-term reform and create the foundations of national existence'. Instead, 'A gulf separated them from the people, into whom they poured rosy liberal views of reality and manipulative technologies with the informational–bureaucratic pump.' He stressed how much effort it had taken in 1996 to get the Russian people to 'vote with their hearts'. He also took issue with liberal arguments that there had been no alternative to the 1998 partial default, in which millions once again lost their savings. In fact, a timely devaluation of the rouble, advocated by Khodorkovsky at the time, could have avoided the worst effects.

The attack on the liberals was comprehensive, noting their personal enrichment while the mass of the population sank into poverty, and the much-vaunted liberal 'freedom of speech' was accompanied, as he put it in the letter, by 'financial and administrative control over the media so as to use this magical arena for their own purposes'. It was hardly surprising that millions of the old Soviet scientific and technical intelligentsia, which 'in the late 1980s were the main motor of the Soviet liberation movement', now voted for Rodina and the KPRF. The liberal elite, in Khodorkovsky's view, showed nothing but contempt for the Russian people. This critique of the Bolshevism of the anti-Bolsheviks could have been written by Putin himself. From the remedial perspective, Putin sought to ameliorate the consequences of the 1990s but not their substance. Khodorkovsky also advanced a remedial agenda, although very different in substance: 'The hour of atonement has come. In the 2003 election the people bid a firm and tearless farewell to official liberals.' Even young people refused to vote for Chubais and the SPS. As for big business, it had cast its lot with the liberal rulers and 'helped them to err and lie', and had thus become 'accomplices to their misdeeds and lies', afraid of jeopardising their own position. They became the scapegoats for what had happened in the country. Attacks on so-called 'oligarchs' obscured, in Khodorkovsky's view, the fact that 'Oligarchy is the totality of the group that dominates power', and the business sector failed to challenge the rules, or indeed 'the absence of rules', and hence 'nurtured official lawlessness and Basmanny justice'. While big business had created 2 million jobs and revived whole sectors of industry, it incurred the wrath of society because of its failure to distance itself from the 'party of irresponsibility' and the 'party of deceit'.

The nascent business group had failed to defend its distinct class identity and had become little more than a subaltern wing of the liberal reform party. Khodorkovsky condemned the failure of the new entrepreneurial elite to become a bourgeoisie in the classical sense of the word, a property-owning class that acts according to the law, while shaping the law to defend its business interests and property rights. Khodorkovsky represented the vanguard of the nascent 'bourgeois' oligarchs and thus sharply distinguished himself from the 'criminal' oligarchy. While the defeat of the bandit capitalism of the Yeltsin era can be justified in terms of overcoming state capture and the end of what the left–nationalist opposition in Russia calls 'comprador capitalism', Khodorkovsky represented a different type of capitalism. Khodorkovsky benefited no less than the criminal oligarchs from the anarcho-capitalism of the 1990s, but he now advanced a new conception of the social role of big business. The flexing of his political muscles in 2003 can be seen as the attempt by this new bourgeoisie to emerge from the shadows of the state and to exist as an autonomous force in Russian politics. Hence the clipping of the wings of the 'criminal' oligarchs in 2000 was, in his view, very different from the attack on the consolidation of a bourgeois class three years later. The second event ultimately changed the nature of the post-Communist state. The relative liberalism of the first years of Putin's leadership now gave way to a far more *dirigiste* form of neo-patrimonial crony capitalism. The crisis of liberalism in Russia, from this perspective, was far deeper than the failings of a particular elite group, but reflected a structural shift in the nature of the Russian polity. Reactionary–remedial policies were compatible with genuine pluralism; however, the system had now moved beyond this to a transformative agenda based on a statist developmental model that negated the bourgeoisie as a class.

Khodorkovsky noted the contradiction between civil society and big business, with the latter seeking maximum profit whereas civil society pursues social goals like environmental and labour protection. Hence business will always find a common language with the state; 'Business does not crave liberal political reforms, nor is it obsessed with freedom.' In addition, 'business can find a home anywhere in the world, and money is not patriotic.' Then there comes a remarkable personal statement:

> As far as I am concerned, Russia is my motherland. I want to live, work and die
> here. I want my offspring to be proud of Russia and proud of me as a small part
> of this country and this unique civilisation. Perhaps I was too late in understand-
> ing this: I only started my involvement in philanthropy and my support for civic
> organizations in 2000. [...] That is why I decided to stop working in business, and

speak not on behalf of the 'business community' but for myself and on behalf of the liberal part of society and the people I consider my comrades-in-arms. There are among our ranks, of course, major businessmen – the world of genuine freedom and democracy is open to all.

Khodorkovsky did not deny the importance of liberalism for Russia, but argued that its practitioners – himself included – had not been up to the task. Hence he now provided his own remedial agenda to draw Russian liberalism out of the impasse of its own making. Unfortunately for him the regime had moved beyond the remedial agenda, and there was no room for the independent political entrepreneur in the new order.

Khodorkovsky nevertheless argued for a programme of constructive work with the regime, rather than engaging in futile condemnations of it. To achieve this he outlined a seven-point programme:

i. Establish a new strategy of interaction with the state: 'The state and the bureaucracy are not synonymous';

ii. 'Learn to seek justice in Russia, not in the West.' He admitted that having a high reputation in the West was 'nice', but this was 'no substitute for the respect of compatriots';

iii. 'Abandon senseless attempts to cast the legitimacy of the president in doubt. Whether we like Vladimir Putin or not, it is time to realise that the head of state is not just an individual. The president is an institution that guarantees the integrity and stability of our country. And God forbid that we should live to see that institution collapse. Russia will not survive another February 1917. The country's history demonstrates that bad power is better than none.' He stressed the important role that the state plays in the development of civil society, something that 'is shaped over the course of centuries';

iv. 'Stop lying to ourselves and to society.' Here he criticised Khakamada's presidential campaign (in March 2004), saying that, unlike his colleague Nevzlin, he refused to sponsor her, because 'I saw troubling signs of mendacity in her campaign', namely the allegations she made that Putin was behind the Dubrovka theatre siege in October 2002;[13]

v. 'Legitimate privatisation.' With 90 per cent of the population viewing the privatisations as unjust there will always be a large constituency ready to attack private property. Privatisation could only be vindicated if business started to share with the people, primarily through taxation, and it would be best if business initiated this itself rather than waiting for this to be imposed upon them;

vi. 'Create real civil society structures' as a way of attracting talented people and at the same time stopping the brain drain: 'Brains always collect in a favourable medium – civil society';

vii. 'To change the nation, we must change ourselves. To bring freedom back to our country, we need to believe in freedom ourselves.' And on this rousing note, reminiscent of Solzhenitsyn's credo, the letter ended.

The article suggested the interplay of six forces in Russia. *Big business* had taken advantage of the opportunities of the 1990s, but had failed to develop its own ethical code and instead had exploited the weakness of both the state and civil society to enrich itself, even though it was aware that its relationship with Yeltsin 'was a sham'. Some of his criticisms of the business world reflected the original criticisms of the National Strategy Council in May 2003, above all the accusation that the Russian business community had displayed a notable lack of 'patriotism'. The *radical liberals* come in for the harshest criticism, since their idealism had quickly turned to cynicism and contempt for the mass of the people. In effect Khodorkovsky argued that the liberal idea was too important to be left to self-styled liberals. The *state* remained a rather foggy presence in his discourse, but his thought was certainly imbued with elements of the 'democratic statism' that was later to triumph in Surkov's thinking, and given specific form in the shallow idea of sovereign democracy. Paradoxically echoing Putin, Khodorkovsky's text on a number of occasions stressed the society-forming and leadership role of the state. The letter thus sought to transcend the sterile confrontation between liberalism and the state, and on balance Khodorkovsky veered towards the latter, in keeping with his national-liberal views, which are given full expression in this letter.

He had little to say about the nature of Putin's *regime*, but had some surprisingly positive words to say about Putin himself. As for *civil society*, it would take a long time to develop, and in this Khodorkovsky shared Putin's awareness of temporality, the historical constraints on the actuation of ideals in the present time and the need to take a long-term approach. As he put it, civil society is formed over generations 'and not in an instant by the wave of a magic wand'. By the same token, despite the 'complexes and phobias' associated with the development of liberalism in the 1990s, the development of liberalism in Russia since the nineteenth century was highly problematic. This is where the final element comes in, namely the role of the *individual*. Everyone should take personal responsibility for what had happened to Russia after the fall of Communism and be prepared for a long struggle for the achievement of freedom in the country. Khodorkovsky's thinking joins the dissident critiques of power and the need for personal responsibility and moral consciousness.[14]

KHODORKOVSKY AS POLITICAL PHILOSOPHER AND COMMENTATOR

Khodorkovsky's decision to start a debate by sending a letter from prison continues a hallowed Russian tradition. Some of Russia's most powerful political philosophy falls into this genre. Characteristically, the relationship of prisoner to captor, victim to tyrant, is as much of interest as the content of the epistle. In the Russian context, the 'power of the powerless' is typically encapsulated in the romantic notion of the power of the written word to challenge the ranks of soldiers and secret policemen, and the power of the martyr to challenge the ease of the throne.

In this case the challenge was notably ambiguous, with some criticising the 'servile' tone, which called for an end to talk of Putin's illegitimacy, while others, like Belkovsky, insisted that Putin should accept Khodorkovsky's repentance. Belkovsky argued that Khodorkovsky challenged 'not Putin and his statehood', but 'his own past and himself'.

> Khodorkovsky has publicly repented for the 1990s and declared that the con-
> temporary crisis of liberalism in Russia is determined not by the intrigues of the
> semi-mythical 'Petersburg siloviki' but the historical mistakes and miscalculations
> of the liberals themselves, in power throughout the last decade.

Khodorkovsky, in Belkovsky's view, was the first to recognise 'the full-scale ideological crisis of Russian liberalism', and he 'exposed the enduring [...] myth about the unrestrained freedom of the 1990s. He openly speaks about the illusory nature of that freedom and the price that was paid for this fairytale illusion.' The article's publication, according to Belkovsky, would only reinforce Khodorkovsky's solitude;

although there was one person who should use the article as the signal to align himself with Khodorkovsky – Vladimir Putin – and to use the document as the 'manifesto of the new Russian elite'.[15]

Khodorkovsky's article outlined a programme up to 2020 and beyond, to be fulfilled, one supposes, by the author himself. The tone of leftist pragmatism grated on the ears of committed liberals, notably in the stress on the need to heal the breach between the state and society, in demanding that civil society work with the state rather than against it, and in arguing that without an end to poverty liberal reforms would run into the sand. In the words of one commentator, 'without restoring a comfortable standard of living to the elites in science, technology and the humanities, there will be no social storehouse for the ideas of freedom.'[16] This was balanced by an insistent patriotic tone that appeared to draw on Dostoevsky-style *pochvennichestvo* ('nativism'), which acted as a corrective to the market cosmopolitanism espoused by the liberals. Indeed, there was more than a hint of a great-power mentality in the letter. Equally, the author's attempt to distance himself from all actually existing liberal forces in Russia not surprisingly won him few friends in the liberal camp.

While the article represented a powerful critique of Russian liberalism, it failed to deal adequately with the classic modernisation dilemma, notably Russian liberalism's traditional reliance on an agent of change outside the modernising dimension itself. From Peter the Great to Lenin, this has traditionally been an enlightened bureaucracy or the state, as it was in the 1990s. Big business and the liberals had allied in 1996 to ensure Yeltsin's re-election, but the liberals objected when in 1997 the group that had begun to rejoice in the term 'oligarchs' really did look as if they wanted to run the country and have a determining say in government decisions. Nemtsov, first deputy prime minister, talked of 'people's capitalism',[17] while Chubais recognised the need to provide a popular social base for reform. Contemporary Russia is faced with a type of 'disembedded liberalism', with the driver of change external to liberalism. Interest groups lack coherent and stable sentiments and preferences, in part because of the constantly shifting background and context in which liberalism operates.[18] Khodorkovsky's views evolved from reliance on spontaneous market forces to generate social order in the 1990s towards a greater emphasis on social justice in the 2000s (on which more below). Khodorkovsky had been ambitious in politics, and now he revealed a different type of ambition: to understand the trajectory of Russian political life. He certainly did not join the Putin camp but sought to salvage something from the liberal experience and to forge a new understanding of the needs of the country on the basis of 'seeking after truth', a politics of parrhesia that was as welcome as it had been delayed.

The article was variously interpreted. For some it signalled Khodorkovsky's attempt to sue for peace with the Kremlin. The demonstrative attempt to distance himself from 'irreconcilables', such as Nevzlin, gives credence to this view. Valeria Novodvorskaya, the leader of Russia's first post-Communist independent political party, the Democratic Union established in May 1998, was typically scathing, condemning Khodorkovsky for 'recanting': 'There are things that are not pardonable even for those held in Matrosskaya Tishina. There can be no forgiveness for betraying one's supporters.' And she sneered at the fact that 'Mikhail Khodorkovsky was desperately defended by the self-same liberals whom he smeared with mud.'[19] Gaidar was no less dismissive of the economic basis of Khodorkovsky's arguments, insisting: 'Even those who gave it a delighted reception have called attention to the banality of what it says and to the fact that all of it has already been repeated many times over by the opponents of Russia's liberals.' What was new was the article's author, not its contents. Gaidar went on to argue that the structural reforms of the 1990s could only produce a positive effect with a time lag and that there had been no way of maintaining people's savings in 1990–1, when there had been a massive monetary overhang created by the lack of goods to purchase in the late Soviet years, and in conditions when from autumn 1990 16 central banks in the USSR were able to 'create liquidity' – that is, to print roubles.[20]

There was little in the way of personal self-criticism in Khodorkovsky's text. His call was for a collective rethink by the neo-liberal enthusiasts of the 1990s and the current liberal leaders, and while he admitted some oversights on his part, there was little sense of a deeper soul-searching about the way in which he had made his fortune. In fact, the article can be seen as very much in line with the pragmatic style that had brought him success in business, a flexibility now adapted, according to his critics, to get him out of his predicament. This may be taking an unduly sceptical approach, and while Khodorkovsky condemned Russia's liberals for having degenerated remarkably swiftly from idealism to cynicism and arrogance, his letter revealed the streak of political romanticism in his character.

Khodorkovsky's concerns had clearly moved on from Yukos, which does not merit a mention in the text. He had become a political figure, and he left the fight to save Yukos to others. Khodorkovsky declared that he would henceforth devote himself to a life as a social activist, if not as a politician. He began by distancing himself from the liberals and sought to position himself as a national leader, including among the leftist forces, to which he appealed in later communications. The letter marked the transformation of Khodorkovsky from business leader to public activist. Hence a very different conclusion can be drawn from that by those who interpreted the letter as Khodorkovsky's attempt to open a dialogue with the regime. With the discrediting of the traditional liberal political leaders a vacuum had opened up, and Khodorkovsky was making a bid for the leadership of democratic forces. Far from a recantation, this represented yet another political challenge. For the Kremlin, this only reinforced fears that Khodorkovsky represented a threat to Putin's regime. The fight continued with this 'turbulent priest'.

PROPERTY AND FREEDOM

In late 2004 Khodorkovsky once again put his thoughts on paper. By then he had been in custody for over a year, and the destruction of Yukos had continued. In December 2004 YNG was auctioned off to Rosneft, and with the tax bill standing at $27.5 billion the company's value had fallen from around $40 billion to little more than $2 billion. In a wide-ranging open letter from prison Khodorkovsky identi-fied a section of the Kremlin bureaucracy as responsible for continuing the attack for their personal benefit, while in his first interview from jail he provided a more political analysis.

In his second open letter Khodorkovsky took a philosophical look at what was happening to the country.[21] Entitled 'Prison and the world: property and freedom', the letter was published just days after YNG had been sold to a shady front company for about half of its estimated real value before being incorporated into Rosneft. He noted that six months earlier he had tried to save Yukos, its minority shareholders and the country by offering to give up his stake as payment of the tax claims.

> But the other side chose a different path: the path of selective application of the law, introducing new provisions and conditions, the public destruction of the first green shoots of business confidence in the arbitration court and government in general.

This was motivated by more than 'political interests alone', and hence the Yukos affair was not so much a conflict between business and the state as an attack by one company on another. He called the culmination of the Yukos case 'the most senseless and economically destructive incident in all of Vladimir Putin's years as president'.

He insisted that loss of his own fortune was not the issue, but the destruction of a company that he and his team had transformed from a loss-making enterprise operating in nine regions and producing only 40 million tonnes of oil a year, with a six-months arrears of wages and $3 billion in debts, to one by 2003 employing

150,000 people, operating in 50 regions and producing 80 million tonnes annually. It had become the country's second-largest taxpayer after Gazprom, comprising 5% of federal budget revenues. He condemned the 'wild imagination' that had conjured up the back-tax claims against the company, in some years exceeding its revenues, and noted: 'It is clear that government officials will stop at nothing in their pursuit of the redistribution of property.' At this point Khodorkovsky's text takes on a philosophical tone:

> It may sound strange to many, but losing my personal wealth is not unbearably pain-ful. Following in the tradition of many prisoners, both known and unknown, I must say thank you to prison. It gave me months for profound thought and time to forge a new outlook on many aspects of life. I now realise that owning property – especially large-scale property – does not make a person free. As part owner of Yukos I had to make enormous efforts to protect this wealth, and had to set limits on myself so as not to jeopardise it. There were many things that I did not permit myself to say, because speaking openly could have harmed those assets. I had to close my eyes and put up with many things, to preserve and increase my personal wealth. I did not control this wealth: it controlled me. [...] Wealth creates opportunities, but it immobilises a person's creative potential, and to the disintegration of a person's individuality as such. That is what this cruel tyranny demonstrates – the tyranny of wealth. And now I have been reborn. I am now an average upper-middle-class person, whose purpose is to live and not just to own things. The struggle is not just to acquire property, but to become oneself – for the right to be an individual. [...] This suggests that the only possible and right choice is the choice of freedom.

This echoes Václav Havel's strictures against the consumerist West,[22] but with the added poignancy that Khodorkovsky was not some isolated intellectual but a man who had been one of the richest people in the world, owning a company that could affect the fate of millions. The narrative of prison as retreat rather than penitentiary, allowing a period of self-reflection and self-realisation, resonates more broadly. There is a tension between penitence, the recognition of wrongdoing and the desire for self-improvement, and self-realisation, the attempt by an individual to find their fate. In Khodorkovsky's case there is no admission that he was guilty in a legal sense, but only that he had been mistaken in an existential sense; now that the burden of defending his property had been lifted, he could realise himself in a new sphere.

He moved on to a disquisition on the appropriate form of government for Russia, insisting that the Russian political tradition is artificial. Russia has always been at the crossroads of civilisations, but for the most part it is a European country. Therefore European political institutions that envisage the separation of powers can be applied in a limited manner to this country.

He then makes the important statement:

However, the other side of the coin should not be ignored. Russian people have traditionally regarded the state as a supreme power that gives them faith and hope. This power cannot be applied until we stop seeing it as supreme. Russian history tells us that the loss of this special, supra-rational respect for the state will inevitably bring the country to chaos, revolt and revolution.

He distinguished between 'authority' and 'governance' (what we call the administrative regime). Government was carried out by officials and bureaucrats who were 'merely mortal'. They could not evoke the patriotism of the people: 'No true patriot would give his life for a bunch of bureaucrats who are only interested in feathering their own nests.' In the Yukos affair the bureaucrats had been let loose and pursued policies that undermined the sanctity of the state. He was unreserved in his condemnation of 'the bureaucracy':

The destruction of Yukos shows that the unrestrained bureaucrats care nothing for the interests of the state [...] They only know that the state machinery exists to promote their interests [...] That is why the Yukos affair is not a conflict between business and government. It is a politically and commercially motivated attack by one company (represented by state officials) on another company. The state, in this particular case, is a hostage to the interests of certain individuals wielding the powers of state officials.

The attempt to manage everything, in his view, was likely to render the country unmanageable because it was 'inconsistent with the traditional rule of authority and the laws of complex systems'. He went further, warning that 'soon the only partner to this omnivorous bureaucracy will be a ferocious, amorphous crowd': 'Then an unmanageable democracy will come into being, with all its innumerable disasters and suffering.' This was a powerful insight that may yet come to pass at the end of the Putin era. In particular, he pitied those in authority who sincerely believed that the action against Yukos was the right thing to do, warning: 'they will eventually realise that political persecution and forced redistribution of property cannot be combined with modern economic development.'

He stressed the political nature of the case:

> My oppressors know that there isn't any solid evidence at all in the criminal case against me – but that doesn't matter. I could always be charged with setting fire to the Manezh building, or plotting an economic counter-revolution. I have been told that the authorities want to keep me in jail for as long as possible: five years, say, or longer. They fear that I will seek revenge.

He would not act like the Count of Monte Cristo and seek revenge:

> Unlike my persecutors, I have realised that making big money is far from the only goal in a person's life (and probably not that important). The time of big bucks is over for me. Now that I have disposed of the burden of the past, I am going to work for the good of the generations who will rule the country very soon – the generations who will usher in new values and new hopes.

As in his earlier letter, Khodorkovsky was careful not to attack Putin personally, but his critique was coming closer to the president. He lambasted elements in the Kremlin for dismantling Yukos and warned that their bureaucratic attempt to manage society would fail. He continued to disassociate himself from his 'oligarchic' past and now recast himself as a Soviet-style political exile. He did not specify how he planned to 'work for the good' of the new generation, but he presented himself as the democratic alternative to the existing bureaucracy that used patriotic slogans to expropriate property and to enrich itself.

FIRST INTERVIEW FROM JAIL

These themes were taken up in his interview published in the Russian version of *Newsweek* at the end of January 2005.[23] He had not anticipated being held in custody for so long, noting that his incarceration depended not on the courts but on 'a few officials and businessmen close to them', afraid that he would seek revenge for the loss of YNG: 'These are people with a criminal mentality. They judge people by their own standards.'[24] Khodorkovsky argued that Putin had been deceived in late October 2003, having been told that Khodorkovsky was planning to become senator for the

Evenk autonomous *okrug*, which would have given him immunity from prosecution. In the event, Khodorkovsky supported his colleague Shakhnovsky to become the region's representative to the Federation Council.

He agreed that in part the reason for his arrest was his active involvement in politics and his attempt to advance his own people into the Duma, but went on:

> I am personally in favour of a strong state, but consider that the strength of the state lies not in a large number of powerful officials, but in the trust of the people, in the ability to attract and use the best people to resolve tasks, in the competition and mutual accountability of state and social institutions. I supported various political parties and social organisations since I am convinced that our society needs various opinions and views, and our country needs a strong opposition not controlled by the authorities.

He then specified why he had been arrested:

> I am now absolutely convinced that the main reason for the 'Yukos affair' was the desire of a group of four–five particular individuals to take over a large and successful oil company. Politics in general and state policy in particular was used as a excuse to convince the country's leadership to use the full power of the state to redistribute property, ignoring the law. Similar things had happened in the last decade, but never before had the object of attack been such a large corporation, and never before had the attackers been such high-ranking individuals.[25]

He admitted that his 'principled and unyielding' attitude in regard to the authorities as well as mistakes in business and social activities had provoked the attack. He went on to say:

> If it was not for my principles I would not be in jail now but abroad or somewhere else, but I did not want to do this and could not do it. Earlier I could, but at a certain moment I felt myself more of a citizen than a businessman.[26]

He noted that in jail he could say less, but he was heard more clearly. 'If I had emigrated, I would have been taken as no more than an oligarch [...] Today it is hard for me physically, but no one can say that I do not have the moral right to speak.'[27]

The discussion moved to Russia's constitutional order in the light of Khodorkovsky's arguments two years earlier that parliament ought to have the power not just to appoint but also to dismiss the prime minister. He now argued that 'Russia needs a concept for a new political system', but revisions should be introduced only after much thought. He argued that the president, as 'guarantor of national stability', should remain 'above the political fray', but some presidential powers should be transferred to the parliamentary majority, above all formation of the cabinet, which should be responsible for the economy. Part of the government would be responsible to parliament, and part to the president: a scheme that already operated, with the security bloc of ministers directly responsible to the president. It was Khodorkovsky's earlier promotion of the idea of a parliamentary republic that had acted as the trigger for the anti-Yukos campaign. As for the appointment of governors (their election had been abolished in December 2004), he argued: 'The authorities are trying to turn all politicians into appointed officials, and thus to "freeze" the ruling class so as not to allow outsiders to enter. [...] This is a typical stagnation project', comparable to the Soviet system in the early 1980s. Touching on the theme of his earlier letters, he agreed that big business should apologise to the people for what it had done in the 1990s, but he extended the act of repentance to encompass the whole 'ruling corporation, which is responsible for the market reforms of the 1990s being anti-social, as a result of which the people's trust in liberal ideas and values was destroyed'.[28]

Asked what he would say to Putin if given the opportunity, he answered:

> Mr President, do not allow power [*vlast'*] to be devalued and profaned. Do not allow it to be transformed into an instrument for the redistribution of property and for the advancement of the private interests of the bureaucracy. This will only multiply the mistakes and problems of the 1990s.[29]

FREEDOM THE RUSSIAN WAY

In response to letters from readers of the *Bolshoi gorod* (*Big City*) magazine, just days before being sentenced in May 2005, Khodorkovsky discussed his understanding of Russian freedom while explaining why a revolution in Russia would be disastrous.[30] He began with the paradoxical statement: 'I am grateful to prison because it has given me a new understanding of freedom – the freedom that is inside a person.' 'This is a freedom', he argued, 'that is difficult to achieve, but for that equally hard to be taken or lost.' As in his earlier communications, he warned against dependence on the material world: 'If a person is critically dependent on something beyond himself, he is already not free.' For him, that had earlier been money, but he now understood:

'When you are forced to think about the fate of your capital every waking day, this is dependence, which means slavery.'

He provided a classical religious understanding of freedom, and one that typified much dissident thinking in the late Soviet period:

> Freedom in my understanding is, first and foremost, the opportunity for a person to think without internal limits, and to act according to his ethical code. In that sense, any political institution is merely the striving of mankind towards freedom, but in no way the source of freedom itself. And even in the most undemocratic environment, a person can be much freer than under the conditions of the broadest democracy. [...] No matter what kind of political system we have had in our country, there has always been freedom and free people in Russia. [...] And that is why freedom cannot be imported the way technology or a natural resource can be.

Thus freedom is not dependent on political institutions but on the inner development and consciousness of the individual. Indeed, for some an authoritarian system, by forcing moral choices, actually enhances the quality of freedom; but faced by legal and administrative arbitrariness, it can only be a partial resolution of the problem.

Khodorkovsky then moved on to the second theme of his article.

> Where a Russian revolution is concerned, it has always been – and remains – a dangerous game on the fine line [echoing Pushkin] between limitless Russian freedom and equally immense Russian slavery. The Russian is always radical and often marginalised – in both positive and negative ways. And that is why the concept of 'revolution' is sacred for him, even if formally he is a counter-revolutionary. It is no wonder the country is dreaming of revolution, even though right now there are no objective grounds for one to occur. But I don't plan to get involved in this game. A revolution in Russia always involves a lot of bloodshed.

This anti-revolutionary theme is one that Khodorkovsky shared with Putin, and it is deeply embedded as part of Russia's post-Communist consciousness. This visceral revulsion against Jacobin-Leninism, shared by figures across the political spectrum, suggests that a distinctive lesson of the Soviet experience has been learnt: violence begets violence, and in the end the country loses. Khodorkovsky's argument, moreover, represents a rupture with the traditional thinking of the Russian intelligentsia, characterised by extreme utopian or nihilistic aspirations.[31] This was a salutary lesson, in that the faults of the intelligentsia were ultimately transcended by an outsider who developed a critique from the perspective of the rising bourgeoisie. This further isolated him from the intelligentsia, although his status as victim was respected (and thus reified). Equally, the reviled dissidents of the Soviet era came into their own during perestroika, but instead of inheriting a free and democratic Russia they were once again marginalised by the brutality of the capitalist revolution. By reaching back into the dissident experience, Khodorkovsky sought to humanise capitalist democracy in Russia.

Four key themes emerge from Khodorkovsky's early writings. First, the business phase of his life was decisively over, and he had now transformed himself into an impartial observer of Russian development. Second, Khodorkovsky advanced a critique of the trajectory of Russian post-Communist political evolution. The architects of Russia's transformation – the liberals – in Khodorkovsky's view failed to engage with the subject of the transformation – the Russian people – and hence they had become politically marginalised. Third, his position became a more clearly delineated one of national liberalism, defending a role for the state as an instrument of modernisation. Fourth, Khodorkovsky turned inwards and defined a new concept of freedom and responsibility for himself. These themes would be further developed in his later writings, to which we now turn.

CHAPTER 10

RUSSIA IS WORTHY
OF FREEDOM

In a pattern that is all too familiar in Russian history, a prominent individual falls foul of the authorities and suffers exile or incarceration, and from that position of relative freedom is able to comment on the system. Khodorkovsky issued numerous missives examining the Russian condition. With his business stolen, Khodorkovsky's other persona was able to emerge – that of a member of the intelligentsia, critical of the authorities but willing to offer constructive criticism and plans. Khodorkovsky avoided personal criticism of Putin and focused his comments on the system and general philosophical problems. In this way he maintained personal dignity and intellectual integrity in adversity. His main argument was that the liberal reforms of the 1990s had given the country freedom but not justice. Khodorkovsky's thinking in this period was paradoxical: while claiming innate rights to freedom and development on the personal and collective level, he remained Soviet in appealing to the principles of social justice and in conceptualising private property not as an inalienable right but as an ethical responsibility.

THE LEFT TURN

From August 2005 Khodorkovsky's writings take on a new tone. His article 'Left turn' reviewed Russia's post-Communist political development and the country's likely future.[1] The key issues were the reconciliation of freedom with justice and the legitimation of privatisation. Belkovsky admitted contributing to the text but denied being the main author.[2] Belkovsky had moved into opposition to Putin, considering him too much of a neo-liberal, and instead called for a more socialist strategy. He was disappointed that the Yukos affair had degenerated into little more than a tawdry struggle over property.

Khodorkovsky began with the striking assertion that 'It is generally accepted today that authoritarian trends are returning to the country', but he disagreed with those who associated this with Putin and his group of 'Leningraders'. Instead Khodorkovsky presented an analysis of the 1996 presidential election, a theme that he had touched on in earlier missives. He noted that in the dreary January of 1996 he, like most other liberals, had been disheartened by the strong showing of Zyuganov's Communists in the parliamentary election held the previous month, and he feared that Zyuganov would win the presidency later that year. Yeltsin's popularity was in single digits and he was ill and depressed. The optimistic tide of of 1990 and 1991 had turned: 'By the mid-1990s it had become evident that the miracle of democracy was not working – freedom did not bring us happiness.' Khodorkovsky now criticised the way that the liberals had manipulated the election, marking the turning point in the erosion of Russian democracy. Honest elections, whatever their outcome, Khodorkovsky suggested, would have averted the emergence of a gulf between the people and the liberal elite.

A whole new set of questions had emerged. He listed these as follows. *Justice*: 'Who should get hold of Soviet socialist property, which three generations had created through blood and sweat?' While people not known for their brains or education made millions, academicians, pilots and others were plunged into poverty. 'Does that not suggest that Soviet socialism, although thrice blessed and maligned at the same time, was not so bad after all?' Khodorkovsky here reveals, like Putin, a broad streak of neo-Sovietism: not so much for the ideology but for its social achievements. *Sense of national dignity*: 'Why were we respected when we lived in the bad Soviet Union [...] yet now in the era of freedom we are looked down on as stupid and penniless?' *Morality in politics*: He noted that people had chafed under the rule of Communist officialdom, 'but did we deserve rulers who are ten times more cynical and a hundred times more thievish than the Party bosses who in comparison look like retired country grandfathers and grandmothers?' *Fear in the face of an uncertain future and unclear goals*: The Russian people had been cast out from their 'dilapidated old Zaporozhets vehicle and had been promised a Mercedes, but instead we were simply tossed out on a muddy road at the end of the world'.

It seemed that only Zyuganov knew the answers to these questions. It was for this reason that in April 1996 the 13 businessmen penned the letter 'Get out of the impasse', proposing that Yeltsin remain president with Zyuganov as prime minister. Social and economic policy, the letter argued, had to become more leftist because of the inevitable post-election conflicts: 'We needed a left turn so that we could reconcile freedom with justice' where there were a few winners and a great mass who felt they had lost during liberalisation. Instead of this compromise, a virulent anti-Communist strategy was adopted:

> millions were poured into the machine to manipulate public opinion that would ensure a Yeltsin victory – unquestionably an authoritarian strategy. The values of the late 1990s were formed at that time, and the most important of them was that the end justifies the means.

'It was at this juncture that journalists changed from being the shapers of public opinion into becoming the servants of their owners, and when independent public institutions became the voice of their sponsors.'

It was impossible, Khodorkovsky argued, 'to prolong the right–liberal Yeltsin regime by democratic means'; this was also the case in 2000, 'when it became clear that the regime could not remain in power without compromises on democracy'. Putin, according to Khodorkovsky, came to power on the back of a gigantic 'bluff': that questions on the agenda since 1995 were being resolved when in fact nothing changed, and political technologies were used to ensure the success of the strategy 'Stability in power and stability in the country'. The contradiction between expectations and reality came to a head in early 2005, with mass demonstrations against the monetisation of benefits, and 'the people's desire for justice and the achievement of change becoming firmer than ever'. Hard questions about the past remained unanswered. The people would not be deceived again, hence the 'Successor 2008' project would be problematic:

> Kremlin spin doctors know that this state course can only continue by undemocratic means. [...] They are convinced that the left would win if there were an honest and fair election. The screws are therefore being tightened [...] electoral law is being changed so that all parties except those that are 102 per cent controlled by the president's administration.[3]

The Kremlin could try to block the course of history, but it lacked the resolve to apply full-blooded authoritarian measures, although it can close down papers and 'seize the assets of those who do not toe the line'. While in most former-socialist-bloc countries leftist parties had come to power in the mid-1990s, they had been able to 'link freedom with justice'. 'As a result the authorities in these countries were able to avoid a severe legitimacy crisis, the crisis that usually marks the start of all revolutions.' The post-Soviet states did not turn to the left in time and engage in real discussions of national priorities; instead they pursued the chimera of 'stability'. This led to the various 'rose', 'orange' and 'tulip' revolutions. In Ukraine the 'orange' authorities were raising the issue of revising privatisation: 'if the question of the legality of the privatisation process had been raised by the authorities five or six years ago there might not have been an orange revolution.' Arguing that the coming to power of a left–nationalist government was inevitable, the letter insisted that

> A left turn in Russia is as inevitable as it is necessary. Putin does not need to do much to allow the left turn to take place. All that he needs to do is to leave within the constitutional framework of his term and ensure democratic conditions for the conduct of the next elections. Only this will guarantee the prospect of sustained democratic development for the country without upheavals and the risk of disintegration.

Putin of course did not leave, and in 2007–8 he engineered the succession to create the tandem, and in due course, in 2012, he once again returned to the Kremlin, exacerbating the legitimacy crisis that Khodorkovsky had identified earlier.

Khodorkovsky's analysis provoked considerable controversy.[4] His attempt to broker some sort of deal between the main competitors in the 1996 election was a pragmatic and realistic response. Primakov's government in 1998–9 demonstrated that a leftist government could work with a right-wing president. Ahead of the 2003 elections Berezovsky proposed a similar arrangement when he called on the Communists to join forces with the liberals. The letter also argued that it was time 'to end the denigration of the Soviet period of Russian history'; but at the same time 'the great ideas of freedom, civility, justice, right and truth' should not be discredited – although the Soviet period did just that.[5] Khodorkovsky was also criticised for exaggerating the prevalence of leftist sentiments in society, although there was support for extensive welfare.[6] Putin's administration reflected these sentiments, ensuring the payment of wages, improved living standards, poverty reduction, restraints on the unmitigated power of capital in the political sphere, and extensive social spending. Quite why the 'entrenchment of a class of effective property owners' would bring about a 'left turn' is unclear, and how the 'left turn' would help legitimise property is no more convincing.

Liberals reacted angrily to the letter. In a considered study Sergei Mitrokhin, the deputy head of Yabloko and in June 2008 Yavlinsky's successor, argued that while coalition politics made some sense in Western countries, in Russian conditions it meant allying with the unreconstructed nationalism and leftism of the KPRF, which had nothing in common with liberalism.[7] Khodorkovsky was right to argue that only a left–right conjuncture could combine aspirations for democracy and social justice, and numerous surveys confirmed this core combination of the Russian value system. Lev Gudkov, of the Levada-Center polling agency, demonstrated that there had been no revolutionary transformation and instead Russia was engaged 'with the slow, very slow, generations-long decay of the Soviet system'.[8] Nevertheless, social democracy remained weak in contemporary Russia.[9] Instead, some of Khodorkovsky's ideas were reflected in Rodina's programme, notably in Sergei Glazev's idea for a natural rent on big business to restore some sense of social justice.[10] RSPP vice president Igor Yurgens argued that he personally was not yet ready for a 'left turn' if there was not equally an opportunity to turn to the right: 'If there is no such possibility, then that will be a dead-end path.'[11] A left turn at this point would only increase the greed of officialdom. For the broadcaster and KPRF member Sergei Dorenko, 'The left turn has already taken place, the country has long been going leftwards.' He argued that in 2003 the Duma turned left, and in 2004 the president followed:

> The thing is that Putin always proceeds with anti-Putinist slogans. That is his essence, and people like this. Putin is politician number one because of his position, and Khodorkovsky is politician number 2, and not only because he is jail.[12]

REALISM OR FATALISM

Soon after publishing the 'Left turn' article, Khodorkovsky issued his sharpest criticism of Putinism:

> The present Kremlin regime has exhausted itself, and its days are numbered. In place of the decayed and disintegrating Putinist system a new generation of leaders must emerge, thinking not of a shameful place at the nomenklatura's trough but of the fate of Russia in the third millennium.[13]

Khodorkovsky still anticipated running in the Duma by-election, hence the inflammatory language. Beginning with his interview with a French journal at the beginning of autumn 2005, and again in his return to the themes of his 'Left turn', the language became noticeably sharper.

While waiting for the outcome of his appeal, the journal *Politique Internationale* published a wide-ranging interview.[14] Asked about the development of civil society in Russia, Khodorkovsky praised the role that the Russian people had played in history, including the overthrow of Communism in 1991:

> I totally disagree with the idea that Russian citizens are unable to be involved in politics. [...] Civil society is just in its formative stages in Russia but it is developing much faster than the Kremlin would like it to do.

He warned that developments were far from irreversible and that

> if no infrastructure is created, we run the risk of losing the next generation. The best brains will leave Russia simply because intelligent, talented and ambitious people will not want to live in a country in which bureaucratic tyranny dominates, as it does today.

He then launched a broadside against the regime:

> Putin's system definitely excludes any public development today. The system needs obedient actors, not creative people. Therefore, as long as Russia is under the reign of this regime, no real progress will be possible. [...] Today absolutely everything – from railroad troops to days off in prisons – depends on the tastes, mood, complexes and quirks of one person. It is sufficient simply to take a look at those who hold key positions in the government: only people coming from Putin's 'narrow circle', who carry out the decisions of the Kremlin without caring about anything.

Asked about what system he would like to see, Khodorkovsky returned to his idea of a presidential–parliamentary republic. He then introduced a new theme, the development of 'true federalism', which included a return to the election of regional leaders (abolished in December 2004) to allow the development of 'new responsible regional elites', and he condemned the bureaucrats 'parachuted in from Moscow', who think only about 'lining their pockets'.

Khodorkovsky noted that the government's failures in social policy would provoke dissatisfaction:

So, in fact, we don't need to do anything to create an influential opposition party – the Kremlin itself will foster its creation through its confused and unpopular policies thereby causing all people of goodwill, both on the 'left' and 'right' wings, to rise up against it.

He went on to warn that Russia's reliance on natural resources was 'not just "risky", it is suicidal!' It depressed growth rates, inhibited the development of a post-industrial economy and encouraged 'irresponsible and corrupt officials' in the much-vaunted 'power vertical'. It would ensure that the state administrative system, which was 'just a shadow of what a real administration should be', would continue to dominate, leading to 'stagnation and degeneration'.

On foreign policy Khodorkovsky argued that 'Russia today does not have the resources necessary to be a world superpower', and while it should concentrate on being a regional power it should also try 'to become the political and intellectual leader of a group of countries that do not want to join the American or the Chinese bloc', a new incarnation of the old non-aligned movement. Europe was Russia's 'historical and cultural partner', but the country should have no illusions about joining the EU soon: 'Russia feels comfortable where it is in the historical role of a natural keeper of the heartland and as a guidepost between Europe and Asia.' Russia should not join NATO but should develop friendly partnership with it, while developing its armed forces. As for the fundamental question about whether 'Western states should be tougher with President Putin', Khodorkovsky gave the wise answer:

Western leaders should deal with Putin while proceeding from the interests of their own countries that invested them with power. As far as Russia is concerned, it should solve its problems itself, mobilising the creative potential of its people and not asking Western countries to become its sponsors, babysitters, or teachers.

ANOTHER LEFT TURN

These points were developed in a second 'left turn' piece, this time written in the corrective colony and responding to the discussion elicited by the first.[15] There is an almost unanimous consensus among even Khodorkovsky's supporters that the article was 'awful and illiterate', allegedly reflecting his isolation from real life in prison.[16] Such a characterisation is unfair. Khodorkovsky sought to answer the following four questions:

i.   Are there effective contemporary opposition forces in Russia today with leftist or left–liberal views?

ii. What is the practical economic programme of the 'left turn'?

iii. Does the country have adequate human potential to ensure a left turn and the realisation of its political and economic programme?

And finally:

iv. Prisoner Khodorkovsky and comrades, do you really think that a change of power in Russia will relieve your fate?

He started with the final question, noting that the 2008 succession raised the issue of what the new leader could do for Russia. He admitted that he owed Russia a lot:

> In the 1970s and 1980s, it gave me an education I can be proud of. In the 1990s, it made me the richest (according to *Forbes*) post-Soviet person. In this decade it took away my property and put me in jail where I had the opportunity to receive a second education, this time human and humane. And I can say that the people who are getting ready to run Russia in two and a half or three years must understand that the parasitic approach is no longer viable. The country is no longer competitive and the reserves of stability laid down by the Soviet Union have run out.[17]

He then listed the major problems that would face Putin's successor: demographic paralysis, crisis in the engineering sector, a systemic crisis of the defence industries, the ageing of the natural-science base, the 'effective loss of Moscow's control over the North Caucasus', 'the collapse of the Russian armed forces' and the 'paralysis of the security system'. To deal with these issues a new political group needed to come to power, with a long-term view of developmental tasks. This would have to be accompanied by a new, creative, mobilisation of the people:

> This can be achieved by a qualitative change in state and social policy, a rebirth of democratic methods of governing the country, including state paternalism as an instrument for unifying the state and the people, acknowledging that the state and economy exist for the people. [...] That is why a left turn is also necessary. To overcome the pathological, existential alienation between elites and the people, the

authorities and those they rule. And not, as some theoreticians of 'Putin's stability' suggest, so that the opposition, winning the parliamentary elections, would let Khodorkovsky out of prison. Without overcoming that alienation, no integrated national idea is possible, and without a national idea, there will be no salvation or rebirth of the country. If people don't like the word 'left', let them find another word. The essence of the turn does not change because of it.[18]

In the event the 2008 succession operation established a new–old leadership, with Medvedev as president and Putin as prime minister. Khodorkovsky once again insisted that a left turn in Russian politics was inevitable and, indeed, had started some time ago. The sooner this 'leftist energy' was incorporated into the system, the better – 'the more constructive and less dangerous it will be.' If the current ruling elite is democratically transformed, 'we will have a peaceful transfer of power. If they delay it, and all the more provoke the less responsible part of the elite to pursue an extremist scenario to justify their authoritarianism, the consequences for the country will be disastrous and absolutely unpredictable.'[19] He outlined a 12-year plan, including the establishment of a presidential–parliamentary republic, the rebirth of genuine federalism, and the 'creation of genuine local government'. He advocated financial incentives to encourage larger families, a measure Putin announced in his 'state of the nation' speech on 10 May 2006. In broad terms, he advocated measures that would achieve 'The transition from the economy of the oil pipeline to the knowledge economy'. One of the key goals of the programme was to ensure the 'Preservation and strengthening [of] its present borders', by ensuring that investment was spread across the country. This required the re-establishment practically from scratch of the armed forces, and the development of education and basic science.

He defended the transformative agenda of the Yeltsin years:

> It cannot be said that the privatisation of the 1990s was absolutely economically ineffective. Yes, many of the largest enterprises in Russia were sold for symbolic prices. But it should not be forgotten that the main goal of that privatisation was not the rapid filling of the exchequer from the sale of those companies, but the establishment of the institution of effective ownership. This task was completely fulfilled.[20]

He then described at length the changes that he had wrought at Yukos:

> I remember what Yukos was like when I joined it in 1996. The company was in relatively satisfactory condition in comparison with other state oil giants. Nonetheless,

oil production was falling by 15 per cent a year, debts to contractors amounted to about $3 billion, wages were six months in arrears and employees were either grumbling to themselves or complaining loudly, the stealing at every turn was frightful. When I left Yukos (in 2003), salaries had reached 30,000 roubles per month, there were no delays in pay and tax payments on all levels reached $3.5 billion–$4 billion per year, and that was when oil stood at $27–30 per barrel, and not $60 as now. Because of privatisation real management was established, which simply did not exist in the era of the 'red directors'.[21]

Privatisation had improved corporate management, but it was 'ineffective politically and socially' since the great mass of the Russian people considered it unjust. He returned to the idea of a legitimating mechanism, a 'windfall tax' on part of a company's turnover at the time of privatisation, which was to be hypothecated for such tasks as stimulating the birth rate. On payment of the tax, the owners were to receive a 'safe conduct pass', and ownership would be considered legal and honest. This would be a 'conscious pact' between the state and owners of big business. For business, Khodorkovsky insisted that it was 'better to give up part today than everything tomorrow', and it would render the legitimisation process open and immune to corruption. He ended with a call for a 'genuine modernisation project', without which Russia would not be able to survive the new century: 'The outline of that project is already visible. There, just beyond the left turn.' These modernisation ideas were to be taken up by Medvedev. The letter looked remarkably like a presidential manifesto. With 'the era of big money' behind him, Khodorkovsky was transformed from an oligarch into a potential national leader.

THE MEDVEDEV YEARS

The rivulet of commentary turned into a flood during the Medvedev years. Khodorkovsky immediately welcomed the new president, and although some of his analysis could be considered naive, Khodorkovsky remained loyal to his vision of a strong and worthy Russia with a free citizenry, independent courts and a dynamic and just business sector. This was to be achieved by evolutionary methods, and hence he considered the Medvedevite option of transcending authoritarianism from within a viable option. This is a coherent position, and it did not mean moderating his critique of the Putinite system, but denoted readiness to embrace within-system change when it appeared. Khodorkovsky was a more sophisticated thinker than even his supporters suspected. Although he may have been misguided on a number of issues, such as the need for a 'left turn' to legitimise capitalist democracy, he was an acute analyst of the dilemmas facing modernisation in Russia.

Khodorkovsky conducted a series of landmark dialogues with the writers Boris Akunin, Boris Strugatsky and Lyudmila Ulitskaya in which he defended his views, while adding more of a personal touch. Discussion ranged over Khodorkovsky's life experience and his time with Yukos, the way that prison had changed him, and reflections on Russia's fate. The constant theme is that in a certain sense 'prison makes a person free'.[22] Some of the questioning is tough, as when Akunin takes Khodorkovsky to task for his attack on Russian liberalism.[23] This interview first appeared in the October 2008 edition of *Esquire* magazine through the exchange of notes with Akunin from the Chita isolator. Khodorkovsky noted that he was not 'especially a liberal', and instead stressed:

> I'm for a strong state in Russia, and I have a whole series of arguments. I'm for an active industrial policy, a social state: in short, the Scandinavian model. Russia is a huge country with difficult climatic conditions, in a complex geopolitical environment. A weak state simply will not be able effectively to deal with all the challenges.

The strong state was to be complemented by the rule of law:

> On the other hand, so that it does not degenerate into yet another totalitarian deformity, a strong state must not only be balanced by a strong civil society but must have an impeccably working system of checks and balances: separation of powers, public control, a strong opposition. In other words, a strong state must be super-legally based, if one can put it that way.[24]

The discussion also ranged over issues of love, life and death, and revealed aspects of Khodorkovsky's character that had not been so clearly expressed in public before. The journal was instantly snapped up from newsstands. Ulitskaya queried his orientation towards governmental action, to which Khodorkovsky admits that he is indeed a 'statist': 'I believe that in the next 20–40 years (I won't look further) the state must play a bigger part in Russian life (Russian society) than it does today. However, I am deeply opposed to an "iron hand".'[25]

In June 2009 Khodorkovsky issued a fundamental statement of his reformist position in an article called 'Russia awaiting justice'. It came in response to the new president's condemnation of 'legal nihilism' and his contradictory attempts to achieve 'modernisation'. Khodorkovsky warned that 'Until Russia has independent courts, it will not have freedom, which, as they say, is "better than unfreedom"', the words used by Medvedev during his election campaign.[26] The article provoked a range of responses focusing on how to liberate the judicial system from subservience to the authorities. The final article in the series disputed Khodorkovsky's view that the creation of independent courts did not require institutional reforms or societal changes.[27] Khodorkovsky admitted: 'Maybe I was too naive in 2003 in believing that certain democratic and legal institutions had already become entrenched in the country.' For his critics, that naivety was once again in evidence in his evaluation of the tandem. Responding to the question about whether he saw a difference between Putin and Medvedev, he responded:

> Many commentators and experts go to extremes. The implication of what they say is that either Medvedev is merely a puppet in Putin's hands or he is just waiting for a chance to rid himself of Putin's influence. I think Medvedev is certainly different from Putin, but at the same time I have no doubt that the current president is completely loyal to the previous one. Will he be able to pursue his own policy, will he deem that to be necessary for himself? These are questions to which I don't have an answer yet.[28]

Khodorkovsky applied a factional model to explain his downfall:

> I know that the Yukos events are the result of a power struggle between various forces around Putin, with the relatively liberal forces on the one side and those that one could call representatives of the security forces on the other.

He argued that 'If President Medvedev realizes his promises to work for independent and fair courts, there will definitely be a fundamental change', although he fully acknowledged the 'piecemeal character' of the changes. He went so far as to argue that 'I think Putin planned for this to happen. The bandit-like style of part of his followers clearly seems to have become uncomfortable for him.'[29] In the event, Putin increasingly identified with the 'hardliners' and unceremoniously displaced Medvedev in September 2011 when he announced his return to the presidency (see Chapter 11).

This does not mean that intra-systemic evolutionary change was a mere chimera. This is why Khodorkovsky reacted positively to Medvedev's programmatic article 'Forward, Russia!', published on 10 September 2009. The article mounted a powerful critique, all the more so since it came from the president, characterising Russian social life as archaic, 'one that unfortunately combines all the shortcomings of the Soviet system and all the difficulties of contemporary life'. Medvedev argued that the country was economically backward and distorted by dependence on extractive industries, and he once again condemned corruption and the 'paternalist mindset' prevalent in Russian society. The fundamental question was whether Russia, with its 'primitive economy' and 'chronic corruption', has a future?[30] Medvedev attacked not Putin but the system that Putin represented, a balancing act that blunted his message. Khodorkovsky noted the passivity of Medvedev's approach and instead argued the need for an agent of change: 'Who will carry out this modernisation?', to which he responded that 'it takes a whole stratum, a real modernising class, to achieve genuine modernisation', and he outlined a 'Generation M' that could achieve this, a group that 'cannot help disliking the power vertical'. He was aware that many dismissed Medvedev's initiative as no more than the 'good cop' act within the tandem, but he insisted that some passages 'suit me just fine, as in the unequivocal assertion that no modernisation was worth human victims on its altar (for example Peter I and Stalin)'.[31]

Khodorkovsky condemned the way that the 'oil curse' allowed the 'authorities to maintain social stability without modernization up to about 2015'. His interlocutor reminded Khodorkovsky about the way that prisoners begin to fear freedom, to which he responded:

> It is a little scary on the outside, because freedom is responsibility, and the burden of responsibility of a rational being is never very light. Our people have long lived in the 'zone' [the colloquial term for the camp system]. [...] but I believe the system will change. [...] Russia is worthy of freedom.[32]

In a regretful article early in 2010, Khodorkovsky noted that 'the past decade started out on optimistic note', with the economy developing and state institutions working more reliably. This all changed. 'Today, many people recall with sadness that Russia once had a real, working parliament, where social and business interests engaged in dialogue, where compromises were sought and found.'[33]

In March 2010 he talked about 'the System' ('Sistema'), the interlocking networks of Russia's judicial and law-enforcement networks.[34]

> You don't know a thing about the System until you find yourself in its claws. The System is, in essence, a single enterprise, whose business is legalised violence. The enterprise is enormous, with a huge number of internal conflicts and clashing interests.

He conjured up its despotic and implacable character as follows:

> The System is like the conveyor belt of a gigantic plant, which lives by a logic of its own that does not submit, in general, to any kind of regulation from outside. [...] Its objective is not to establish the truth, but to carry out its own internal agenda.[35]

In an interview in August 2010 Khodorkovsky stressed:

> I was not a robber in the past, just as I'm not a martyr today. Besides, I don't like stereotypes. It was almost a foregone conclusion that I would become active socially and a patron of the arts. Unfortunately, this had an unpleasant side effect: my public involvement was seen as an attack on the Russian system of power. I had no interest in being an enemy of the Kremlin, or a martyr or hero. In retrospect, however, I wouldn't change anything about my life.[36]

In September 2010 he wrote a letter in support of Yevgeniya Chirikova, the leader of the Ecodefence movement to preserve the Khimki forest against the Moscow–St Petersburg highway. She stressed that 'Khimki, corruption, Khodorkovsky's imprisonment – are connected'.[37] She would go on to become one of the most charismatic figures in the opposition protests against electoral manipulation and Putin's return in 2011–12. In the same month Khodorkovsky warned the new David Cameron-led coalition government in Britain not to establish improved relations with Russia without first establishing 'principled conditions' over democracy, civil liberties and human rights: 'I, as a Russian political prisoner, would very much like Britain to understand the fate of 150 million people, capable and talented, that are searching for their way out of the darkness of totalitarianism into the light of freedom.'[38]

COMMENTATOR ON RUSSIAN POLITICS

A number of themes emerge from Khodorkovsky's writings. The early texts argued that the oligarchs and the Kremlin 'democrats' in the 1990s were jointly responsible for the crisis of liberalism, although in different ways. Big business had not been able to withstand the neo-liberal approach. Quite how it could have done so is a matter that Khodorkovsky does not explore. In 'The crisis of Russian liberalism', 'Property and freedom' and 'Left turn' he stresses the enormous inequalities of wealth, accompanied by advocacy of a policy of state paternalism. He also talks about the need to legitimate the process of privatisation, and by doing so to establish the foundations on which a secure property regime could be established. The mechanism to achieve this legitimation remains rather vague, although he does suggest that a rotation of power and the coming to power of a leftist government would secure the political basis for a permanent settlement of the property question, accompanied by some sort of restitution payment. Khodorkovsky's writings assert the belief that a new 'social contract' had to be forged between the authorities and the people, based on a paternalistic state run by a selfless and patriotic officialdom. Another part of the contract involved the operation of the market and its associated property rights; these had to be 'normalised', digested by the public as the only way to live. Khodorkovsky's focus was on the technical legitimation of the privatisations of the 1990s, but the deeper problem is the concern that capitalism itself had not yet been accepted as legitimate by Russian public consciousness.

Khodorkovsky's critique was directed not only against the corrupt and self-seeking bureaucracy of the Putin era, or the mistakes made by big business leaders in taking advantage of the weakness of the state in the 1990s, but also the liberals of that period and later. This critique of the right takes two forms. The first is of the economic liberals for the way in which they shaped the privatisation process, and their lack of concern for the social consequences of their programme. The second critique focused on the inadequacies of the political liberals, the leaders of the various parties who failed to connect with the people or to offer a viable programme. The partial exception is the Yabloko party. Mitrokhin insisted: 'Liberalism cannot enjoy any success or influence in Russia without recourse to the ideology of social justice,' and hence had long ago understood what Khodorkovsky was now saying about 'Russia being a country with very strong left tendencies'.[39] Khodorkovsky, however, paid little attention to them and instead placed his hopes on leftist forces, despite the lack of evidence that appropriate left parties were available. Khodorkovsky's interventions were greeted with little greater warmth on the liberal side of the political spectrum than they were by Kremlin functionaries. His position, however, is logical if one accepts his structural argument about the need for the bourgeois business class to shake itself free not only from the era of criminal oligarchy, but also from its subordination to political liberalism.

Khodorkovsky's concerns were in part shared by democratic statists within the regime, those who would go on to back Medvedev. In his *Delovaya Rossiya* speech on 16 May 2005 Surkov argued that the country needed a 'national elite', thinking not of Monte Carlo but of the country, the basis of a 'national bourgeoisie'. He insisted that Yukos had represented no threat to the Kremlin leadership, asserting that even if Khodorkovsky had been free the elections results (in December 2003 and March 2004) would have been exactly the same: 'This company represented no political threat', and he went on to report a conversation with Khodorkovsky: 'I told him that power, like love, cannot be bought. It was naive to think that a few corrupt factions would make someone prime minister. He had some strange ideas.' He insisted that the Yukos affair, 'which was so heavy and unpleasant for us, has no crude political colouring. It was a combination of factors, as happens in life':

> There was this task [for the Kremlin] to send a negative message to business tycoons. They've got it all wrong if they think that they can do what they please. From the very start we kept saying that we will not allow a small group of companies to rule the country. As well as this small number of people another 140 million 'poor relations' also live here. Their views also need to be taken into account.[40]

When asked about Surkov's speech, Khodorkovsky noted: 'I am in agreement with much of what Slava Surkov said,' in particular the passage about 140 million average Russians, and 'I am glad that they have not yet jailed Surkov, and I hope that they won't jail him in the future.' He agreed that numerous factors had provoked the Yukos affair, and one of them was that Yukos had been worth $40 billion and was now burdened by debt: 'Indeed, you cannot buy people's love, but you can serve them. Not everyone achieves this.'[41] Surkov spent the early 1990s working with Khodorkovsky, and they came out of a single milieu. They converged in their analysis of Russia's fate in the 1990s and indeed in their evaluation of contemporary social realities. There were also some similarities in their prescriptions, since the state paternalism advocated by Khodorkovsky complemented Surkov's democratic statism. Khodorkovsky's strictures in 'The crisis of Russian liberalism' for Russian liberals to 'renounce the cosmopolitan understanding of the world', and that the liberal project in Russia 'can only exist in the context of national interests' echoed many of Surkov's sovereignty themes.

However, fundamental differences emerged when it came to the specific nature of the political system required to lead the country out of crisis. Surkov was unequivocal: the only force capable of doing so was a group of enlightened individuals using the state to achieve developmental and sovereignty-enhancing goals, the developmental state model. Democracy and sovereignty were important, Surkov insisted, but he clearly prioritised the latter. In his briefing to foreign journalists on 28 June 2006, on the eve of the G8 summit in St Petersburg, Surkov quoted from the foreign press of 1997 and 1998, describing Russia as riddled by criminality in economic life and cronyism in politics, and stating that 'Russia is not a democracy'. With Russia facing a barrage of criticism for alleged democratic backsliding, brought to the fore by its chairmanship of the G8, Surkov then made the point: 'This is how you and your colleagues viewed our country in the 1990s. This is what we are backpedalling from and this is what we will continue to backpedal from.' As a close associate of Khodorkovsky's in the 1990s, Surkov knew whereof he spoke, and he now advocated the robust defence of Russia's national interests and its own democratic path.[42]

Khodorkovsky distanced himself from the radical anti-Putinists, who brought together exiled oligarchs and marginalised liberals, but was unequivocal that much of the existing Kremlin leadership had to be changed. Khodorkovsky's leftism was more social than socialist, since his writings lack any detailed systemic critique of capitalist society, its class structures and its dynamics of class power, or any valorisation of the working class or institutions such as trade unions. Much the same, it may be added, can be said about most of the left parties in Russia. From the 'Left turn' onwards it was clear that he had in mind not just the KPRF but also Rodina and its successors. Khodorkovsky argued that the left would come to power either as a result of elections or a popular revolution demanding social justice. He noted the danger from renascent neo-leftist and neo-imperial tendencies, but rather idealistically assumed they could be constrained by a vigorous civil society. Throughout he called on people to vote, condemning those for example who in 2007 called for a boycott, arguing that this 'would only encourage the bureaucratic class to greater arbitrariness' and would be taken as a sign of popular apathy, and called for people to cast their ballots for smaller parties that 'did not inspire contempt'.[43] Kasyanov People's Democratic Union, which had tried to stand, condemned Khodorkovsky's call as 'giving legitimacy to the forthcoming theatrical performance' and called for a boycott of the 'farce that is called Duma elections'.[44]

From jail Khodorkovsky released a steady stream of commentary on current affairs, providing a strategic perspective on current events and searching for a substantive national idea. In an article for *The Economist* he predicted that 2007 would be decisive for the creation of a 'new world order'. The world in his view would be less 'Americocentric' as China emerged as a superpower, and the US, Europe and Russia would become 'hostages' to China. 'Sinification', in Khodorkovsky's view, was the main threat to Russia.[45] He returned to this theme in his first face-to-face interview since his arrest, held in a courtroom in Chita on 6 February 2008. Facing a second trial, Khodorkovsky remained unbroken. In the ninth day of a hunger strike in support of Aleksanyan, Khodorkovsky 'looked gaunt and drawn', yet remarkably robust. He was wading through some 200 pages of trial documentation a day. He feared that Russia's next president, Medvedev, would be unable to 'undo the damage to the rule of law inflicted during the Putin era':

> It will be so difficult for him, I can't even imagine [...] Tradition, and the state of people's minds, and the lack of forces able to [support] any movement towards the rule of law, everything's against him. So [...] may God grant him the strength to do it. All we can do is hope.

Khodorkovsky rejected the extreme views of some of his supporters and, in the words of the reporter, 'did not share the concerns of some civil society and opposition leaders that democratic freedoms would continue to be eroded in Russia'. As Khodorkovsky put it, 'People can leave freely, the internet works.' It was just 'not possible' for Russia to return to the dark days of the Soviet past.

He argued that China's model of authoritarian modernisation could not be borrowed: 'I'm convinced that Russia is a European country, it's a country with democratic conditions which more than once have been broken off during its history, but nonetheless there are traditions.' He dismissed with contempt the charges against Yukos: 'The accusations are not connected with a real crime, but with a desire – the desire to take away people's conscience, the desire to convince a witness to give evidence. It's all about their various, conflicting desires.' He showed no bitterness about the break-up of Yukos, noting that 'I used up all my nerves in 2004, when a company that was working well was seized and handed over to Rosneft [...] Rosneft today is basically Yukos with a bit added on.' As for his living conditions, he called them 'standard'.[46] He noted that he was treated better in Chita than in Moscow: 'Here [Chita] the word "conscience" has not yet disappeared.' He refused to comment on rumours that he had embraced the Russian Orthodox faith: 'That's a complicated question. I have thought a lot about this. And I'd rather keep it to myself.' Despite the erosion of democracy and the rule of law, he remained optimistic about the country's future: 'It's a question of my personality. I can't provide a lot of arguments for and against but, on the whole, I'm optimistic.'[47]

Khodorkovsky's strongly delineated patriotic instinct was evident at the time of the Russo-Georgian war of August 2008, when he defended Russia's robust reaction to the Georgian assault on Tskhinvali (the capital of South Ossetia) on 7 August.[48] He argued that 'President Medvedev had no other choice, taking into account the situation on 8 August [the commitment of massive Russian forces] and 26 August [when South Ossetia's independence was recognised]. He adopted the only possible decision.'[49] This was not an attempt to curry favour with the authorities but reflected his deeply patriotic instincts.[50] Khodorkovsky retained 'guarded optimism' about Medvedev's reforms. On arriving in Moscow from Chita for his second trial, Khodorkovsky noted 'positive institutional changes'. 'These are just early indications: attempts for the emergence of a normal opposition, a sane reaction to international events in parts of the elite and the beginning of recognition of the judiciary as a separate branch of power.'[51] In the event, the second trial turned out to be a trial of Medvedev's presidency, and both were found to be deeply flawed. Medvedev had called for a state based on the rule of law, and the trial demonstrated precisely the opposite – the continuation of 'legal nihilism'.

Khodorkovsky refused to conform to stereotypes, but the effect of his missives and other interventions was ambiguous. They certainly helped him endure the long years of imprisonment, but they had little direct impact on the shaping of policy. However, the obdurate persecution of Khodorkovsky and his colleagues discredited the regime and came to symbolise its failings, while the struggle for his release became the rallying call for the opposition. Imprisonment endowed Khodorkovsky with the character of a Soviet dissident and prisoner of conscience. Like Becket, suffering bestowed him with the martyr's halo. In the Soviet years Havel argued that even a minor act of resistance could demonstrate 'the power of the powerless', but this applied to a public domain monopolised by a single coercive authority. In post-Communist Russia there is a far more tumultuous babel of discordant opinions, and Khodorkovsky's was a lone, brave, but isolated, voice. However, 'The "Khodorkovsky affair" is gradually changing Russia. The longer the former co-owner of Yukos stays in jail, the higher the country holds him in esteem.'[52] In a familiar pattern, Khodorkovsky was 'expelled from Official Russia and cast into the depths of Popular Russia'.[53] It is far from clear whether he would be able to take 'the long walk to freedom' that led Nelson Mandela to the presidency of South Africa, but he had certainly taken the first steps.[54]

CHAPTER 11

RETURN, RESISTANCE AND REFORM

It had proved relatively easy for the Putin system to break Yukos and to jail Khodorkovsky, but by 2011 there were clear signs of exhaustion in the Putinite methods of co-optation and coordination. His system of rule was at its most effective when the terms of a deal were left imprecise, the limits of autonomy unspecified, and when political and economic actors subjected themselves to internal constraints. Pavlovsky notes: 'A social contract usually emerges in unfavourable conditions; when no one can resolve a question unilaterally, and thus both sides have reason to come to terms, as should have been with the Yukos affair in 2003.' Instead, Khodorkovsky went to jail, millionaires became billionaires, and 'business was threatened with popular vengeance, and became a resource of the power system.'[1] He goes on to argue that 'Every agreement or reform here turns into a power resource.'[2] It was this system, consolidated in the Yukos affair, that sought to perpetuate itself in the 2011–12 elections, but it encountered a profound popular resistance. The fate of the fallen oligarch would be a constant theme of the succession crisis as Putin clawed his way back to the Kremlin.

PUTIN'S RETURN

Parliamentary elections were held on 4 December 2011, followed on 4 March by the presidential ballot. It was clear that both Putin and Medvedev had ambitions to return to the presidency, provoking a succession crisis. Khodorkovsky called on Medvedev to launch a major political reform, above all to transform Russia from a 'super-presidential' into a presidential–parliamentary country, an idea that Khodorkovsky had long propounded. Irrespective of who won, he insisted that Russia objectively needed political change. His specific ideas included reform of the State Duma to give it responsibility over the major branches of the federal government (with the exception of law-enforcement agencies), the holding of genuine parliamentary hearings, the restoration of direct elections to the Federation Council, and the revival of federalism through the election of governors by regional parliaments. He warned against 'uncontrolled presidential power' that allowed wholesale corruption.

> Being a citizen of Russia, I do not want to pin my hopes on a celestial ruler who acts by an algorithm known only to himself. It is necessary to create institutional conditions in which a transparent team of responsible professionals can govern the country. That team must be ready to assume and leave power.[3]

These aspirations lay at the heart of the protest movement that swept the country in the wake of the flawed elections, the biggest challenge to Putin's rule since he had first come to power in 2000.

In 2010 Khodorkovsky was named by the *Foreign Policy* journal as one of the world's most powerful prisoners, an intriguing oxymoron that captures the truth. Khodorkovsky is quoted as arguing that without fundamental reform, 'destruction will occur in the traditional way for Russia – from below and with bloodshed.'[4] Khodorkovsky released a stream of commentary from his camp in Karelia, where he had been assigned to the maintenance brigade. Even the justice minister, Alexander Konovalov, conceded that conditions in prisons and colonies remained inhumane and were not much better than under Stalin.[5] This was reflected in Khodorkovsky's observations on prison life for the journal *New Times*. Khodorkovsky started a column in August 2011, and in his first contribution to the series 'Prison people' he described the moving case of fellow prisoner Kolya, jailed repeatedly for drug possession, but who had agreed to admit to other offences to help the police with their clear-up rates in exchange for certain mild favours. Assuming that this would amount to little more than admitting to the theft of a mobile phone, instead they pinned on him the mugging of a pensioner. He refused and, after being beaten, slashed open his stomach. The moral of the tale was that even prisoners have principles: 'I look at this serially convicted man and with bitterness think of many people on the outside who value their honour far less.'[6] In January 2012 he provided a portrait of 'the investigator', noting that the fate of the prisoner depends on this person, many of whom in the camps were newly graduated young people. The system reproduced itself through negative selection: 'Only the worst remain in the system: some lack brains, others lack conscience [...] Fools or scoundrels – fine material to build a state machine. And that is our state.'[7]

Answering questions submitted by Reuters in early September 2011, Khodorkovsky noted: 'The hopes for internal reform of the current power system would disappear' if Putin returned to the Kremlin, and the 'Emigration of socially active and intellectual Russians would accelerate'. Looking back at his arrest, he noted: 'It was a demonstration of the authorities' readiness to prevent unsanctioned opposition activities by business. The main prize for the raiders was Yukos.' He warned of a forthcoming crisis; hence, 'The real question is: will the elections appear fair enough so that the legitimacy of the president is sufficient when the crisis comes'? He dismissed speculation that he would seek revenge: 'Forgive? I doubt it. But spend time on revenge? I am too pragmatic.'[8] Even the courts in Russia were forced to recognise that Khodorkovsky and Lebedev had been illegally held in pre-trial detention rather than in jail. Disregarding Medvedev's April 2010 amendments, which softened punishments for economic crimes, the Moscow City Court twice ruled to keep the two in Matrosskaya Tishina – from mid-May to mid-August, and then from mid-August to mid-November 2010. The Supreme Court on 15 April 2011 ruled that the second extension was illegal; on 13 September it judged that the decisions were a 'gross violation' of the new legislation and ruled that the first period was illegal as well.[9] The decision had little practical effect, yet signalled a rare victory for Yukos.

The regime sought to deliver a pre-emptive blow by airing a programme about the Yukos case on the state-owned Rossiya 2, in early September 2011. The commentator was Sergei Kurginyan, a political analyst with eccentric pro-regime views. He thoroughly traduced Khodorkovsky and went even further than the formal charges to accuse him of murder, a trope already started by Putin, showing an interview with the child-killer Korovnikov that allegedly implicated Khodorkovsky. In a classically Soviet manner, the aim was to whip up sentiment against a 'bestial' enemy of the people.[10] Mikhail Prokhorov, one of Russia's richest oligarchs, who in 2011 turned his hand to politics, briefly leading the Right Cause liberal party before falling out with Surkov and being deposed in a Kremlin-inspired inner-party putsch on 14 September, called for Khodorkovsky and Lebedev to be freed, but he insisted that he should not be compared to the two.

As for the case of Mikhail Khodorkovsky and mine, I believe they are incomparable. I publicly left business and became the head of a political party. I did it in the framework of Russian law. I am not doing anything illegal. I think that if Khodorkovsky had done the same, the result would have been different. One should not engage in politics while heading a major company.[11]

Prokhorov condemned the Gaidar–Chubais neo-liberal line and called for radical political reform. He was the first businessman to enter public politics for over a decade and fought the presidential election as the champion of the liberals, although he was careful to temper his criticism. It was this sort of stifling tutelage that the opposition, with Khodorkovsky as their symbolic head, sought to change.

Khodorkovsky had undergone a profound ideological evolution. From the rip-roaring neo-liberal of his book (with Nevzlin) *Man with a Rouble*, Khodorkovsky now espoused a left–centre social-democratic philosophy. Khodorkovsky pinned his hopes on Medvedev and argued that Russia 'objectively needs political reform regardless of the personality of the chief of state and party or corporate preferences'. He argued that if Medvedev wanted 'to enter Russian history with a positive image', he would need a second term of six years to implement 'a fundamental political reform'.[12] Putin sought to demonstrate his strength by imposing a harsh sentence on the Yukos defendants, yet the revelation of crude manipulation over the court and the judge only exposed the flaws of the Putinite system. Already Khodorkovsky warned that attempts to return to an irreproducible past would provoke a societal reaction. He insisted that 'Medvedev represents a chance to enter the path of normal development', and that 'a significant part of society will not accept Putin's return', accentuating the 'gulf between the authorities and society'.[13] Even locked away in a prison camp, Khodorkovsky was sensitive to popular sentiment disgusted by the pervasive corruption and degradation.

THE SEEDS OF MODERNITY

When the decision was announced, it was brutal and effective. At the United Russia congress on 24 September 2011 Putin declared that he would seek to return to the Kremlin and would nominate Medvedev as prime minister. The castling move provoked a wave of antipathy, since it appeared gratuitously to add insult to injury.[14] Not only did the regime plan once again to short-circuit a competitive democratic process, but it effectively treated the people as cattle, an affront to their civic dignity.

Two days later Kudrin was summarily dismissed by Medvedev, the first major sign of intra-elite splits. Khodorkovsky noted soon after, as a result of the reshuffle, 'disillusionment reigns among the active part of the Russian population'. The reason for this was not so much the personal qualities of Putin or Medvedev,

> But rather that the continuation of the Putin era is a step into the past. For any political system or political elite a move backwards into the past is a bad thing since it kills hope, and, together with it – the prerequisites for a consolidation of the active section of the people and mutual understanding between them and the regime.

He was sceptical about the modernisation programme announced by the regime, since it was perceived by the elite not as a 'subject for dialogue with society but as a thing in itself, a "black box", which may on checking turn out to be empty'. The events of 24 September 'killed the last hopes' for 'Generation M', those who saw themselves as the modernising class, leaving them with three options: to emigrate, to integrate into 'the economy and politics of the pipeline', or to act as citizens, pushing for modernisation and democratisation, acting 'as conscience dictates'.[15]

On 8 November Khodorkovsky announced that he would not seek parole, even though he had served two-thirds of his sentence, on the grounds that the authorities would block it. A district court upheld the decision by prison officials to issue him with a reprimand for sharing his cigarettes with inmates, an infringement of prison rules.[16] At that time Khodorkovsky warned that Putin's government would be toppled by a revolution. In comments collected by the Ekho Moskvy radio station, Khodorkovsky argued that Putin had 'passed the point of no return' and that he would stay in power as long as he could, 'fostering a long period of stagnation, a political crisis and a revolutionary (I hope bloodless) change of power. Alas, Putin will not leave of his own accord and he cannot prepare a real successor.'[17] In the event, things moved rather faster than he had anticipated. The relatively poor result for United Russia in the parliamentary elections, in which the party lost its constitutional majority, demonstrated the sharp drop in support for the regime. Widespread ballot rigging provoked thousands to demonstrate 'for honest elections' and a 'Russia without Putin'. One of the main demands of the protesters was the release of political prisoners, prominent among them Khodorkovsky and Lebedev. One can imagine the effect that Khodorkovsky's presence would have had on the tens of thousands of demonstrators at Bolotnaya Ploshchad on 10 December or Prospekt Akademika Sakharova on 24 December. He would undoubtedly have acted as a unifying force for the opposition (like Andrei Sakharov), combining patriotic and liberal principles, and would have acted as a symbol of resistance to the regime as a whole.

With his back to the wall, Putin typically came out fighting. During the presidential campaign Putin vigorously engaged with various interest groups. Meeting with political scientists on 6 February 2012, Putin criticised Zhirinovsky's idea of a political, economic and criminal amnesty:

> Are we talking about releasing all convicts, like they did in 1953? Frankly, I'm not sure what he means when he says political amnesty. I don't think that we have any political prisoners, although they keep talking about them without providing any names. Why don't they show us at least one person who is in prison for political reasons? I don't know any.[18]

His comments provoked widespread criticism and the compilation of lists of political prisoners containing between two- and four-dozen names – with Khodorkovsky at the head of them all. On 8 February Memorial and the Moscow Helsinki Group, along with some other NGOs, gave the Presidential Council for Civil Society and Human Rights a list of over 30 names of alleged political prisoners, which the council passed on to the president. The composition of the list was controversial, notably excluding Russian nationalists. The compilers argued that the issue was not whether the people were innocent or guilty, but that their trials had been conducted with gross violations.

On 9 February Putin took up one of Khodorkovsky's key themes. Meeting with the RSPP, Putin talked about the need to improve the business climate and to close the book on the 'dishonest' privatisation of the 1990s. Khodorkovsky had repeatedly argued that the property settlement of the 1990s would have to be legitimated before Russia could set out on the path of normal capitalist democratic development. Putin argued that a 'one-off levy' on people who had benefited would ensure 'the social legitimacy of private property' and could 'draw the curtain' on the issue of the 'unfair privatisation' of the 1990s.[19] Putin acknowledged that the idea of a windfall tax had been mooted by Yavlinsky, but not surprisingly ignored Khodorkovsky's repeated disquisitions on the subject. In 2003 the Audit Chamber issued a report outlining the unfair practices employed in the privatisations, and this sword of Damocles remained suspended over Russian business. Shortly after the end of the second trial Khodorkovsky argued:

If the current authorities were truly concerned with the unfair distribution of property, they could have accepted the proposal that I formulated back in 2003 on behalf of a number of my colleagues about a compensation tax. And yet, in the years since, the billionaires who are close to power have only increased their wealth.[20]

Now Putin returned to the idea as part of his populist electoral campaign, to which Kasyanov tweeted: 'Khodorkovsky and I suggested this. His reaction: I was sacked, Khodorkovsky sent to jail.'[21] The idea of such a tax was probably a decade too late, since much of the property in question had changed hands, some of it several times. In such cases it was not clear who would pay the fine.[22] A windfall tax would have legitimating functions, but it was also designed to pay for the extensive promises outlined in Putin's presidential campaign. The attack on the oligarchs, accompanied by the idea of a 'luxury tax', represented a populist move in a tough electoral environment, but was dropped as soon as Putin returned to power.

Khodorkovsky was sceptical. In a considered evaluation of the political situation, he noted that Putin did not trust the bona fides of the demonstrators, believing that they were either in the pay of Western powers or marginal figures, who sought to use the movement for their careerist ambitions. Putin thought of himself as a successful ruler using the correct methods, hence any concessions to the protestors would be individual rather than systemic, since the latter would throw in doubt Putin's whole approach. Khodorkovsky argued that the 'new opposition' could only use Kudrin as an intermediary to establish the rules of the game; he could not act as a substantive negotiator. Putin was now set against 'the square' (the protest movement), and there was no need for a 'new Putin'; what was required was a whole new philosophy of cooperation to replace the archaic 'vertical'. Russia's opposition should hold a dialogue with Putin since the country needed more political cooperation. The demands of the new opposition in his view could be reduced to the need for honest government; this required fair elections, for which independent courts and media were needed, as well as zero tolerance of corruption and a coalition government. Not least, the powers of the presidency had to be reduced; otherwise a new leader would soon engage in the discredited practices of old. The new opposition in his view needed to escalate peaceful protest until it achieved its goals. However, asked about the acceptable limits to the protest actions, he argued that the authorities had 'not yet crossed the boundary' to become wholly morally illegitimate, even though some of its officials had crossed the line. Asked about whether the protest movement could push Putin to make a concession, possibly by releasing him and Lebedev, Khodorkovsky was doubtful: 'I have received no signal from the current authorities associated with the latest changes in society. It is impossible for me to compromise with conscience. I do not wish to speculate on my future.'[23]

Khodorkovsky was sensitive to the dilemma of the new opposition, walking a fine line between asserting its demands and drawing back from the brink that could escalate into violence. In his comment for the eighth 'Khodorkovsky Colloquium' (*Khodorkovskie chteniya*) he argued that the change in social consciousness had occurred as a result of the confluence of two factors. First, the coming to an end of an extended political cycle that usually lasts for some 15 years (Putin had already been in power for 12), and thus people were fed up with him and he had become a less effective leader. Second, the numerical growth of the educated middle class; or, in Marxist terminology, the authorities had created their own gravediggers, 'the contemporary "proletariat" of office workers'. Khodorkovsky noted Putin's personal characteristic whereby a filter prevented information that could challenge his fixed views from entering his mind. Hence he retains 'the sincere conviction that he is doing everything correctly'. Khodorkovsky anticipated a 'conservative scenario' for the future development of politics, accompanied by a more or less liberal economy in which 'real democratisation and liberalisation is excluded, since it is not organic for Putin', and thus modernisation would at best be sluggish. The key challenge facing 'our generation is to change paradigms without civil war', and thus change should avoid revolution and too much haste; instead he advocated 'a slow and gradual influencing of the authorities through cooperation or refusal to work with some of its features'. The 'demonstrations' were designed not so much to change the authorities 'but ourselves'. Once again he urged participation in the presidential ballot,[24] against the advice of those who urged a boycott or spoiling of ballots (the 'Nakh Nakh – Vote Against All' movement).

Rattled by the scale of protests, Putin published a series of articles on developments in the country. Much of what Putin proposed, Khodorkovsky insisted, was 'unacceptable, because specialists have long known what they lead to (for example, governing in "manual control mode", the "vertical power structure", etc.)'. However, some was 'adequate and sometimes even useful' and the liberal opposition 'could agree to the implementation of much of what he has spoken about'. Why then, did Putin allow his own proposals 'to be talked out of existence'? The problem was that Putin was afraid of getting on the wrong side of the *siloviki* and thus 'watered down even his own initiatives'. Although Putin was trying to win over the middle class, whose growing numbers in Khodorkovsky's view made them a major electoral factor, 'Our future president does not want to antagonise the *siloviki* who surround him,' and hence he remains loyal to his friends, 'no matter how incompetent they may be'. It was this that made government so inefficient, comprising 'an eclectic set of methods poached from different systems', and, 'far from creating a new system, [it was] simply dysfunctional, even if you call it "sovereign democracy"'.[25]

Khodorkovsky insisted that real change was inevitable. The protest movement 'exploded the long-held myth that the people want to stick with Putin just for the sake of stability'. He condemned the mocking tone with which Putin had initially scorned the demonstrators, but recognised that the 'authorities also responded – quietly – with reform', easing party-registration laws and restoring gubernatorial elections: 'These steps are capable of changing much in Russia, a catalyst, perhaps unintended, for a more fundamental transformation. They give hope that the seeds of modernity can be planted', to allow genuine multi-party competition, but for that the opposition 'will have to consolidate into two or three parties, avoiding the Kremlin trap of divide and rule among myriad rivals'. He hoped for a high turnout, consistent with his long-held view that engagement rather than abstention could more effectively bring about change. Forcing Putin into a second round

> would confirm that an evolutionary and not a revolutionary approach can be the way forward. We do not want the bloodshed seen elsewhere – but we do want things to be different. It must be the role of our generation to change the paradigm without civil war.

The abuse of power and presidential lack of responsibility had flourished for too long: 'From Cairo to Damascus, from Moscow to Magadan, people want to be treated with dignity and respect – and Russia is no exception.'[26] Khodorkovsky thus outlined an evolutionary path in which the mass protests were channelled into constructive political change, repudiating the extremism that so often only perpetuates authoritarianism in new forms. This would be Russia's long-awaited arrival into a modernity in which political participation would be genuinely pluralist and the authorities would be accountable to the people.

Putin won the 4 March vote in the first round by a handsome margin (65.6%), followed by the veteran Communist leader Zyuganov with 17.18%, but Prokhorov gained an impressive third-place finish with 8% of the vote. Running on a liberal platform, Prokhorov's achievement indicated that the old popular animus against 'oligarchs' was waning. As Inozemtsev put it:

> Prokhorov's success refutes many of the myths about Russian politics. It shows that Russians do not hate oligarchs as much as they used to, that the memory of

the 'wild 90s' is fading, and that they desperately want a new political figure who answers to the needs of a rising middle class. Prokhorov's success was due not so much by his personal capacities but by these new aspirations.[27]

Prokhorov had long argued that the jailing of Khodorkovsky and the attack on Yukos set 'a very bad precedent'. 'A lot of small businessmen suffered from the same methods all over the country. It was a key signal for lower-ranking policemen, or judges, or ex-KGB guys to do the same.'[28] The raid against Yukos rendered business vulnerable to attack, a problem that had greatly exercised Medvedev, and the issue remained to confront Putin as he returned for a third term.

PRESIDENTIAL REVIEW

The Yukos affair had always been Putin's project and not Medvedev's, and the latter's failure to resolve the issue blighted his presidency. Failing more open and demonstrative actions, it would have taken little more than a telephone call to Yegorova's Moscow City Court in December 2010 to prevent the second prison sentence. With Medvedev declaring his political ambitions, including a return to the presidency, a gesture such as the release of the Yukos victims would have given him enormous political capital. It would also have had a positive social impact. A survey in April 2012 found that one in ten Russians considered Khodorkovsky a political prisoner, even though 40% struggled to define the term, with a plurality (26%) considering that they were people out of favour with the authorities. Nearly a quarter rejected the idea that such a group existed. Other polls found that when specifically asked why Khodorkovsky was in jail, 44% named economic crimes, 27% did not know anything about him, and 19% considered that he was being persecuted for political reasons.[29]

The Presidential Council for Human Rights and Civil Society, now headed by Mikhail Fedotov, showed considerable activism in the Yukos case. The council was established in 1993 with consultative and advisory powers, and the 40-member body was composed of some of Russia's most renowned and respected human-rights advocates and experts. Under Medvedev the council had been joined by a number of nonconformists, such as the political analyst Dmitry Oreshkin, who sought to challenge the system from within. Responding to widespread public criticism of abuses in the conduct of the second trial, at a meeting of the council in Ekaterinburg on 1 February 2011, broadcast live, Medvedev ordered 'a legal analysis of the relevant decisions' in the case.[30] This was challenged by some Constitutional Court judges, who argued that the 'introduction of a special procedure to verify judicial decisions in certain high profile cases is against the principle of equality of all citizens before the law'.[31] However, the court's chair, Valery Zorkin, defended public monitoring of judicial decisions and the review went ahead. A multidisciplinary nine-person team, including leading Russian and international experts from America, Germany and Holland, worked on the report from April to December, with the brief to avoid a political assessment of the case and to ensure the confidentiality of their work.[32] The experts were asked to examine the second Khodorkovsky trial for compliance with Russian and international norms, to identify trends in Russia's judicial and law-enforcement practices and to make appropriate recommendations for reform. The group worked in great secrecy and finally presented the result of their endeavours on 21 December 2011. The 400-page report was adopted and formally submitted to Medvedev.

The report comprised three volumes of closely argued analytical material.[33] It identified serious and widespread violations of the law in the second trial, some of which have been noted earlier. The experts rejected the court's findings about the illegality of Yukos's operations, arguing that the company's vertically integrated structure and the use of offshore companies for trading oil and oil products were industry norms and far from exceptional, both in Russia and abroad. The report was scathing about the verdict, which was held to have misunderstood and misapplied basic concepts of Russian civil and criminal law. The report found no evidence to substantiate charges of embezzlement or money laundering. Differences between intra-Yukos pricing and external market pricing could not be held to represent embezzlement of oil, and thus the experts found 'no evidence or substance behind the accusations of embezzlement' and indeed noted the absence of evidence connected to a coherent legal theory. Consequently, they found that the verdict was 'illegal and subject to repeal' and was issued in 'gross violation' of the Russian constitution. They noted that the case contradicted the evidence provided in other Yukos-related trials, which had not been overturned. Above all, the first trial had focused on punitive taxation on oil sales, whereas now the same oil was found to have been stolen, which by definition would preclude it from being taxed. A string of violations were found on procedural matters and due process, including deprivation of the presumption of innocence, lack of independence of the court and its 'bogus' jurisdiction, non-consideration and rejection of evidence favourable to the defendants, and the granting of procedural advantage to the prosecution over the defence. The judge's verdict, moreover, simply copied large portions verbatim from the indictment and thus lacked indicia of reasoned judgment; in any case it failed to respect the statute of limitations.

The council found that the 'miscarriage of justice' in the second case was so egregious that the verdict should be annulled through recognised legal channels. The reforms proposed included the extension of the use of jury trials, greater efforts to ensure judicial independence, reinforcement of the right to effective defence at a trial, limitations on the interpretation and application of criminal law, the abolition of abusive procedural obstacles that prevented the granting of deserved parole, and a reduction in the use of pre-trial detention in cases of alleged economic crime. The report recommended a broad amnesty for wrongfully imprisoned entrepreneurs (including Khodorkovsky and Lebedev), noting the socially disruptive and economically repressive impact of the wrongful imprisonment of thousands of Russian businesspeople who had fallen victim to corrupt state officials.

In a press release accompanying the report, the council called for the second sentence to be reviewed, arguing: '(We) suggest that the Investigative Committee should initiate a new inquiry into newly revealed circumstances (of the case) and study the grounds to review the criminal case due to fundamental violations.'[34] Yurgens noted that 'In the second Yukos case the violations are so serious that we should either pardon the defendants or start a new investigation'. The former Constitutional Court judge Tamara Morshchakova argued: 'This subject is becoming a public issue. Society has matured to understand the problem, in part because of this report. The authorities are witnessing an awakening of civil society.'[35] The scandals attending the Khodorkovsky and Magnitsky cases for television journalist and political expert Nikolai Svanidze demonstrated that the 'ice has broken up in the country's judicial system'. Vasileva's revelations of political interference, the outcry in society, and the investigation by the Presidential Council reinforced the need for reform: 'After all, a proper judicial system is the cornerstone for the renovation of the entire system of state power.'[36]

On 5 March 2012 Medvedev ordered the PGO to review the legal foundations of the sentences against Khodorkovsky and Lebedev, as well as 30 other people (including the scientist Valentin Danilov, convicted of spying in November 2004). The next day the Supreme Court requested materials from the first-instance courts concerning the criminal case against the Yukos executives. The names were taken from the list of political prisoners, which the leaders of the non-parliamentary opposition took to Medvedev when they met him at his residence in Barvikha on 20 February. Numbers 15 and 28 on the list were Lebedev and Khodorkovsky, while Pichugin was number 21. Chaika, the prosecutor general, had until 1 April to review the 32 cases that reached back over the last decade. The publication of the list the day after the election was probably not accidental. With the hard-fought contest over, some concessions could be made to those dissatisfied with the system. As Yurgens put it:

> Scenting blood, even a democratic mob wants more and all this usually ends in serious failure for the reformer. Putin could not back down. This is not part of his rules. It is not his style. Today, after the elections, it would be logical to make some concessions – especially since the concessions are being made by an outgoing liberal president. But one who leaves himself hope of continuing his own career in precisely this vein.[37]

Medvedev had already announced that freeing Khodorkovsky would not be dangerous, and the review was intended to bolster his reputation among the intelligentsia as he left the Kremlin to become prime minister.

Asked about the review at a press conference on 7 March, Putin was typically forthright:

> Look, I have made my point many times. There are court rulings, they came into legal effect. And there are legal procedures concerned with a possible release. If anybody wishes to implement these procedures, they are welcome. Mr Medvedev has given this instruction, indeed, I do not see any special point in that. The Presidential Human Rights Commission submitted this petition to him and he filed a relevant instruction with the Prosecutor's Office. I think it is right. [...] But, my friends, we keep talking about some political component in this case, but you have eyes and ears and you have read the European Court verdict? Have you read it or not? It is written there that the European Court of Human Rights does not see a political motive there. And yet they go on insisting. There are many people held for economic reasons. What about them?
>
> What am I trying to say? There is a way. Such a way exists! It is stipulated in the law. Let this person take this way. Nobody is against it. Everybody is seeking a political solution, but there are legal solutions. You are welcome. But nobody wants to do that.

In other words, those who wished to free Khodorkovsky and his associates should follow legal procedures. Asked about what qualities in Sechin Putin valued, he answered: 'For his professionalism and grasp, for his ability to see something through to the end'.[38] This characteristic was certainly much in evidence in his dogged pursuit of Yukos and its managers. On the last day of his premiership on 6 May 2012, Putin nominated Sechin to become a board member of Rosneftegaz, the holding company of the Rosneft oil company with also a small stake in Gazprom, and soon after he became CEO of Rosneft – the company that he had so assiduously fostered.

PARDON AGAIN

All presidential candidates, with the notable exception of Putin, announced that they would pardon the Yukos managers. On 3 February 2012 the Human Rights Council announced that it would be reviewing the rules for pardons so as formally to exclude admission of guilt as the requirement for issuing a pardon or release on parole. They also planned to pardon all those convicted of non-violent offences, including financial crimes.[39] On 16 March the council argued that Khodorkovsky could in fact be pardoned without an admission of guilt. The council cited two rulings from the Constitutional Court and the Supreme Court in 2004 and 2008, respectively, to demonstrate that the president had the right to pardon a convicted person irrespective of their status in the criminal-justice system. Fedotov announced that the matter would be taken up with Medvedev in April, in his last days in office. 'The president has the right to pardon whomever he wants,' Fedotov argued.[40] However, in late March Medvedev rejected expert advice from ten top Russian lawyers on constitutional law that a convict could be pardoned without their application, consent or approval, or even against their will. Although they unequivocally argued that no personal request from the prisoner was required for a presidential pardon, Medvedev asserted that he saw no reason to pardon someone who did not ask to be pardoned, a view that had wide resonance in and beyond the legal profession. There is no law on pardon, but as noted Article 89 of the constitution states that the president has this unique right, and it does not stipulate that the prisoner has to repent.

Speculation continued that some political prisoners would be released before Medvedev left office on 7 May. Nemtsov believed that Khodorkovsky and Lebedev would be among those freed. Yurgens argued that while their release would split the elite, with the law-enforcement vertical opposed to their release, but the reputational damage caused by their continued incarceration needed to be resolved.[41] Pardons and the whole Yukos affair became one of the main items of discussion in the media. A programme on NTV on 18 March was devoted to the case, with a discussion of whether political motives were responsible for their imprisonment or whether they really were guilty of criminal offences. The presenter, Pavel Khrekov, noted that the programme had been planned before the parliamentary elections, but the producers could not find anyone willing publicly to defend the trials. Bakhmina, who had served four years in jail, spoke movingly of her experiences and argued that Yukos had not been given a chance to pay off its claimed tax arrears. Pereverzin, the former deputy director of Yukos's foreign debt directorate who served over seven years in prison, stated that he had been accused of plotting with Khodorkovsky in 2002, even though they had not met, and revealed that the investigators had offered him a deal to admit his guilt and slander Khodorkovsky and Lebedev in return for his release. A fifth of the studio audience considered the whole affair a show trial, and 70% voted for their immediate release. On a line from Paris, Akunin argued that freeing Khodorkovsky and Lebedev would mean that the authorities wanted a real dialogue with civil society.[42]

The contradictory signals continued. The PGO denied the possibility of having made a mistake. On 2 April the PGO completed its review of the cases of alleged political prisoners. Confirming the sceptics' view, no violations were found (except in the case of Taisia Osipova, whose verdict had already been quashed in Smolensk).[43] It was clear that a review lasting barely a month could not hope to do justice to the complexity of the cases. An appeal by some leading Russian human-rights activists, including Lyudmila Alekseeva, Sergei Kovalev, Svetlana Gannushkina, and Lev Ponomarev, called on president Medvedev to act immediately:

> We ask you to pardon the political prisoners included on the lists that were handed to you at a personal meeting. We are aware of your view about the need for personal appeals to you for pardon. So we, Russian citizens, all together and every one of us personally, appeal to you. [...] An act of pardon will be a brilliant finale of your presidential term, thanks to which you will be remembered by the people of Russia and the entire international community as a magnanimous person.[44]

In a rather testy exchange during his live interview with five television journalists on 26 April 2012, Medvedev reaffirmed his view that he could not pardon Khodorkovsky unless the latter effectively recognised his guilt by asking for mercy.[45] Only three days earlier he had pardoned Sergei Mokhnatkin, a passer-by who intervened to help an elderly lady being beaten by the police during an unsanctioned demonstration on 31 December 2009 on Triumfalnaya Ploshchad. In June 2010 he was sentenced to two and a half years for assaulting a police officer, and in March 2012 he wrote to ask for a pardon, without admitting guilt. Mokhnatkin, who was on the list of political prisoners compiled by human-rights activists, had nearly completed his sentence when he was released. Mokhnatkin's pardon turned out to be an isolated gesture by the outgoing president, disappointing those who looked for a final act of political courage as he left office. It was clear from those who met Medvedev at this time that he was morally ready to take the step, but for political reasons he was unable to liberate himself from the evident constraints, a feature of his entire presidency. The only hope now was that that the presidential inauguration could be accompanied by an amnesty. There is a long tradition in Russia of an amnesty to accompany the inauguration of a new tsar and on major Orthodox Church festivals. The release of the fallen oligarch would have provided a clear signal that Putin's return to the presidency did not simply mean more of the same. In the event, Putin failed to seize the opportunity to gain considerable political capital in the West and at home.

Elements of Medvedev's attempts to strengthen the constitutional state remained. On 24 July 2012 the head of the Supreme Court, Vyacheslav Lebedev, a judge of the old school and a respected figure in the profession, ordered the Moscow City Court to examine the defence argument that Khodorkovsky and Lebedev had been tried twice for the same offence. The resolution suggested that the authorities were aware that they had gone too far, and were now looking to row back a little.[46] The Supreme Court sought to demonstrate its independence, but by referring the matter to a notoriously hard-line lower court, nothing of consequence would emerge. Shortly afterwards, the Velsk District Court on 8 August accepted Lebedev's appeal and reduced his sentence by three years and four months, citing the changes to Article 171(1) of the Criminal Code, which reduced punishment for white-collar crimes.[47] By February 2012 Pereverzin had been released from prison early because of the change in legislation. He had been sentenced to 11 years for stealing and laundering $13 billion, but ended up serving seven years and two months.[48]

The Velsk court was responding to a request to review the case from the procuracy, and thus it in effect endorsed a decision taken elsewhere, although the extent of the cut was greater than that demanded by the prosecutors.[49] The ruling was overturned by the Arkhangelsk Regional Court.[50] On 1 November the Velsk court confirmed a reduction, this time by three years; however, this was also rejected by the higher court on 14 December, and a third hearing by the Velsk court was ordered.[51] On 19 March 2013 the presidium of the Arkhangelsk Regional Court upheld the ruling by the lower courts for parole to be denied to Lebedev. Khodorkovsky had not filed a similar appeal and instead challenged his conviction on other grounds. Rather than releasing him, persistent rumours suggested that a third case was being prepared. The trial of Ivan Kolesnikov, a Yukos lawyer who had fled to Cyprus, accused him of stealing Yukos shares. The Cyprus authorities had refused an extradition request, but the holding of a trial *in absentia* suggested that those behind the Yukos affair were intent on keeping the case alive. Sentences for 'embezzlement and money laundering' were now subject to the milder regime, whereas charges of membership of an 'organised criminal group' entail up to 20 years in jail.[52]

In June 2012 a new Presidential Commissioner for Entrepreneurs' Rights was appointed: Boris Titov, who immediately declared that he would press for pardons for the 13,000 people jailed for economic crimes, including Khodorkovsky.[53] In August Khodorkovsky asked Titov to conduct an independent review of the second Yukos case. In his letter Khodorkovsky stated: 'it is useful for entrepreneurs to know what risks they are taking when they rely on our "justice" [and] how the entrepreneurs' ombudsman can realistically help them.'[54] As noted, the Human Rights Council under Fedotov had already investigated the matter; it had recommended a review of the sentence because of 'some fundamental violations during the investigation into the case, demonstrating judicial violations', yet there had been no follow-up, and so yet another review was unlikely to change the situation.[55] Indeed, Fedotov endorsed Khodorkovsky's appeal to the new business ombudsman: 'This is a natural step, since Titov is a commissioner for businessmen's rights, and Khodorkovsky has been convicted exactly as a businessman.'[56] The review would be conducted by the Business Against Corruption Centre, an independent NGO. Titov noted Khodorkovsky's scepticism about his independence, but stressed that within months of starting work he had looked into 160 appeals, and 'many have been rendered legal support and real assistance'.[57]

In a twist that is all too common in the Yukos case, the Russian members of the international review, which had exposed the irregularities in the second trial, came under pressure shortly after Putin's return to the Kremlin. In September 2012 the Investigative Committee searched the home of Mikhail Subbotin and two of his colleagues, as well as the offices of the Centre for Legal and Economic Research (which has received European and Canadian funding), which he heads. The IC was apparently investigating the old charge that Yukos money had been laundered in the West and then channelled back to Russian NGOs in exchange for them reaching 'deliberately false conclusions' about Khodorkovsky's conviction 'under the guise of independent public expertise'. Subbotin was named as a 'witness' in the case. Three more of the six Russians on the expert commission were targeted: Sergei Guriev, Oksana Oleinik and Astamur Tedeev were also called in for questioning. Fedotov, who had commissioned the review, called the persecution of the legal experts 'absolutely shocking', and insisted that 'Their activity was absolutely within the framework of the law'.[58] Jeffrey Kahn, one of the Western experts, noted:

Punishing the leaders to quiet the herd is an old practice for authoritarian regimes. […] With Mr. Putin back in the Kremlin, it is no longer safe to express an opinion on public affairs, even if that opinion was requested by the state itself.[59]

The attack against the experts was part of a more general increase in activity in Yukos-related cases and added further to the speculation that a third trial was being prepared.

Paradoxically, rather than facilitating Khodorkovsky's freedom, the protest movement – one of whose main demands was his release – complicated it politically. In conditions where the regime faced a genuine threat from the street, with its legitimacy cast in doubt, Andrei Kolesnikov argues that the authorities could not allow Khodorkovsky out. They may well have been concerned that 'in a situation lacking leadership, he [Khodorkovsky] could become the leader of the opposition', and in any case it was a continuation of the 'policy of counter-reform and thermidor that has been pursued for the last ten years'. He dismissed any possibility of 'self-democratisation' of the regime and mocked illusions regarding reform peddled by Medvedev in the tandem years.[60] If he was right, then many more years of jail awaited Khodorkovsky.

In the event, on 20 December 2012 the presidium of the Moscow City Court reduced the sentences on Khodorkovsky and Lebedev by two years, clearing the way for them to be released on 25 October and 2 July 2014, respectively, after 11 years in jail. The guilty verdict was upheld, but citing the recent liberalisation of legislation on economic crimes, an early release was sanctioned, although the ruling could be overturned on appeal. The judge also dropped the charge of laundering 2.5 billion roubles ($81 million), which the pair had been accused of embezzling.[61] The court rejected as unsubstantiated the claim that the Yukos case had been biased: 'Claims of the accusatory trend and the court's obstruction of defensive procedures made in the appeals are unfounded and not confirmed with materials of the case.' The resolution rejected the argument that there had been 'the deliberate infringement of procedural rights of the defendants and their lawyers by the presiding judge' and went on to argue, rather surprisingly, that the defence should not have referred to the results of public reviews, such as the report of the Presidential Civil Society and Human Rights Council or the report of the Institute of Human Rights of the International Bar Association. Despite the cut in his sentence, Khodorkovsky was not impressed:

The prison term reduction is an ostrich policy of the court, decisions of which many educated people in Russia and the world are laughing at. It is a pity that the already not quite flawless reputation of Moscow courts is being dented further.[62]

In February 2013 the Supreme Court requested the case materials on the two from the Meshchansky and Khamovnichesky district courts, apparently to look into claims of irregularity in the proceedings.[63]

The City Court judgment appeared timed to coincide with Putin's extended press conference, also held on 20 December. The Reuters correspondent noted that although the decision was made by 'an apparently independent Russian court, all the same it cannot be taken without your agreement'. Putin took umbrage at the idea that the courts in Russia could be less than independent, but expressed a sanguine view of Khodorkovsky's early release:

> For four years I was not head of state, and despite that the courts upheld their deci-
> sions. I wish to make it clear that there was no way for me to exert influence. I did
> not influence the work of the law enforcement or judicial authorities in any way.
> I did not get involved in those matters. I got on with my work, and still the courts
> stuck to their well-known views. [...] As regards my opinion that a thief must sit
> in jail, who is against that? Should he walk the streets? [...]
>
> As for Mikhail Borisovich, there is no personal persecution here. Nothing
> that some try to present as a political case. Did Mikhail Borisovich go into politics?
> Was he a deputy? Did he lead a political party? There was nothing of the sort. The
> case is entirely economic. These questions should not be politicised. I am sure that
> when in accordance with the law everything will be sorted, Mikhail Borisovich will
> walk free. God give him health.[64]

This was classic Putinism, distancing himself from something with which he had been intimately involved from the very first, accompanied by the gratuitous injunction against politicising what had from the first been the major political trial of post-Communist Russia. Nevertheless, Putin made it understood that he would not object to an early release if granted by the courts, and this represented a significant advance. With the succession out of the way and the tide of political protest ebbing, Khodorkovsky no longer represented an immediate political threat.

PUTINISM AND THE FUTURE

Watching the succession crisis unfold from his camp, Khodorkovsky remained an acute observer of events. He approved of the main opposition demand to hold repeat parliamentary elections: 'The country needs a fully fledged, honestly elected parliament and it must be a legitimate one.' As for recent events, he thanked the Presidential Expert Council, 'which probably made more understandable the legal deficiency of the Khamovnichesky court sentence'. He would avail himself of 'all the opportunities offered by the judiciary system to obtain a just ruling even though I have profound doubts about its ability "to independently cleanse the case of its political elements"'. He welcomed the idea of an amnesty proposed by the Council, not just for himself, but for all the others 'caught between the grinding stones of a vile system'.[65]

In a 'public lecture' prepared for *Novaya gazeta* in April 2012 called 'Contemporary social liberalism and the economy' he distinguished social liberals from 'neo-liberals', with the former approaching social democrats in social matters, favouring taxes on the super-rich and an active role for the state, while defending the free market as the engine of development. He questioned the notion of the 'resource curse', arguing that it was regime type that was the problem: authoritarian systems were susceptible to corruption and the wasteful use of resources. He provided a wide-ranging prescription of what he considered should be the liberal position on fundamental questions facing Russia. He advocated a special tax on the wealthy and on luxury goods, including the introduction of an inheritance tax, accompanied by the introduction of a graduated tax rate to replace the current flat-rate system. On security matters, he argued:

> Law enforcement agencies should be relatively small in number, should be well-equipped technically, be strongly motivated for stable and honest work and engaged only in fighting real crime and dangerous violations of law and order rather than serve as a tool to exert pressure on society and political opponents.

He warned against 'criminals in epaulettes', no doubt having the Hermitage Capital case in mind. On the question of defence spending, 'another issue on which liberals are criticised for being irresponsible', he argued that effective national defence required a strong economy and society, since 'A weak country will have a weak army'. Above all, he insisted that 'Patriotism, love for one's homeland and willingness to defend it is absolutely not something alien to a modern liberal'.[66] Khodorkovsky thus continued to provide detailed recommendations for a future liberal government in Russia.

This did not mean that if released he would directly enter politics. In his Ekho Moskvy interview of November 2011, Khodorkovsky was asked directly whether he would run for president when released.

No, even though I know about the lives of different sorts of Russian people – nevertheless, I consider myself a representative of the liberal intelligentsia and everything that I have written over these years has been written for them. The role of the intelligentsia in Russia is not to struggle for power but to change society. This is what interests me.

He once again denied that he would seek revenge. He insisted on the need for social justice and defended his earlier views expressed in the 'Left turn' missives, insisting: 'I am still a "social liberal".' As for the alleged 'founding pact' of the Putin era, that the oligarchs could keep their assets if they kept out of politics, Khodorkovsky was unequivocal:

> This assertion, which has become so widespread, is in actual fact a lie. […] The nature of the agreement was different and the involvement of business in politics, as everyone knows, remained a common thing. The issue was about not using companies in politics.[67]

The distinction is a fine one, and not everyone would accept its validity.

In a revealing interview on the Dozhd TV station on 20 March 2012, Vladimir Yevtushenkov, the head of the AFK Sistema telecoms and minerals conglomerate, confirmed that this was Khodorkovsky's stance. He knew 'Misha' very well, since the two had graduated from the same institute. Khodorkovsky had even worked for him when Yevtushenkov was a production foreman in a plastics plant:

> I knew exactly what motivated him: what drove him, the rationale behind his actions. […] I'll put it this way: he is a profoundly talented man. He lived according to the American model, where you have to change positions every 5–7 years. His aim was to merge Yukos with Gazprom. When he realised that he wasn't going to be able to do this, he wanted to get involved in political activities and so on. On this path it is merciless.

He reports a conversation held about a month before his arrest: 'Misha, you'll lose your company.' Khodorkovsky replied, 'I don't care about the company any more – I have other tasks.' Yevtushenkov noted that 'when you enter another field [i.e. politics] you need to live by different laws. These are harsher than in business.' Khodorkovsky in his view could no longer be considered a 'businessman', since he had now turned to politics.

> At some stage Misha started getting high and mighty. […] from a sense of self-worth, a sense that you see and do everything better than everyone else […] That's not good. You soon lose touch with the real world and you need to constantly look at yourself in the mirror and take a reality check. If you don't do this, then you start living in a distorted space, a virtual world. This is the most dangerous scenario possible.

Yevtushenkov outlined the rules of doing business in Russia, where 'If the amount of political influence the owners of a business have is in line with the size of their enterprise, then they need not worry about their business, as they have enough energy and resources to defend it.' However, 'if the size of a business significantly exceeds the amount of political influence its owners have, then it will be very difficult to hang on to it,' which was the case with Yukos. When the business is small and the political influence is high, then the person is called a 'politician'. 'The size of Yukos's business exceeded the political influence that Khodorkovsky and his ilk had.' Yevtushenkov argued that the start of the Yukos affair was 'not a one-act affair': he likened it to a man walking with a rucksack, in which more and more is placed, and when finally a small screw is added the man buckles. He was not felled by the screw; 'It had accumulated over some time – this needs to be clearly understood. A man does not get rooted out for uttering one word. It's complete nonsense.' Yevtushenkov would not commit himself to predicting when Khodorkovsky would be freed, but argued: 'He will certainly be released, with his spirit intact. He will certainly get involved in some kind of charitable activity.' Asked if this would be political, Yevtushenkov was adamant: 'No, he will not get involved in political activity.'

> I don't think that a man who has been deprived of his family, his loved ones for so long, would go headlong into politics, where at every turn they lie in wait for you and could throw you in jail again.[68]

Khodorkovsky's son, Pavel, now assumed an increasingly public profile. He left Russia in 2003 to go to university and has been in New York ever since. He now works for a media company as well as managing the Institute of Modern Russia. Commenting on the protests on the eve of Putin's inauguration on 7 May 2012, he noted:

> His [Putin's] regime fails to understand that Russia in 2012 is a different place than it was in 2004, when he was last president. The Russian people are now seeing the future of our country beyond the bounds of autocracy and beginning to express themselves in a peaceful and democratic way.[69]

Pavel noted: 'I remain abroad in self-imposed exile, unwilling to return to my own country, like thousands of other young Russians educated overseas. Many more are leaving Russia daily.' After a brief moment of hope that 'reforms could come overnight' following the Duma elections,

> Many subsequently became disenchanted when Mr Putin did not suffer defeat. Yet the protests will continue, reinforcing the idea that his ascension is illegitimate, and their momentum will be sustained by focusing on small goals rather than on the Kremlin itself.

Pavel thus echoed his father's philosophy of gradualism, engagement and non-retribution. The key was on challenging the 'self-serving interests of the *siloviki*', on 'registering political parties' and securing 'justice against those who violated the rights of Yukos employees such as Vasily Aleksanyan'. He noted that 'our country yearns for reform', in conditions in which 'one in six Russian businessmen has been on trial, and prisons hold thousands of them – many of whom are victims of abuse of the criminal-justice system through fabricated cases'.[70]

Although the protest movement spluttered on and resistance took on a variety of forms, Russian politics soon assumed accustomed patterns: Putin was back in the Kremlin, Medvedev was in the White House and Khodorkovsky was in prison. Putin issued decrees and directives, whereas Khodorkovsky published commentary and analysis. In a nasty reminder of how little had changed, some of the opposition leaders faced fabricated criminal charges, notably those against Navalny and his associates by the Investigative Committee headed by Putin's bulldog, Bastrykin. Some things had changed, and a popular movement now stalked the land. The regime itself was dissolving from within, or, as Khodorkovsky put it, 'The authoritarian system is alienating its own creators and true believers'; and although the Russian state enjoyed 'enormous powers, it was weak'.[71] Abroad, his son supported sanctions against the Russian officials involved in the Magnitsky case. As Pavel put it:

> This is now the most effective means of pressuring the Russian government, one that could bring about real changes in the legal system and a return to the promised reforms aimed at combating legal nihilism, as President Medvedev often loved to talk about.

The US Congress repealed the 1974 Jackson–Vanik amendment, and Russia was at last granted Permanent Normal Trade Relations (so that American businesses could take advantage of Russia's accession to the WTO in August 2012), but this was accompanied in December 2012 by the adoption of the Sergei Magnitsky Rule of Law Accountability Act, penalising 18 officials allegedly involved in the lawyer's death in November 2009. Pavel held out little hope for his father's immediate release, but sought at least a transfer to a prison closer to Moscow and improved conditions.

> I am sure that ultimately the key to my father's release is in the hands of Russian society – not in the hands of Mr. Putin. I think his release will come as a response to the demands of Russian society that, under today's conditions, cannot be ignored for long.[72]

Khodorkovsky warned the liberal democratic opposition against 'looking for allies exclusively among "liberals" and [that] it is even more of a mistake to refuse unity with clever trained "statists"'.[73] He remained true to his national-liberal convictions, favouring a 'state industrial policy designed to develop social infrastructure and a knowledge economy'.[74] In the third of his lectures published in *Novaya gazeta* in June 2012 he argued that Russia was stuck between an empire and a nation state, with the latter not yet formed while the former had not yet been transcended. He argued that liberals and nationalists should cooperate rather than compete, since the two were essentially similar. 'Real nationalists should be liberal. People become a nation when liberty becomes one of the basic values.' He noted that in Russia liberals were suspicious of nationalists, fearing a descent into chauvinism. He sought to traverse the fine line between the two, condemning the idea of the non-national character of liberalism. He wanted to achieve a reconciliation that would release Russia's huge potential. 'After all, liberals have always supported a nation's right to self-determination, including the right to create their own state. And there is no reason to deny this right to the Russian people.'[75] In sombre tones he warned that 'Russia today is on the brink. We are rich, but possibly because of this we are closer to self-destruction as a historical community.'[76] His voice now resonated across Russia and abroad. The Kremlin had turned Khodorkovsky into a political martyr, and the authorities became hostages to the hero that they had created.

FREEDOM

When asked about the so-called third 'Yukos case' during his four-hour press conference on 19 December 2013, Putin noted: 'As to the third case, I do not want to go into details but honestly speaking I, as a person watching this from the outside, do not see great prospects for this'. Barely an hour later, after the formal press conference had ended, when asked again about Khodorkovsky, Putin unexpectedly announced that he would 'in the nearest future' pardon him. Asked about the various amnesties, including the one announced the previous day that would see Greenpeace activists and others freed, Putin responded as follows:

> As for Khodorkovsky, you know that I have already spoken of this. Mikhail Borisovich should in line with the law have written the necessary document – a petition for clemency. He did not do this. But just recently he did write this document and addressed me with an appeal for clemency. He has already spent ten years in jail, which is a serious punishment. He bases his appeal on humanitarian grounds – his mother is ill. I think that taking into account all these circumstances, we can take the appropriate decision and in the nearest future a decree on his pardon will be signed.[77]

Putin signed the pardon shortly afterwards, and already at 2.30 a.m. on 20 December Khodorkovsky was woken in his prison cell in the Segezha camp in Karelia and driven to Petrozavodsk, where a short flight took him to Pulkovo airport in St Petersburg, from which a chartered German plane flew him to Berlin. In his first talk that evening with *The New Times*, the Russian magazine that had published his sketches of prison life, he said: 'After 10 years, I now have an unbelievable feeling of freedom. I am grateful to you and to everyone who supported me all this time [...] I love everyone, I am happy. The most important thing now is freedom, freedom, freedom'.[78]

In his first statement, Khodorkovsky announced that on 12 November 2013 he had written to the president for a pardon 'due to my family situation, and I am glad that his decision was positive'. He stressed that 'The issue of admission of guilt was not raised'. He did not mention that he wrote another letter to Putin stating that he had no intention of entering current politics and that he would not fight for the return of Yukos assets expropriated by the Kremlin.[79] His statement gave special thanks to the former German foreign minister (1974–92), Hans-Dietrich Genscher, for 'his personal participation in my fate', and looked forward to celebrating the holidays with his family.[80] It now became known that only two weeks after Khodorkovsky and Lebedev were sentenced for the second time, that is, in early 2011, evidence began to be collected for a third case, and the investigations intensified from February 2013 with new searches and interviews.[81] On 6 December the deputy prosecutor general, Alexander Zvyagintsev, raised the prospect of new criminal charges being filed against him. A third trial appeared imminent, focusing on an episode related to the main case launched in 2003 regarding the alleged laundering of $10 billion outside

Russia. There were fears that Khodorkovsky could also be accused of sponsoring experts and scholars to promote 'liberalisation of the criminal law in 2008–11' with money obtained from selling oil embezzled from Yukos subsidiaries.[82]

Khodorkovsky had been due for release in August 2014. Instead, the pardon indicated Putin's confidence that the oligarch no longer represented a threat. The protest movement provoked by his return to power had fizzled out, accompanied by some political reforms that would not change the tutelary powers of the regime but did allow a mild degree of greater pluralism and electoral competitiveness. The model of state–business relations in operation since the Yukos affair, with business largely absent from open politics, was still operating satisfactorily from the regime's perspective. With the Sochi Winter Olympics due to start in February 2014, the amnesty of most political prisoners and Khodorkovsky's release removed some of the major human rights issues poisoning relations with the West. Russian economic performance, moreover, was deteriorating, with only 1.4% growth registered in 2013. Nevertheless, the manner in which Putin made the announcement suggested that there remained powerful forces in the regime opposed to Khodorkovsky's release. A pardon, unlike an amnesty, does not require the State Duma's approval but is a presidential prerogative.

In his first major interview, with *The New Times*, on 21 December in the Adlon Hotel in Berlin, Khodorkovsky speculated that his departure for Berlin, in connection with his mother's illness, made Putin's decision rather easier. There had been no deal of any sort. Khodorkovsky did not consider himself in exile and wished to return to Moscow, but only on condition that he would be able to leave again. He insisted that the Yukos affair could not be over until the last of the Yukos prisoners was free. As for why Putin allowed his release, Khodorkovsky considered that it was intended above all to send a signal to his own entourage, to limit their fractiousness and greed. To impose order in his own group, Khodorkovsky argued, required either a ten-year sentence on the former minister of defence, Anatoly Serdyukov (accused of major corruption), or Khodorkovsky's release: 'I am glad that he took the latter option'. It was also a signal to society and the wider world that Putin felt himself back on top: 'I am not afraid. That was the signal'. More personally, when asked about why he had not been killed in jail, Khodorkovsky asserted that Putin had given two orders: that neither Khodorkovsky nor his family should be harmed. 'This was absolutely forbidden'.[83]

In his first press conference, held in Berlin on 22 December, Khodorkovsky thanked all those who had supported him, including the media, the German authorities and Chancellor Angela Merkel personally, who had 'made it possible for me to be free today'. He stressed that many victims of the Yukos affair still remained in jail, notably Lebedev and Pichugin. He was not planning an immediate return to Russia, since there was no guarantee for his immunity from further prosecution due to a court order to pay $550 million in damages dating back to his first conviction in 2005. If he returned, 'Russian law has the power of not allowing me to leave for abroad'. He opposed a boycott of the Sochi Olympics, arguing that 'a festival of sport should not be spoilt'. As for his appeal for clemency, Khodorkovsky explained that Genscher informed him on 12 November that Putin, unlike Medvedev, was not insisting that a pardon could only be granted if he accepted guilt. Since his release, Khodorkovsky explained, in any case depended on Putin personally, whether through clemency or the end of his term, a pardon for Khodorkovsky thus became a mere formality. He had no intention of funding the Russian opposition, and stressed that his involvement in politics was over:

> There is no question of politics, if politics is understood as a struggle for power, for me either. I am not interested or willing to take the way politicians in Russia have to a stance that is not quite frank. I believe that I have won for myself one right which is worth much – the right not to say what I what think.

Neither was he planning to go back into business: 'The question of business is closed to me, including from the point of view of fighting for my previous assets. I will not take part in it for the simple reason that I don't want to waste my time on that'.[84] Instead, he would get involved in unspecified public activities.

Had Khodorkovsky given up? Did the request for clemency automatically imply recognition of the lawfulness of all the court rulings against him? Formally, as argued above, there is no legal relation between pardon and admission of guilt, but politically, the circumstances attending his release undermined the case for his exoneration domestically, while impeding attempts to regain Yukos property abroad. It was not clear whether any conditions had been attached to his release. He had certainly not 'betrayed' his supporters, and Khodorkovsky insisted that he would continue to fight for the release of the remaining political prisoners, including Yukos officials. His political stature was somewhat diminished by the circumstances attending his release, allowing Putin to pose as the moral victor and supreme arbiter, but his personal prestige was unaffected. Abroad and at home, Khodorkovsky remained one of the moral leaders of post-Communist Russia. After ten years of imprisonment he retained his characteristic balance and composure, avoiding populist anti-Putin demagoguery while advancing a piercing analysis of the problems facing his country. His commitment to the peaceful but resolute improvement of Russia remained undimmed.

CHAPTER 12

CONCLUSION

In March 2000 Putin promised that if elected president, 'Russia's oligarchs will be abolished as a class'. Within five years a new system of state–business relations was created. Independent oligarchs like Khodorkovsky ceased to exist and business became dependent on the state, while a shadow class of 'beneficiaries' intercepted natural-resource rents and enjoyed a privileged relationship with the power system. The extractive power of the state was greatly enhanced, not only in terms of direct taxes but also in its ability to manage rents as a whole. The new system was forged in the crucible of the Yukos affair. The case exercised a profound influence on Russian politics in the early part of the twenty-first century, but it also raised universal issues about the role of the state in developmental agendas, the quality of political relationships and, indeed, the very category of 'freedom'. The selective application of the law against Khodorkovsky and his colleagues demonstrated not the power of the state but its weakness, unable to resolve genuine problems by means other than those that undermined the constitutional foundations of the state and legitimacy of the regime. The Yukos case turned into one of the most important political trials of the early twenty-first century.

While 'freedom' may have come to Russia in the 1990s following the collapse of Communism, the unaccustomed conditions meant that the necessary framework of constraints, limits and mutual responsibilities was lacking. Society lost its moral compass, and individuals and the state as a whole were deprived of the usual signifiers that transmit the moral code of a society down the generations. The Yukos affair acts as a prism through which the elements making up the new society can be identified. For his defenders, the attack on Khodorkovsky and his associates was provoked by his political activities and the threat that his independence posed to the regime. For others, he was an over-ambitious oligarch who headed a 'corporate criminal group' with the aim of defrauding the state and imposing his policies on society. Charges of financial and other crimes camouflaged a politically motivated prosecution. This book has demonstrated that the attack on Yukos was indeed political and highly selective, yet it reflected some profound dilemmas in Russia's developmental path. The regime's response only exacerbated these problems, reducing the efficacy of law and reinforcing archaic practices. From prison Khodorkovsky issued calm and measured analytical articles and became for many a spiritual and moral hero. When martyrdom came, Khodorkovsky claimed the moral right to speak for Russia.

The well-researched 113-minute film about Khodorkovsky by the German filmmaker Cyril Tuschi shows Putin telling the oligarchs that they could make money, but that politics was the Kremlin's business. The power of the film, shot between 2005 and 2011, lies in its presentation of contrasting versions of the Khodorkovsky affair, told from different perspectives of high-profile eyewitness and observers, revealing the contradictory nature of the case. In an interview filmed in 2009 during the second trial, with Khodorkovsky in the 'aquarium', Khodorkovsky tells Tuschi that he did not want to escape abroad to avoid arrest, since that would have left Lebedev 'hostage' to the Kremlin. He added that he was perhaps too naive to believe that law would rule in Putinite Russia.[1] The film's balanced and judicious approach makes it a worthy commentary on the Yukos affair and a fitting commemoration of Khodorkovsky's tribulations. With many people still critical of Khodorkovsky for his oligarch days, Tuschi insisted that his main aim was to show how people could change. 'I'm happy that I didn't do propaganda, so people can have their own opinions.'[2] The composer Arvo Pärt in 2009 dedicated his fourth symphony to Khodorkovsky, adding to the cultural iconography of the case.

The oligarchic factor was stressed in Hubert Seipel's documentary film *Ich, Putin: Ein Porträt* (*I, Putin: A Portrait*), aired on Gazprom-owned NTV on 7 May 2012. It portrayed Putin's tough childhood in the postwar courtyards of Leningrad and his lonely rise to the top. Putin describes how in the 1990s the state had been weak and oligarchs ran the show. Khodorkovsky is then shown, shortly before his arrest, and the narrator states:

> This billionaire, within a few years, thanks to dubious deals and the best connections in government, becomes one of the richest people in Russia. He declares war on the new president, financing the opposition and relying on the West. He wants to sell his Yukos oil business, the second largest in the country, to an American

oil conglomerate. He accuses the Kremlin of corruption. Putin fends of the allegations with accusations of tax evasion. The question is about who runs the country.

Footage of the fateful exchange on 19 February 2003 is shown, with Khodorkovsky raising the issue of corruption and Putin the question of tax evasion. The narrator continues: 'A few months later Khodorkovsky was arrested on charges of tax evasion and sentenced to eight years in prison.' Putin also defended his statement that 'A thief should sit in prison', just days before the second verdict, explaining that his comments referred to the first sentence.

Khodorkovsky the businessman was the product of a world in which a group of individuals were able to exploit their skills and connections and to establish the basis for a capitalist democracy characterised by the mega-wealth of the few and the immiseration of the many. Russia endured a virulent form of what in the 1990s was known as 'shock therapy', but tempered economically by entrenched and new interests who exploited the weakened state to their own advantage. A plutocratic social order was created in which the political and economic elites converged (although did not merge, allowing the political elites in due course to exact a type of revenge), and wealth was concentrated in the hands of a few. From a Marxist viewpoint this was once again a period of 'primitive accumulation', building on two earlier industrialisation campaigns in the late tsarist and early Soviet periods and accompanied therefore less by 'extra-economic coercion' than by 'intra-economic' violence. Encouraged by the rhetoric of neo-liberal globalisation, a disaster was inflicted upon the nation that was exploited by economic entrepreneurs, notably the so-called oligarchs, along with their Western allies.[3] This was 'creative destruction' on a grand scale.[4]

Russia swiftly became one of the most unequal societies in the world, and one in which a select group was able to forge mutually beneficial ties between the political and economic levels. However, in these years the foundations of Russian capitalism were established, and the basis laid for the economic boom that began in 1999 and lasted throughout Putin's first two-term presidency up to 2008, fuelled by high commodity prices. Yukos thrived in the environment of the 1990s, where connections with power were one of the most important business assets and the courts were used to ensure the necessary outcomes. With Putin's ascent to power a new model of state–business relations was imposed, dubbed the policy of 'equidistance': independent tycoons would no longer be allowed to have a privileged relationship with the state, while the state in theory would hold them all equally at arm's length. However, from the dual-state perspective it was not so much the state that was strengthened as the regime, which fought for its autonomy from both the state and the oligarchs. Within the regime, a new combination of political and economic power was forged and a group in due course emerged to take advantage of the new conditions.

The new system worked well enough in the first years of Putin's leadership. Some of the more egregiously political of the so-called 'oligarchs' were humbled, notably Gusinsky and Berezovsky, and both ended up in exile. The business community as a whole was not unhappy to see them go, since their flamboyant model of capitalism tended to discredit the system as a whole. Yukos continued to thrive, and moved towards the Western model of corporate governance. By early 2003 there were plans to merge with the Sibneft oil company, which would have created a major world energy company. At the same time, Yukos took on more of a political role, and Khodorkovsky made little secret of his political ambitions. Since at least 1998 he had undergone a type of spiritual evolution, what he called 'an internal reorientation of values'.[5] After an initial period of enthusiasm, he came to see Putin as a usurper. By 2003 all this had come together in a sustained attempt to create an alternative model: independent business, parliamentary opposition and a new free generation. This was the real struggle for Russia.

We have examined the many reasons for the estrangement between the regime and Yukos, and personally between Putin and Khodorkovsky. The case raised some fundamental political questions: 'What did Yukos and its shareholders actually represent? An organized criminal group of tremendous complexity and power, or an extremely powerful group of individuals who were regarded as a danger to the interests of Putin's ruling elite?'[6] Or simply a successful business that sought to become part of a multinational corporation and to operate according to the normal laws of international business, although with the mission to 'normalise' Russia so that business could operate autonomously and society could free itself from state tutelage? Russia always had exceptionally concentrated companies in core industries, accompanied by their closeness to the Russian state. In most periods of Russian history the state dominated, but in the 1990s the position was reversed. The Putinite strategy now sought to free the state from what it perceived to be the excessive power of financial–industrial groups.[7]

Russia had begun the transition with a large state apparatus but 'an exceptionally weak state', although its coercive capacities were greater than its regulatory potential, which permitted agents to enjoy freedom to privatise 'transition rents'.[8] The Yukos affair allowed a renascent state to 'de-privatise' these rents and use them for state-defined national priorities. It did not put an end to conflicts over resource rents, but it did change the environment in which these conflicts were conducted. Struggles were now primarily conducted within the regime rather than between independent economic actors in society. The extractive capacity of the state was greatly enhanced as the government learnt how to tax more effectively. The state could not entirely bypass the need to negotiate with society over the terms of rent extraction, although it did this in both constitutional and para-constitutional ways. The reform of the oil-tax regime in 2004, including the indexation of taxes with prices, allowed the government to benefit from the later rise in prices. The net result was an enormous enhancement of the fiscal capacity of the state. As Appel notes:

> Yet for all of the corruption and political failures of the Putin presidency, the improved fiscal situation of the country and the fact that not all of the oil wealth was stolen, but instead directed in large part towards improving Russia's fiscal health and future autonomy from foreign lenders, deserves much more recognition.[9]

The Yukos affair signalled that the oligarchs were no longer to fund political parties, independent think tanks or the media, and thus independent sources of finance were choked off, stifling the development of an autonomous civil society.[10]

Ira Straus, the American coordinator of the Committee on Russia in NATO, notes that

> The shunting of the Communists and ultra-nationalists out of their formerly joint hegemony in Parliament was Putin's proudest achievement as a centrist, making possible a working relationship with Parliament – an achievement for freedom and stability that, for a while, the democrats and the West appreciated.[11]

There was far more to the attack on Yukos than its funding of liberal (and other) parties in 2003, yet the regime expended enormous effort in creating a dominant party in the form of United Russia, and it was not ready to see the consolidation of a bloc of parliamentary deputies beholden to the maverick oligarch. In the end it was surprisingly easy for the regime to destroy Yukos and expropriate its assets, but the political costs were high and overshadowed both Medvedev's presidency and Putin's return to the Kremlin in 2012. Medvedev was unable to break his unspoken dependence on Putin, and his failure to resolve the Yukos case diminished his presidency as a whole. Khodorkovsky's challenge to the system of power and property consolidated in the Putin years is far from over.

In an interview with the BBC Russian Service on 10 May 2012, Andrei Borodin, the former head of Bank of Moscow, confirmed the extent to which the attack on

Yukos marked a turning point. Borodin had headed the bank since its foundation in 1994 at Luzhkov's request, but in April 2011 he joined the growing tide of exiles in London. Borodin noted that the bank had operated like all others, quoting Lenin to the effect that 'one cannot live in society and be free from society'. He accepted that

> Perhaps it was easier for us to operate, in the sense that we were a bank that worked a lot with state organisations. And the Moscow government was one of the principal shareholders. In fact, that was why we didn't have to pay bribes, since, when a state organisation is your main shareholder, it is in the interests of that organisation to support the business rather than to suck money out of it.

The tipping point according to Borodin was the 'Yukos affair':

> After that, the *siloviki* and officials had been given a clear signal – you can do the same as was done to Yukos right at the top – and, as they say in Russia, 'here we go again'. Some people right away understood what was happening. But the majority (including me), seem to have thought: well, it won't affect us anyway. [We thought] that we'd lie low, we'd get by [...] if we didn't stick our necks out and didn't engage in politics, perhaps the danger would pass us by. I'll tell you no lies – I don't know how I'd act [in that situation now]. But there's no doubt that the conclusions I'd have had to draw from that affair would have been drawn earlier.

He noted that entrepreneurs working in Russia have set up 'emergency airfields' so that they can make a quick exit, 'to leave the country in short order and at a fast pace'.[12] This is not exactly a promising business environment.

The Yukos affair revealed the clash between the logic of two different spheres. While Khodorkovsky represented the claim that the business world had the right to engage in political life to shape conditions suitable for its own purposes, Putin insisted that the state had the right to pre-eminence not only in the political sphere, but also over the broad directions of economic policy. Indeed, Putin went further in insisting that the state had the right to a dominant voice in detailed issues, including the direction of pipelines and access to resources and markets. Above all, the model of politics that Putin operated meant that the regime claimed a specific tutelary right over the management of the political system. For Putin, democracy was less a set of institutions than, to paraphrase Michael Mann, 'an ideology of equality, one that legitimates itself through a claim to represent the people and aims at a popular redistribution of social power'.[13] Equally, Amitai Etzioni argues that security is the prerequisite for the development of democratic institutions, and not the other way round, as the occupying forces understood in Germany and Japan after World War II, but not in Iraq in 2003[14] – a sentiment that fully accords with Putin's views. As far as Putin was concerned, politics was far too important to be left to the free play of political forces or an autonomous civil society, and thus the regime not only had the right but the duty to manage day-to-day political matters. Market forces came up against the concept of *dirigisme* in economic and political life, accompanied by a redistribution of power from independent economic actors (notably the oligarchs) to the bureaucracy: not quite a 'popular redistribution of social power' in Mann's sense, but a corrective to previous policies that was initially undoubtedly popular.

The Yukos affair has a resonance in debates and renewed leftist political programmes in Latin America, in particular in the Venezuela of Hugo Chávez and the Bolivia of Evo Morales. The hegemony of neo-liberalism was challenged on both theoretical and empirical grounds, and above all in the political sphere. How can we speak of freedom when there is gross inequality and the aggregative role of the state is undermined by particularistic interests?[15] The Yukos affair also poses the problem more broadly about the transferability of Western-style liberalism and its universality; it stands at the vortex of fundamentally different appreciations of the relationship between the right of citizens to develop political forms of representation, and the demand by modern states that in certain fundamental respects people are subjects, to be subordinated to the military and developmental projects of the government.

Conflicting demands in an unformed system such as Russia's assumed a particularly sharp character. In conditions of post-Communism, there were obvious tensions between citizenship and market subjectivity, as well as between political and economic representations of political activism. Khodorkovsky in effect claimed his right as a businessman and citizen to become involved in political life on his terms, without deferring to the existing power system. He carved out a vision of what an oppositional political figure could look like and how such a figure should act. Khodorkovsky forcefully asserted his claim to exercise his political rights and personal freedoms in the public domain. For him, freedom increasingly meant 'expression of individuality, or self-expression'.[16] Freedom became interpreted as the absence of impediments, a classical liberal approach that helped align his aspirations with the dominant values in the Euro-Atlantic political community, but which are not predominant in Russia.[17] Khodorkovsky repudiated the stoicism that is characteristic of Russian political subjectivity, which was accentuated (particularly in the business class) as a result of the Yukos affair, and asserted that indifference was not a political category that he could accept. Instead, in a number of ways, includ-ing the creation of the Open Russia Foundation, Khodorkovsky sought to shape the political environment.

The tension between freedom and justice is a theme repeatedly taken up by Khodorkovsky in his prison correspondence. Democracy, of course, is 'a constantly and painfully calculated combination of freedom and justice, the opposites mani-fested in dialectical unity'; however, in the context of managed democracy in the 2000s, the symbols and substance of both freedom and justice were appropriated into a discourse of state reconstitution. For the Putinites, the reassertion of the presumed prerogatives of the state was the only road to freedom and justice, but liberals lamented their inability to 'make the breaking up of the state monopoly on power irreversible',[18] an extraordinary ambition in any circumstances. Discussion in the late perestroika period onwards, according to a recent study, 'extolled the virtues of liberalism, which invariably proved to be, upon closer examination, a copy of crisis-stricken Western democracy', and 'A confusion of liberalism and democracy made it possible to sidestep the issue of the class nature of democracy and the socio-economic and political structures of liberalism taking shape within it'. Even worse:

> It was assumed that the reforms had to be carried out by the state, which at the same time had to withdraw from the market. At that time this patent nonsense did not strike the eye, because the public consciousness functioned in the logic of elementary abstractions.[19]

The sheer scope and the contradictory nature of the reforms set the stage for the Yukos affair later. This was, as Colton notes, 'the largest divestiture of state resources *anywhere* in history'.[20]

Putin stressed state autonomy and socially contextualised freedom. In his 'Russia at the turn of the millennium' manifesto on the eve of taking over the reins of power he argued that Russia had turned its back on Communism not so much because of the lack of freedom but because it led the country into a developmental impasse: 'The main thing is that Soviet power did not make the country prosperous, the society dynamic, or the people free. [...] We spent seven decades heading away from the main highway of civilisation towards a dead end.'[21] In his Federal Assembly address on 25 April 2005 he was unequivocal:

> We are a major European nation, we have always been an integral part of Europe and share all its values and the ideals of freedom and democracy. But we will carry

out this process ourselves, taking into account all our specific characteristics, and do not intend to report to anyone on the progress we make.[22]

This reflected Alexander Solzhenitsyn's thinking when he argued that 'the realisation of freedoms should not threaten the existence of the motherland or offend against people's religious feelings or ethnic sentiments' and that sacred things are values on a par with 'human rights'.[23]

The notion of 'managed democracy' from 2005 gave way to the idea of 'sovereign democracy', assuming a paternalist model of political engagement. As Stanley Benn notes,

> To protest against paternalism is not therefore necessarily to claim that the subjects are being treated contrary to their best interests, but that they are deprived of their right to decide for themselves what their interests are, and how best they would be served.[24]

Khodorkovsky was alive to the element of moral conflict in the case, and in his various publications from jail he reflected on the problem of how to legitimise a property settlement that not only had negative social consequences, in that it swiftly reduced Russia to the level of Brazil in terms of inequality, but also posed grave ethical issues: property that had been created by the Soviet people was transferred at a huge discount to a small group of people well-placed to lever access to power into property. Stephen Fortescue may well be right to argue that they key thing is what the new property owners did with their new assets, and mostly, and certainly in the case of Khodorkovsky, they created new value in the form of modern corporations and thus generated wealth that in the form of taxation was in part returned to the people.[25] However, the 'original sin' of the 1990s settlement is a stain that Khodorkovsky argued could not be removed so easily.

The Yukos affair is a modern representation of the Orthodox struggle for unity and diversity, testing the limits of individual freedom and collective responsibility. The tension between these various sets of binary values, Yury Lotman argued, is characteristic of Russian culture. He identifies a number of polar opposites, including charity versus justice, love versus the law, personal morality versus state law, and holiness versus politics. The tension between these is a universal theme, yet in Russia, Lotman argues, they take the form of a binary opposition: it's one or the other, politics or *pravda* ('truth'); you can't have both, and instead he advanced an evolutionary perspective.[26] The leitmotif of Putin's leadership was precisely the repudiation of revolution, yet the Yukos affair showed how deeply ingrained the polarising dynamic was in cultural terms. Khodorkovsky sought to portray his struggle as one of the free citizen against the despotic state, and his writings enunciate an evolutionary strategy. As typical products of the late Soviet era, the two shared a profoundly anti-revolutionary mentality (that is, opposed to the very logic of revolution);[27] however, finding themselves in a profoundly revolutionary historical process – the establishment of post-Communist Russian statehood and economy – the two ended up on opposite sides of the barricades.

In his final interview Berezovsky was asked whether he would have been prepared to go to jail if he had stayed in Russia. He responded: 'I don't have an answer to this question. Khodorkovsky saved himself [...] This doesn't mean that I have lost myself. But I've lived through a lot more of my own revaluations and disappointments than Khodorkovsky. I lost the meaning.'[28] Paradoxically, Khodorkovsky in jail remained truer to himself than the oligarch in London. Khodorkovsky's persecution can be compared to the Dreyfus affair in France, when the Jewish army officer Alfred Dreyfus was accused of treason in 1894 for allegedly having passed information to the Germans. After a massive public campaign in his defence, including Émile Zola's famous open letter 'J'accuse', in 1906 Dreyfus was exonerated. Although initially there was little public agitation in Russia on Khodorkovsky's behalf, a groundswell of support developed. There is a further similarity, well drawn-out in the historian Vincent Duclert's argument for Dreyfus's remains to be transferred to the Panthéon, the mausoleum for the great and the good of France, including Zola himself:

> Although he was a victim of a conspiracy at the heart of state Dreyfus was a heroic fighter for justice. Even after undergoing this terrifying deportation he refused to behave like a condemned man. He behaved like someone who was innocent. He did not see himself as a victim because he was Jewish but a citizen fighting for the truth.[29]

Khodorkovsky acknowledged the similarities, but stressed that in the Dreyfus case others had not been taken hostage to provide false evidence, there had been no 'marauding' to seize property and there had not been such intense personal feelings 'as Putin has towards me, otherwise Dreyfus would not have been pardoned five years after his arrest at the government's request, without any "repentance" or personal request'.[30]

In an exaggerated but exemplary form, Khodorkovsky's fate reflects that of Russia's larger transition out of Communism and into an era of brutal conflict over the fate of the country. He was a loyal Komsomol activist, a proponent of neo-liberal capitalism, a patriotic Russian citizen and a concerned philanthropist. As his co-author Natalya Gevorkyan puts it:

> Russia's future richest man was born during Khrushchev's thaw, grew up in Brezhnev's stagnation, gained his first fortune during Gorbachev's perestroika, became a millionaire under Yeltsin and a billionaire in the 2000s. He then lost his freedom, company and business.[31]

His trajectory follows that of Putin's by a decade, shaped by the same Soviet experience followed by astonishing upward mobility, yet ultimately finding themselves enemies. This epochal confrontation exposed the condition of suppressed civil war that for so long has haunted Russia.

In the end, Putin and Khodorkovsky became locked into a type of mutual dependency that tested them both. Khodorkovsky admitted that 'He [Putin] is very similar to me (or me to him, since he is older). But I was able (forced to?) change; but he has stayed the same. He sees only the game, and not the players.'[32] Both were educated with a sense of 'duty to the country' but ended up with very different representations of 'the good life'.[33] It may seem not paradoxical but absurd to suggest that a man twice sentenced to a corrective colony and enduring long days of deprivation, humiliation and the most direct loss of freedom could exercise such power over a man at the pinnacle of the political tree, the presidency of one of the world's great powers. Yet we have seen this type of relationship before, and Mandela's 'long walk to freedom' from incarceration in Robben Island ended with him becoming president of South Africa. The Yukos affair represented a confrontation between two personalities, each of whom in their own way believed they were pursuing the path of freedom most appropriate for the good of Russia. In this struggle, the man in the Kremlin and the man in the labour camp were equals, and it is not difficult to envisage circumstances where their positions could be reversed. Khodorkovsky's release in December 2013 signalled perhaps the beginning of the reconciliation of the contrasting visions of Russian development represented by the two men. Khodorkovsky could not avoid becoming a symbol of aspirations for strengthened democratic constitutionalism, while Putin had learnt that the 'oligarch' was not after all such a threat.

LIST OF ACRONYMS

AAR	Alfa Group, Access Industries and Renova Group (aka Alfa–Access–Renova)
AOZT	Closed joint-stock company (*Aktsionernoe obshchestvo zakrytogo tipa*)
BAM	Baikal–Amur Mainline
CNPC	China National Petroleum Corporation
KPRF	Communist Party of the Russian Federation (*Kommunisticheskaya partiya Rossiiskoi Federatsii*)
KPSS	Communist Party of the Soviet Union (*Kommunisticheskaya partiya Sovetskogo Soyuza*)
ECHR	European Convention on Human Rights and Fundamental Freedoms
ECtHR	European Court of Human Rights
FIG	Financial–industrial group
FSB	Federal Security Service (*Federal'naya sluzhba bezopasnosti*)
FSIN	Federal Penitentiary Service (*Federal'naya sluzhba ispolneniya nakazanii*)
GAAP	Generally Accepted Accounting Principles
GML	Group Menatep Ltd
IBAHRI	International Bar Association Human Rights Institute
IC	Investigative Committee (previously within the Prosecutor General's Office but now autonomous)
INS	National Strategy Institute (*Institut natsional'noi strategii*)
IVTAN	High Temperatures Institute of the Academy of Sciences (*Institut vysokikh temperature* AN SSSR), now Joint Institute for High Temperatures RAS

KGB	Committee for State Security (*Komitet gosudarstvennoi bezopasnosti*)
MERT	Ministry of Economic Development and Trade
MVD	Ministry of Internal Affairs (*Ministerstvo vnutrennikh del*)
NEP	New Economic Policy (*Novaya economicheskaya politika*)
NIUIF	Samoilov Research Institute for Fertilisers and Insectofungicides (*Nauchno-issledovatel'skii institut po udobreniyam i insektofungitsidam imeni Ya.V. Samoilova*)
NTTM	Centre for the scientific and technical creativity of youth (*Tsentr nauchno-tekhnicheskogo tvorchestva molodezhi*)
OSI	Open Society Institute
OVR	Fatherland–All Russia (*Otechestvo–Vsya Rossiya*)
PFIG	Politicised financial–industrial group
PGO	Prosecutor General's Office
PSA	production-sharing agreements
RAO UES	Unified Energy System of Russia (*RAO Edinaya energeticheskaya sistema Rossii*)
RGGU	Russian State Humanities University (*Rossiiskii gosudarstvennyi gumanitarnyi universitet*)
RSPP	Russian Union of Industrialists and Entrepreneurs (*Rossiiskii soyuz promyshlennikov i predprinimatelei*)
SIZO	Pre-trial detention centre (*Sledsvennyi izolyator*)
SNS	Council for National Strategy (*Sovet po natsional'noi strategii*)
SPS	Union of Right Forces (*Soyuz pravykh sil*)
TNK	Tyumen Oil Company (*Tyumenskaya neftyanaya kompaniya*)
UDO	Parole (*Uslovno-dosrochnoe osvobozhdenie*)
UPK	Criminal Procedure Code (*Ugolovno-protsessual'nyi kodeks*)
USAID	United States Agency for International Development
VNK	Eastern Oil Company (*Vostochnaya neftyanaya kompaniya*)
VTSIOM	All-Russian Centre for the Study of Public Opinion (*Vserossiiskii tsentr izucheniya obshchestvennogo mneniya*)
WTO	World Trade Organisation
YNG	Yuganskneftegaz
ZATO	Closed administrative-territorial formation (*Zakrytoe administrativnoe-territorial'noe obrazovanie*)

NOTES

INTRODUCTION

1   John Harvey, *The Plantagenets* (London: Fontana/Collins, [1948] 1967), p. 45.
2   The idea of the dual state is drawn from Ernst Fraenkel, *The Dual State: A Contribution to the Theory of Dictatorship*, translated from the German by E.A. Shils, in collaboration with Edith Lowenstein and Klaus Knorr (New York: Oxford University Press, 1941; reprinted by The Lawbook Exchange Ltd, 2006).
3   This is analysed in Richard Sakwa, 'The regime system in Russia', *Contemporary Politics*, 3(1), 1997, pp. 7–25; id., 'The dual state in Russia', *Post-Soviet Affairs*, 26(3), July–September 2010, pp. 185–206; id., *The Crisis of Russian Democracy: The Dual State, Factionalism and the Medvedev Succession* (Cambridge: Cambridge University Press, 2011).
4   Valerii Panyushkin, *Mikhail Khodorkovskii: Uznik tishiny* (Moscow: Sekret Firmy, 2006), frontispiece.
5   Ibid., p. 7.

1. RISE OF THE CITIZEN OLIGARCH

1   Valerii Butaev, 'Khodorkovskii priznalsya v $7 mlrd. s kopeikami', *Komsomol'skaya pravda*, 22 June 2002, p. 3. Please also note that here and throughout the book, US dollars are used unless otherwise specified.
2   'Kratkii kurs istorii milliarderov', *Izvestiya*, 1 March 2003, p. 2.
3   For an outstanding analysis of the way in which the oligarchs made their fortunes, including a detailed study of Khodorkovsky's rise (pp. 100–26), see David E. Hoffman, *The Oligarchs: Wealth and Power in the New Russia* (New York: PublicAffairs, 2002).
4   Mumin Shakirov, 'Khodorkovsky's parents worry and remember', *Moscow Times*, 2 June 2008.
5   Mikhail Khodorkovskii and Nataliya Gevorkyan, *Tyur'ma i volya* (Moscow: Howard Roark, 2012), p. 69.
6   Inna Luk'yanova, 'Chelovek s rublem', *Profil'*, 43, 23 November 1998.
7   Vera Chelishcheva, *Zaklyuchennyi No. 1: Neslomlennyi Khodorkovskii* (Moscow: Eksmo, 2011), p. 29.

8   Khodorkovskii and Gevorkyan, *Tyur'ma i volya*, p. 71.
9   Ibid., p. 99.
10   Ibid., pp. 33–5.
11   Author's interview with Gleb Pavlovsky, Russia House, 28 January 2008.
12   Larisa Kallioma, "'U Mishi ruki ne ottuda rastut, emu nel'zya eksperimental'noi khimiei'", *Izvestiya*, 6 June 2005, p. 3.
13   Khodorkovskii and Gevorkyan, *Tyur'ma i volya*, p. 73.
14   Ibid., p. 74.
15   Ibid., p. 75.
16   Luk'yanova, 'Chelovek s rublem'.
17   Ol'ga Kryshtanovskaya, *Anatomiya rossiiskoi elity* (Moscow: Zakharov, 2005), pp. 296–7.
18   *Kommersant*, 42, 22–9 October 1990; cited in Mikhail Khodorkovskii and Leonid Nevzlin, *Chelovek s rublem* (Moscow: Menatep-Inform, 1992), p. 7.
19   Khodorkovskii and Gevorkyan, *Tyur'ma i volya*, p. 77.
20   Ibid.
21   The academic Aleksandr Sheindlin, the rector of IVTAN at the time, has fond memories of how he helped Khodorkovsky and Leonid Nevzlin build up their business empire at the suggestion of the USSR State Committee on Science and Technology, and later he joined the Advisory Board of Menatep. He claimed to have no regrets and argued that as a good judge of character he questioned whether they had committed any misdeeds; see Irina Timofeeva, 'Prezhde chem poiti v biznes, byvshie komsomoltsy posovetovalis' s akademikami', *Novaya gazeta*, 92, 9 December 2003. Khodorkovsky also has warm memories of him; see Khodorkovskii and Gevorkyan, *Tyur'ma i volya*, pp. 79–80.
22   Kryshtanovskaya, *Anatomiya rossiiskoi elity*, p. 299.
23   Rose Brady, *Kapitalizm: Russia's Struggle to Free Its Economy* (New Haven, CT: Yale University Press, 1999), p. 55.
24   Kryshtanovskaya, *Anatomiya rossiiskoi elity*, p. 303.
25   Khodorkovskii and Gevorkyan, *Tyur'ma i volya*, p. 83.
26   *Moskovskaya pravda*, 28 December 1990.
27   Marshall I. Goldman, *The Piratization of Russia: Russian Reform Goes Awry* (London and New York: Routledge, 2003), p. 147.
28   Khodorkovskii and Nevzlin, *Chelovek s rublem*, p. 203.
29   This information surfaced following the search of the basement of Media-Most's security department in 2000, in which a database was found with telephone transcripts; see Rimma Akhmirova, *Ya sidel s Khodorkovskim: Dokumental'nye khroniki* (Moscow: Sobesednik, 2005), p. 133. See also V.M. Kartashov, *Who Is Mr. Hodorkowsky?* (Rostov-on-Don: Feniks, 2007), pp. 83–4.
30   In 1992 Menatep's board of directors comprised 11 members: in addition to Khodorkovsky and Nevzlin there were Marina Kuzkina, Mikhail Brudno, Alexei Golubovich, Ruslan Dakhaev, Vladimir Dubov, Boris Zolotarev, Platon Lebedev, Sergei Monakhov and Vladislav Surkov – overwhelmingly male, with an average age of 30; see Khodorkovskii and Nevzlin, *Chelovek s rublem*, p. 94.
31   Ibid., p. 121.
32   Khodorkovskii and Gevorkyan, *Tyur'ma i volya*, p. 81.
33   For details of the scheme, see Sergei Mavrodi, *Vsya pravda o 'MMM': Istoriya pervoi piramidy. Tyuremnye dnevniki* (Moscow: RIPOL klassik, 2007).
34   Kryshtanovskaya, *Anatomiya rossiiskoi elity*, p. 305.
35   Valery Kryukov and Arild Moe, 'Banks and the financial sector', in David Lane (ed.), *The Political Economy of Russian Oil* (Lanham, MD: Rowman & Littlefield, 1999), p. 52.

36   Kirill Venediktov, 'Roman s neft'yu: Zek i gubernator', *Smysl*, 1(20), January 2008, pp. 28–9, at p. 28. This activity was handled by N. Kruchina, head of administration at the Central Committee of the KPSS; he committed suicide immediately after the August 1991 coup.

37   Kartashov, *Who Is Mr. Hodorkowsky?*, pp. 105, 114–15. One of them, the Russian Exchange Bank, funded Yeltsin's presidential campaign in June 1991, thus making him financially independent of the democratic movement that brought him to power. In turn, the head of the bank, Alex Konanykhin, received privileges and free access once Yeltsin displaced Gorbachev in the Kremlin in late December 1991, making him Russia's richest man before his spectacular fall the following year, when he was an early victim of a 'raiding' attack. In exile in New York, he later became Menatep's vice president for international development.

38   Khodorkovskii and Gevorkyan, *Tyur'ma i volya*, p. 123.

39   Ibid., pp. 120–1.

40   Ibid., pp. 124–5.

41   Ibid., p. 125.

42   Ibid., p. 126.

43   For an account of this early period, see Paul Klebnikov, 'The oligarch who came in from the cold', *Forbes*, 18 March 2002, [online]. Available at http://www.forbes.com/forbes/2002/0318/110_print.html (accessed 18 September 2013).

44   David Satter, *Darkness at Dawn: The Rise of the Russian Criminal State* (New Haven, CT: Yale University Press, 2003), pp. 272–3, footnote 5. For further details of these alleged machinations, see Matt Bivens and Jonas Bernstein, 'The Russia you never met', *Demokratizatsiya: The Journal of Post-Soviet Democratization*, 6(4), Fall 1998, pp. 613–47.

45   Valerii Panyushkin, *Mikhail Khodorkovskii: Uznik tishiny* (Moscow: Sekret Firmy, 2006), p. 63.

46   Kartashov, *Who Is Mr. Hodorkowsky?*, p. 85.

47   Hoffman, *The Oligarchs*, pp. 122–3.

48   Khodorkovskii and Nevzlin, *Chelovek s rublem*, p. 92.

49   Khodorkovskii and Gevorkyan, *Tyur'ma i volya*, p. 167.

50   Vladimir Perekrest, 'Za chto sidit Mikhail Khodorkovskii', Part 1, *Izvestiya*, 17 May 2006.

51   Natal'ya Gotova, 'Mikhail Khodorkovskii ukhodit v promyshlennost'', *Segodnya*, 29 March 1996.

52   Khodorkovskii and Gevorkyan, *Tyur'ma i volya*, p. 196.

53   Marshall I. Goldman, *Oilopoly: Putin, Power, and the Rise of the New Russia* (Oxford: Oneworld Publications, 2008), p. 109. There were persistent reports about Menatep's links with organised crime, notably in laundering the funds of the Ingush mafia. Khodorkovsky immediately sought to bring the CIA onside and organised a major event for them and influential Americans at the Russian embassy in Washington, the first major case of his independent foreign-policy entrepreneurship. See Kartashov, *Who Is Mr. Hodorkowsky?*, p. 101.

54   *Kommersant*, 13 October 1992; Kartashov, *Who Is Mr. Hodorkowsky?*, pp. 86–7.

55   Kartashov, *Who Is Mr. Hodorkowsky?*, p. 196.

56   Ibid., p. 88. The Media-Most group headed by Gusinsky also supported Gaidar, but his main party-building effort went into supporting the social-liberal Yabloko party headed by Grigory Yavlinsky.

57   John Lloyd, *Rebirth of a Nation: An Anatomy of Russia* (London: Michael Joseph, 1998), p. 306.

58   Thane Gustafson, *Capitalism Russian-Style* (Cambridge: Cambridge University Press, 1999), p. 89.

59   Arkady Ostrovsky, 'Putin oversees rise of security apparatus', *Financial Times*, 31 October 2003.

60   Paul Klebnikov, *Godfather of the Kremlin: Boris Berezovsky and the Looting of Russia* (New York: Harcourt, 2000); we shall be citing the Russian version, Pavel Khlebnikov, *Krestnyi otets kremlya Boris Berezovskii, ili Istoriya razgrableniya Rossii* (Moscow: Detektiv-Press, 2001), p. 6. The security service of Vladimir Gusinsky's Most group numbered over 1,000, with its largest part headed by Filipp Bobkov, a former deputy head of the KGB; see Khlebnikov, *Krestnyi otets kremlya*, p. 151.

61   Interview with Anthony Latta, 'Khodorkovsky, Menatep and Yukos', *Moscow News*, 24 March 2004, p. 1.

62   For the development of the Soviet oil industry, see Thane Gustafson, *Crisis Amid Plenty: The Politics of Soviet Energy under Brezhnev and Gorbachev* (Princeton: Princeton University Press, 1989).

63   Nina Poussenkova, *From Rigs to Riches: Oilmen vs. Financiers in the Russian Oil Sector* (Houston, TX: The James A. Baker III Institute for Public Policy of Rice University, October 2004), p. 1.

64   For the birth of the Russian oil majors, Lukoil, Surgutneftegaz and Yukos, see Thane Gustafson, *Wheel of Fortune: The Battle for Oil and Power in Russia* (Cambridge, MA: Belknap Press, 2012), pp. 98–144.

65   See Nina Poussenkova, 'Rosneft' kak zerkalo russkoi evolyutsii', *Pro et Contra*, 10(2–3), March–June 2006, pp. 91–104.

66   The three oil refineries were Kuibyshev, Syzran and Novokuibyshev.

67   For a general analysis of the loans-for-shares scheme, see Duncan Allan, 'Banks and the loans-for-shares auctions', in David Lane (ed.), *Russian Banking: Evolution, Problems and Prospects* (Cheltenham: Edward Elgar, 2002), pp. 137–59.

68   Kryukov and Moe, 'Banks and the financial sector', p. 62.

69   Khodorkovskii and Gevorkyan, *Tyur'ma i volya*, pp. 186–7.

70   Ibid., p. 223.

71   Ibid., p. 184.

72   Daniel Treisman, '"Loans for shares" revisited', *Post-Soviet Affairs*, 26(3), 2010, pp. 207–27, with the quotation at p. 225.

73   Vladimir Putin, 'Poslanie prezidenta Federal'nomu Sobraniyu', 12 December 2012. Available at http://kremlin.ru/news/17118 (accessed 23 September 2013).

74   Quoted in Khodorkovskii and Gevorkyan, *Tyur'ma i volya*, p. 199.

75   The hitherto unknown company was registered in Taldom, in Moscow region, and the whole process was conducted in a manner prefiguring the role that the unknown Baikal Finance Group would play in December 2004 in allowing Rosneft to buy Yukos's main production field, YNG. The state had learnt how to play by the same rules as the oligarchs.

76   The third bid represented a consortium of Alfa bank, Inkombank and Rossiyskiy Kredit Bank, and was rejected for 'the absence of properly filled out banking documents' (Satter, *Darkness at Dawn*, p. 108). See: Khlebnikov, *Krestnyi otets kremlya*, p. 203; Panyushkin, *Mikhail Khodorkovskii*, pp. 72–3.

77   Khlebnikov, *Krestnyi otets kremlya*, p. 262.

78   Valery Kryukov and Arild Moe, *The Changing Role of Banks in the Russian Oil Sector* (London: RIIA, 1998).

79   Kryshtanovskaya, *Anatomiya rossiiskoi elity*, p. 325.

80   Juliet Johnson, 'Russia's emerging financial–industrial groups', *Post-Soviet Affairs*, 13(4), 1997, pp. 333–65.

81   Peter Glatter, 'Federalization, fragmentation, and the West Siberian oil and gas province', in David Lane (ed.), *The Political Economy of Russian Oil* (Lanham, MD: Rowman & Littlefield, 1999), p. 156.

82   Panyushkin, *Mikhail Khodorkovskii*, pp. 69–70. For Khodorkovsky's own account, see Khodorkovskii and Gevorkyan, *Tyur'ma i volya*, pp. 134–6.
83   For a vivid description of Berezovsky's conflict with Gusinsky in 1994–5, and their alliance in 1996–7 on the basis of common support for Yeltsin's re-election, see Aleksandr Korzhakov, *Boris El'tsin: ot rassveta do zakata* (Moscow: Interbuk, 1997).
84   Aleksandr Korzhakov, *Boris El'tsin: ot rassveta do zakata. Posleslovie* (Moscow: Detektiv-Press, 2004), pp. 482–3.
85   The others were Boris Berezovsky, Vladimir Gusinsky, Vladimir Potanin and Mikhail Fridman, and the meeting was called at their request. Boris Yeltsin, *Midnight Diaries* (London: Weidenfeld & Nicolson, 2000), pp. 20–1.
86   Timothy J. Colton, *Yeltsin: A Life* (New York: Basic Books, 2008), p. 355.
87   Marina Shakina, 'Biznesmeny vykhodyat iz-za kulis', *Nezavisimaya gazeta*, 27 April 1996.
88   'Get out of the impasse', *Current Digest of the Post-Soviet Press*, 48(17), 22 May 1996, pp. 1–3; from 'Vyiti iz tupika!', *Kommersant*, 27 April 1996, p. 1. The letter, published on that day in all the major papers, was signed by Khodorkovsky, Nevzlin and Muravlenko from Mentaep–Yukos as well as Berezovsky, Gusinsky, Potanin, Smolensky, Fridman and five others.
89   'Get out of the impasse', p. 1.
90   Ibid.
91   Mikhail Khodorkovskii, *Levyi povorot 2* (Moscow: Galleya-Print, 2006), p. 5; discussed in Chapter 10.
92   Khlebnikov, *Krestnyi otets kremlya*, p. 10.
93   The seven bankers were Boris Berezovsky, Mikhail Fridman, Vladimir Gusinsky, Mikhail Khodorkovsky, Vladimir Potanin, Alexander Smolensky and Vladimir Vinogradov. Chrystia Freeland, John Thornhill and Andrew Gowers, 'Moscow's group of seven', *Financial Times*, 1 November 1996, p. 17. Petr Aven is listed when in fact the seventh was Vinogradov, head of Inkombank.
94   Ibid.
95   Cited by Andrei Piontovsky, 'Modern-day Rasputin', *Moscow Times*, 12 November 1997.
96   Kryshtanovskaya, *Anatomiya rossiiskoi elity*, p. 330.
97   Satter, *Darkness at Dawn*, p. 54.
98   Stephen Fortescue, *Russia's Oil Barons and Metal Magnates: Oligarchs and State in Transition* (Basingstoke: Palgrave Macmillan, 2006), p. 59.
99   Martin Gilman, *No Precedent, No Plan: Inside Russia's 1998* (Cambridge, MA, and London: MIT Press, 2010).
100 The struggle with Dart focused in particular on his ownership of Acirota Ltd, which owned 13% of Tomskneft, technically a subsidiary of VNK. See Panyushkin, *Mikhail Khodorkovskii*, pp. 120–1; see also Fortescue, *Russia's Oil Barons*, p. 63.
101 Chelishcheva, *Zaklyuchennyi No. 1*, pp. 70–1.
102 Hoffman, *The Oligarchs*, pp. 448–52.
103 Klebnikov, 'The oligarch who came in from the cold'.
104 However, Yukos type 1 American Depositary Receipts (ADRs) were traded earlier.
105 Aleksei Osipov, 'Khodorkovskii i "Yukos": khronika "ideal'nogo prestupleniya"', *Novaya gazeta*, 4 October 1999.
106 'Oproverzhenie', *Novaya gazeta*, 9 November 2000.
107 Matthew Brzezinski, *Casino Moscow: A Tale of Greed and Adventure on Capitalism's Wildest Frontier* (New York: Free Press, 2001), p. 308.
108 Panyushkin, *Mikhail Khodorkovskii*, p. 96.
109 The letter to Panyushkin was written from pre-trial detention after October 2003 and is cited in Panyushkin, *Mikhail Khodorkovskii*, p. 110.

110   Gustafson, *Wheel of Fortune*, pp. 185–230.
111   In 1999 Yukos invested 1.7 billion roubles, but planned to increase this to 11 billion roubles in 2000, of which 8.35 billion roubles would go directly into raising output. See Tat'yana Lysova, 'Kuda devat' den'gi', *Vedomosti*, 25 October 1999.
112   Surgutneftegaz covered its ownership structure in a complicated cross-holding scheme and in 2003 stopped publishing GAAP-compliant financial reports. See Catherine Belton and Neil Buckley, 'On the offensive: how Gunvor rose to the top of Russian oil trading', *Financial Times*, 14 May 2008.
113   Chrystia Freeland, *Sale of the Century: Russia's Wild Ride from Communism to Capitalism* (New York: Crown Business, 2000), p. 157.
114   Simon Pirani, 'Oligarch? No, I'm just an oil magnate', *The Observer*, 4 June 2000.
115   'Who owns Russia?', *Forbes*, 18 March 2002. Available at http://www.forbes.com/forbes/2002/0318/110tab.html (accessed 23 September 2013).
116   'The world's richest people', *Forbes*, 26 February 2004. Available at http://www.forbes.com/2004/02/25/bill04land.html (accessed 18 October 2013).
117   Serge Schmemann, 'In going legit, some Russian tycoons resort to honesty', *New York Times*, 12 January 2003.
118   Klebnikov, 'The oligarch who came in from the cold'.
119   Panyushkin, *Mikhail Khodorkovskii*, p. 149.
120   Oleg Chernitskii, 'Eshche odin chestnyi oligarkh', *Vremya novostei*, 16 May 2001, p. 4.
121   Judy Sarasohn, 'Russia's jailed titans have Washington ally', *Washington Post*, 25 December 2003.

2. THE STATE AND THE OLIGARCHS

1   'Vystuplenie pri predstavlenii ezhegodnogo poslaniya prezidenta Rossiiskoi Federatsii Federal'nomu Sobraniyu Rossiiskoi Federatsii', 8 July 2000.
2   'Vladimir Putin – "Rossiya ne dol'zhna byt' i ne budet politseiskim gosudarstvom": prezident Rossii dal interv'yu "Izvestiyam"', *Izvestiya*, 14 July 2000, p. 1.
3   Lee S. Wolosky, 'Putin's plutocrat problem', *Foreign Affairs*, 79(2), March–April 2000, p. 18.
4   Vladimir Putin, 'Otkrytoe pis'mo Vladimira Putina k rossiiskim izbiratelyam', *Izvestiya*, 25 February 2000, p. 5.
5   Interview on Radio Mayak, 18 March 2000, in BBC Summary of World Broadcasts, SU/3793 B/3; also cited in David E. Hoffman, *The Oligarchs: Wealth and Power in the New Russia* (New York: PublicAffairs, 2002), p. 475.
6   'Vladimir Putin: Pozitivnye tendentsii est', no poka eto tol'ko tendentsii. Prezident Rossii v interv'yu ORT, RTR i Nezavisimoi gazete podvodit itogi 2000 goda', *Nezavisimaya gazeta*, 26 December 2000, p. 1.
7   'Vstupitel'noe slovo na vstreche s rukovoditelyami krupneishikh rossiiskikh kompanii i bankov', 28 July 2000. Available at http://www.kremlin.ru/appears/2000/07/28/0000_type63376_28808.shtml (accessed 24 September 2013).
8   William Tompson, 'Putting Yukos in perspective', *Post-Soviet Affairs*, 21(2), April–June 2005, p. 168.
9   Wolfgang Merkel, 'Embedded and defective democracies', *Democratisation*, 11(5), December 2004, p. 49.
10   Mikhail Zygar and Valerii Panyushkin, *Gazprom: Novoe russkoe oruzhie* (Moscow: Zakharov, 2008).
11   Brian Killen, 'Interview: Russian oil baron impressed by Putin', *Johnson's Russia List*, No. 4085, 2 February 2000, item 7.

12 'Dialogi: Lyudmila Ulitskaya – Mikhail Khodorkovskii', in Mikhail Khodorkovskii, *Stat'i, dialogi, interv'yu* (Moscow: Eksmo, 2010), p. 116; see also Vera Chelishcheva, *Zaklyuchennyi No. 1: Neslomlennyi Khodorkovskii* (Moscow: Eksmo, 2011), pp. 112–13.

13 Mikhail Khodorkovskii and Nataliya Gevorkyan, *Tyur'ma i volya* (Moscow: Howard Roark, 2012), pp. 305–6.

14 All this is described well in Paul Klebnikov, *Godfather of the Kremlin: Boris Berezovsky and the Looting of Russia* (New York: Harcourt, 2000).

15 Cited in Dale R. Herspring and Jacob Kipp, 'Understanding the elusive Mr. Putin', *Problems of Post-Communism*, 48(5), September–October 2001, p. 9.

16 For his analysis of the anti-oligarch investigations and his dismissal, see Yurii Skuratov, *Variant drakona* (Moscow: Detektiv-Press, 2000); for a larger review, see id., *Kremlevskie podryady: Poslednee delo genprokurora* (Moscow: Algoritm, 2012).

17 Natal'ya Arkhangel'skaya et al., 'Provokatsiya', *Ekspert*, 27, 17 July 2000, in *Ekspert: Luchshie materialy*, 2, 2007, pp. 14–16.

18 Ibid., p. 15.

19 Ol'ga Kryshtanovskaya, 'Transformatsiya biznes-elity Rossii, 1998–2002', *Sotsiologicheskie issledovaniya*, 8, 2002, p. 23.

20 Putin, 'Rossiya ne dolzhna byt' i ne budet politseiskim gosudarstvom', p. 1.

21 Arkady Ostrovsky, 'Berezovsky hits at Putin campaign', *Financial Times*, 18 July 2000, p. 10.

22 Amelia Gentleman, 'Tycoon resigns from Duma as relations with Kremlin cool', *Guardian*, 18 July 2000, p. 12.

23 Sarah Karush, 'Berezovsky says he's quitting the Duma', *Moscow Times*, 18 July 2000, p. 1.

24 Amelia Gentleman, 'Putin picks off opponents who matter most', *Guardian*, 14 July 2000, p. 20.

25 For a good study of the background to these events, see Laura Belin, 'The Russian media in the 1990s', in Rick Fawn and Stephen White (eds), *Russia after Communism* (London: Frank Cass, 2002), pp. 139–60.

26 Timothy J. Colton, *Yeltsin: A Life* (New York: Basic Books, 2008), p. 405.

27 A.A. Yakovlev, 'Vlast', biznes i dvizhushchie sily ekonomicheskogo razvitiya v Rossii: do i posle "dela YUKOSa"', *Obshchestvennye nauki i sovremennost'*, 1, 2005, pp. 35–44.

28 The points were outlined by Nemtsov, in Arkady Ostrovsky, 'Oligarchs to seek peace deal with Putin', *Financial Times*, 24 July 2000.

29 A.Yu. Zudin, 'Rezhim V. Putina: kontury novoi politicheskoi sistemy', *Obshchestvennye nauki i sovremennost'*, 2, 2003, pp. 67–83. See also: id., 'Oligarchy as a political problem of Russian postcommunism', *Russian Social Science Review*, 41(6), November–December 2000, pp. 4–33; id., 'Neokorporativizizm v Rossii', *Pro et Contra*, 6(4), 2001, pp. 171–98.

30 Yakovlev, 'Vlast', biznes i dvizhushchie sily', p. 37.

31 Alexander Budberg, 'Gryaznaya osen' 2003 goda', *Moskovskii komsomolets*, 12 September 2003, p. 3.

32 Richard Sakwa, 'Systemic stalemate: *Reiderstvo* and the dual state', in Neil Robinson (ed.), *The Political Economy of Russia* (Lanham, MD: Rowman & Littlefield, 2013), pp. 69–96. See also A. Kireev, 'Reiderstvo na rynke korporativnogo kontrolya: rezultat evolyutsii silovogo predprinimatel'stva', *Voprosy ekonomiki*, 8, 2007, pp. 80–92.

33 Vadim Volkov, 'Violent entrepreneurship in post-communist Russia', *Europe–Asia Studies*, 51(5), July 1999, pp. 741–54. See also id., *Violent Entrepreneurs: The Use of Force in the Making of Russian Capitalism* (Ithaca, NY: Cornell University Press, 2002).

34 Wojciech Konończuk, 'The "Yukos affair": its motives and implications', *Prace OSW/CES Studies*, 25, Centre for Eastern Studies, Warsaw, August 2006, p. 38.

35 There was a division of labour in the group, with each company responsible for 'its' party:

Lukoil worked with the Party of Russian Regions, TNK with the Union of Right Forces, and Yukos with Yabloko; see ibid., p. 56, n. 32.

36 Andrew Barnes, 'Russia's new business groups and state power', *Post-Soviet Affairs*, 19(2), 2003, p. 155; see also id., *Owning Russia: The Struggle over Factories, Farms and Power* (Ithaca, NY: Cornell University Press, 2006).

37 Konstantin Smirnov, 'Vol'skomu volya', *Kommersant-Vlast'*, 39, 3 October 2005, p. 42.

38 Ol'ga Kryshtanovskaya, *Anatomiya rossiiskoi elity* (Moscow: Zakharov, 2005), p. 361.

39 Barnes, 'Russia's new business groups and state power', pp. 155–6.

40 'Poslanie Federal'nomu Sobraniyu Rossiiskoi Federatsii', 16 May 2003. Available at http://www.president.kremlin.ru/text/appears/2003/05/44623.shtml (accessed 24 September 2013).

41 Gleb Pavlovskii interviewed by Vladimir Demchenko, 'Nalitso popytka usilit' boyarstvo', *Izvestiya*, 9 September 2003, p. 1; Gleb Pavlovskii, '"Brat – 3"', *Ekspert*, 32, 1 September 2003, in *Ekspert: Luchshie materialy*, 2, 2007, p. 63.

42 Pavlovskii, '"Brat – 3"', p. 66.

43 Mancur Olson, *Power and Prosperity: Outgrowing Communist and Capitalist Dictatorships* (Oxford: Oxford University Press, 2000).

44 The SNS included 23 experts across the political spectrum, a number of whom disagreed with the findings of the report and resigned (see below); see Vladimir Pribylovsky, 'What's the scandal about?', *Moscow Times*, 11 June 2003, p. 8.

45 A leaked version was published on 26 May 2003 on the nationalist website http://www.utro.ru, titled 'V Rossii gotovitsya oligarkhicheskii pereverot'. The full version of 'Gosudarstvo i oligarkhiya' was available at http://www.strategeia.ru/news_453.html (accessed 7 November 2007). An abbreviated version was republished as 'Gosudarstvo i oligarkhiya', *Zavtra*, 27 June 2003, p. 3.

46 'Bol'shaya igra v Rossii'. Previously available at http://www.strategeia.ru/news_451.html (link no longer valid).

47 'Riski i ugrozy dlya Rossii v 2003 godu'. Previously available at http://www.strategeia.ru/news_452.html (link no longer valid).

48 There is much circumstantial and some direct evidence that Putin was not the initiator of the assault against Yukos, but was convinced by others that it was necessary. Eberhard Schneider, for example, drawing on sources in the Kremlin close to Voloshin and Kasyanov, is unequivocal about Putin's initially secondary role; see Eberhard Schneider, 'The Russian Federal Security Service under President Putin', in Stephen White (ed.), *Politics and the Ruling Group in Putin's Russia* (London: Palgrave Macmillan, 2008), pp. 49–52.

49 Andrew Wilson, *Virtual Politics: Faking Democracy in the Post-Soviet World* (New Haven, CT: Yale University Press, 2005), pp. 109–10.

50 Karl Polanyi, *The Great Transformation: The Political and Economic Origins of Our Time*, with a foreword by Joseph E. Stiglitz and an introduction by Fred Block (Boston: Beacon Press, [1944] 2001).

51 Daniel Kimmage, 'Putin's restoration: consolidation or clan rivalries?', in Geir Flikke (ed.), *The Uncertainties of Putin's Democracy* (Oslo: NUPI, 2004), p. 129.

52 Peter Baker and Susan Glasser, *Kremlin Rising: Vladimir Putin's Russia and the End of Revolution* (New York and London: Scribner, 2007), p. 286.

53 Khodorkovskii and Gevorkyan, *Tyur'ma i volya*, p. 16.

54 'Sobytiya', *Vedomosti*, 28 June 2005, p. A3.

55 Irina Sandul, 'Corporate Russia reaches into its pockets', *The Russia Journal*, 19 July 2002.

56 Valerii Panyushkin, *Mikhail Khodorkovskii: Uznik tishiny* (Moscow: Sekret Firmy, 2006), p. 146.

57 Khodorkovskii and Gevorkyan, *Tyur'ma i volya*, p. 295.

58   Ibid., p. 296.

59   Mikhail Vasil'ev, 'Khodorkovskii znaet, kak proiti v biblioteku', *Rossiiskaya gazeta*, 28 May 2002, p. 3.

60   Sarah L. Henderson, *Building Democracy in Contemporary Russia: Western Support for Grassroots Organizations* (Ithaca and London: Cornell University Press, 2003), p. 52.

61   Vladimir Perekrest, 'Za chto sidit Mikhail Khodorkovskii', Part 4, *Izvestiya*, 18 June 2006.

62   Taken from http://openrussiafoundation.com/About_the_Foundation.asp; the site is no longer available.

63   'Den'gi: s kem delit den'gi M. Khodokovskii?', *Argumenty i fakty*, 16, 16 April 2003, p. 9.

64   Author's interview with Irina Yasina, 18 June 2008, Moscow.

65   Marina Filippovna's interview with Anna Żebrowska, which gives much interesting background on Khodorkovsky's family, was featured in *Gazeta Wyborcza*, 17 March 2008. Available at http://www.khodorkovsky.info/personal/136221.html (accessed 24 September 2013).

66   Notes by Charles Grant, head of the Centre for European Reform, to whom I am most grateful.

67   Perekrest, 'Za chto sidit Mikhail Khodorkovskii', Part 4.

68   Elena Tokareva, *Kto podstavil Khodorskovskogo* (Moscow: Yauza, 2006), p. 133.

69   Interview with Yevgeny Kiselev, '"I'm doing the same in the U.S."', *Moscow News*, 5 November 2003, p. 1.

70   Alfa Bank was also active on the charitable front, supporting a number of orphanages as well as helping the 75 children of crew members of the Kursk submarine, sunk in the Barents Sea in August 2000, but few heard of this activity.

71   Timothy O'Brien, 'How Russian oil tycoon courted friends in US', *New York Times*, 5 November 2003.

72   Published in English as Alexander M. Yakovlev, *A Century of Violence in Soviet Russia* (New Haven, CT: Yale University Press, 2004).

73   Lera Arsenina and Viktoriya Malyutina, '100 million humanitarian petrodollars', *Gazeta. ru*, 25 April 2003. Available at http://gazeta.ru/2003/04/25/100millionhu.shtml (accessed 24 September 2013).

74   Panyushkin, *Mikhail Khodorkovskii*, p. 166.

75   The group was led by Sergei Miroshnikov, a professor at Tomsk State University and later the chairman of the International Cooperation Committee of the Tomsk regional administration. Author's interview, 8 July 2005.

76   'Valdai: participant quotes', *Russia Profile*, 3(8), October 2006, p. 46.

77   Peter Rutland, 'Business and civil society in Russia', in Alfred B. Evans, Jr, Laura A. Henry and Lisa McIntosh Sundstrom (eds), *Russian Civil Society: A Critical Assessment* (Armonk, NY: M.E. Sharpe, 2005), p. 78.

78   For an overview, see Andrei Yakovlev, 'The evolution of business–state interaction in Russia: from state capture to business capture?', *Europe–Asia Studies*, 58(7), November 2006, pp. 1033–56.

79   Timothy Frye, 'Capture or exchange? Business lobbying in Russia', *Europe–Asia Studies*, 54(7), November 2002, pp. 1017–36. See also Andrei Yakovlev and Timoti Frai [Timothy Frye], 'Reformy v Rossii glazami biznesa', *Pro et Contra*, 11(4–5), July–October 2007, pp. 118–34.

80   Panyushkin, *Mikhail Khodorkovskii*, pp. 63–5, 213–17.

81   Laurence A. Groen, 'The "Iukos affair": the Russian judiciary and the European Court of Human Rights', *Review of Central and East European Law*, 38(1), 2013, p. 86.

82   Kryshtanovskaya, *Anatomiya rossiiskoi elity*, p. 363.

83   A biography and full details of the Pichugin case can be found in Vera Vasil'eva, *Aleksei Pichugin: Puti i pereput'ya (biograficheskii ocherk)* (Prague: Human Rights Publishers, 2011).

84   For biographical details, character assessment and trials, see the notes by Lebedev's lawyer, Konstantin Rivkin, *Khodorkovskii, Lebedev, dalee vezde: Zapiski advokata o "dele Yukosa" i ne tol'ko o nem* (Moscow: Sterna, 2013), pp. 27–36 and *passim*.

3. WHY KHODORKOVSKY?

1   Wojciech Konończuk, 'The "Yukos affair": its motives and implications', *Prace OSW/CES Studies*, 25, Centre for Eastern Studies, Warsaw, August 2006, p. 34.
2   Andrei Piontovskii, 'Luchshe nachat' s yuridicheskikh garanti', *Ekspert*, 33, 8 September 2003, in *Ekspert: Luchshie materialy*, 2, 2007, p. 73.
3   Igor' Klyamkin and Lev Timofeev, *Tenevaya Rossiya: Ekonomiko-sotsiologicheskoe issledovanie* (Moscow: RGGU, 2000), p. 12.
4   Valerii Panyushkin, *Mikhail Khodorkovskii: Uznik tishiny* (Moscow, Sekret Firmy, 2006), p. 81.
5   Ibid., p. 91.
6   Vladimir Perekrest, 'Za chto sidit Mikhail Khodorkovskii', Part 2, *Izvestiya*, 18 May 2006. Available at http://www.izvestia.ru/investigation/article3092896/index.html (accessed 24 September 2013).
7   Yuliya Latynina, 'Imperiya Khodorkovskogo: kuda ubegayut neftedollary', *Sovershenno sekretno*, August 1999.
8   Reported by Shakhnovsky; see Elena Tokareva, *Kto podstavil Khodorskovskogo* (Moscow: Yauza, 2006), p. 143.
9   Perekrest, 'Za chto sidit Mikhail Khodorkovskii', Part 2.
10   Kosals, Leonid, 'Klanovyi kapitalizm v Rossii', *Neprikosnovennyi zapas: Debaty o politike i kul'ture*. Previously available at http://www.nz-online.ru/print.phtml?aid=80022545 (link no longer valid).
11   Marshall I. Goldman, *Oilopoly: Putin, Power, and the Rise of the New Russia* (Oxford: Oneworld Publications, 2008), p. 112.
12   Michael Specter, 'Kremlin, inc.: why are Vladimir Putin's opponents dying?', *New Yorker*, 29 January 2007, p. 58.
13   The same process is visible in the heartlands of globalised neo-liberal capitalism, where giant corporations and financial institutions implicitly make sovereignty claims against the state.
14   Tokareva, *Kto podstavil Khodorskovskogo*, p. 129.
15   Thane Gustafson, *Wheel of Fortune: The Battle for Oil and Power in Russia* (Cambridge, MA: Belknap Press, 2012), p. 316.
16   Ibid., p. 273.
17   Perekrest, 'Za chto sidit Mikhail Khodorkovskii', Part 2.
18   See Andrei Yakovlev, 'The evolution of business–state interaction in Russia: from state capture to business capture?', *Europe–Asia Studies*, 58(7), November 2006, pp. 1033–56.
19   'Settle Yukos: still time for the Kremlin to limit economic damage', *Financial Times*, 8 November 2004.
20   Andrew Jack, *Inside Putin's Russia* (London: Granta Books, 2004), pp. 306–13.
21   Danilin et al., *Vragi Putina* (Moscow: Evropa, 2007), p. 158.
22   Reported in 'Intervyu: Mikhail Khodorkovskii – "Ya uveren, chto prigovor budet otmenen"', *Vedomosti*, 4 August 2005, p. 5.
23   Author's interview with Alexei Venediktov, Moscow, 19 June 2008.
24   John Browne, *Beyond Business: An Inspirational Memoir from a Remarkable Leader* (London: Phoenix, 2010), p. 145.
25   Ibid.
26   Ibid., p. 149.

27   Khodorkovsky sought some official documentation so that he could explain the situation to the workers, but Putin refused to engage in discussion. See Mikhail Khodorkovskii and Nataliya Gevorkyan, *Tyur'ma i volya* (Moscow: Howard Roark, 2012), p. 329.

28   Ibid., p. 330.

29   Ibid., p. 333.

30   Ibid., p. 339.

31   Ibid., p. 340.

32   Ol'ga Kryshtanovskaya, *Anatomiya rossiiskoi elity* (Moscow, Zakharov, 2005), p. 366.

33   Dmitrii Kamyshev and Nikolai Gul'ko, 'Protsess: gde vy byli v mae 2005-go?', *Kommersant-Vlast'*, 20, 23 May 2005, p. 17.

34   Author's interview with Dimitri K. Simes, Director of the Nixon Center, 8 November 2007.

35   For a vivid account, see Andrei Kolesnikov, *Vladimir Putin: Ravnoudalenie oligarkhov* (Moscow: Eksmo, 2005), pp. 17–21.

36   Vladimir Putin, 'Vstupitel'noe slovo na vstreche s predstavitelyami Rossiiskogo soyuza promyshlennikov i predprinimatelei', 19 February 2003. Available at http://archive.kremlin.ru/text/appears/2003/02/29787.shtml (accessed 18 October 2013).

37   Vera Chelishcheva, *Zaklyuchennyi No. 1: Neslomlennyi Khodorkovskii* (Moscow, Eksmo, 2011), p. 118.

38   Elena Dikun, '"Delo Yukosa" v sude kreml': Yukos neokonchennaya voina', *Moskovskie novosti*, 18, 21 May 2004, p. 4.

39   Mikhail Khodorkovskii, 'Korruptsiya v Rossii – tormoz ekonomicheskogo rosta', Powerpoint presentation. Available at http://www.khodorkovsky.ru/faq/2636.html (accessed 24 September 2013) in section 'Voprosy i otvety: za chto on sidit'.

40   Aleksandr Pumpyanskii, 'Protsess', in Aleksandr Pumpyanskii, Sergei Kovalev and Boris Zhutovskii, *Delo Khodorkovskogo* (Moscow: Zebra, 2011), p. 37.

41   Panyushkin, *Mikhail Khodorkovskii*, pp. 158–62.

42   Goldman, *Oilopoly*, p. 114.

43   'Vladimir Putin vzyal ostroe interv'yu u oligarkhov', *Kommersant*, 20 February 2003.

44   Viktor Gerashchenko, 'Ya stolknulsya s pravovym bespredelom', *Novaya gazeta*, 49, 10 July 2008, pp. 1–3. Khodorkovsky later denied that such an exchange took place; see Khodorkovskii and Gevorkyan, *Tyur'ma i volya*, p. 52.

45   Valerii G. Shiryaev, *Sud mesti: pervaya zhertva dela Yukosa* (Moscow: OGI, 2006), p. 17.

46   Mikhail Kasyanov, *Bez Putina* (Moscow: Novaya gazeta, 2009), pp. 199–203.

47   Vladimir Putin, *First Person: An Astonishingly Frank Self-Portrait by Russia's President Vladimir Putin*, with Nataliya Gevorkyan, Natalya Timakova and Andrei Kolesnikov, translated by Catherine A. Fitzpatrick (London: Hutchinson, 2000), p. 179.

48   '"Man sollte die active Rolle Putins nicht überschätzen": der russiche Politologe Belkowski sieht wirtschaftliche Kräfte am Werk im Kreml und prophezeit den Niedergang Russlands', *Die Welt*, 12 November 2007.

49   Cited by Daniel Kimmage, 'Putin's restoration: consolidation or clan rivalries?', in Geir Flikke (ed.), *The Uncertainties of Putin's Democracy* (Oslo: NUPI, 2004), p. 131. The official record of the meeting at Novo-Ogarevo makes no mention of Yukos; it is available at http://archive.kremlin.ru/text/appears/2003/09/52624.shtml (accessed 24 September 2013).

50   Stephen Fortescue, *Russia's Oil Barons and Metal Magnates: Oligarchs and State in Transition* (Basingstoke: Palgrave Macmillan, 2006), pp. 126, 141–2.

51   For analysis of the fraught development of the company, including the flight in July 2008 of its chief executive, Robert Dudley, see Shamil Yenikeyeff, 'BP, Russian billionaires, and the Kremlin: a power triangle that never was', *Oxford Energy Comment* (Oxford: Oxford Institute for Energy Studies, November 2011).

52   Tat'yana Lysova, 'Deistvuyushchie litsa: interv'yu – Mikhail Khodorkovskii, predsedatel' pravleniya NK "Yukos", *Vedomosti*, 16 June 2003.

53   Nina Poussenkova, *From Rigs to Riches: Oilmen vs. Financiers in the Russian Oil Sector* (Houston, TX: The James A. Baker III Institute for Public Policy of Rice University, October 2004), p. 36.

54   A.A. Yakovlev, 'Vlast', biznes i dvizhushchie sily ekonomicheskogo razvitiya v Rossii: do i posle "dela YUKOSa", *Obshchestvennye nauki i sovremennost'*, 1, 2005, p. 38.

55   Thierry Wolton, *Le KGB au pouvoir: Le système poutine* (Paris: Buchet–Chastel, 2008), pp. 186–7.

56   Dominic Midgley and Chris Hutchins, *Abramovich: The Billionaire from Nowhere* (London: Harper Collins, 2005), p. 9.

57   Panyushkin, *Mikhail Khodorkovskii*, p. 186.

58   The company was known as ChevronTexaco between 2000 and 2005, when it dropped the Texaco moniker and reverted to Chevron.

59   For full details, see Gustafson, *Wheel of Fortune*, pp. 297–300.

60   Tat'yana Gurova and Aleksandr Privalov, 'My teryaem ego!', *Ekspert*, 41, 3 November 2003, in *Ekspert: Luchshie materialy*, 2, 2007, p. 80.

61   Ajay Goyal, 'Analysis: sale of a state', *The Russia Journal*, 31 October 2003, p. 10.

62   *ITAR-TASS Weekly News*, 3 October 2003.

63   See: *New York Times*, 6 October 2003, p. 1; *ITAR-TASS Weekly News*, 6 October 2003; Denis Rebrov, 'Ne dozhdetes', *Vremya novostei*, 7 October 2003, p. 2.

64   Valeria Korchagina, ''93 tender won by Exxon annulled', *Moscow Times*, 30 January 2004.

65   V.V. Putin, 'O nashikh ekonomicheskikh zadachakh', *Vedomosti*, 30 January 2012.

66   'Exxon in talks over $25bn deal with Yukos', *Financial Times*, 3 October 2003. The article reports that ExxonMobil was considering the purchase of 40%, and possibly over 50%, of Yukos–Sibneft.

67   Author's interview with Iosif Diskin, Moscow, 4 March 2008.

68   Maria Levitov, 'Ministry drafts criteria for strategic companies', *Moscow Times*, 30 January 2006.

69   Gurova and Privalov, 'My teryaem ego!', pp. 80–1.

70   Nelli Sharushkina, head of the Moscow branch of the Energy Intelligence Group, quoted in Lyudmila Romanova and Andrei Bobrov, '"Yukossibneft'" snova prodaetsya', *Gazeta*, 16 September 2003, p. 8.

71   Christopher Kenneth, 'Russian corporations eye global markets', *The Russian Journal*, 14 February 2003, pp. 6–7.

72   'Talks on Yukos–Exxon–Chevron merger suspended', *ITAR-TASS Weekly News*, 27 October 2003.

73   Henry E. Hale, *Why Not Parties in Russia? Democracy, Federalism and the State* (Cambridge: Cambridge University Press, 2006), pp. 163–95.

74   'Khodorkovskii podderzhivaet "Yabloko"', *Novye izvestiya*, 11 November 1999.

75   Vladimir Perekrest, 'Za chto sidit Mikhail Khodorkovskii', Part 3, *Izvestiya*, 7 June 2006.

76   Ibid.

77   Vyacheslav Kostikov, 'I viden uroven' g-na', *Argumenty i fakty*, 25, 2006, p. 8.

78   Natal'ya Arkhangel'skaya, 'Dumskaya monopol'ka', *Ekspert*, 3, 26 January 2004, in *Ekspert: Luchshie materialy*, 2, 2007, p. 90.

79   PSAs allowed foreign partners to receive 90% of the oil and gas until they had recouped their investments, paying only a small royalty fee to the Russian government.

80   Danilin provides a table with details; see Danilin et al., *Vragi Putina*, pp. 171–4.

81   Konstantin Simonov, *Russkaya neft': Poslednii peredel* (Moscow: Eksmo Algoritm, 2005), p. 101. The deputy in question was Sergei Shtogrin; see Danilin et al., *Vragi Putina*, p. 183.

82   Marshall Goldman in an interview with Bernard Gwertzman, 2 June 2005. Available at http://www.cfr.org/publication/8155/goldman.html (accessed 24 September 2013).

83   Angus Roxburgh, *The Strongman: Vladimir Putin and the Struggle for Russia* (London: I.B.Tauris, 2013), p. 76.

84   Vadim Visloguzov, 'Okhotnyi ryad: deputat barrelya', *Kommersant-Vlast'*, 48, 8 December 2003, pp. 26–7.

85   Jack, *Inside Putin's Russia*, p. 310.

86   *Ekspert*, 41, 3 November 2003, in *Ekspert: Luchshie materialy*, 2, 2007, p. 79.

87   Perekrest, 'Za chto sidit Mikhail Khodorkovskii', Part 3.

88   Carl Mortishead, 'Power struggle follows shift in influence towards oligarchs', *The Times*, 18 September 2003.

89   Valery Vyzhutovich, 'Tycoon puts his cards on the table', *Moscow News*, 16 April 2003, p. 3.

90   Kseniya Veretennikova, 'I pravym i levym', *Vremya novostei*, 8 April 2003, p. 4.

91   David Nowak, 'This economist keeps on swinging', *Moscow Times*, 5 October 2007, p. 1.

92   Maksim Mironov, '"Yukos" partiyam ne platit', *Trud*, 23 July 2003, p. 2.

93   'Yabloko list', *Moscow Times*, 5 December 2003.

94   Vladimir Gel'man, 'Political opposition in Russia: a dying species?', *Post-Soviet Affairs*, 23(3), 2005, p. 240.

95   Visloguzov, 'Deputat barelya'; Simonov, *Russkaya neft'*, p. 102.

96   Panyushkin, *Mikhail Khodorkovskii*, p. 185.

97   For a detailed study of the issue, see David White, *The Russian Democratic Party Yabloko* (Aldershot: Ashgate, 2006).

98   Khodorkovskii and Gevorkyan, *Tyur'ma i volya*, pp. 138–9.

99   Francesca Mereu, 'Capitalists signing up as Communists', *Moscow Times*, 2 December 2003, p. 1.

100   Tokareva, *Kto podstavil Khodorskovskogo*, p. 136.

101   Boris Kagarlitsky, 'Storm warning: corruption in Russia's political parties', in Stanislav Gyandzhinskii, 'Politicheskaya sreda: shtormovoe preduprezhdenie', *Rossiiskie vesti*, 13, 5 April 2006, p. 3.

102   Kirill Benediktov, 'Roman s neft'yu: zek i gubernator', *Smysl'*, 1(20), January 2008, p. 29.

103   Khodorkovskii and Gevorkyan, *Tyur'ma i volya*, p. 352.

104   Panyushkin, *Mikhail Khodorkovskii*, p. 187; Pumpyanskii, 'Protsess', p. 39.

105   Peter Baker and Susan Glasser, *Kremlin Rising: Vladimir Putin's Russia and the End of Revolution* (New York and London: Scribner, 2007), p. 283.

106   Catherine Belton, 'Kasyanov reveals Putin's pursuit of tycoon', *Moscow Times*, 21 July 2009.

107   Anna Skornyakova, 'Mikhail Khodorkovskii prodolshit lichno zanimat'sya politikoi', *Nezavisimaya gazeta*, 1 September 2003, p. 4.

108   Hale, *Why Not Parties in Russia?*, p. 62.

109   Ibid., p. 66.

110   Sergei Mulin, 'Son chinovnikov', *Novaya gazeta*, 1, 12 January 2006, p. 8.

111   Yulia Latynina, 'What really happened to Medvedev', *Moscow Times*, 23 November 2005.

112   The quotation is from Stanislav Belkovsky, in Khodorkovskii and Gevorkyan, *Tyur'ma i volya*, p. 361.

113   'Poslanie Federal'nomu Sobraniyu Rossiiskoi Federatsii', 16 May 2003. Available at http://www.president.kremlin.ru/text/appears/2003/05/44623.shtml (accessed 24 September 2013).

114   Andrei Kolesnikov, 'Vladimir Putin pozvolil sebe svobodu slov', *Kommersant*, 1 February 2006, p. 2.

115   'Stenogramma press-konferentsii dlya rossiiskikh i inostrannykh zhurnalistov', 31 January 2006.

116 In April 2003 the report commissioned indirectly through the Foundation for the Development of Parliamentarianism by Open Russia to the Systems Analysis Research Foundation, called 'An investigation in constitutional–legal problems of state development, improving the constitutional foundations of the Russian Federation', argued that a shift to a government of the parliamentary majority would not require changes to the constitution but the adoption of a straightforward federal constitutional law. Vladimir Perekrest, 'Za chto sidit Mikhail Khodorkovskii', Part 5, *Izvestiya*, 19 June 2006.

117 Mikhail Khodorkovskii, 'Rossiya, za kotoruyu menya posadili', *Kommersant-Vlast*, 37, 19 September 2011.

118 Andrei Panov and Aleksandr Bekker, 'Rossiya bez tsarya', *Vedomosti*, 1 February 2005.

119 Khodorkovskii, 'Rossiya, za kotoruyu menya posadili'.

120 Panov and Bekker, 'Rossiya bez tsarya'.

121 Perekrest, 'Za chto sidit Mikhail Khodorkovskii', Part 5.

122 'Conversation of writer Grigory Chkhartishvili (B. Akunin) with Mikhail Khodorkovsky', *Esquire*, October 2008, p. 159.

123 Yuliya Bushueva and Elizaveta Osetinskaya, 'Khodorkovskii otmeril sebe srok', *Vedomosti*, 4 April 2003; also in *Finans*, 14 April 2003.

124 Karsten Mattkhoiz [Carsten Matthäus], 'Neftyanoi korol' Khodorkovskii', *Der Spiegel*, 24 April 2003. Available at http://www.inosmi.ru/translation/179334.html (accessed 24 September 2013).

125 Baker and Glasser, *Kremlin Rising*, p. 281.

126 Nick Paton Walsh, 'Moscow court says tycoon must stay in jail', *Guardian*, 16 January 2004.

127 Caroline McGregor, 'Powell frets over state of democracy', *Moscow Times*, 27 January 2004.

128 Martin Sixsmith, *Putin's Oil: The Yukos Affair and the Struggle for Russia* (London: Continuum, 2010), p. 86.

129 Michael Wines, 'Coddling Iraq a $40bln gamble', *Moscow Times*, 4 February 2002, p. 9.

130 Not long before his overthrow, Saddam Hussein had repudiated the interests of Russian companies, since Russia had supported Western sanctions, and following his fall the Americans continued Hussein's policy.

131 The conversation was reported by Stanislav Belkovsky, in Perekrest, 'Za chto sidit Mikhail Khodorkovskii', Part 5; also mentioned by Tokareva, *Kto podstavil Khodorskovskogo*, p. 133. Neither gives the date.

4. THE STATE STRIKES BACK

1 Mikhail Khodorkovskii and Nataliya Gevorkyan, *Tyur'ma i volya* (Moscow: Howard Roark, 2012), p. 126.

2 Ibid., p. 128.

3 Svetlana Babaeva and Georgii Bovt, 'Novyi kontrakt Putina', *Izvestiya*, 18 September 2003, p. 1.

4 Khodorkovskii and Gevorkyan, *Tyur'ma i volya*, p. 128.

5 Philip Hanson, 'The turn to statism in Russian economic policy', *The International Spectator*, 42(1), March 2007, pp. 29–42.

6 David M. Woodruff, *Khodorkovsky's Gamble: From Business to Politics in the YUKOS Conflict*, *PONARS Policy Memo*, 308, November 2003, p. 2.

7 *Energeticheskaya strategiya Rossii na period do 2020 goda*, 28 August 2003. Available at http://web.archive.org/web/20101028025814/http://www.minprom.gov.ru/docs/strateg/1 (accessed 18 October 2013).

8 Konstantin Simonov, *Russkaya neft': Poslednii peredel* (Moscow: Eksmo Algoritm, 2005), p. 35.

9   Miriam Elder, 'How the state got a grip on energy', *Moscow Times*, 14 March 2008, p. 1.

10 Marshall I. Goldman, *Oilopoly: Putin, Power, and the Rise of the New Russia* (Oxford: Oneworld Publications, 2008), p. 113.

11 A.A. Mukhin, *Novye pravila igry dlya bol'shego biznesa, prodiktovannye logikoi pravleniya V.V. Putina* (Moscow: Tsentr politicheskoi informatsii, 2002), p. 252.

12 A. Makarkin, *Politiko-ekonomicheskie klany sovremennoi Rossii* (Moscow: Tsentr politicheskikh tekhnologii, 2003), p. 99.

13 Ibid., p. 100.

14 Khodorkovskii and Gevorkyan, *Tyur'ma i volya*, p. 64. Nevzlin suggests that the group only really swung into action in late February or early March 2003; see ibid., p. 353.

15 Elena Kiseleva, 'Lubyanskii PR', *Kommersant-Den'gi*, 27, 17 July 2002.

16 Bortnikov's appointment as head of the FSB on 11 May 2008 was variously seen as a victory for Medvedev or a confirmation of Putin's continued control over the security agency. As for Ustinov, his role is unequivocal: 'Ustinov was a key figure in the legal onslaught against Yukos and its former CEO, Mikhail Khodokovsky. He also led other politically tinged legal campaigns during his six-year tenure as prosecutor general under Putin.' Nabi Abdullaev and Miriam Elder, 'Putin appears to be the big winner', *Moscow Times*, 13 May 2008.

17 For more details, see Catherine Belton and Neil Buckley, 'On the offensive: how Gunvor rose to the top of Russian oil trading', *Financial Times*, 14 May 2008.

18 Valerii Popov, 'Gromkoe delo: kto-to skoro mozhet poteryat' pogony', *Novaya gazeta*, 20 October 2003, p. 3; Vitalii Ivanov, 'Pereshli na lichnosti', *Vedomosti*, 21 October 2003.

19 Embezzlement charges were first made against Burganov in January 2002; see Daniel Kimmage, 'Table, chair, Yukos', RFE/RL, *Newsline*, 14 July 2003.

20 Vladimir Demchenko, 'Dorogie svideteli: Mikhail Khodorkovskii i Leonid Nevzlin doprosheny i opushcheny', *Izvestiya*, 5 July 2003, p. 1.

21 Hanson, 'The turn to statism in Russian economic policy', p. 36.

22 Valeria Korchagina and Caroline McGregor, 'Oligarchs to appeal to Putin on Yukos', *Moscow Times*, 10 July 2003, p. 1.

23 Ibid.

24 Ivan Sas, 'Khodorkovskii uezhaet', *Nezavisimaya gazeta*, 7 October 2003, p. 1.

25 Catherine Belton and Alex Nicholson, 'Probe of Yukos hits Yabloko', *St Petersburg Times*, 24 October 2003.

26 Louise L. Shelley, 'Crime and corruption: enduring problems of post-Soviet development', *Demokratizatsiya*, 11(1), Winter 2003, pp. 110–14.

27 Simonov, *Russkaya neft'*, p. 87.

28 Peter Lavelle, 'Voloshin: between mea culpa and get a good lawyer', *Untimely Thoughts*, 17 September 2003.

29 Gleb Pavlovskii, 'O negativnykh posledstviyakh "letnego nastupleniya" oppozitsionnogo kursu prezidenta RF men'shinstva', 29 August 2003. His analytical report is analysed and quoted in Valerii Shiryaev, 'Predvybornaya likhoradka: "Sem'ya" prinyala vyzov "khunty"', *Novaya gazeta*, 66, 8 September 2003, pp. 1–3.

30 Valerii Panyushkin, *Mikhail Khodorkovskii: Uznik tishiny* (Moscow: Sekret Firmy, 2006), p. 177.

31 Ajay Goyal, 'Analysis: sale of a state', *The Russia Journal*, 31 October 2003, p. 10.

32 Sergei Kez, 'Neft', Datsin i Yukos', *Nezavisimaya gazeta*, 8 September 2003, p. 4.

33 Peter Baker and Susan Glasser, *Kremlin Rising: Vladimir Putin's Russia and the End of Revolution* (New York and London: Scribner, 2007), p. 289.

34 Daniel Kimmage, 'Putin's restoration: consolidation or clan rivalries?', in Geir Flikke (ed.), *The Uncertainties of Putin's Democracy* (Oslo: NUPI, 2004), p. 132.

35 Svetlana Smetanina, "'Krome nekrupnykh politicheskikh intrig, vse ostal'noe v strane razvivaetsya normal'no'", *Gazeta*, 17 July 2003, p. 7.

36 Ibid.

37 Evgeniya Obukhova, "'Lyudi iz okruzheniya prezidenta" boryutsya s biznesom', *Nezavisimaya gazeta*, 13 August 2003, p. 3.

38 Mikhail Khodorkovsky, 'Keynote address', *Russian Business Watch*, 11(3), Fall 2003, p. 2.

39 Ibid., p. 3.

40 *Constitutional and Due Process Violations in the Khodorkovsky/Yukos Case*, a white paper prepared by defence lawyers on behalf of Mikhail Khodorkovsky, Platon Lebedev, Alexei Pichugin (Moscow: n.d.), compiled by Robert Amsterdam and Charles Krause, p. 24.

41 Author's interviews with participants. Nevertheless, on 11 October he met with his lawyers to discuss actions in case of his arrest, Goldman, *Oilopoly*, p. 115.

42 Khodorkovskii and Gevorkyan, *Tyur'ma i volya*, p. 63.

43 Ibid., p. 61.

44 Author's interview with Dimitri K. Simes, 8 November 2007.

45 'President Bush meets with Russian President Putin at Camp David', Office of the Press Secretary, 27 September 2007. Available at http://web.archive.org/web/20090110081953/ http://www.whitehouse.gov/news/releases/2003/09/20030927-2.html (accessed 18 October 2013).

46 Ibid.

47 The journalists were from the *Wall Street Journal* and the *Financial Times*. See Kimmage, 'Putin's restoration', p. 131.

48 Goyal, 'Analysis: sale of a state', p. 10.

49 Evgeniya Pis'mennaya, 'Medved' s chelovecheskim litsom', *Russkii Newsweek*, 51, 17–23 December 2007.

50 Pavel Sedakov, Mikhail Fishman and Konstantin Gaaze, 'Putin: Ostavil ten' v istorii', *Russkii Newsweek*, 20, 12–18 May 2008.

51 Simonov, *Russkaya neft'*, p. 48.

52 Interview in *Ekspert*, 4 April 2005, p. 72.

53 Tat'yana Vitebskaya, Vladimir Demchenko, Mariya Ignatova, Susanna Oganezova, Natal'ya Pashkalova, 'Mikhail Khodorkovskii, president kompaniya "Yukos": "Eto – poslednii boi"', *Izvestiya*, 27 October 2003, p. 1.

54 Valerii Popov, 'Kto-to mozhet poteryat' pogony', *Novaya gazeta*, 78, 20 October 2003, p. 3.

55 Questions collated by Ekho Moskvy, BBC Monitoring, 'Jailed ex-Yukos head answers questions from Russian radio listeners', 7 November 2011; in *Johnson's Russia List*, No. 203, 2011, item 16.

56 Khodorkovskii and Gevorkyan, *Tyur'ma i volya*, p. 55.

57 Svetlana Bocharova and Andrei Bondarenko, 'Khodorkovskii na Volge', *Nezavisimaya gazeta*, 24 October 2003, p. 4.

58 Wojciech Konończuk, 'The "Yukos affair": its motives and implications', *Prace OSW/CES Studies*, 25, Centre for Eastern Studies, Warsaw, August 2006, p. 57, n. 52.

59 This was repeated to me on several occasions by people who talked with Khodorkovsky at this time, including Yasina. See also Panyushkin, *Mikhail Khodorkovskii*, p. 162.

60 Catherine Belton, 'Khodorkovsky arrested on 7 charges', *Moscow Times*, 27 October 2003, p. 1.

61 Tat'yana Gurova and Aleksandr Privalov, 'My teryaem ego!', *Ekspert*, 41, 3 November 2003, in *Ekspert: Luchshie materialy*, 2, 2007, p. 78.

62 Author's interview with Stanislav Belkovsky, Moscow, 3 March 2008.

63 Author's interview with Andrei Kolesnikov, Moscow, 19 June 2008.

64   Vladimir Fedosenko, 'Mikhail Khodorkovskii ostaetsya za reshetkoi', *Rossiiskaya gazeta*, 2 December 2004, p. 2.

65   Author's interview with Angela Stent, Director of the Center for Eurasian, Russian and East European Studies at Georgetown University, 29 November 2007, who was present at the meeting.

66   Martin Sixsmith, *Putin's Oil: The Yukos Affair and the Struggle for Russia* (London: Continuum, 2010), p. 152.

67   Author's interview with Alexei Vendediktov, Moscow, 19 June 2008.

68   Gurova and Privalov, 'My teryaem ego!', p. 78; Ol'ga Kryshtanovskaya, *Anatomiya rossiiskoi elity* (Moscow: Zakharov, 2005), p. 364.

69   Andrei Kolesnikov, *Anatolii Chubais: Biografiya* (Moscow: AST Moskva, 2008), p. 204.

70   Ibid., p. 206.

71   *Ekspert*, 41, 3 November 2003, in *Ekspert: Luchshie materialy*, 2, 2007, p. 78.

72   Cited by Vadim Volkov in 'The Yukos affair: terminating the implicit contract', *PONARS Policy Memo*, 307, November 2003, p. 5.

73   Gurova and Privalov, 'My teryaem ego!', p. 79.

74   Vladimir Putin, 'Statement to the Cabinet', Moscow, 27 October 2003. Available at http://www.kremlin.ru/text/appears/2003/10/54587.shtml (accessed 26 September 2013).

75   Vladimir Putin, 'Zaklyuchitel'noe slovo na s''ezde Rossiiskogo soyuza promyshlennikov i predprinimatelei', 14 November 2003. Available at http://web.archive.org/web/20050221004235/http://www.kremlin.ru/text/appears/2003/11/55586.shtml (accessed 18 October 2013).

76   Andrei Kolesnikov, *Vladimir Putin: Ravnoudalenie oligarkhov* (Moscow: Eksmo, 2005), pp. 130–1.

77   Peter Rutland, 'Business and civil society in Russia', in Alfred B. Evans, Jr., Laura A. Henry and Lisa McIntosh Sundstrom (eds), *Russian Civil Society: A Critical Assessment* (Armonk, NY: M.E. Sharpe, 2005).

78   'Eks-glava Yukosa fakticheski vyveden iz sostava byuro RSPP', *Gazeta*, 17 November 2005, p. 2.

79   Fedor Chaika, 'Mikhaila Khodorkovskogo osvobodili: Ego mesto v "profsoyuze oligarkhov" zanyal Viktor Veksel'berg', *Izvestiya*, 17 November 2005.

80   Peter Baker, 'Putin finding power in the pump', *Washington Post*, 11 August 2004, p. A01; Philip Hanson and Elizabeth Teague, 'Big business and the state in Russia', *Europe–Asia Studies*, 57(5), July 2005, p. 664.

81   Elena Tokareva, *Kto podstavil Khodorskovskogo* (Moscow: Yauza, 2006), p. 226.

82   For comment on the letter, authored by talk-show host Alexander Gordon, see Yulia Latynina, 'Ideology is for intellectuals', *Moscow Times*, 8 February 2006.

83   Miriam Elder, 'Pas de Putin', *Guardian*, 5 February 2011, p. 30.

84   Woodruff, *Khodorkovsky's Gamble*, p. 4.

85   Simonov, *Russkaya neft'*, pp. 175–6.

86   'Illarionov says Yukos affair is political', *Eurasia Daily Monitor*, 1(126), 12 November 2004.

87   Andrei Gromov, Tat'yana Gurova, Oleg Kashin and Maksim Rubchenko, 'Ne po tsarskoi vole', *Ekspert*, 44, 21 November 2005, in *Ekspert: Luchshie materialy*, 2, 2007, p. 114.

88   Valeriya Korchagina, 'Kasyanov steps up criticism of Putin, *Moscow Times*, 20 May 2005, p. 3.

89   Masha Gessen, *The Man without a Face: The Unlikely Rise of Vladimir Putin* (New York: Riverhead Books, 2012), p. 234. The later downfall of Hermitage and the death of Sergei Magnitsky are described at pp. 243–8.

90   Bill Browder, 'Turning the tables on Russia's power elite: the story behind the Magnitsky act', 25 July 2012. Available at http://www.opendemocracy.net/od-russia/bill-browder/turning-tables-on-russia%E2%80%99s-power-elite-%E2%80%94-story-behind-magnitsky-act (accessed 25 September 2013).

91 Tat'yana Gurova, Aleksandr Privalov and Valerii Fadeev, 'Nasha malen'kaya svoboda', *Ekspert*, 33, 8 September 2003, in *Ekspert: Luchshie materialy*, 2, 2007, p. 73.

92 Valerii Fadeev, 'Opasnost' prostoty', *Ekspert*, 1, 12 January 2004, in *Ekspert: Luchshie materialy*, 2, 2007, p. 87.

93 See Valerii Fadeev, 'Sokhranit' effektivnoe gosudarstvo v sushchestvuyushchikh granitsakh', *Ekspert*, 13, 4 April 2005, in *Ekspert: Luchshie materialy*, 2, 2007, p. 100.

94 Ibid., p. 104.

95 Daniel Treisman, 'Presidential popularity in a hybrid regime: Russia under Yeltsin and Putin', *American Journal of Political Science*, 55(3), July 2011, pp. 603–6.

96 Konstantin Sonin, 'Election still waiting for the big question', *Moscow Times*, 11 September 2007, p. 10.

97 Vladimir Putin, 'Poslanie Federal'nomu Sobraniyu Rossiiskoi Federatsii', *Rossiiskaya gazeta*, 27 May 2004.

98 For an accusation that the letter was inspired by people funded by Khodorkovsky, see Eric Kraus, 'Return to sender', *Moscow Times*, 6 October 2004.

5. BASMANNY JUSTICE

1   Marie Mendras, *Russian Politics: The Paradox of a Weak State* (London: Hurst & Company, 2012), p. 238.

2   Martin Sixsmith, *Putin's Oil: The Yukos Affair and the Struggle for Russia* (London: Continuum, 2010), p. 195.

3   Konstantin Rivkin, *Khodorkovskii, Lebedev, dalee vezde: Zapiski advokata o "dele Yukosa" i ne tol'ko o nem* (Moscow: Sterna, 2013), pp. 51–2. Rivkin was one of the lawyers and provides an insider's account of the work of the team, including details of pressure put on them by the authorities.

4   For a description of life in Matrosskaya Tishina, see the prison memoirs of the nationalist Ivan Mironov: Ivan Mironov, *Zamurovannye: Khronika Kremlovskogo tsentrala* (Moscow: Vagrius, 2009). Mironov ended up on one occasion in Khodorkovsky's former cell (see p. 61).

5   Ibid., p. 74.

6   Yuliya Mikhailina, 'Sud i tyur'mu soedinili mostom dlya Mikhaila Khodorkovskogo', *Gazeta*, 12 November 2003, p. 1.

7   Anastasiya Samotorova, '168 chasov: Khodorkovskii smeyalsya v mosgorsude', *Moskovskie novosti*, 16 January 2004, p. 2

8   Ol'ga Roshchina, 'Pod strazhei: "Ya ne schitayu vozmozhnym podvesti kollektiv"', *Gazeta*, 16 January 2004, p. 3.

9   William Burnham and Jeffrey Kahn, 'Russia's criminal procedural code five years out', *Review of Central and East European Law*, 33, 2008, pp. 1–2.

10 *Ugolovno-protsessual'nyi kodeks Rossiiskoi Federatsii*, 12th ed., with all changes up to 1 February 2008 (Moscow: Os'-89, 2008), p. 13.

11 Burnham and Kahn, 'Russia's criminal procedural code', p. 3.

12 Council of Europe, *The European Convention on Human Rights, Rome, 4 November 1950, and its Five Protocols*. Available at http://www.hri.org/docs/ECHR50.html (accessed 26 September 2013).

13 Rimma Akhmirova, *Ya sidel s Khodorkovskim: Dokumental'nye khroniki* (Moscow: Sobesednik, 2005), p. 16.

14 Ibid., p. 23.

15 Valerii Panyushkin, *Mikhail Khodorkovskii: Uznik tishiny* (Moscow: Sekret Firmy, 2006), p. 31.

16   Akhmirova, *Ya sidel s Khodorkovskim*, p. 11.

17   Ibid., p. 27.

18   Ibid., p. 83.

19   See Leon Aron, 'A champion for the bourgeoisie: reinventing virtue and citizenship in Boris Akunin's novels', *The National Interest*, Spring 2004.

20   Akhmirova, *Ya sidel s Khodorkovskim*, p. 93.

21   Ibid., p. 87.

22   Ibid., p. 35.

23   Daniel Kimmage, 'Putin's restoration: consolidation or clan rivalries?', in Geir Flikke (ed.), *The Uncertainties of Putin's Democracy* (Oslo: NUPI, 2004), p. 130.

24   Dmitry Gololobov, 'The Yukos money-laundering case: a never-ending story', *Michigan Journal of International Law*, 28, 2007, p. 750.

25   Vera Vasil'eva, *Aleksei Pichugin: Puti i pereput'ya (biograficheskii ocherk)* (Prague: Human Rights Publishers, 2011), pp. 159–60.

26   Valerii G. Shiryaev, *Sud mesti: pervaya zhertva dela Yukosa* (Moscow: OGI, 2006), p. 47.

27   Ibid., p. 39.

28   Ibid., pp. 65–6.

29   Ibid., pp. 73–96; Vasil'eva, *Aleksei Pichugin*, pp. 71–3.

30   Sarah E. Mendelson and Theodore P. Gerber, 'Soviet nostalgia: an impediment to Russian democratization', *The Washington Quarterly*, 21(1), Spring 2008, p. 92.

31   Listed in *Constitutional and Due Process Violations in the Khodorkovsky/Yukos Case*, a white paper prepared by defence lawyers on behalf of Mikhail Khodorkovsky, Platon Lebedev, Alexei Pichugin (Moscow: n.d.), compiled by Robert Amsterdam and Charles Krause.

32   Details in Mariya Lokotetskaya and Lyudmila Romanova, 'Sud idet: Lebedev i Khodorkovskii ponyali, v chem ikh obvinyayut i ne priznali vinu', *Gazeta*, 16 July 2004, p. 3.

33   See, for example, Lev Romanov, 'Zhestokie igry', *Komsomol'skaya pravda*, 20 May 2005; the paper has close links with the Kremlin.

34   Aleksandr Pumpyanskii, 'Protsess', in Aleksandr Pumpyanskii, Sergei Kovalev and Boris Zhutovskii, *Delo Khodorkovskogo* (Moscow: Zebra, 2011), p. 7.

35   Gleb Pavlovskii, *Genial'naya vlast'! Slovar' abstraktsii kremlya* (Moscow: Evropa, 2012), p. 101.

36   Panyushkin, *Mikhail Khodorkovskii*, p. 220.

37   Aleksei Grishin, 'Svideteli s raz"yasneniem', *Vremya novostei*, 25 August 2004, p. 2.

38   Andrei Skrobot and Roman Ukolov, 'Khodorkovskii sekonomil vremya sudu', *Nezavisimaya gazeta*, 25 August 2004, p. 11.

39   Anfisa Voronina, 'Khodorkovskii obvinil prokurorov', *Vedomosti*, 13 January 2005.

40   Dmitrii Simakin, 'Khodorkovskii: "Eto kriminal'no-khudozhestvennoe delo"', *Nezavisimaya gazeta*, 28 February 2005, p. 7.

41   Vladimir Perekrest, 'Mikhail Khodorkovskii: "Vse, v chem menya obvinyayut, – eto normal'naya praktika vedeniya biznesa"', *Izvestiya*, 28 February 2005, p. 2.

42   Vladimir Perekrest, 'Prokuror otkazalsya doprashivat' Khodorkovskogo', *Izvestiya*, 28 February 2005, p. 3.

43   Dmitrii Simakin, '"Prestupleniya voobshche ne bylo": Genrikh Padva nachal dolguyu rech' v zashchitu Khodorkovskogo', *Nezavisimaya gazeta*, 6 April 2005, p. 1.

44   Dmitri Simakin, 'V poiskakh zerna istiny', *Nezavisimaya gazeta*, 8 April 2005, p. 7.

45   Viktor Yasmann, 'Khodorkovskii case is a sign of the times', RFE/RL, *Russian Political Weekly*, 5(15), 14 April 2005.

46   Larisa Kallioma, '"Ya byl nepravil'nym oligarkhom": Mikhail Khodorkovskii skazal svoe poslednee slovo', *Izvestiya*, 12 April 2005, p. 1.

47   A. Rodionov, *Nalogovye skhemy, za kotorye posadili Khodorkovskogo* (Moscow: Vershina, 2006), pp. 209–26.

48   Ekaterina Butorina, 'Nepravil'nyi oligarkh: Mikhail Khodorkovskii skazal sudu poslednee slovo', *Vremya novostei*, 12 April 2005, p. 1; Anfisa Voronina, 'Khodorkovskii uveren, chto delo "Yukosa" zaterano radi razgrableniya kompanii', *Vedomosti*, 12 April 2005.

49   Marina Gridneva and Lina Panchenko, '"Ne vinovat, sniskhozhdeniya ne proshu"', *Moskovskii komsomolets*, 12 April 2005, p. 3. Later Khodorkovsky was jailed where the Decembrists had been exiled, and Inna could truly reveal her Decembrist qualities.

50   Larisa Kallioma, 'Sadites' poka', *Izvestiya*, 17 May 2005, p. 1; the article provides details of the NIIUIF, Apatit and income-tax cases.

51   Lyuba Pronina, '9 years for Khodorkovsky and Lebedev', *Moscow Times*, 1 June 2005, p. 1.

52   For a good overview, see Peter Clateman, 'Yukos affair, Part VII: review of the criminal sentence and appeal', 29 March 2006, *Johnson's Russia List*, No. 77, 30 March 2006, item 19. See also: Dmitrii Simakin and Mikhail Tolpegin, 'Upryatali', *Nezavisimaya gazeta*, 1 June 2005, p. 1; Yurii Sergeev, 'Iz dos'e "KP"', *Komsomol'skaya pravda*, 1 June 2005, p. 2.

53   Rodionov, *Nalogovye skhemy*, pp. 106–13.

54   Ibid, pp. 191–208.

55   Ibid, pp. 8–57.

56   Igor' Smirnov, 'Protsess: privesti nagovor v ispolnenie', *Moskovskaya Pravda*, 22 April 2005, p. 2.

57   Dmitrii Simakin and Mikhail Tolpegin, 'Upraytili: rasprava nad Khodorkovskim i Lebedevym byla ozhidaema, no vse ravno shokirovala svoei zhestokost'yu', *Nezavisimaya gazeta*, 1 June 2005, p. 1. Lebedev's sentence was later reduced on appeal to eight years.

58   'Nakanune vyneseniya prigovora prokuratura grozit Khodorkovskomu novym obvineniyami', Newsru.com, 13 May 2005.

59   Peter Lavelle, 'The Kremlin's "cartridge clip"', *Untimely Thoughts: Analysis*, 7 June 2005.

60   Nick Paton Walsh, 'Prosecutors warn Russian oligarchs', *Guardian*, 7 June 2005, p. 12.

61   Catherine Belton, 'Shock and then boredom in court', *Moscow Times*, 1 June 2005, p. 1; Anna Arutunyan, 'Khodorkovsky sentenced to 9 years in prison', *Moscow News*, 1 June 2005, p. 2.

62   Qutoations here and in subsequent paragraphs are taken from 'Zayavlenie Mikhaila Khodorkovskogo', *Nezavisimaya gazeta*, 1 June 2005, p. 3; Lyuba Pronina, '9 years for Khodorkovsky and Lebedev', *Moscow Times*, 1 June 2005, p. 1.

63   The date of the interview is not given, but it was published three days after his article 'Left turn' came out in the same paper, discussed in Chapter 10. See: 'Intervyu: Mikhail Khodorkovskii – "Ya uveren, chto prigovor budet otmenen"', *Vedomosti*, 4 August 2005, p. 5; Catherine Belton, 'Khodorkovsky says Sechin led Yukos attack', *Moscow Times*, 5 August 2005, p. 3.

64   'Ya uveren, chto prigovor budet otmenen'.

65   Anton Malyavskii, 'Tot chelovek', *Moskovskie novosti*, 23, 17 June 2005, p. 12. Malyavskii was a member of the Moscow city SPS Political Council.

66   Sabine Leutheusser-Schnarrenberger, Press Release, 31 May 2005, mimeo.

67   Amnesty International public statement, AI Index: EUR 46/012/2005 (public). News Service No. 087, 11 April 2005.

68   'Russia: Khodorkovsky sentencing illuminates erosion of rule of law', *Freedom House*, 31 May 2005. Available at http://web.archive.org/web/20051210130043/http://www.freedomhouse.org/media/pressrel/053105.htm (accessed 18 October 2013).

69   President George W. Bush's press conference, the Rose Garden, 31 May 2005; *Vedomosti*, 1 June 2005.

70   US State Department news briefing, 31 May 2005; political transcripts by Federal Document Clearing House.

71   Nick Paton Walsh, 'Russian oligarch jailed for nine years', *Guardian*, 1 June 2005, p. 15.

72   Untitled report, Mosnews.com, 23 November 2004.

73   Alla Bossart, 'Ra-by-ne-my', *Novaya gazeta*, 3 November 2005.

74   Daniel Brössler, 'Interview with Mikhail Khodorkovsky', *Süddeutsche Zeitung*, 11 September 2005.

75   Mikhail Khodorkovskii, 'Obrashchenie k izbiratelyam, vsem grazhdanam rossii', *Nezavisimaya gazeta*, 1 September 2005, p. 1.

76   A Levada poll gave him no less than 30%; see Rustem Falyakhov, 'K urne: Mikhail Khodorkovskii mozhet rasschityvat' na tret' golosov', *Gazeta*, 14 September 2005, p. 3.

77   Aleksandr Kolesnichenko, 'Kamernaya druzhba', *Novye izvestiya*, 14 September 2005, p. 2.

78   Mikhail Khodorkovskii, 'Vinovnym menya priznal ne sud, a gruppa byurokratov', speech of 22 September 2005. Available at http://web.archive.org/web/20070208184406/http://www.khodorkovsky.ru/speech/3548.html (accessed 18 October 2013).

79   'Pozdravlenie', *Kommersant*, 7 October 2005, in V.M. Kartashov, *Who Is Mr. Hodorkowsky?* (Rostov-on-Don: Feniks, 2007), p. 6.

80   A 'colony', or in Russian *koloniya*, is the contemporary term for the old labour camps of the Gulag; very few long-term convicts serve their sentences in prisons proper, known as *tyurmy*.

81   'A statement by Mikhail Khodorkovsky: to everyone who has supported me and continues to support me', *Financial Times*, 2 November 2005, p. 9. This was an advertisement placed with the support of Leonid Nevzlin, Vladimir Dubov and Mikhail Brudno; an earlier version appeared as Mikhail Khodorkovskii, 'Vsem, kto menya podderzhival i podderzhivaet', *Novaya gazeta*, 31 October 2005, which was rather more explicit about the threat from China.

82   Vladislav Kulikov, 'Khodorkovskii sekretno pokinul tyur'mu', *Rossiiskaya gazeta*, 11 October 2005, p. 2.

83   Oleg Kashin, 'Kak doekhat' do Khodorkovskogo', *Izvestiya*, 24 October 2005, p. 1. This account also has rich details about the camp and the region.

84   Vitalii Cherkasov, 'Ot Rokossovskogo do Khodorkovskogo', *Novaya gazeta*, 21 November 2005.

85   For an interesting study of the world of contemporary Russian prisons, including the structure of internal order, 'folklore', culture and customs, see E.S. Efimova, *Sovremennaya tyur'ma: Byt, traditsii i fol'klor* (Moscow: OGI, 2004).

86   Larisa Kallioma and Vladimir Perekrest, 'Kuda podal'she', *Izvestiya.ru*, no date available.

87   For a good description of the camp, see Vladislav Kulikov, 'Kandidat tyuremnykh nauk', *Rossiiskaya gazeta*, 27 October 2005, p. 2.

88   Mikhail Khodorkovskii and Nataliya Gevorkyan, *Tyur'ma i volya* (Moscow, Howard Roark, 2012), p. 37.

89   Mark Franchetti, 'Oligarch plots political revenge from jail', *Sunday Times*, 13 November 2005.

90   'Khodorkovskii vestretilsya s dochkoi', *Moskovskii komsomolets*, 13 September 2006, p. 2.

91   'Khodorkovskii mnogo pishet', *Moskovskii komsomolets*, 18 December 2006, p. 2.

92   '"On nazyvaet eto mesto antimirom"', *Presstsentr Mikhaila Khodorkovskogo*, 6 June 2006. Available at http://web.archive.org/web/20070416214625/http://www.khodorkovsky.ru/bio/5320.html (accessed 18 October 2013).

93   RFE/RL, *Russian Political Weekly*, 6(14), 7 August 2006.

94   'Reiting pyat' zvezd: Mikhail Khodorkovskii, zaklyuchennyi', *Gazeta*, 20 March 2006, p. 2; Irina Vlasova, 'Khodorkovskii "zaeli"', *Novye izvestiya*, 7 June 2006, p. 6.

95   Eduard Lomovtsev, 'Manual'naya terapiya', *Vremya novostei*, 26 October 2007, p. 3.

96 Andrei Pankov, 'Khodorkovskii pobedil ShIZO', *Novye izvestiya*, 19 April 2006, p. 6.
97 There are various versions of what happened, with the prison administration asserting that the two got into an argument at 3 a.m., and that Kuchma then punched Khodorkovsky. Khodorkovsky refused to press charges against his assailant, noting that he was 'inadequate'; see Ivan Sas, 'Shvy na informatsii', *Nezavisimaya gazeta*, 17 April 2006, p. 7.
98 Andrei Sharov, 'Khodorkovskii popal pod nozh', *Rossiiskaya gazeta*, 17 April 2006, p. 2.
99 Sergei Dyupin, 'V rezhime myagkoi posadki', *Kommersant-Den'gi*, 46, 21 November 2005, p. 20. Some of the detail above about the camp and the region is drawn from Dyupin's rather sanguine account.
100 Interview with Igor' Kovalevskii, 'Advokat Karinna Moskalenko – o visite v koloniyu Krasnokamenske', *Novaya gazeta*, 15 December 2005.
101 Aleksandr Stepanov, 'Khodorkovskii zaimetsya ukladkoi rukavits', *Izvestiya*, 15 August 2006, p. 3.
102 Lina Panchenko, 'Khodorkovskii sdaet ekzamen na shveyu-motorista', *Moskovskii komsomolets*, 2 February 2006, pp. 1–2.

6. COLLATERAL DAMAGE

1 'A conversation with Vladimir Putin', 3 December 2009.
2 Valerii G. Shiryaev, *Sud mesti: Pervaya zhertva dela Yukosa* (Moscow: OGI, 2006).
3 Vera Vasil'eva, *Aleksei Pichugin: Puti i pereput'ya (biograficheskii ocherk)* (Prague: Human Rights Publishers, 2011).
4 Ibid., pp. 164–5.
5 Lev Romanov, 'Zhestokie igry', *Komsomol'skaya pravda*, 20 May 2005.
6 Shiryaev, *Sud mesti*, Chapter 4.
7 Ibid., p. 79.
8 The incident and its implications are described in detail in Shiryaev, *Sud mesti*, pp. 82–5, with a general discussion of the use of pharmacological substances by the security police on pp. 85–93.
9 'Pichugin denies murder accusations', *Moscow Times*, 24 April 2008.
10 Vera Vasil'eva, *Kak sudili Alekseya Pichugina: Sudebnyi reportazh* (Prague/Moscow: Human Right Publishers, 2007); Vasil'eva, *Aleksei Pichugin*, pp. 90–100, which includes an account of how the jurors were selected to ensure a conviction.
11 Valentina A. Korneeva, untitled article, 22 January 2007. Available at http://www.alexey-pichugin.ru/index.php?id=253 (accessed 27 September 2013).
12 Vladimir Perekrest, 'Za chto sidit Mikhail Khodorkovskii', Part 2, *Izvestiya*, 18 May 2006. Available at http://www.izvestia.ru/investigation/article3092896/index.html (accessed 24 September 2013).
13 Mariya Rogacheva and Elena Vlasova, 'Alekseya Pichugina budut sudit' vo vtoroi raz', *Izvestiya*, 20 March 2006.
14 Vasil'eva, *Aleksei Pichugin*, p. 166.
15 David Holley, 'Former Yukos oil official is convicted of 2 murders', *Los Angeles Times*, 18 August 2006.
16 Evgenii Vladimirovich Reshetnikov, untitled article, 22 January 2007. Available at http://www.alexey-pichugin.ru/index.php?id=264 (accessed 27 September 2013).
17 Mikhail Viktorovich Ovsyannikov, untitled article, 22 January 2007. Available at http://www.alexey-pichugin.ru/index.php?id=261 (accessed 27 September 2013).
18 Vladimir Vasil'evich Shapiro, untitled article, 22 January. Available at http://www.alexey-pichugin.ru/index.php?id=266 (accessed 27 September 2013).

19 Vasil'eva, *Aleksei Pichugin*, p. 167.

20 The issue is fully examined by Sergei Kovalev, 'Posleslovie k protsessu', in Aleksandr Pumpyanskii, Sergei Kovalev and Boris Zhutovskii, *Delo Khodorkovskogo* (Moscow: Zebra, 2011), pp. 143–50.

21 Gregory White, 'Russia's Sechin defends investment climate', *Wall Street Journal*, 22 February 2011.

22 'Former Yukos head says he has never resorted to violence to achieve goals', Interfax, 5 April 2011.

23 The news came to Khodorkovsky early in the morning, Moscow time, and he immediately cancelled his birthday celebrations.

24 Marshall I. Goldman, *Oilopoly: Putin, Power, and the Rise of the New Russia* (Oxford: Oneworld Publications, 2008), p. 109.

25 Mikhail Khodorkovskii and Nataliya Gevorkyan, *Tyur'ma i volya* (Moscow, Howard Roark, 2012), pp. 222, 232–3; for a general discussion, see pp. 260–5, 267–70.

26 Steve Allen, 'Is Khodorkovsky Russia's Al Capone', *Business New Europe*, 16 June 2011.

27 David Satter, *Darkness at Dawn: The Rise of the Russian Criminal State* (New Haven, CT: Yale University Press, 2003), p. 108.

28 Catherine Belton, 'The oil town that won't forget Yukos', *Moscow Times*, 25 April 2006, p. 1.

29 Khodorkovskii and Gevorkyan, *Tyur'ma i volya*, p. 270.

30 Belton, 'The oil town that won't forget Yukos'.

31 Satter, *Darkness at Dawn*, p. 109.

32 Ibid., p. 107, with more details on p. 110.

33 The default of 17 August 1998 diverted attention away from Yukos, but Nefteyugansk was heavily represented in a mass demonstration of oil workers outside the White House in October 1998.

34 Romanov, 'Zhestokie igry'. The Chechen link is possibly deeper, since a delivery of oil intended to pay off a 450-billion-rouble non-denominated debt owed to the city from before Menatep took over in 1995 disappeared into the coffers of trading firm Rondo-S, possibly linked to a financier of Chechen rebel groups, Khozh-Akhmed Nukhaev, who is none other than the person suspected of involvement in organising the murder of Paul Khlebnikov in July 2004; see Belton, 'The oil town that won't forget Yukos'. The book by Khlebnikov is called *Razgovor s varvarom: Besedy s chechenskim polevym komandirom Khozh-Akhmedom Nukhaevym o banditizme i islame* (Moscow: Detektiv-Press, 2003). The title *Conversations with a Barbarian* probably did not go down too well with Nukhaev.

35 Two alleged members of the Kamyshinsky criminal gang, Popov and Prikhodko, were identified by witnesses as having exactly the features of the murderers, but were nevertheless released on bail and soon after died in mysterious circumstances, as a result of which the case was closed; see Vladimir Arkad'evich Petukhov, untitled article, 22 January 2007. Available at http://www.alexey-pichugin.ru/index.php?id=263 (accessed 27 September 2013). Reshetnikov has Caucasian features (in the Russian sense), whereas witnesses described the killers as classically Slavic types.

36 At the same time Tsigelnik confessed to the attack on the Rosprom director Viktor Kolesov and also to two attacks on the businessman Yevgeny Rybin.

37 Petukhov, untitled article.

38 Arkady Ostrovsky, 'Yukos workers shed few tears for jailed ex-boss', *Financial Times*, 17 November 2003.

39 Matt Siegel, 'Widow puts blame on Khodorkovsky', *Moscow Times*, 28 March 2008, p. 7.

40 Ibid.

41 Aleksei Nikol'skii, 'Sud poshel na krainyuyu meru', *Vedomosti*, 4 August 2008, p. 2.

42 Perekrest, 'Za chto sidit Mikhail Khodorkovskii', Part 2.

43   Il'ya Zhegulev, 'Diagnoz – Yukos: pochemu Vasilii Aleksanyan tak dorog sledovatelyam', *Vedomosti*, 18 February 2008.

44   Romanov, 'Zhestokie igry'.

45   Perekrest, 'Za chto sidit Mikhail Khodorkovskii', Part 2.

46   Vera Vasil'evna, 'Nespravedlivo i nekachestvenno', Grani.ru, 17 August 2006, cited in Evgenii L'vovich Rybin, untitled article, 22 January 2007. Available at http://www.alexey-pichugin. ru/index.php?id=265 (accessed 27 September 2013).

47   Author's interview, London, 25 October 2005.

48   Charles Gurin, 'Prosecutors raid Yukos one more time', *Eurasia Daily Monitor*, 1(5), 7 May 2004.

49   Guy Chazan, 'Yukos case fuels legal fears', *Wall Street Journal*, 3 January 2005. Available at http://online.wsj.com/news/articles/SB110470214638614707 (accessed 18 October 2013).

50   The case is described by Rachel Polonsky, 'Russia in the dock', *Spectator*, 2 April 2005, pp. 18–19.

51   Mikhail Fishman, 'Zamknutyi srok', *Kommersant-Vlast'*, 16, 24 April 2006, p. 36.

52   Aleksandr Shadrin, 'Zhelanie poprizhat'', *Kommersant*, 29 March 2006, p. 8.

53   Fishman, 'Zamknutyi srok', p. 36.

54   Anna Arutunyan, 'Bakhmina parole may come with strings', *Moscow News*, 23 April 2009.

55   Alexander Osipovich, 'From legal eagle to dying in a cage', *Moscow Times*, 7 February 2008, p. 1.

56   Statement to the RF Supreme Court, 22 January 2008. Quoted at http://web.archive.org/ web/20101217114603/http://khodorkovsky.ru/objective/7880.html (accessed 18 October 2013).

57   Zhegulev, 'Diagnoz – Yukos'.

58   Christian Lowe, 'Ex-Yukos executive tells of blackmail', *Moscow Times*, 17 January 2008, p. 5.

59   Aleksandr Yakovlev and Roman Ukolov, 'Aleksyanu uluchshili usloviya', *Nezavisimaya gazeta*, 1 February 2008, p. 4; Marina Lepina and Yurii Yudin, 'Mikhail Khodorkovskii golodaet za Vasiliya Aleksanyana', *Kommersant*, 31 January 2008, p. 5.

60   The letter is dated 29 January 2008. Available at http://web.archive.org/web/20090513072922/ http://khodorkovsky.ru/speech/7762.html (accessed 18 October 2013).

61   Svetlana Osadchuk and Natalya Krainova, 'Aleksanyan says he is receiving care', *Moscow Times*, 1 February 2008, p. 3.

62   Neil Buckley, 'Unbowed in face of "absurd" charges', *Financial Times*, 7 February 2008, p. 9.

63   Svetlana Osadchuk, 'Aleksanyan denied release for illness', *Moscow Times*, 4 February 2008, p. 5.

64   Marina, Lepina, '"Kto-to reshil vzyat' menya i unichtozhit"', *Kommersant*, 1 February 2008, p. 5.

65   Mikhail Khodorkovsky, writing from SIZO No. 75/1, Chita, 11 February 2008. Available at http://web.archive.org/web/20080416201701/http://www.khodorkovsky.ru/speech/7956. html (accessed 18 October 2013).

66   Jonas Bernstein, 'Aleksanyan's plight: a case of the "legal nihilism" Medvedev has vowed to fight', *Eurasian Daily Monitor*, 5(21), 4 February 2008.

67   'Vasilii Aleksanyan peresel s nar na tsep'', *Kommersant-Vlast'*, 7, 25 February 2008, p. 22.

68   Vera Chelishcheva, 'V dush puskaet nadziratel'', *Novaya gazeta*, 15, 3 March 2008, p. 15.

69   ECtHR First Section, 'Case of Aleksanyan v. Russia (application no. 46468/06)', Strasbourg, 22 December 2008.

70   Ekaterina Zapodinskaya, 'Provornyi invalid', *Kommersant*, 16 January 2007, p. 1.

71   'Spanish citizen pronounced a new guilty party in Yukos case', *ITAR-TASS*, 19 July 2011.

72   'Fugitive Spanish businessman makes accusations against YUKOS investigators', MosNews, 23 April 2009.

73   Central Criminal Investigation Court No. 001, Madrid, Extradition Case 11/2009 2, 'Order of the court', 6 July 2009. Pilar Bonet, 'Spain will not extradite to Russia a Spanish citizen sought for his link to the oil company Yukos', *El País*, 29 July 2009.

74   Dmitry Gololobov, 'The Yukos money-laundering case: a never-ending story', *Michigan Journal of International Law*, 28, 2007, p. 714.

75   For an early list of cases, see Robert Coalson, 'All Yukos's men', RFE/RL, *Russian Political Weekly*, 5(21), 31 May 2005.

76   'Former Yukos executives jailed for 11 and 12 years', *Moscow Times*, 6 March 2007, p. 5.

77   For a moving personal account, see Vladimir Pereverzin, *Zalozhnik: Istoriya menedzhera Yukosa* (Moscow: Howard Roark, 2013).

78   Vera Chelishcheva, 'Vyshel na svobodu odin is figurantov "delo Yukosa"', *Novaya gazeta*, 16 January 2012.

79   The institute's website is available at http://imrussia.org/ (accessed 27 September 2013). The present author acts as an adviser to the institute.

7. THE TRIAL OF THE CENTURY

1   Aleksandr Pumpyanskii, 'Protsess', in Aleksandr Pumpyanskii, Sergei Kovalev and Boris Zhutovskii, *Delo Khodorkovskogo* (Moscow: Zebra, 2011), p. 68.

2   Richard Sakwa, 'The trials of Khodorkovsky in Russia', in Devin Pendas and Jens Meierhenrich (eds), *Political Trials* (Cambridge: Cambridge University Press, forthcoming).

3   Dmitrii Golubovskii and Svetlana Reiter, '"Zhizn' menyaet printsipy: No ne vse"', *Esquire*, 29 September 2012.

4   Although found guilty of the last of these charges, the two were not sentenced on this count due to the expiration of the statute of limitation.

5   Mariya Lokotetskaya, 'Mikhail Khodorkovskii ostalsya pod strazhei', *Gazeta*, 4 April 2007, p. 10. The new charges were based on Articles 160 and 174 of the RF Criminal Code.

6   The former head of Fargoil, Valdés-García, as we have seen fled Moscow in January 2007, just days before he and former Ratibor president Vladimir Malakhovsky were due to be sentenced for this alleged embezzlement; see Miriam Elder, 'Bank of New York sued for $22 Bln', *Moscow Times*, 18 May 2007, p. 1.

7   Ekaterina Zapodinskaya, 'Sudu podbrosili prilichnye den'gi', *Kommersant*, 6 February 2007, p. 1.

8   Yurii Shmidt, 'Chto dal'she', *Presstsentr Mikhaila Khodorkovskogo i Platona Lebedeva*, 25 October 2007. Available at http://web.archive.org/web/20080602010813/http://www.khodorkovsky.ru/cassation/comments/7430.html (accessed 18 October 2013).

9   Ivan Romanov, 'Delo Mikhail Khodorkovskogo stalo srochnym', *Kommersant*, 16 November 2007, p. 6.

10   Zoya Eroshok, 'Grazhdanin oligarkh', *Novaya gazeta*, 25 October 2007, p. 6.

11   Mikhail Khodorkovskii, 'Ne znayu, skazhet li im za eto Putin "spasibo"', *Presstsentr Mikhaila Khodorkovskogo i Platona Lebedeva*, 7 February 2007. Available at http://web.archive.org/web/20090603001049/http://khodorkovsky.ru/speech/6273.html (accessed 19 October 2013).

12   'Judgement of the Ingodinsky District Court of the City of Chita', 18 May 2007, mimeo.

13   Schmidt, 'Chto dal'she', 25 October 2007.

14   'Khodataistvuem o prekrashchenii ugolovnovo dela', *Presstsentr Mikhaila Khodorkovskogo i Platona Lebedeva*, 22 December 2007. Available at http://web.archive.org/web/20101217124641/http://khodorkovsky.ru/cassation/petitions/7637.html (accessed 19 October 2013).

15   Dmitrii Medvedev, 'Speech at the 2nd all-Russia civic forum', 22 January 2008. Available at http://
      web.archive.org/web/20111205005737/http://www.medvedev2008.ru/english_2008_01_22.
      htm (accessed 19 October 2013).

16   Schmidt, 'Chto dal'she', 25 October 2007.

17   Miriam Elder, 'Khodorkovsky faces 15 more years', *Moscow Times*, 2 July 2008.

18   Ibid.

19   Vera Chelishcheva, *Zaklyuchennyi No. 1: Neslomlennyi Khodorkovskii* (Moscow: Eksmo,
      2011), p. 212.

20   Mikhail Khodorkovskii and Nataliya Gevorkyan, *Tyur'ma i volya* (Moscow: Howard Roark,
      2012), p. 46.

21   Andrei Kolesnikov, 'Vladimir Putin: dayu vam chestnoe partiinoe slovo', *Kommersant*, 30
      August 2010, p. 1.

22   Chelishcheva, *Zaklyuchennyi No. 1*, p. 251.

23   Golubovskii and Reiter, '"Zhizn' menyaet printsipy: No ne vse"'.

24   The case is made by Otto Luchterhandt, *Report of the Presidential Council of the RF for the
      Development of Civil Society and Human Rights on the Results of the Public Scholarly Analysis
      of the Court Materials of the Criminal Case against M.B. Khodorkovsky and P.L. Lebedev (tried
      by the Khamovnichesky District Court of the City of Moscow; the verdict issued on 27.12.2010)*
      (Moscow, 2011), p. 210.

25   Ferdinand Feldbrugge makes this point in his submission. See *Report of the Presidential
      Council*, pp. 63–4.

26   For a discussion, see Dmitry Gololobov, 'The Yukos money-laundering case: a never-ending
      story', *Michigan Journal of International Law*, 28, 2007.

27   Chelishcheva, *Zaklyuchennyi No. 1*, p. 233.

28   For a transcript, see 'Pervym svidetelem zashchity stal Mikhail Kasyanov', *Presstsentr
      Mikhaila Khodorkovskogo i Platona Lebedeva*, 24 May 2010. Available at http://web.archive.
      org/web/20101125004220/http://khodorkovsky.ru/documents/2010/05/24/13335/ (accessed
      19 October 2013).

29   Mikhail B. Khodorkovsky, 'Reform must, and will, come to Russia', *Los Angeles Times*, 20
      October 2010.

30   'Text of closing statement by Mikhail Khodorkovsky', RFE/RL, *Russia Report*, 2 November
      2010.

31   'A conversation with Vladimir Putin', 16 December 2010. Available at http://web.archive.
      org/web/20120128002331/http://www.premier.gov.ru/eng/events/news/13427/ (accessed
      19 October 2013).

32   Alexandra Odynova, 'Yukos verdict tests balance of ruling tandem', *Moscow Times*, 11 January
      2011.

33   Mikhail Khodorkovskii, 'Vlasti ne khvataet dobra i terpimosti', *Nezavisimaya gazeta*, 24
      December 2010, p. 3.

34   Jeffrey Kahn subjects the verdict to detailed analysis, *Report of the Presidential Council*,
      pp. 200–4. In particular, he notes the 'extensive duplication of the indictment [which itself
      consists of 14 volumes containing 3,460 pages]. [...] Astonishingly, the first 130 pages
      of the verdict (and, quite possibly, much more) is a near exact copy of the indictment',
      p. 147.

35   'Khodorkovsky, Lebedev lawyers appeal new 14-year sentence', RIA Novosti, 31 December
      2010.

36   Aleksandra Samarina, 'Na kryuchke neopredelennosti', *Nezavisimaya gazeta*, 25 January
      2011.

37   'The Khodorkovsky verdict', *The Economist*, 29 December 2010.

38   Mikhail Khodorkovskii interview with Veronika Kutsyllo, "'Slepo verit ne nado ne tol'ko mne – nikomu'", *Kommersant-Vlast'*, 7, 21 February 2011, pp. 4–7.

39   Marie Jégo, 'Affaire Khodorkovski: "Vladimir Poutine me considère comme son opposant personnel'", *Le Monde*, 26 January 2011.

40   Evgeniya Albats interview with Khodorkovskii, 'Oni zhili, kak schitali dolzhnym: seichas – moya ochered', *New Times*, 44–5, 27 December 2010, pp. 4–7.

41   Mikhail Khodorkovskii, 'Zima pravosudiya: slovi i real'nost', *Vedomosti*, 2 February 2011, p. 4.

42   Natal'ya Vasil'eva, "'Prigovor byl privezen iz Mosgorsuda, ya tochno znayu": otkrovennoe interv'yu o dele Yukosa pomoshchnika sud'i Khamovnicheskogo suda', *Gazeta.ru*, 14 February 2011. Available at http://web.archive.org/web/20131009064156/http://www.gazeta.ru/politics/2011/02/14_a_3524202.shtml (accessed 19 October 2013).

43   'Pravosudie zadnim chislom', *New Times*, 14, 18 April 2011, p. 1.

44   'Rezolyutivnaya chast' prigovora Mikhailu Khodorkovskomu i platonu lebedevu', 14 June 2011. Available at http://www.echo.msk.ru/blog/echomsk/784249-echo/ (accessed 30 September 2013).

45   On 14 June the Investigative Committee refused to launch criminal proceedings against Danilkin, dismissing Vasileva's charges. The IC's spokesman, Vladimir Markin, insisted that 'There are no signatures or handwritten notes which would identify authorship', hence 'the interviews she [Vasileva] gave to journalists is only based on her guesses and assumptions and is not backed by any objective data'; see: 'Allegations about pressure on Yukos judge "conjecture" – Investigative Committee', Interfax, 14 June 2011; Tom Washington, 'A rival Khodorkovsky verdict appears', *Moscow News*, 15 June 2011.

46   In a further ruling on the complaint of political motivation by the two defendants' lawyers, on 16 November 2011 the Moscow City Court rejected 'the presence of a political motivation in the criminal prosecution' and appeal arguments that the two were essentially being tried for the second time on the same charges.

47   'M.B. Khodorkovsky's submission in the cassation instance', 24 May 2011, mimeo, p. 1, retranslated.

48   Ibid., p. 3.

49   Ibid., p. 5.

50   Ibid., p. 22.

51   Ibid., p. 26.

52   'Russia's Khodorkovsky appeals new jail term', AFP, 24 May 2011.

53   'M.B. Khodorkovsky's submission in the cassation instance', 24 May 2011, mimeo, p. 1. This is a different text to the one cited above, and represents a more general statement distributed by Khodorkovsky's defence lawyers.

54   REF/RL *Russia Report*, 14 September 2011.

55   Reznik noted that Putin had pardoned the American spy Edmund Pope, and Medvedev the actress Natalya Zakharova. Interview with Genri Reznik, 'Sudovladel'tsy', *Profil'*, 15, 2012, p. 18.

56   Anatoly Medetsky, 'Khodorkovsky not eligible for parole', *Moscow Times*, 26 October 2007, p. 7.

57   Sergei Dyupin, "'S Mikhailom Borisovichem ya postupil ne po ponyatiyam'", *Kommersant-Vlast'*, 25, 30 June 2008, pp. 20–5. Gnezdilov provides much interesting information about Khodorkovsky's time in pre-trial detention in Chita.

58   Valerii Panyushkin, *Mikhail Khodorkovskii: Uznik Tishiny 2* (St Petersburg: Piter, 2009), p. 278.

59   Ibid., p. 279.

60   Mark Franchetti, 'Jailed tycoon Mikhail Khodorkovsky "framed" by key Putin aide', *Sunday Times*, 18 May 2008.

61   Ibid.

62   Vladimir Putin, 'Otvety na voprosy zhurnalistov po okonchanii peregovorov s Federal'nym kantslerom Germanii Angeloi Merkel", 8 March 2008. Available at http://www.kremlin.ru/text/appears/2008/03/161952.shtml (accessed 30 September 2013).

63   'En visite à Paris, le premier ministre russe explique au "Monde" les choix stratégiques de son pays', *Le Monde*, 1 June 2008, pp. 1–2.

64   'Press-konferentsiya po okonchanii rossiisko-germanskikh peregovorov', 5 June 2008. Transcript available at http://web.archive.org/web/20081019041328/http://kremlin.ru/text/appears/2008/06/202120.shtml (accessed 19 October 2013).

65   Miriam Elder, 'Khodorkovsky challenges Medvedev', *Moscow Times*, 17 July 2008.

66   Ryan Chilcote, 'Interview to Bloomberg Television', *Kremlin.ru*, 27 January 2011; Alexandra Odynova, 'At Davos, Medvedev defends Yukos trial', *Moscow Times*, 28 January 2011.

67   'Press-konferentsiya Prezidenta Rossii', 18 May 2011. Available at http://www.kremlin.ru/transcripts/11259 (accessed 30 September 2013).

68   Alexandra Odynova, 'Signaling thaw: Khodorkovsky pops up on state TV', *Moscow Times*, 31 May 2011; Yan Gordeev, 'V sud'be Khodorkovskogo nastupili teleperemeny', *Nezavisimaya gazeta*, 31 May 2011.

69   Typically, when asked whether he considered Khodorkovsky's prosecution a mistake, he said: 'No, I don't think so, because I was taught at university to respect a verdict', 'Transcript: Interview with President Dmitry Medvedev', *Financial Times*, 19 June 2011.

70   For example, an unsigned article, 'Medvedev dolzhen postavit' tochku v zatyanuvsheisya istorii s Khodorovskim', *Nezavisimaya gazeta*, 3 June 2011, p. 2.

71   'Russian court rejects tycoon Khodorkovsky's parole application', Reuters, 7 June 2011.

72   Catherine Belton, 'Jailed Yukos chief in Medvedev plea', *Financial Times*, 15 July 2011.

73   Ibid.

74   Aleksandr Kukolevskii, 'Platonu Lebedevu pripomnili tapochki', *Kommersant-Vlast'*, 30, 25 July 2011, p. 17.

75   Town of Velsk, 'Judgment', 27 July 2011, mimeo.

76   'RF ombudsman says Lebedev should be released under economic amnesty', *ITAR-TASS*, 28 July 2011.

77   Lyudmila Alexandrovna, 'Rights activists call refusal to release Lebedev "disgraceful"', *ITAR-TASS*, 29 July 2011.

78   'Khodorkovsky unabridged: the full transcript of the replies that Mikhail Khodorkovsky sent to the *Wall Street Journal Europe* and other newspapers', *Wall Street Journal*, 15 June 2011.

79   Alexei Navalny's interview with Yevgenia Albats, 'Russian protest icon Navalny discusses plans, ambitions in marathon interview', Ekho Moskvy Radio, 26 December 2011, BBC Monitoring, *Johnson's Russia List*, No. 233, 2011, item 29.

80   Paul Goble, 'Window on Eurasia: Khodorkovsky's failure to turn his "show trial" against his accusers raises some disturbing questions, Pavlova suggests', 9 January 2011, in *Johnson's Russia List*, No. 6, 2011, item 13.

81   Irina Pavlova, 'Tema ne raskryta', 5 January 2011. Available at http://grani.ru/Politics/Russia/yukos/m.185090.html (accessed 30 September 2013).

82   'Stenogramma programmy "Razgovor s Vladimirom Putinym. Prodolzhenie"', 15 December 2011. Available at http://web.archive.org/web/20120510200221/http://premier.gov.ru/events/news/17409/index.html (accessed 19 October 2013).

83   Various polls available at http://www.levada.ru/category/rubrikator-oprosov/sudebnaya-sistema (accessed 30 September 2013). The findings are summarised in Maria Kuchma,

'Russian presidential candidates play Khodorkovsky card', RIA Novosti, 12 January 2012.

84   'Communist leader pledges pardon for Khodorkovsky if elected president', RIA Novosti, 13 January 2012. Available at http://en.rian.ru/news/20120111/170708548.html (accessed 30 September 2013).

8. RUSSIA ON TRIAL

1   Andrew Jack, *Inside Putin's Russia* (London: Granta Books, 2004), p. 310.

2   Leandro Despouy, *Promotion and Protection of All Human Rights, Civil, Political, Economic, Social and Cultural Rights, Including the Right to Development, Report of the Special Rapporteur on the Independence of Judges and Lawyers*, Addendum, Mission to the Russian Federation, Human Rights Council, Eleventh session, Agenda item 3, A/HRC/11/41/add.2, 23 March 2009.

3   *The Circumstances Surrounding the Arrest and Prosecution of Leading Yukos Executives*, Doc. 10368, 29 November 2004, Committee on Legal Affairs and Human Rights, Parliamentary Assembly of the Council of Europe.

4   PACE, 'Resolution 1418 (2005)', 25 January 2005.

5   PACE, 'Recommendation 1692 (2005) 1', 25 January 2005.

6   'PACE rapporteur in Moscow calls for support of judges "who take their independent role seriously"', press release, 281 (2009).

7   Sabine Leutheusser-Schnarrenberger, 'Allegations of politically-motivated abuses of the criminal-justice system in council of Europe member states', 7 August 2009, report for the Legal Affairs and Human Rights Committee, PACE, Doc. 11993.

8   IBAHRI, *The Khodorkovsky Trial: A Report on the Observation of the Criminal Trial of Mikhail Borisovich Khodorkovsky and Platon Leonidovich Lebedev, March 2009 to December 2010* (London: International Bar Association, September 2011).

9   Laurence A. Groen, 'The "Iukos affair": the Russian judiciary and the European Court of Human Rights', *Review of Central and East European Law*, 38(1), 2013, p. 107.

10   ECtHR (first section), 'Decision as the admissibility of application No. 5829/04 by Mikhail Borisovich Khodorkovsky against Russia, sitting on 7 May 2009', mimeo. All decisions and judgments are available at www.echr.coe.int/echr/en/hudoc (accessed 30 September 2013).

11   ECtHR Former First Section, 'Case of Khodorkovsky v. Russia (application No. 5829/04): Judgment', 31 May 2011, Strasbourg.

12   The minister was in fact Mikhail Lesin, endorsing the deal in July 2000 to drop criminal charges in return for Gusinsky selling his media empire to Gazprom.

13   'First Mikhail Khodorkovsky trial "not political", European court upholds', RIA Novosti, 17 December 2011. Available at http://en.rian.ru/russia/20111217/170320637.html (accessed 30 September 2013).

14   'Khodorkovsky unabridged: the full transcript of the replies that Mikhail Khodorkovsky sent to the *Wall Street Journal Europe* and other newspapers', *Wall Street Journal*, 15 June 2011.

15   'Lebedev v. Russia (application no. 4493/04): judgment', 25 October 2007.

16   Vera Chelishcheva, 'Narusheno pravo na spravedlivyi sud', *Novaya gazeta*, 121, 24 October 2012, p. 7.

17   Groen, 'The "Iukos Affair"', p. 108.

9. FROM OLIGARCH TO DISSIDENT

1   Yurii Sergeev, 'pis'mo na volyu: Khodorkovskii ne stanet grafom Monte-Kristo', *Komsomol'skaya Pravda*, 29 December 2004, p. 5.

2   Maksim Kantor, 'Kazarmennyi kapitalizm', *Moskovskie novosti*, 31, 12–18 August 2005, p. 16.

3   The interview was with Nataliya Gevorkyan, with whom he later wrote a book, 'Mikhail Khodorkovskii: Rokefelleru bylo namnogo tyazhelee', *Kommersant*, 1 June 2005.

4   Mikhail Khodorkovskii, 'Krizis liberalizma v Rossii', *Vedomosti*, 29 March 2004, p. 17. According to the editor, Tatyana Lysova, the article appeared at the paper without prior consultation. Khodorkovsky's lawyer, Anton Drel, affirmed that his client had been working on the article for three months; see Catherine Belton, 'Khodorkovsky seeks peace with Putin', *Moscow Times*, 30 March 2004, p. 1.

5   At the time there was considerable controversy over its authenticity, with the ubiquitous anti-oligarchic fighter Stanislav Belkovsky allegedly playing his part. It had originally appeared under the title 'Russian liberalism in the twentieth century: manifesto' on the website Utro. ru on 18 March, with the author line 'Initiative Group, Chair Yu. A. Stepanov'. The website stated that it had received the article on 17 March, and about half of it was similar to the version that came out in *Vedomosti* later under Khodorkovsky's name. This was the website where Belkovsky's article on behalf of the National Strategy Council 'The state and oligarchs' had first appeared on 26 May 2003. For a discussion, with much contradictory information, see Irina Nagornykh, Nataliya Gevorkyan and Ilya Bulavinov, 'Oligarkh raspisalsya v liberalizme', *Kommersant*, 30 March 2004, p. 1. Khodorkovsky himself comments ironically on the issue in Mikhail Khodorkovskii and Nataliya Gevorkyan, *Tyur'ma i volya* (Moscow: Howard Roark, 2012), p. 7, confirming his authorship.

6   Valeria Korchagina, 'Khodorkovsky essay causes stir', *Moscow Times*, 31 March 2004, p. 5.

7   Kalinin declared that 'Khodorkovsky did not pass any articles out of jail', and announced that an investigation had been launched to determine 'the circumstances that – if it were really true – allowed the prisoner to prepare an article and pass it to the newspaper'; see Korchagina, 'Khodorkovsky essay causes stir'.

8   Aleksei Nikol'skii and Sevast'yan Kozitsyn, 'Po kusochkam', *Vedomosti*, 7 April 2004.

9   Leonid Berres, 'Khodorkovskii otreksya ot svoei stat'i: radi advokatov', *Izvestiya*, 7 April 2004, p. 6.

10   Nikol'skii and Kozitsyn, 'Po kusochkam'.

11   Khakamada's campaign was financed by Nevzlin and managed by Anatoly Yermolin from Yukos, a former security official; see Elena Tokareva, *Kto podstavil Khodorskovskogo* (Moscow: Yauza, 2006), p. 215.

12   Karl Polanyi, *The Great Transformation: The Political and Economic Origins of Our Time*, with a foreword by Joseph E. Stiglitz and an introduction by Fred Block (Boston: Beacon Press, [1944] 2001), p. 40.

13   In an interview with *Izvestiya* on 1 April 2004 in the immediate wake of the publication of the letter, Nevzlin stated that he would stop funding Khakamada's party and that since it was impossible to discuss matters with Khodorkovsky in person he was obliged to 'depart the political scene'. Ivan Gordeev, *Vremya novostei*, 5 April 2004, p. 2.

14   See Philip Boobbyer, *Conscience, Dissent and Reform in Soviet Russia* (London: Routledge, 2005).

15   Stanislav Belkovskii, 'Pokayanie: odinochestvo Khodorkovskogo', *Vedomosti*, 30 March 2004.

16   Aleksandr Arkhangel'skii, 'A poutru oni prosnulis'', *Izvestiya*, 30 March 2004, p. 2.

17   Jonas Bernstein, 'Liberalism gets the blame', *Moscow Times*, 16 January 1998.

18   See Axel Kaehne, *Political and Social Thought in Post-Communist Russia* (London and New York: Routledge, 2007).

19   Valeriya Novodvorskaya, 'Grovelling before the Inquisition', *New Times*, 30 June 2004, p. 21.

20   Egor Gaidar, 'Liberalizm: slukhi o smerti preuvelicheny', *Vedomosti*, 14 April 2004. For a more developed analysis, see id., *Gibel' imperii: uroki dlya sovremmennoi Rossii* (Moscow: Rosspen, 2006).

21   Mikhail Khodorkovskii, 'Tyur'ma i mir: sobstvennost' i svoboda', *Vedomosti*, 28 December 2004. Note that the word *mir* can also be translated as 'peace', and the idea that prison had allowed Khodorkovsky to achieve a type of inner peace and reconciliation with his fate is reflected in the text. As he puts it: 'Breathing the spring air, playing with children who study at a normal Moscow school, reading wise books – all these things are more important, pleasant and right than dividing property and settling scores with one's own past.'

22   Václav Havel and John Keane, *The Power of the Powerless: Citizens against the State in Central-Eastern Europe* (London: Hutchinson, 1985).

23   'Mikhail Khodorkovsky: vpervye – interv'yu iz tyur'my, "Tyazhelo, chto sovsem net solntsa"', *Russkii Newsweek*, 31 January 2005, pp. 14–17. The questions were passed to Khodorkovsky via his lawyers, and the answers returned in the same way.

24   Ibid., p. 14.

25   Ibid., p. 15.

26   Ibid.

27   Ibid., p. 16.

28   Ibid.

29   Ibid., p. 17.

30   Mikhail Khodorkovskii, untitled article, *Bol'shoi gorod*, No. 9 (135), 25 May 2005. Available at http://web.archive.org/web/20061005212159/http://www.bg.ru/article?id=4787 (accessed 19 October 2013).

31   Condemned already in *Vekhi: Sbornik statei o russkoi intelligentsia* (Moscow, 1909; reissued Frankfurt: Posev, 1967).

10. RUSSIA IS WORTHY OF FREEDOM

1   Mikhail Khodorkovskii, 'Levyi povorot', *Vedomosti*, 139, 1 August 2005, p. A5.

2   Interview with the present author, Moscow, 3 March 2008. Following the report the Council for National Strategy split, and in April 2004 Belkovsky established the National Strategy Institute (INS).

3   He cites a Levada-Center poll.

4   For reactions, see Catherine Belton, 'Khodorkovsky says a left turn is inevitable', *Moscow Times*, 2 August 2005, p. 1.

5   This contradiction is pointed out by an editorial in the same issue in which 'Left turn' was published, 'Levyi put', *Vedomosti*, 1 August 2005, p. 1.

6   Dmitrii Polikanov, 'Lodka dlya "sverkh-Putina"', *Vedomosti*, 8 August 2005, p. A4. The author, director of international links at VTsIOM, argued this on the basis of extensive opinion polling.

7   Sergei Mitrokhin, 'Izobretatel'nost' d'yavola: ob uchastii demokratov v "pravo-levoi" koalitsii', *Nezavisimaya gazeta*, 20 June 2008, p. 11.

8   *Khodorkovskikh chtenii*, Konferentsii 'Rossiiskie al'ternativy', 10 July 2007. Available at http://www.polit.ru/dossie/2007/10/05/conf.html (accessed 2 October 2013).

9   For an interesting discussion of the (poor) prospects of the Social Democratic Party of Russia, see Elena Rudneva, Anna Nikolaeva and Aleksei Nikol'skii, 'Gel'man podkhvatil znamya u Gorbacheva', *Vedomosti*, 4 August 2005, p. A2.

10 Khodorkovsky's failure to mention United Russia is also enigmatic. Some officials of the latter party accused Rodina of supporting Khodorkovsky, suggesting that mercenary motives were involved. Georgii Il'ichev, "'Edinaya Rossiya" edet na "Rodinu"', *Izvestiya*, 8 August 2005, p. 2. See also Syuzanna Farizova, 'Zaklyuchennyi Khodorkovsky zapyatnal "Rodinu"', *Kommersant*, 6 August 2005, p. 2.

11 'Vy gotovy k povorotu nalevo?', *Kommersant-Vlast'*, 31, 8 August 2005, p. 5.

12 Ibid.

13 'Nedelya/Rossiya', *Kommersant-Vlast'*, 35, 5 September 2005, p. 29.

14 The questions were posed by Grigory Raiko in an untitled article in *Politique Internationale*, 10 November 2005.

15 Mikhail Khodorkovskii, 'Levyi povorot-2', *Kommersant*, 11 November 2005, p. 8; Mikhail Khodorkovskii, *Levyi povorot 2* (Moscow: Galleya-Print, 2006), p. 3.

16 For example, Alexei Venediktov, author's interview, 19 June 2008, Moscow; the view is shared by Irina Yasina, author's interview, 18 June 2008.

17 Khodorkovskii, *Levyi povorot 2*, p. 4.

18 Ibid., p. 6.

19 Ibid., p. 7.

20 Ibid., p. 11.

21 Ibid.

22 'Razgovor pisatelya Grigoriya Chkhartishvili (B. Akunin) s Mikhailom Khodorkovskim', in Mikhail Khodorkovskii, *Stat'i, dialogi, interv'yu* (Moscow: Eksmo, 2010), p. 78.

23 Ibid., p. 81.

24 'Conversation of writer Grigory Chkhartishvili (B. Akunin) with Mikhail Khodorkovsky', *Esquire*, October 2006, p. 161; 'Razgovor pisatelya Grigoriya Chkhartishvili (B. Akunin) s Mikhailom Khodorkovskim', pp. 82–3.

25 'Dialogi: Lyudmila Ulitskaya – Mikhail Khodorkovskii', in Mikhail Khodorkovskii, *Stat'i, dialogi, interv'yu* (Moscow: Eksmo, 2010), p. 130.

26 Mikhail Khodorkovskii, 'Rossiya v ozhidanii suda', *Kommersant-Vlast'*, 23, 15 June 2009; reprinted in Mikhail Khodorkovskii, *Stat'i, dialogi, interv'yu* (Moscow: Eksmo, 2010), p. 59.

27 Evgenii Semenyako, "'My imeem takoi sud, kotoryi zasluzhivaem"', *Kommersant-Vlast'*, 35, 7 September 2009, pp. 26–7, in which all previous contributions are listed.

28 'Maybe I was too naïve', *Newsweek*, published 15 August 2009, from the magazine issue dated 31 August 2009. A longer version was published in *Russkii Newsweek*, 15 August 2009.

29 Boris Reitschuster, 'Mikhail Khorkovsky interviewed by Germany's *Focus* magazine', *Focus*, 7 September 2009.

30 Dmitrii Medvedev, 'Rossiya, vpered!', 10 September 2009. Available at http://www.gazeta.ru/comments/2009/09/10_a_3258568.shtml (accessed 2 October 2013).

31 Mikhail Khodorkovskii, 'Modernizatsiya: pokolenie M', *Vedomosti*, 21 October 2009, p. 4. Natalya Timakova, Medvedev's press secretary, revealed that Medvedev read Khodorkovsky's article as he prepared his annual address, *ITAR-TASS*, 21 October 2009.

32 Elena Skvortsova, 'Eksklyuzivnoe interv'yu. Mikhail Khodorkovskii: Rossiya dostoina svobody, i sud'by strany reshat' nam', *Sobesednik*, 50, 29 December 2009.

33 Mikhail Khodorkovsky, 'A time and a place for Russia', *New York Times*, 29 January 2010.

34 See Alena V. Ledeneva, *Can Russia Modernise? Sistema, Power Networks and Informal Governance* (Cambridge: Cambridge University Press, 2013).

35 Mikhail Khodorkovskii, 'Uzakonennoe nasilie', *Nezavisimaya gazeta*, 3 March 2010, p. 5.

36 Christian Neef and Matthias Schepp, '*Spiegel* interview with Mikhail Khodorkovsky', *Der Spiegel*, 9 August 2010.

37 Elena Vlasenko and Elena Polyakovskaya, 'Epistles of Russia's opposition', RFE/RL, *Russia Report*, 7 September 2010.

38 Mikhail Khodorkovsky, 'Russia's democratic future lies with Britain', *Observer*, 19 September 2010.

39 'Propisnye istiny', *Argumenty i fakty*, 32, 11 August 2005, p. 11.

40 Surkov's 'secret speech' was published on the Radio Liberty website on 11 July. Available at http://web.archive.org/web/20070528074604/http://www.mosnews.com/interview/2005/07/12/surkov.shtml (accessed 19 October 2013).

41 'Intervyu: Mikhail Khodorkovskii – "Ya uveren, chto prigovor budet otmenen"', *Vedomosti*, 4 August 2005, p. 5.

42 Natalya Melikova, 'Kreml' skazal vrazheskim SMI svoe tverdoe slovo', *Nezavisimaya gazeta*, 29 June 2006.

43 'Khodorkovskii prizyvaet golosovat' za malye partii', *Nezavisimaya gazeta*, 8 November 2007, p. 3.

44 Mariya-Luiza Tirmaste, 'Mikhail Khodorkovskii nachal agitatsiyu', *Kommersant*, 8 November 2007, p. 3.

45 Boris Popov, 'Iz glubiny sibirskikh rud', *Novye izvestiya*, 27 November 2006, p. 7; 'Mikhail Khodorkovskii – v stat'e dlya zhurnala the economis' [*sic*], *Moskovskii komsomolets*, 22 November 2006, p. 2.

46 Neil Buckley, 'Khodorkovsky still defiant', *Financial Times*, 7 February 2008, p. 1.

47 Neil Buckley, 'Unbowed in face of "absurd" charges', *Financial Times*, 7 February 2008, p. 9.

48 'Khodorkovskii odobril deistviya Medvedeva v Yuzhnoi Osetii', *Obshchaya gazeta*, 11 September 2008. Available at http://og.ru/news/2008/09/11/41296.shtml (accessed 2 October 2013).

49 Nadia Popova, 'Interview transcript: Mikhail Khodorkovsky', *Moscow Times*, 11 September 2008.

50 Ul'yana Makhkamova and Roman Ukolov, 'Shag v storonu osvobodozhdeniya', *Nezavisimaya gazeta*, 12 September 2008, p. 4.

51 Mikhail Khodorkovskii, 'Zametny priznaki pozitivnykh institutsional'nykh izmenenii', 2 March 2009. Available at http://web.archive.org/web/20090306041937/http://www.khodorkovsky.ru/speech/9399.html (accessed 19 October 2013).

52 Nikolai Smorodin, 'Vtoroi srok Khodorkovskogo', *Novye izvestiya*, 11 March 2005, p. 7.

53 Robert Sharlet, 'Politics of the Yukos affair', in William Simons (ed.), *Private and Civil Law in the Russian Federation: Essays in Honor of F.J.M. Feldbrugge* (Leiden and Boston: Martinus Nijhoff Publishers, 2009), p. 348.

54 Nelson Mandela, *A Long Walk to Freedom: The Autobiography of Nelson Mandela* (London: Abacus, 1995).

11. RETURN, RESISTANCE AND REFORM

1 Gleb Pavlovskii, *Genial'naya vlast'! Slovar' abstraktsii kremlya* (Moscow: Evropa, 2012), p. 64.

2 Ibid., p. 65.

3 Mikhail Khodorkovskii, 'Rossiya, za kotoruyu menya posadili', *Kommersant-Vlast*, 37, 19 September 2011.

4 Joshua E. Keating, 'The world's most powerful prisoners', *Foreign Policy*, 10 August 2010.

5 BBC Monitoring, 'Justice minister says Russian prisons not changed much since Stalin', *Ekho Moskvy*, 21 September 2011, *Johnson's Russia List*, No. 172, 2011, item 31.

6 Mikhail Khodorkovskii, 'Tyuremnye lyudi', *New Times*, 27, 29 August 2011. Further articles were published in issues 29, 35, 38 and 42 in 2011.

7 Mikhail Khodorkovskii, 'Tyuremnye lyudi: Sledovatel'', *New Times*, 1, 23 January 2012.

8   Guy Falconbridge, 'Forget reform if Putin stays in power: Khodorkovsky', Reuters, 18 September 2011.

9   Alexandra Odynova and Jonathan Earle, 'Top court hands Khodorkovsky rare token victory', *Moscow Times*, 14 September 2011.

10   Aleksandra Samarina, 'Khodorkovskii pugayut stranu pered vyborami: telekanal "Rossiya" obsudil delo Yukosa', *Nezavisimaya gazeta*, 5 September 2011, p. 3.

11   'Prokhorov about Khodorkovsky', *Gazeta.ru*, 9 September 2012; reported by Interfax on that day.

12   Mikhail Khodorkovskii, 'Rossiya, za kotoruyu menya posadili', *Kommersant-Vlast*, 37, 19 September 2011.

13   Mikhail Khodorkovskii interview with Veronika Kutsyllo, '"Slepo verit ne nado ne tol'ko mne – nikomu"', *Kommersant-Vlast'*, 7, 21 February 2011.

14   This is how it was described by Boris Makarenko in discussion with the author.

15   Mikhail Khodorkovskii, 'Okonchanie, ili prodolzhenie', *Vedomosti*, 12 October 2011, p. 16.

16   Alexey Eremenko, 'Khodorkovsky warns of revolution', *Moscow Times*, 9 November 2011, p. 2.

17   BBC Monitoring, 'Jailed ex-Yukos head answers questions from Russian radio listeners', 7 November 2011; in *Johnson's Russia List*, No. 203, 2011, item 16.

18   'Predsedatel' pravitel'stva Rossiiskoi Federatsii V.V. Putin vstretilsya s politologami', 6 February 2012. Available at http://web.archive.org/web/20120209115545/http://premier.gov.ru/events/news/18008/ (accessed 19 October 2013).

19   'Predsedatel' pravitel'stva Rossiiskoi Federatsii V.V. Putin prinyal uchastie v rabote s"ezda Rossiiskogo soyuza promyshlennikov i predprinimateli', 9 February 2012. Available at http://web.archive.org/web/20120607094526/http://premier.gov.ru/events/news/18052/ (accessed 19 October 2013).

20   Mikhail Khodorkovsky, 'A prisoner in Russia', *New York Times*, 27 January 2011.

21   Konstantin von Eggert, 'Wooing the oligarchs', *Moscow News*, 13 February 2012.

22   Oleg Nishenkov, 'Investors skeptical on "oligarch" tax', *Moscow News*, 13 February 2012.

23   Evgeniya Albats, 'Chto zhdat' ot vlasti? Mikhail Khodorkovskii – the New Times', *New Times*, 3, 30 January 2012.

24   Mikhail Khodorkovskii, 'Kak vesti sebya na prezidentskikh vyborakh 4 marta', *Novaya gazeta*, 2 February 2012.

25   'Mikhail Khodorkovskii: "On prosto boitsya konkurentsii"', *Novaya gazeta*, 10 February 2012.

26   Mikhail Khodorkovsky, 'Real political change is unavoidable', *Guardian*, 27 February 2012, p. 26.

27   Vladislav Inozemtsev, 'Creating a two-party system', *Moscow Times*, 15 March 2012.

28   Tai Adelaja, 'Cleaning up the house', *Russia Profile*, 19 March 2012.

29   'One in ten Russians describe ex Yukos chief as political prisoner', poll conducted by VTsIOM, Interfax, 9 April 2012. A Levada-Center poll conducted on 24–7 February 2012 found that 48% of Russians believed that there were political prisoners in the country, Interfax, 12 March 2012.

30   Natal'ya Kostenko and Anastasiya Kornya, 'Ogromnaya pobeda prezidenta', *Vedomosti*, 2 February 2011, p. 1.

31   Tom Washington, 'Court gets Kremlin off the Khodorkovsky hook', *Moscow Times*, 11 February 2011.

32   The experts comprised six Russians and three foreigners: Ferdinand Feldbrugge (Leiden University, Holland), Sergei Guriev (Rector of the New Economic School, Moscow), Jeffrey Kahn (SMU Dedman School of Law, Dallas, Texas), Otto Luchterhandt (Hamburg University,

Germany), Anatoly Naumov (Academy of the PGO, Moscow), Oksana Oleinik (Higher School of Economics, Moscow), Alezei Proshlyakov (Urals State Law Academy, Ekaterinburg), Mikhail Subbotin (IMEMO, Moscow) and Astamur Tedeev (Higher School of Economics, Moscow).

33 *Report of the Presidential Council,* quoted in Chapter 7.

34 Thomas Grove and Alexei Anishchuk, 'Kremlin rights council urges Khodorkovsky review', Reuters, 21 December 2011. Available at http://www.reuters.com/article/2011/12/21/us-russia-council-khodorkovsky-idUSTRE7BK1R920111221 (accessed 2 October 2013).

35 Aleksandra Samarina, 'Novaya politicheskaya real'nost' v dele Yukosa', *Nezavisimaya gazeta,* 22 December 2011, p. 3.

36 Nikolay Svanidze, 'One small step for Russia's courts, one big step for Russian society', Russiatoday.com, 16 February 2011.

37 Aleksandra Samarina, 'Spisok nemedlennogo reagirovaniya', *Nezavisimaya gazeta,* 6 March 2012, p. 3.

38 'Prime Minister Vladimir Putin wishes Russian women a happy upcoming holiday and takes questions from female members of the government press pool', 7 March 2011. Previously available at http://www.premier.gov.ru/events/news/18379/ (link no longer valid).

39 'Presidential council proposes to pardon Khodorkovsky and Lebedev', *ITAR-TASS,* 3 February 2012.

40 Ilya Arkhipov and Henry Meyer, 'Khodorkovsky pardon won't need guilt admission, council says', Bloomberg, 16 March 2012.

41 Aleksandra Samarina, 'Tret'ya sila v dele Khodorkovskogo', *Nezavisimaya gazeta,* 26 March 2012, p. 3.

42 The programme was called 'Khodorkovsky go home' on the 'NTVshniki' talk show. A summary was drafted by BBC Monitoring, 'Russian TV show debates reasons behind former Yukos boss' imprisonment', 18 March 2012; in *Johnson's Russia List,* No. 53, 2012, item 20.

43 Alexander Litoi, 'Kompromis', *RBC Daily,* 5 April 2012.

44 'Russian rights activists ask president to pardon political prisoners', Interfax, 4 April 2012.

45 'Interv'yu rossiiskim telekanalam', 26 April 2012. Available at http://news.kremlin.ru/transcripts/15149 (accessed 2 October 2013).

46 Sergei Mashkin and Fedor Maksimov, 'Mikhail Khodorkovskomu postanovili osvobozhdenie', *Kommersant,* 1 August 2012, p. 1.

47 Aleksei Sokovnin, 'Platonu Lebedevu rano na svobodu', *Kommersant,* 11 August 2012, pp. 1, 3.

48 Alexander Bratersky, 'Court cuts prison sentence of Khodorkovsky's partner', *Moscow Times,* 9 August 2012.

49 *Ekspert,* 32, 13 August 2012, pp. 6–7.

50 Vera Chelishcheva, '"Chto by vnizu ni reshili – sverkhu vsegda podpravyat"', *Novaya gazeta,* 24 September 2012, pp. 3–4.

51 'Yukos's Lebedev denied early release – again', RIA Novosti, 14 December 2012.

52 Aleksandra Samarina, 'Sikvel dela Yukosa', *Nezavisimaya gazeta,* 21 August 2012, p. 1.

53 'Business ombudsman in Khodorkovsky release plea', RIA Novosti, 23 June 2012.

54 'Khodorkovsky asks business ombudsman to review term', *Moscow Times,* 10 August 2012, p. 3.

55 Anastasiya Kornya, Liliya Biryukova and Natal'ya Kostenko, 'Vtoraya exspertiza', *Vedomosti,* 3 August 2012, p. 2.

56 'Presidential human rights council backs Khodorkovsky appeal to businessman's ombudsman', Interfax, 2 August 2012.

57 'Khodorkovsky case to get independent assessment', Russia Today, 9 August 2012. Previously available at http://rt.com.politics/khodorkovsky-espertise-case-documents-237/ (link no longer valid).

58   Tom Balmforth, 'Critics of Khodorkovsky verdict in crosshairs', RFE/RL *Russia Report*, 27 March 2013.

59   Jeffrey D. Kahn, 'In Putin's Russia, shooting the messenger', *New York Times*, 26 February 2013.

60   Andrei Kolesnikov, 'Razvorot nad Arkhangel'skom: v chem politicheskii smysl otmeny resheniya o sokrashenii sroka Platona Lebedeva', *Novaya gazeta*, 22 September 2012, p. 2.

61   'Khodorkovsky, Lebedev to walk free in 2014', RIA Novosti, 20 December 2012.

62   'Moscow City Court does not find artificial criminalization of Khodorkovsky/Lebedev business', Interfax, 16 January 2013.

63   'Russian Supreme Court requested the criminal cases against Mikhail Khodorkovsky and Platon Lebedev', *ITAR-TASS*, 21 March 2013.

64   'Press-konferentsiya Vladimira Putina', 20 December 2012. Available at http://kremlin.ru/news/17173 (accessed 2 October 2013).

65   'Mikhail Khodorkovskii: "On prosto boitsya konkurentsii"'.

66   Mikhail Khodorkovskii, 'Sovremennyi sotsial'nyi liberalizm i ekonomika', *Novaya gazeta*, 42, 16 April 2012, pp. 7–9.

67   BBC Monitoring, 'Jailed ex-Yukos head answers questions'.

68   'Vladimir Evtushenkov na dozhde. Polnaya versiya. Chast' 2', *TVrain.ru*, 21 March 2012. Available at http://tvrain.ru/teleshow/harddaysnight/vladimir_evtushenkov_na_dozhde_polnaya_versiya_chast_2-205417/ (accessed 2 October 2013).

69   'IMR president Pavel Khodorkovsky on the police actions against peaceful protesters in Moscow', Institute of Modern Russia, 8 May 2012. Available at http://www.imrussia.org/index.php?option=com_content&view=article&id=236&Itemid=124&lang=en (accessed 2 October 2013).

70   Pavel Khodorkovsky, 'My father's message to Putin from a prison camp', *Financial Times*, 5–6 May 2012, p. 9.

71   Dmitrii Golubovskii and Svetlana Reiter, '"Zhizn' menyaet printsipy: No ne vse"', *Esquire*, 29 September 2012.

72   'Interview: son says Khodorkovsky's freedom "in the hands of Russian society"', RFE/RL, *Russia Report*, 26 June 2012.

73   Mikhail Khodorkovskii and Nataliya Gevorkyan, *Tyur'ma i volya* (Moscow: Howard Roark, 2012), p. 382. His ideas were developed in a wide-ranging programmatic last chapter called 'On the future of Russia', in ibid., pp. 376–92.

74   Ibid., p. 380.

75   Mikhail Khodorkovskii, 'Mezhdu imperiei i natsional'nym gosudarstvom', *Novaya gazeta*, 65, 15 June 2012.

76   Khodorkovskii and Gevorkyan, *Tyur'ma i volya*, p. 346.

77   'Press-konferentsiya Vladimira Putina', 19 December 2013; http://kremlin.ru/news/19859.

78   Shaun Walker and Philip Oltermann, 'Airlift to Berlin as Khodorkovsky celebrates "freedom, freedom, freedom" after 10 years', *Guardian*, 21 December 2013, p. 3.

79   'Mikhail Khodorkovsky: in from the cold', Economist.com, 23 December 2013.

80   'Khodorkovsky's first message in freedom', 20 December 2013; http://www.khodorkovsky.com/featured-articles/khodorkovskys-first-message-in-freedom/.

81   'Evidence collection for third Yukos case started directly after 2nd conviction – source', Interfax, 18 December 2013.

82   'Russia mulls new case against Khodorkovsky – paper', RIA Novosti, 9 December 2013.

83   Evgeniya Al'bats, 'Mikhail Khodorkovskii, "Ya vernus' v Rossiyu"', *New Times*, No. 43–44, 25 December 2013.

84   Mikhail Khodorkovskii, 'Esli by ne usiliya ochen' mnogikh lyudei i u nas v strane, i vo vsem

mire, ya by segodnya byl ne zdes", Presstsentr Mikhaila Khodokovskogo i Platona Lebedeva, 22 December 2013; http://khodorkovsky.ru/news/2013/12/22/18545.html.

12. CONCLUSION

1   *Khodorkovsky*, directed by Cyril Tuschi, premiered in Washington on 2 May 2011 and was released in the UK on 2 March 2012. A final version of the film was stolen in early 2011 from the production company's offices in Berlin, described by the police as a 'very professional break-in', just days before it was due to premiere at the Berlin Film Festival in February. Helen Pidd and Miriam Elder, 'Suspicions fall on Kremlin as documentary on jailed oligarch is stolen before festival premiere', *Guardian*, 8 February 2011, p. 17.

2   'Khodorkovsky film premieres in Moscow despite cinema snub', RIA Novosti, 25 November 2011. On its release in Russia in late 2011 only a handful of cinemas agreed to its screening.

3   Cf. Naomi Klein, *The Shock Doctrine: The Rise of Disaster Capitalism* (London and New York: Allen Lane, 2007). Klein writes about the early 1990s and the launching of 'shock therapy': 'many of Washington's power brokers were still fighting a Cold War. They saw Russia's economic collapse as geopolitical victory, the decisive one that ensured U.S. supremacy' (p. 250).

4   Joseph A. Schumpeter, *Capitalism, Socialism and Democracy*, 5th edn (London: George, Allen & Unwin, 1976).

5   Valerii Panyushkin, *Mikhail Khodorkovskii: Uznik Tishiny 2* (St Petersburg: Piter, 2009), p. 191.

6   Dmitry Gololobov, 'The Yukos money-laundering case: a never-ending story', *Michigan Journal of International Law*, 28, 2007, p. 764.

7   Cf. Sergei Vasil'ev, 'Ekonomicheskie predposylki oligarkhii i avtoritarizma v sovremennoi Rossii', Moscow Carnegie Centre, *Brifing*, 3(6), June 2001.

8   William Tompson, 'The political implications of Russia's resource-based economy', *Post-Soviet Affairs*, 21(4), October–December 2005, p. 341.

9   Hilary Appel, 'Is it Putin or is it oil? Explaining Russia's fiscal recovery', *Post-Soviet Affairs*, 24(4), October–December 2008, p. 321.

10   On think tanks, see Anders Aslund, 'Rise and fall of Russia's economic think tanks', *Moscow Times*, 19 December 2012.

11   Ira Straus in 'Russia Profile weekly experts panel: did the Kremlin signal Khodorkovsky's release?', *Russia Profile.org*, 6 October 2011. Previously available at http://russiaprofile.org/experts_panel/38338/ (link no longer valid).

12   'Andrei Borodin, my dumali, chto otsidimsya', BBC Russian Service, 10 May 2012, Available at http://www.bbc.co.uk/russian/multimedia/2012/05/120504_borodin_interview.shtml (accessed 19 October 2013).

13   The paraphrase can be found at Dylan Riley, 'Democracy's graveyards?', *New Left Review*, 48, November–December 2007, p. 125, reviewing Michael Mann, *The Dark Side of Democracy: Explaining Ethnic Cleansing* (Cambridge: Cambridge University Press, 2005).

14   Amitai Etzioni, *Security First: For a Muscular, Moral Foreign Policy* (New Haven, CT: Yale University Press, 2007).

15   Cf. Ernest Gellner and César Cansino (eds), *Liberalism in Modern Times: Essays in Honour of José G. Merquior* (Budapest: Central European University Press, 1996).

16   Christian Bay, *The Structure of Freedom* (Stanford: Stanford University Press, 1958), p. 15.

17   For a fascinating discussion of 'the free person in an unfree world', see the correspondence Ol'ga Romanova, 'Perepiska s nauchnym rukovoditelem: Khodorkovskim Mikhailom Borisovichem', *New Times*, 34, 17 October 2011, pp. 22–5.

18   Vadim Dubnov, 'The folly of the right', *New Times*, 11, 30 November 2005, p. 31.

19   Lyudmila Evstigneeva and Ruben Evstigneev, 'Ot uskoreniya k uskoreniyu: razmyshleniya nad itogami dvadtsatiletiya', *Obshchestvennye nauki i sovremennost'*, 3, 2005, p. 26.

20   Timothy J. Colton, *Yeltsin: A Life* (New York: Basic Books, 2008), p. 233.

21   Vladimir Putin, 'Russia at the turn of the millennium', in Richard Sakwa, *Putin: Russia's Choice*, 2nd edn (London and New York: Routledge, 2008), p. 320 [revised translation].

22   Vladimir Putin, 'Poslanie Federal'nomu Sobraniyu Rossiiskoi Federatsii', 25 April 2005. Available at http://www.kremlin.ru/text/appears/2005/04/87049.shtml (accessed 4 October 2013).

23   Interview with Vitalii Tret'yakov, 'Aleksandr Solzhenitsyn: "Sberezhenie naroda – vysshaya izo vsekh nashikh gosudarstevennykh zadach"', *Moskovskie novosti*, 15, 28 April 2006, p. 1.

24   Stanley I. Benn, *A Theory of Freedom* (Cambridge: Cambridge University Press, 1988), p. 11.

25   Stephen Fortescue, *Russia's Oil Barons and Metal Magnates: Oligarchs and State in Transition* (Basingstoke: Palgrave Macmillan, 2006), Chapter 4.

26   Yurii Lotman, *Kultura i vzryv*, cited in Tim McDaniel, *The Agony of the Russian Idea* (Princeton: Princeton University Press, 1996), p. 17.

27   Cf. Richard Sakwa, 'From revolution to *krizis*: the transcending revolutions of 1989–91', *Comparative Politics*, 38(4), July 2006, pp. 459–78.

28   Interview with Ilya Zhegulev on 22 March 2013, the day before his death, 'Russian oligarch Boris Berezovsky's final interview: "I want to go home"', *Forbes*, 23 March 2013. Available at http://www.forbes.com/sites/clareoconnor/2013/03/27/russian-oligarch-boris-berezovskys-final-interview-i-want-to-go-home/ (accessed 4 October 2013).

29   Kim Willsher, 'Dreyfus saga goes on amid calls for reburial with France's finest', *Guardian*, 28 June 2006, p. 19.

30   Dmitrii Golubovskii and Svetlana Reiter, '"Zhizn' menyaet printsipy: No ne vse"', *Esquire*, 29 September 2012.

31   Mikhail Khodorkovskii and Nataliya Gevorkyan, *Tyur'ma i volya* (Moscow: Howard Roark, 2012), p. 91.

32   Ibid., p. 279.

33   Ibid., p. 280.

BIBLIOGRAPHY

Akhmirova, Rimma, *Ya sidel s Khodorkovskim: otkroveniya sokamernikov znamenitogo uznika Matrosskoi Tishiny* (Moscow: Sobesednik, 2005).

Akunin, Boris, 'Conversation of writer Grigory Chkhartishvili (B. Akunin) with Mikhail Khodorkovsky', *Esquire*, October 2008, pp. 148–63.

Allan, Duncan, 'Banks and the loans-for-shares auctions', in David Lane (ed.), *Russian Banking: Evolution, Problems and Prospects* (Cheltenham: Edward Elgar, 2002), pp. 137–59.

Amnesty International, 'Annual report 2009: Russian Federation' (London: Amnesty International, 2009).

——, 'Annual report 2011: the state of the world's human rights' (London: Amnesty International, 2011).

Appel, Hilary, 'Is it Putin or is it oil? Explaining Russia's fiscal recovery', *Post-Soviet Affairs*, 24(4), October–December 2008, pp. 301–23.

Baker, Peter, and Susan Glasser, *Kremlin Rising: Vladimir Putin's Russia and the End of Revolution* (New York and London: Scribner, 2005; revised 2007).

Barnes, Andrew, 'Russia's new business groups and state power', *Post-Soviet Affairs*, 19(2), 2003, pp. 154–86.

——, *Owning Russia: The Struggle over Factories, Farms and Power* (Ithaca, NY: Cornell University Press, 2006).

Bay, Christian, *The Structure of Freedom* (Stanford: Stanford University Press, 1958).

Belin, Laura, 'The Russian media in the 1990s', in Rick Fawn and Stephen White (eds), *Russia After Communism* (London: Frank Cass, 2002), pp. 139–60.

Benediktov, Kirill, 'Roman s neft'yu: zek i gubernator', *Smysl*, 1(20), January 2008, pp. 28–9.

Benn, Stanley I., *A Theory of Freedom* (Cambridge: Cambridge University Press, 1988).

Bivens, Matt, and Jonas Bernstein, 'The Russia you never met', *Demokratizatsiya: The Journal of Post-Soviet Democratization*, 6(4), Fall 1998, pp. 613–47.

Boobbyer, Philip, *Conscience, Dissent and Reform in Soviet Russia* (London: Routledge, 2005).

Brady, Rose, *Kapitalizm: Russia's Struggle to Free Its Economy* (New Haven, CT: Yale University Press, 1999).

Browne, John, *Beyond Business: an Inspirational Memoir from a Remarkable Leader* (London: Phoenix, 2010).

Brzezinski, Matthew, *Casino Moscow: A Tale of Greed and Adventure on Capitalism's Wildest Frontier* (New York: Free Press, 2001).

Burnham, William, and Jeffrey Kahn, 'Russia's criminal procedural code five years out', *Review of Central and East European Law*, 33, 2008, pp. 1–93.

Chelishcheva, Vera, *Zaklyuchennyi No. 1: Neslomlennyi Khodorkovskii* (Moscow: Eksmo, 2011).

Colton, Timothy J., *Yeltsin: A Life* (New York: Basic Books, 2008).

Danilin, Pavel, Natal'ya Kryshtal' and Dmitrii Polyakov, *Vragi Putina* (Moscow: Evropa, 2007).

Despouy, Leandro, *Promotion and Protection of All Human Rights, Civil, Political, Economic, Social and Cultural Rights, Including the Right to Development, Report of the Special Rapporteur on the Independence of Judges and Lawyers*, Addendum, Mission to the Russian Federation, Human Rights Council, Eleventh session, Agenda item 3, A/HRC/11/41/add.2, 23 March 2009.

Efimova, E.S., *Sovremennaya tyur'ma: Byt, traditsii i fol'klor* (Moscow: OGI, 2004).

Etzioni, Amitai, *Security First: For a Muscular, Moral Foreign Policy* (New Haven, CT: Yale University Press, 2007).

Fortescue, Stephen, *Russia's Oil Barons and Metal Magnates: Oligarchs and State in Transition* (Basingstoke: Palgrave Macmillan, 2006).

Fraenkel, Ernst, *The Dual State: A Contribution to the Theory of Dictatorship*, translated from the German by E.A. Shils, in collaboration with Edith Lowenstein and Klaus Knorr (New York: Oxford University Press, 1941; reprinted by The Lawbook Exchange Ltd, 2006).

Freeland, Chrystia, *Sale of the Century: Russia's Wild Ride from Communism to Capitalism* (New York: Crown Business, 2000).

Friedman, Milton, *Capitalism and Freedom* (Chicago: University of Chicago Press, 1962).

Frye, Timothy, 'Capture or exchange? Business lobbying in Russia', *Europe–Asia Studies*, 54(7), November 2002, pp. 1017–36.

Gaidar, Egor, *Gibel' imperii: uroki dlya sovremmennoi Rossii* (Moscow: Rosspen, 2006).

Gellner, Ernest, and Cesar Cansino (eds), *Liberalism in Modern Times: Essays in Honour of José G. Merquior* (Budapest: Central European University Press, 1996).

Gel'man, Vladimir, 'Political opposition in Russia: a dying species?', *Post-Soviet Affairs*, 21(3), July–September 2005, pp. 226–46.

Gessen, Masha, *The Man without a Face: The Unlikely Rise of Vladimir Putin* (New York: Riverhead Books, 2012).

Gilman, Martin, *No Precedent, No Plan: Inside Russia's 1998* (Cambridge, MA, and London: MIT Press, 2010).

Goldman, Marshall I., *The Piratization of Russia: Russian Reform Goes Awry* (London and New York: Routledge, 2003).

——, *Oilopoly: Putin, Power, and the Rise of the New Russia* (Oxford: Oneworld Publications, 2008).

Gololobov, Dmitry, 'The Yukos money-laundering case: a never-ending story', *Michigan Journal of International Law*, 28, 2007, pp. 711–64.

Golubovskii, Dmitrii, and Svetlana Reiter, '"Zhizn' menyaet printsipy: no ne vse"', *Esquire*, 29 September 2012.

Goyal, Ajay, 'Analysis: sale of a state', *The Russia Journal*, 31 October 2003, pp. 10–13.

Groen, Laurence, A., 'The "Iukos affair": the Russian judiciary and the European Court of Human Rights', *Review of Central and East European Law*, 38(1), 2013, pp. 77–108.

Gustafson, Thane, *Crisis Amid Plenty: The Politics of Soviet Energy under Brezhnev and Gorbachev* (Princeton: Princeton University Press, 1989).

——, *Capitalism Russian-Style* (Cambridge: Cambridge University Press, 1999).

——, *Wheel of Fortune: The Battle for Oil and Power in Russia* (Cambridge, MA: Belknap Press, 2012).

Hale, Henry E., *Why Not Parties in Russia? Democracy, Federalism and the State* (Cambridge: Cambridge University Press, 2006).

Hanson, Philip, 'The turn to statism in Russian economic policy', *The International Spectator*, 42(1), March 2007, pp. 29–42.

Hanson, Philip, and Elizabeth Teague, 'Big business and the state in Russia', *Europe–Asia Studies*, 57(5), July 2005, pp. 657–80.

Harvey, John, *The Plantagenets* (London: Fontana/Collins, [1948] 1967).

Havel, Václav, and John Keane, *The Power of the Powerless: Citizens against the State in Central-Eastern Europe* (London: Hutchinson, 1985).

Henderson, Sarah L., *Building Democracy in Contemporary Russia: Western Support for Grassroots Organizations* (Ithaca and London: Cornell University Press, 2003).

Herspring, Dale R., and Jacob Kipp, 'Understanding the elusive Mr. Putin', *Problems of Post-Communism*, 48(5), September–October 2001, pp. 3–17.

Hoffman, David E., *The Oligarchs: Wealth and Power in the New Russia* (New York: PublicAffairs, 2002).

IBAHRI, *The Khodorkovsky Trial: A Report on the Observation of the Criminal Trial of Mikhail Borisovich Khodorkovsky and Platon Leonidovich Lebedev, March 2009 to December 2010* (London: International Bar Association, September 2011).

Jack, Andrew, *Inside Putin's Russia* (London: Granta Books, 2004).

Johnson, Juliet, 'Russia's emerging financial–industrial groups', *Post-Soviet Affairs*, 13(4), 1997, pp. 333–65.

Kaehne, Axel, *Political and Social Thought in Post-Communist Russia* (London and New York: Routledge, 2007).

Kartashov, V.M., *Who Is Mr. Hodorkowsky?* (Rostov-on-Don: Feniks, 2007).

Kasyanov, Mikhail, *Bez Putina* (Moscow: Novaya gazeta, 2009).

Khlebnikov, Pavel, *Krestnyi otets Kremlya Boris Berezovskii, ili Istoriya razgrableniya Rossii* (Moscow: Detektiv-Press, 2001); see also Klebnikov.

——, *Razgovor s varvarom: besedy s chechenskim polevym komandirom Khozh-Akhmedom Nukhaevym o banditizme i islame* (Moscow: Detektiv-Press, 2003).

Khodorkovsky, Mikhail B., 'Keynote address', *Russian Business Watch*, 11(3), Fall 2003, pp. 2–3.

——, 'Krizis liberalizma v Rossii', *Vedomosti*, 29 March 2004, p. 17.

——, 'Levyi povorot', *Vedomosti*, 1 August 2005, p. A5; republished as Mikhail Khodorkovskii, *Levyi povorot* (Moscow: Galleya-Print, 2006).

——, 'Levyi povorot-2', *Kommersant*, 11 November 2005, p. 8; republished as Mikhail Khodorkovskii, *Levyi povorot 2* (Moscow: Galleya-Print, 2006).

——, 'Novyi sotsializm: levyi povorot-3', *Vedomosti*, 7 November 2008, p. A5.

——, 'Rossiya v ozhidanii suda', *Kommersant-Vlast'*, 23, 15 June 2009.

——, *Stat'i, dialogi, interv'yu* (Moscow: Eksmo, 2010).

——, 'Rossiya, za kotoruyu menya posadili', *Kommersant-Vlast*, 37, 19 September 2011.

——and Leonid Nevzlin, *Chelovek s rublem* (Moscow: Menatep-Inform, 1992).

——and Nataliya Gevorkyan, *Tyur'ma i volya* (Moscow: Howard Roark, 2012).

——(ed.), *Mir v 2020 godu* (Moscow: Algoritm, 2007).

Khodorkovskikh chtenii, Konferentsii 'Rossiiskie al'ternativy', 10 July 2007. Available at http://www.polit.ru/dossie/2007/10/05/conf.html (accessed 3 October 2013).

Kimmage, Daniel, 'Putin's restoration: consolidation or clan rivalries?', in Geir Flikke (ed.), *The Uncertainties of Putin's Democracy* (Oslo: NUPI, 2004), pp. 129–43.

Kireev, A., 'Reiderstvo na rynke korporativnogo kontrlya: rezultat evolyutsii silovogo predprinimatel'stva', *Voprosy ekonomiki*, 8, 2007, pp. 80–92.

Klebnikov, Paul, 'The oligarch who came in from the cold', *Forbes*, 18 March 2002. Available at http://www.forbes.com/forbes/2002/0318/110_print.html (accessed 3 October 2013).

——, *Godfather of the Kremlin: Boris Berezovsky and the Looting of Russia* (New York: Harcourt, 2000).

Klein, Naomi, *The Shock Doctrine: The Rise of Disaster Capitalism* (London and New York: Allen Lane, 2007).

Klyamkin, Igor', and Lev Timofeev, *Tenevaya Rossiya: ekonomiko-sotsiologicheskoe issledovanie* (Moscow: RGGU, 2000).

Kolesnikov, Andrei, *Vladimir Putin: ravnoudalenie oligarkhov* (Moscow: Eksmo, 2005).

———, *Anatolii Chubais: Biografiya* (Moscow: AST Moskva, 2008).

Konończuk, Wojciech, "'Sprawa Jukosu": przyczyny i konsekwencje' ['The "Yukos affair": its motives and implications'], *Prace OSW/CES Studies*, 25, Centre for Eastern Studies, Warsaw, August 2006; English version pp. 33–60. Available at http://www.osw.waw.pl/files/PRACE_25.pdf (accessed 3 October 2013).

Korzhakov, Aleksandr, *Boris El'tsin: ot rassveta do zakata* (Moscow: Interbuk, 1997).

———, *Boris El'tsin: Ot rassveta do zakata – Posleslovie* (Moscow: Detektiv-Press, 2004).

Kosals, Leonid, 'Klanovyi kapitalizm v Rossii', *Neprikosnovennyi zapas: debaty o politike i kul'ture.* Previously available at http://www.nz-online.ru/print.phtml?aid=80019312 (link no longer valid).

Kryshtanovskaya, Ol'ga, 'Transformatsiya biznes-elity Rossii, 1998–2002', *Sotsiologicheskie issledovaniya*, 8, 2002, pp. 17–29.

———, *Anatomiya rossiiskoi elity* (Moscow: Zakharov, 2005).

Kryukov, Valery, and Arild Moe, *The Changing Role of Banks in the Russian Oil Sector* (London: RIIA, 1998).

——— and ———, 'Banks and the financial sector', in David Lane (ed.), *The Political Economy of Russian Oil* (Lanham, MD: Rowman & Littlefield, 1999), pp. 47–74.

Lane, David (ed.), *The Political Economy of Russian Oil* (Lanham, MD: Rowman & Littlefield, 1999).

———(ed.), *Russian Banking: Evolution, Problems and Prospects* (Cheltenham: Edward Elgar, 2002).

Ledeneva, Alena V., *Can Russia Modernise? Sistema, Power Networks and Informal Governance* (Cambridge: Cambridge University Press, 2013).

Lloyd, John, *Rebirth of a Nation: An Anatomy of Russia* (London: Michael Joseph, 1998).

Luchterhandt, Otto, *Report of the Presidential Council of the RF for the Development of Civil Society and Human Rights on the Results of the Public Scholarly Analysis of the Court Materials of the Criminal Case against M.B. Khodorkovsky and P.L. Lebedev (tried by the Khamovnichesky District Court of the City of Moscow; the verdict issued on 27.12.2010)* (Moscow, 2011).

McDaniel, Tim, *The Agony of the Russian Idea* (Princeton, NJ: Princeton University Press, 1996).

Mandela, Nelson, *A Long walk to Freedom: The Autobiography of Nelson Mandela* (London: Abacus, 1995).

Makarkin, A., *Politiko-ekonomicheskie klany sovremennoi Rossii* (Moscow: Tsentr politicheskikh tekhnologii, 2003).

Mavrodi, Sergei, *Vsya pravda o 'MMM': Istoriya pervoi piramidy. Tyuremnye dnevniki* (Moscow: RIPOL klassik, 2007).

Mendelson, Sarah E., and Theodore P. Gerber, 'Soviet nostalgia: an impediment to Russian democratization', *The Washington Quarterly*, 21(1), Spring 2008, pp. 131–50.

Mendras, Marie, *Russian Politics: The Paradox of a Weak State* (London: Hurst & Company, 2012).

Merkel, Wolfgang, 'Embedded and defective democracies', *Democratisation*, 11(5), December 2004, pp. 33–58.

Midgley, Dominic, and Chris Hutchins, *Abramovich: The Billionaire from Nowhere* (London: Harper Collins, 2005).

Mironov, Ivan, *Zamurovannye: khronika Kremlovskogo tsentrala* (Moscow: Vagrius, 2009).

Mukhin, A.A., *Novye pravila igry dlya bol'shogo biznesa, prodiktovannye logikoi pravleniya V.V. Putina* (Moscow: Tsentr politicheskoi informatsii, 2002).

Olson, Mancur, *Power and Prosperity: Outgrowing Communist and Capitalist Dictatorships* (Oxford: Oxford University Press, 2000).

Panyushkin, Valerii, *Mikhail Khodorkovskii: uznik tishiny* (Moscow: Sekret Firmy, 2006).

——, *Mikhail Khodorkovskii: uznik tishiny 2* (St Petersburg: Piter, 2009).

Pavlovskii, Gleb, *Genial'naya vlast'! Slovar' abstraktsii kremlya* (Moscow: Evropa, 2012).

Perekrest, Vladimir, 'Za chto sidit Mikhail Khodorkovskii', *Izvestiya*, 17, 18 May, 7, 8, 9, 16 June 2006.

Pereverzin, Vladimir, *Zalozhnik: Istoriya menedzhera Yukosa* (Moscow: Howard Roark, 2013).

Polanyi, Karl, *The Great Transformation: The Political and Economic Origins of Our Time*, with a foreword by Joseph E. Stiglitz and an introduction by Fred Block (Boston: Beacon Press, [1944] 2001).

Polonsky, Rachel, 'Russia in the dock', *The Spectator*, 2 April 2005, pp. 18–19.

Poussenkova, Nina, *From Rigs to Riches: Oilmen vs. Financiers in the Russian Oil Sector* (Houston, TX: The James A. Baker III Institute for Public Policy of Rice University, October 2004).

——, 'Rosneft' kak zerkalo russkoi evolyutsii', *Pro et Contra*, 10(2–3), March–June 2006, pp. 91–104.

Pumpyanskii, Aleksandr, Sergei Kovalev and Boris Zhutovskii, *Delo Khodorkovskogo* (Moscow: Zebra, 2011).

Putin, Vladimir, *First Person: An Astonishingly Frank Self-Portrait by Russia's President Vladimir Putin*, with Nataliya Gevorkyan, Natalya Timakova and Andrei Kolesnikov, translated by Catherine A. Fitzpatrick (London: Hutchinson, 2000).

Riley, Dylan, 'Democracy's graveyards?', *New Left Review*, 48, November–December 2007, pp. 125–36.

Rivkin, Konstantin, *Khodorkovskii, Lebedev, dalee vezde: zapiski advokata o "dele Yukosa" i ne tol'ko o nem* (Moscow: Sterna, 2013).

Robinson, Neil, 'The myth of equilibrium: winner power, fiscal crisis and Russian economic reform', *Communist and Post-Communist Studies*, 34(4), December 2001, pp. 423–46.

Rodionov, A., *Nalogovye skhemy, za kotorye posadili Khodorkovskogo* (Moscow: Vershina, 2006).

Roxburgh, Angus, *The Strongman: Vladimir Putin and the Struggle for Russia* (London: I.B.Tauris, 2011).

Rutland, Peter, 'Business and civil society in Russia', in Alfred B. Evans, Jr., Laura A. Henry and Lisa McIntosh Sundstrom (eds), *Russian Civil Society: A Critical Assessment* (Armonk, NY: M.E. Sharpe, 2005), pp. 73–94.

Sakwa, Richard, 'The regime system in Russia', *Contemporary Politics*, 3(1), 1997, pp. 7–25.

——, 'From revolution to *krizis*: the transcending revolutions of 1989–91', *Comparative Politics*, 38(4), July 2006, pp. 459–78.

——, *Putin: Russia's Choice*, 2nd edn (London and New York: Routledge, 2008).

——, 'The dual state in Russia', *Post-Soviet Affairs*, 26(3), July–September 2010, pp. 185–206.

——, *The Crisis of Russian Democracy: The Dual State, Factionalism and the Medvedev Succession* (Cambridge: Cambridge University Press, 2011).

——, 'Raiding in Russia', *Russian Analytical Digest*, 105, 5 December 2011, pp. 9–13.

——, 'Systemic stalemate: reiderstvo and the dual state', in Neil Robinson (ed.), *The Political Economy of Russia* (Lanham, MD: Rowman & Littlefield, 2013), pp. 69–96.

——, 'The trials of Khodorkovsky in Russia', in Devin Pendas and Jens Meierhenrich (eds), *Political Trials* (Cambridge: Cambridge University Press, forthcoming).

Satter, David, *Darkness at Dawn: The Rise of the Russian Criminal State* (New Haven, CT: Yale University Press, 2003).

Schneider, Eberhard, 'The Russian Federal Security Service under President Putin', in Stephen White (ed.), *Politics and the Ruling Group in Putin's Russia* (London: Palgrave Macmillan, 2008), pp. 42–62.

Schumpeter, Joseph A., *Capitalism, Socialism and Democracy*, 5th edn (London: George, Allen & Unwin, 1976).

Sharlet, Robert, 'Politics of the Yukos affair', in William Simons (ed.), *Private and Civil Law in the Russian Federation: Essays in Honor of F.J.M. Feldbrugge* (Leiden and Boston: Martinus Nijhoff Publishers, 2009), pp. 347–59.

Shelley, Louise L., 'Crime and corruption: enduring problems of post-Soviet development', *Demokratizatsiya*, 11(1), Winter 2003, pp. 110–14.

Shiryaev, Valerii G., *Sud mesti: Pervaya zhertva dela Yukosa* (Moscow: OGI, 2006).

Simonov, Konstantin, *Russkaya neft': Poslednii peredel* (Moscow: Eksmo Algoritm, 2005).

Sixsmith, Martin, *Putin's Oil: The Yukos Affair and the Struggle for Russia* (London: Continuum, 2010).

Skuratov, Yurii, *Variant drakona* (Moscow: Detektiv-Press, 2000).

——, *Kremlevskie podryady: Poslednee delo genprokurora* (Moscow: Algoritm, 2012).

Specter, Michael, 'Kremlin, inc.: why are Vladimir Putin's opponents dying?', *The New Yorker*, 29 January 2007, pp. 50–63.

Tarbell, Ida Minerva, *The History of the Standard Oil Company* (London: Lightning Source, 2012).

Tokareva, Elena, *Kto podstavil Khodorskovskogo* (Moscow: Yauza, 2006).

Tompson, William, 'Putting Yukos in perspective', *Post-Soviet Affairs*, 21(2), April–June 2005, pp. 159–82.

——, 'The political implications of Russia's resource-based economy', *Post-Soviet Affairs*, 21(4), October–December 2005, pp. 335–59.

Treisman, Daniel, '"Loans for shares" revisited', *Post-Soviet Affairs*, 26(3), 2010, pp. 207–27.

——, 'Presidential popularity in a hybrid regime: Russia under Yeltsin and Putin', *American Journal of Political Science*, 55(3), July 2011, pp. 590–609.

Vasil'eva, Vera, *Kak sudili Alekseya Pichugina: Sudebnyi reportazh* (Prague and Moscow: Human Rights Publishers, 2007).

——, *Aleksei Pichugin: Puti i pereput'ya (biograficheskii ocherk)* (Prague: Human Rights Publishers, 2011).

Vekhi: Sbornik statei o russkoi intelligentsia (Moscow, 1909; reissued by Frankfurt: Posev, 1967).

Volkov, Vadim, 'Violent entrepreneurship in post-Communist Russia', *Europe–Asia Studies*, 51(5), July 1999, pp. 741–54.

——, *Violent Entrepreneurs: The Use of Force in the Making of Russian Capitalism* (Ithaca, NY: Cornell University Press, 2002).

——, 'The Yukos Affair: Terminating the Implicit Contract', *PONARS Policy Memo*, 307, November 2003.

White, David, *The Russian Democratic Party Yabloko* (Aldershot: Ashgate, 2006).

Wilson, Andrew, *Virtual Politics: Faking Democracy in the Post-Soviet World* (New Haven, CT: Yale University Press, 2005).

Wolosky, Lee S., 'Putin's plutocrat problem', *Foreign Affairs*, 79(2), March–April 2000, pp. 18–31.

Wolton, Thierry, *Le KGB au pouvoir: Le système poutine* (Paris: Buchet–Chastel, 2008).

Woodruff, David M., *Khodorkovsky's Gamble: From Business to Politics in the YUKOS Conflict*, *PONARS Policy Memo*, 308, November 2003.

Yakovlev, Alexander, *A Century of Violence in Soviet Russia* (New Haven, CT: Yale University Press, 2004).

Yakovlev, Andrei A., 'Vlast', biznes i dvizhushchie sily ekonomicheskogo razvitiya v Rossii: do i posle "dela YUKOSa"', *Obshchestvennye nauki i sovremennost'*, 1, 2005, pp. 35–44.

——, 'The evolution of business–state interaction in Russia: from state capture to business capture?', *Europe–Asia Studies*, 58(7), November 2006, pp. 1033–56.

——, and Timoti Frai (Timothy Frye), 'Reformy v Rossii glazami biznesa', *Pro et Contra*, 11(4–5), July–October 2007, pp. 118–34.

Yeltsin, Boris, *Midnight Diaries* (London: Weidenfeld & Nicolson, 2000).

Yenikeyeff, Shamil, 'BP, Russian billionaires, and the Kremlin: a power triangle that never was', *Oxford Energy Comment* (Oxford: Oxford Institute for Energy Studies, November 2011).

Yudenich, Marina, *Neft'* (Moscow: Popularnaya literature, 2007).

Zudin, Aleksei Yu., 'Oligarchy as a political problem of Russian postcommunism', *Russian Social Science Review*, 41(6), November–December 2000, pp. 4–33.

——, 'Neokorporativizism v Rossii', *Pro et Contra*, 6(4), 2001, pp. 171–98.

——, 'Rezhim V. Putina: kontury novoi politicheskoi sistemy', *Obshchestvennye nauki i sovremennost'*, 2, 2003, pp. 67–83.

Zygar, Mikhail, and Valerii Panyushkin, *Gazprom: Novoe russkoe oruzhie* (Moscow: Zakharov, 2008).

INDEX

<u>Final</u>

<u>Essay Q on Reading & Discussion</u>

You need:

Clear grasp on evolution of events from USSR collapse → Putin's power → Phases of Putin's Power.

- 1990's Effect on Society
- Economic Factors

<u>Identifications</u>

readings & discussions

→ - Dilemas confronting various actors

    ex). What did Russia look like when he gets back from GDR & KGB.

    " What are Putin's biggest confronted crisis of last 6 yrs.

- Why is Putin today described as a Conservative.

- What is the System

    - Sistema.